Vide Page 30

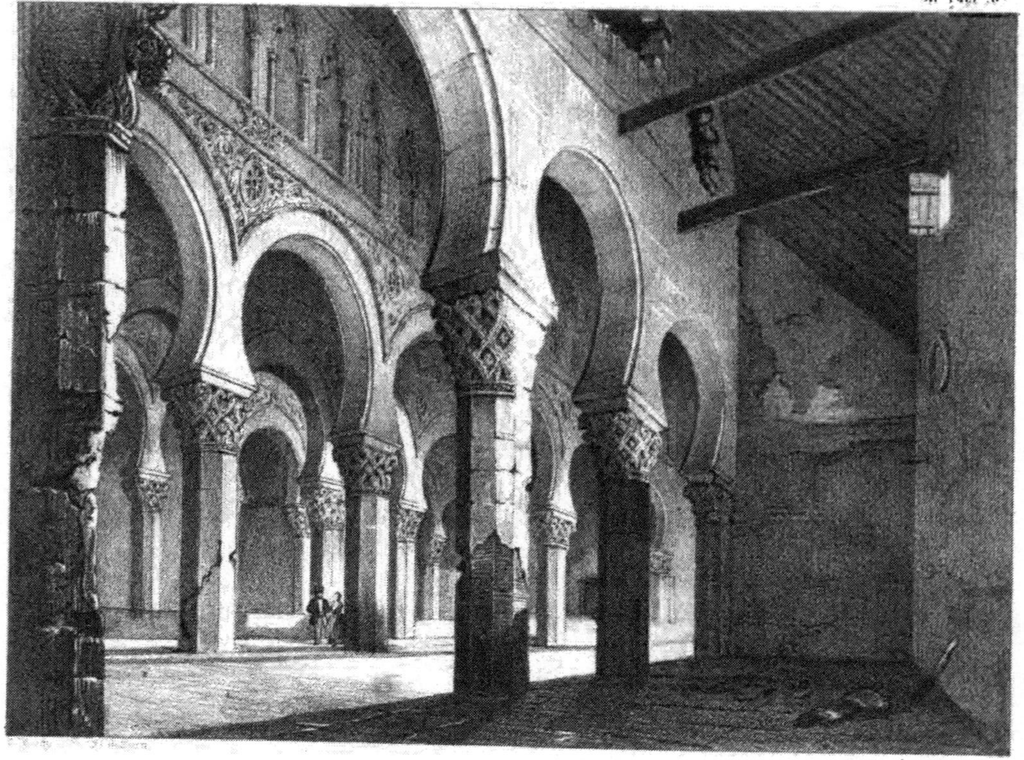

# THE HISTORY

OF

# THE JEWS OF SPAIN AND PORTUGAL,

FROM THE EARLIEST TIMES TO THEIR FINAL
EXPULSION FROM THOSE KINGDOMS, AND
THEIR SUBSEQUENT DISPERSION;

WITH COMPLETE TRANSLATIONS OF ALL THE LAWS
MADE RESPECTING THEM DURING THEIR
LONG ESTABLISHMENT IN THE
IBERIAN PENINSULA.

By E. H. LINDO,

AUTHOR OF "THE JEWISH CALENDAR," AND TRANSLATOR OF "THE CONCILIATOR"
OF R. MANASSEH BEN ISRAEL.

LONDON:
LONGMAN, BROWN, GREEN & LONGMANS,
PATERNOSTER ROW.

M.DCCC.XLVIII.

LONDON:
PRINTED BY J. WERTHEIMER AND CO.,
CIRCUS PLACE, FINSBURY.

## PREFACE.

An impartial history of the Jews of Spain and Portugal has long been a desideratum. It is a link uniting the Hebrews of the present day with the Israelites of antiquity; for, during the many centuries they resided in the Iberian Peninsula, they continued to pursue their studies and cultivate the arts and sciences.

The writings of the learned Rabbins of Spain, served to preserve the works of the ancient philosophers, while Europe in the Gothic ages was exclusively occupied in the art of war. Seeking only to live in tranquillity, "every man under his vine, and under his fig-tree," from their peaceable habits they could dedicate themselves to study, in which their powerful intellects and cultivated minds gave them greater facilities than the other inhabitants of Europe, and in proportion to their population, even in the present enlightened age, they can boast a much larger number of men of genius and learning than any single country in the world can produce.

The Jesuit, Huarte, in his "Examination of Genius," in the 16th century, considered that the Jewish mind was better fitted for learning than that of others; and the author of "Coningsby" would lead to the supposition that it yet remains unchanged.

In the present volume by arranging those Hebrew authors, in the respective ages in which they flourished, their learning can be better appreciated by a comparison with other writers of the same periods, than in a modern work[1] where that order has not been observed.

The digressive chapters in that work have no connection with the history of the Jews of Spain and Portugal, but appear solely as a tirade against the Talmud and Cabala, subjects not understood by the author; but, from the influence he mentions in his preface, it is not surprising that the work is written more in the style of a conversionist than in that of an impartial historian. Nor does he seem to have been better acquainted with the idiom of the Spanish language, or he could not have committed so gross an error as to state, in Law VI., of the " Fuero Real," that the legal interest was three per cent., where the original says, *tres por quatro,* " three for four," that is thirty-three and a third per cent.

Basnage, Maynard, and Jost, in their general histories of the Jews; and Milman, in his excellent abridgement, give tolerably correct accounts of the Spanish and Portuguese Hebrews; but the author, during a visit to Spain, having had access to many ancient Spanish manuscripts, has obtained information from sources with which those able historians were probably unacquainted.

[1] " Sephardim," by James Finn.

The petitions to the various Cortes and the answers of the sovereigns, are all from manuscripts which, until now, have never been printed, even in the original Spanish, and therefore are for the most part unknown. In a work of this description many events recorded by other historians must be found; but the author has derived his information from many original and most authentic Spanish, Portuguese, and Hebrew sources; he has only to regret that some more able pen has not undertaken the task of giving to the world a detailed account of the persecutions the descendants of Israel suffered in the Peninsula; the causes that led to them, and an exact translation of the edicts of the Catholic sovereigns that affected them.

Their history, from the high position they held in those countries, is so connected with the histories of Spain and Portugal, that many events in the histories of those kingdoms are necessary for its elucidation; therefore, there will be found, in the following pages, circumstances recorded that apparently do not belong to Jewish history.

This work being confined to the Hebrews of the Peninsula, is the reason the names of numerous celebrated writers in France, Germany, and Italy, are not mentioned; as R. Solomon ben Isaac (Rashi), R. Levi ben Gershon, and others, although terming themselves Spaniards from following the Spanish ritual, which differs in some minor points from the

German. But that Germany, at those periods, gave birth to men of first-rate talents and learning, is evident from the enlightened Spanish Jews appointing Rabenu Asher, of Rottenburg, Chief Rabbi of the Jews of all Spain.

Hoping for the same indulgent consideration, the author has received for his "Jewish Calendar," and his translation of the "Conciliator of Rabbi Manasseh Ben Israel," he ventures to submit this work to the British public.

# CONTENTS.

### Chapter I.
Early settlement of the Jews in Spain and Portugal . . . 1

### Chapter II.
Edict of Augustus.—Philosophy taught by Jews at Cordova, Toledo, and Oxford.—Proficiency in Astronomy.—Causes of their Medical knowledge.—Council of Elvira in 304.—Gothic Invasion.—Persecution at Minorca —Third Council of Toledo. —Persecution by Sizebut.—Fourth Council of Toledo. . . 8

### Chapter III.
Sixth, Eighth, Ninth, Tenth, Twelfth, and Sixteenth Councils of Toledo.—Settlements in Africa.—Seventeenth Council of Toledo. . . . . . . . . . . . . . . . 18

### Chapter IV.
The Fuero Juzgo, or " Visigothic Code." . . . . . . . 28

### Chapter V.
The Jews recalled by Witiza.—Invasion of the Moors.—Jews protected by them.—Capitulation of Toledo.—Pelage forms a Christian Monarchy.—Manuscripts of Granada burnt.—Muley Hassan's Library at Tunis destroyed.—Change of Moorish Dynasty.—The Persian Schools closed.—R. Moses clad in Sackcloth.—Heroic Conduct of his Wife.—Talmud translated into Arabic. . . . . . . . . . . . . . . . 37

## CHAPTER VI.

Abderachman III. his remarkable Opinion. — Saracens form petty States.—The Kingdoms of Navarre, Aragon, and Portugal commence.— Rabbinical establishments in Spain.— R. Samuel a Levi, the Prince.— R. Joseph his son succeeds him. — Assassinated.—Sufferings at Granada.—Council at Coyaca.—Learned Men. — R. Solomon ben Gabriol, comparison of his writings with Rousseau. — Five Isaacs. — Anecdote of Alfez. . . . 48

## CHAPTER VII.

Ferdinand I.— Persecutions prevented.— Jews protected by Alphonso VI.—Capitulation of Toledo. — Claim of Exemption from Capitation Tax.—Peter of Aragon.—Nicholas de Valencia, Physician of Alphonso, interferes with the Marriage of the Princess Urraca.— Assist in the Attack on Burgos. — Learned Men.— R. Judah a Levi — his Opinions of the Deity compared with Voltaire's. — Maimonides, his Opinion of Aben Ezra.— Extracts from some of his Writings.—Anecdote of Saladin. . 56

## CHAPTER VIII.

Learned Men.—Nachmanides, his Conference with Fr. Paul.— Riot at Toledo. — Synagogue at Estella taken from them. — Privileges in Aragon.—Alphonso II. of Aragon has two Christians executed for the murder of a Jew.—Letter of Innocent III. — Fuero Viejo. — Caraites. — Alphonso IX. opposed to their innovations. — Fuero Real. . . . . . . . . . . , . . 66

## CHAPTER IX.

Learned Men. — Poignard of Faith. — Christian Conquest.— Moorish Dissensions. — Cortes of Barcelona — of Saragossa. — Capitulation of Cordova.— Valencia surrendered. — Rescript at Gerona.—Ordinance of Lerida.—Seville reduced.—Kindness of Ferdinand. — College of Cordova transferred to Toledo. — Reported Crucifixion of a Chorister. — Alphonso X. the Wise, succeeds his Father.—Astronomers employed by him.—Jealousy of the Catalans.—A Duty levied on Foreign Jews and Moors.—

CONTENTS. ix

Page

Protected by Alphonso — his ordinance respecting Pledges. — Charter of Alcala — of Salamanca — of Sahagun. — Bull of Alexander IV. . . . . . . . . . . . . . . . . 78

CHAPTER X.

Las Siete Partidas, or " Seven Codes." . . . . . . . . 92

CHAPTER XI.

Jews accused of Murder at Ossuna. — Discovery of the Plot. Sahudano, Minister to James II. — Clement IV. wishes James to expel the Jews and Moors. — An additional Tax laid on them. — Join the Authorities to preserve Estella for Donna Johanna. — Orders respecting Debts due to them in Navarre. — Their Petition to the Cortes of Barcelona.—Alphonso's conduct to Don Zag de la Malea. — Cortes of Palencia. — Hebrew Population in Castile and Murcia.—Assessment.—Physician to Don Sancho.— His Treatment of Fever.—Learned Men.—Cortes of Valladolid. 103

CHAPTER XII.

Privileges enjoyed in Castile.— State of Society.—Ordinance respecting the Capitation Tax at Segovia. — Cortes of Medina del Campo. — Ferdinand's attachment to them. — Council at Zamora. — Cortes of Carrion.—The Shepherds — the Infante Alphonso and the Jews repulse them. — Riot at Barcelona. — Council of Salamanca. — Relative Population of the towns of Aragon. . . . . . . . . . . . . . . . . . 117

CHAPTER XIII.

Alphonso XI. — Their Petitions to him. — Amount of their Debts reduced. — Protection afforded them. — Revolt at Valladolid against Don Joseph of Ecija. — Murders at Estella, the instigator punished, and the City fined.—Cortes of Valladolid.— Ordinance respecting Bonds at Vittoria.—Council of Salamanca. —Martinez's plan to destroy them—his end.—Cortes of Alcala. — The Plague. — Massacre of the Jews. — Rabenu Asher.— Suicide of his Son. — Ordinance respecting Usury. — Riot at Barcelona.—Physicians and Men of note. . . . . . . . . 131

## CONTENTS.

### Chapter XIV.

Peter the Cruel.—Samuel Levi.—New Synagogue at Toledo. — Murderers executed at Miranda del Ebro.— Sentences of the Jew Magistrates in Navarre, to be executed by the Bailiff. — Abu Said beheaded.—Henry, Count of Trastemar, crowned at Burgos. — Cortes of Burgos. — Gallant Defence of Briviesca, Toledo, and Burgos. — Protection offered to Jews of Castile on settling in Navarre.—Cortes of Toro.—Massacre at Granada. —Cortes of Burgos.—Learned Men. . . . . . . . . 147

### Chapter XV.

John I.—Joseph Pico.—Prevented leaving Navarre.—Cortes of Soria. — John of Castile claims the Crown of Portugal.— David Negro saves the King by his timely notice. — Cortes of Segovia. — Cortes of Saragossa.—Laws at Briviesca.—Council of Salamanca.—Cortes of Palencia. — Representation of Seville against the Archdeacon of Niebla. . . . . . . . . . 160

### Chapter XVI.

Henry III.—Riot at Seville —Massacre at Palma. —Jewries of Cordova, Toledo, Burgos, Valencia, Barcelona, etc. attacked and plundered. — The consequences. — Anecdote of Queen Leonora, of Henry. — His Physicians. — State of the Jews in Spain at the end of the 15th century. . . . . . . . . 171

### Chapter XVII.

Cortes of Madrid.— Regency of John II.— Ordinance of the Regent.—Vincent Ferrer.—The ancient Synagogue of Toledo converted into a Church.—False Accusation against Don Meir Algudes. — Another False Accusation at Segovia. — Learned Men and celebrated Physicians. . . . . . . . . . . 181

### Chapter XVIII.

Ordinance of the Queen Regent at Valladolid—of Don Ferdinand, the other Regent, at Cifuentes.—Memorial of the Jews.— Continued in Public Offices. . . . . . . . . . . . 196

CONTENTS.

CHAPTER XIX.

Jerome of Santa Fé.—Disputation at Tortosa.—Benedict's Address to the Rabbins.—Termination of the Conference.—Bull of Benedict.—Riot at Toledo.—Council of Tortosa.—Cortes of Burgos.—Comparative Population in Aragon.—Alphonso de Spina.—Fortress of Faith.—Jews and Converts of Toledo plundered by Don Henry. . . . . . . . . 209

CHAPTER XX.

Ordinance of John for the Protection of Jews and Moors.—Henry IV. succeeds his Father.—Abraham Benevista, negotiator between Castile and Aragon.—Cortes of Toledo.—Gaon sent to Biscay to raise the Pedido.—Murdered.—Answer of the Basques to the King's Demand. . . . . . . . . . 221

CHAPTER XXI.

Laws made at Medina del Campo.—Accused of crucifying a Child.—Persecution of Converts, the Causes.—John II. of Aragon operated on for Cataract.—The Jewry of Pampluna ordered to be repaired.—Cortes of Ocana.—Mock Deposition of Henry.—Persecution in Andalusia.—Riot at Segovia.—Outrages in Sicily.—Assessment in Castile.—Isabella becomes Queen.—The Crowns of Castile and Aragon united.—Cortes of Toledo.—The Inquisition founded. . . . . . . . . 235

CHAPTER XXII.

The Inquisition.—Opposition to its establishment.—Usque's picture of it.—Torquemada.—Llorente's observation on it.—Its Power.—Number of Victims.—Indications of Judaism of the New Christians.—Inscriptions on the Offices at Seville.—Inquisitors of Toledo.—Extracts of Llorente's History of it. . 248

CHAPTER XXIII.

Employed in Public Offices.—Town Council of Vittoria.—Appeal of the Jews.—Cortes of Tafalla.—Learned men.—Don Isaac Abarbanel and his Sons.—Donna Leonora of Toledo, Wife of Cosmo de Medici, educated by Benvenida Abarbanel. . 259

## CONTENTS.

### Chapter XXIV.

War of Granada.—Assistance rendered by the Jews.—Four Hundred and Fifty Captives redeemed by Abraham Senior.—Improbable Accusations.—Overcharge of Taxes refunded.—Fall of Granada.—The Edict of Banishment. . . . . 270

### Chapter XXV.

The offer of Abarbanel.—Conduct of Torquemada.—Jews of Vittoria save their Cemetery from Desecration.—Abarbanel's Account of their Departure.—Bernaldez's.—Jews of Segovia.—Sufferings.—Some are baptised.—Number that go to Portugal—to Navarre.—Orders of the King to assist the Refugees.—Embark.—Cruelties and Misery experienced in their Voyages.—The Synagogues converted into Churches. . . . 281

### Chapter XXVI.

Review of the Consequences of Ferdinand's Conduct.—Condemned by Mariana.—Surprise of Bajazet.—Declarations of the Grandees.—Forgeries to impose on the People.—Ten ages of Rabbanim.—Opinions thereon of Spaniards of the present Day.—The Consequences of the Expulsion.—Extracts from Morejon on the Act.—Assistance.—The second Inquisitor-general, Deza.—Additional Decree obtained by him.—A private Synagogue discovered at Valencia. . . . . . . . . . . 293

### Chapter XXVII.

Jews of Portugal.—Don Solomon Jachia holds the highest Offices of State.—Order of Gregory IX.—Favoured by all the Sovereigns.—Their Civil and Religious Government.—Privileges.—Laws respecting Converts.—Bull of Clement VI.—Cortes of Lisbon—of Evora.—Paid a Property Tax of Two per Cent.—Ordinance of Duarte—of Alphonso V.—Cortes of Santarem—of Lisbon. . . . . . . . . . . 303

### Chapter XXVIII.

John II.—Cortes of Evora.—The Exiles from Spain

CONTENTS.  xiii

Page

admitted.— Forced to quit.—Cruelties they suffered.—Emanuel succeeds to the Throne. — Banishes them. — Deliberations of the Council. — Their Children taken from them. — Bishop Osorio's Account. — Usque's Relation of their Sufferings. . . 317

CHAPTER XXIX.

The Exiles protected by the Papal See. — The Senate of Venice welcomes them. — Privileges granted them at Leghorn, and other Italian States. — Heroism of Esther Cohen. — Solomon Rophé — in the Barbary States, raised to the Highest Offices. — Egypt.— Morocco. — Heroism of Alvarensi. —Noble Conduct of the Jews to the Portuguese Prisoners.—Parliament of Paris.— Settle at Bourdeaux and Bayonne. — Deputation to Charles V. — Independence of Holland. — The Jews protected there — at Hamburgh — in South America and the West Indies — the North of Europe — England. — Sir Moses Montefiore, Baronet of the United Kingdom — Employed and ennobled by Spain and Portugal. — An Article of the Treaty of Utrecht. . 332

CHAPTER XXX.

New Christians. — Massacres at Lisbon. — John III. — Inquisition established in Portugal. — Jew Physicians.— Anecdote of Francis I.— Learned Men.— Amatus Lusitanus — Solomon Malcho, etc. . . . . . . . . . . . . . . 351

CHAPTER XXXI.

New Christians who escape from Spain and Portugal — R. Manasseh ben Israel. — Learned Men. — R. Isaac Cardozo— Specimen of his Writings. — Isaac Orobio, his sufferings in the Inquisition.— R. David Nieto — Prevented from quitting Portugal.—Sugar introduced by them into South America and the West Indies. — Jews permitted to trade in Portugal.— Anecdote of the Marquis of Pombal.— Re-admitted into Portugal.— Sir I. L. Goldsmid created a Portuguese Baron. — Laws of Spain unrepealed. — Some established and trade with it unmolested.— Opinions of the enlightened Spaniards of the present day. . . . . . . . . . . . . . . . 364

## APPENDIX.

|  | Page |
|---|---|
| No. I.—Extract from Power's History of the Empire of the Mussulmans. | 379 |
| II.—Extract from Epitaph of R. Joseph Ben Shoshan. | 380 |
| III.—Extract from Epitaph of R. Joseph Ben Daoud. | 381 |
| IV.—Extract from Epitaph of R. Joseph Levi Abulaphia. | ib. |
| V.—Extract from a Poetical Satire on Sancho the Brave for his Protection of the Jews. | ib. |
| VI.—Extract from Epitaph of R. Abraham Alnakova. | ib. |
| VII.—Privileges granted by the British Government to the Jews of Surinam. | ib. |
| VIII.—Fac-simile of the Inscription in the Synagogue of Toledo, taken in 1752. | 383 |

# THE JEWS IN SPAIN AND PORTUGAL.

## CHAPTER I.

*Early Settlement of the Jews in Spain and Portugal.*

THE first settlement of the Jews in the Iberian Peninsula is lost in the obscurity of ages; but no doubt can exist of its having been at a very early period; for if Tarshish was, as is supposed by many learned writers, the ancient Tartessus, a city of the Peninsula, some may have established themselves in this part of Europe in the time of Solomon, upwards of seven centuries before the Christian Era, or even earlier.

The Bible leads us to this conclusion; and the inference may fairly be drawn from the following passages.

"For the king had at sea a fleet of Tarshish: with the fleet of Hiram, triennially came the fleet of Tarshish bringing gold, and silver, ivory, and apes, and peacocks."[1]

"And King Solomon constructed a fleet of ships at Ezion-geber, which is close to Eloth, on the shore of the Red Sea in Idumea.

"And Hiram sent in the fleet his servants, navi-

[1] 1 Kings, x. 22.

gators who had a knowledge of the sea, with the servants of Solomon.

"And they came to Ophir, and took from thence four hundred and twenty talents of gold, and brought it to King Solomon."[2]

This shews that Solomon had two fleets; one that took its departure from Ezion-geber for Ophir, in the East Indies; and one for the Mediterranean that sailed from Joppa, which we learn from Jonah, was the port of embarkation for Tarshish.[3]

Therefore, there is no reason to suppose, although the fleet arrived triennially, that they took the same route as that of Pharaoh Necho, who, it is recorded, employed skilful Phœnician mariners, who having sailed out of the Red Sea, to discover the coasts of Africa, went successfully round them, and the third year after their setting out returned to Egypt, through the straits of Gibraltar.[4]

The closest friendship and connection existed not only between the two kings, but likewise between their subjects, the Hebrews and Phœnicians. The immediate vicinity of the kingdoms, their similarity of language, habits and dress, contributed to render them, as it were, one people. Jews appear to have resided at Tyre, even before the reign of Solomon, for it is said:—

"And King Solomon sent and took Hiram from Sor [Tyre]. The son of a widow woman, he was[5] of the tribe of Napthali, and his father was a man of Tyre.[6]

[2] 1 Kings, ix. 26.   [3] Jonah, i. 3.   [4] Rollin's Anc. Hist. vol. i.
[5] 2 Chro. ii. 14. This is the exact translation from the Hebrew. From the words *he was* being misplaced in the English version, the widow might be supposed to have been of the tribe of Napthali instead of the son.   [6] 1 Kings, vii. 13.

"The son of a widow woman of the daughters of Dan, and his father was a man of Tyre."

He being a Naphthalite proves that his father, who was married to a daughter of the tribe of Dan, belonged to that tribe; and from being termed a man of Tyre, it must be supposed he enjoyed the same rights of citizenship as the inhabitants of that city, and that the Hebrews settled in foreign countries at that early period.

From ancient history we learn, that the Phœnicians were among the earliest navigators. They founded Carthage five centuries before the foundation of Rome, and made voyages to Spain, from which country they drew incredible quantities of silver; for Aristotle assures us that when the Phœnicians first arrived in Spain, they exchanged their naval commodities for such immense quantities of silver, that their ships could neither contain nor sustain its weight, although they used it for ballast, and made their anchors, and other implements of silver. And Jeremiah informs us that "plates of silver were brought from Tarshish."[7]

The Hebrew and Phœnician fleets sailing together for Tarshish, accounts for the incalculable quantity and superabundance of silver at that time in Jerusalem, as stated in Scripture.

"Silver was accounted as nought in the time of Solomon."[8]

"And the king made silver to be in Jerusalem as stones for abundance."[9]

When the Carthaginians first went to Spain, they found the quantity of silver undiminished, as the inhabitants at that time made all their utensils, and even their mangers, of that precious metal.

[7] Jer. x. 9.   [8] 1 Kings, x. 21.   [9] Ibid. x. 27.

After the Romans gained possession of Spain, this immense quantity was greatly reduced; but yet in the space of nine years they carried away 111,542 pounds of silver, and 4,095 of gold, besides a large quantity of coin, and other articles of value. Making allowance for the exaggerations of fabulous historians, there is no doubt Spain at this time was exceedingly rich, for if we may believe Strabo, there was a mine near Carthagena, that yielded daily 25,000 drams of silver, or about £300,000 per annum.

According to the Targum of Onkelos, he considers Tarshish to have been in Africa. That he may have been led into that opinion is easily accounted for. The Phœnicians are known to have been very jealous of strangers knowing from whence they drew their riches. It is even said, that if at any time they observed a strange sail keeping them company, or following in their track, they were sure to get rid of him if they could, or deceive him if possible; in which policy they went so far as to venture the loss of their vessels and even their lives, so jealous were they of foreigners and so tenaciously bent on keeping the whole trade to themselves.[10]

This being the case, and Carthage being a colony of theirs, it is probable that, in later times, to deceive other nations and particularly the Romans when Rome became their powerful rival, the Tarshish fleet touched there in their voyages, which led Onkelos and the Romans to suppose that they drew their wealth from Africa.

This early settlement of the Jews in Spain is further corroborated by an ancient history of Toledo,[11] wherein it is stated that 500 years before the Chris-

[10] Ency. Brit.    [11] Rojas.

tian Era, their population had so increased in that city (which could not have been the case unless they had been long settled there), that they spread and built the towns of Escalona, Magueda, Cadaholsa, Guardia, Romeria, Almoroz, Noves, Nombleca, and the present Tembleque, which they had named Bethlehem. Toledo is also said to have been built by them on their first establishment in that country, to which they gave the name of Toledoth; although the Hebrew writers of the middle ages call it Tolitola, probably the name given to it by the Moors, who held possession of it for four centuries, or a corruption of its Latin name Toletanum.

Some authors of high authority, and to whom the greatest erudition cannot be denied, entertain the opinion that Jews existed in Spain from the earliest times.

Mariana, and some other Spanish historians, date the establishment of the Jews after the destruction of Jerusalem and the temple by Nebuchadnezzar; and that many came to Hispania with Hispan, who had accompanied him as an auxiliary in his expedition against Judea; as this event only took place 550 years before the Christian Era, they could not then have built the above-named towns at the period stated, yet Father Mariana, who was no friend to the Jews, and acquainted with the assertion, says, he will neither affirm nor attempt to disprove it; which he would readily have done if he could.

Some assert it to have been seventy years later, on the restoration to freedom by Cyrus; at which period they say, one of his captains named Pyrrhus came to Spain, and brought many Hebrews with him.

Whether at the former or latter periods, their early settlement is confirmed by Don Isaac Abarbanel; for in his commentary on Zechariah, he states that his and another family resided at Seville during the time of the Second Temple.

Many probably emigrated from the Holy Land during the troubles in the time of the Judges, as we learn Elimelech did[12]; and also during the wars between the kings of Judah and Israel.

Later writers assume the great influx to have taken place after the destruction of the Second Temple. One says, "'After Titus the son of Vespasian subjected Judea, many of those that could escape from the swords of the Roman legions, or the flames that reduced the beautiful Jerusalem to ashes, fled, seeking an asylum, some in the East, some in Babylon, some in Egypt; and the families of the greatest consideration were brought to Spain, among whom were the remnants of Benjamin and Judah, descendants of the house of David."[13]

At this period many went to Merida; for the historian of that city states, " that they always made their residence in the best towns of a state, and from their general endeavours to assist each other, those expatriated from Jerusalem after the second destruction being destitute, came to seek their brethren, who had long resided in that city.[14]

The anonymous author of the Memorias of Majorca, considers their settling in the Balearic Islands to have been sixty-five years before the Christian Era.

After the conquest of Bither, and the suppression of the revolt against the Roman power caused by Barchochab, the last effort of the Jewish nation to

[12] Ruth i. 1, 2.   [13] Morejon.   [14] Vargas.

regain their independence, Adrian, who was a native of Spain, transported to it a large number of prisoners from Judea; some authors say as many as 50,000 families, thus greatly increasing the Hebrew population of those Roman provinces.

Although the Spanish title of *Don* is generally supposed to be derived from an abbreviation of the Latin *Dominus*, and for which, seeing its universal application, there might be good grounds were the word *Dom*, yet, when the ancient establishment of the Jews in that country is considered, it is by far more probable that it originated from the Hebrew word אדון *Adon* (Lord, Master), which is used by Jews, as commonly as *Sir* in English conversation.

This opinion has also been entertained by some ancient learned lexicographers.[15]

[15] Minsheu, Guichard, and others.

## CHAPTER II.

*Edict of Augustus—Philosophy taught by Jews at Cordova, Toledo, and Oxford — Proficiency in Astronomy— Causes of their Medical knowledge— Council of Elvira in 304— Gothic Invasion — Persecution at Minorca — Third Council of Toledo—Persecution by Sizebut—Fourth Council of Toledo.*

THE edict of Augustus in the year 15 B.C., upwards of half a century before the destruction by Titus, addressed to all the Governors of the Roman provinces even to Britain,[1] in favour of the Jews, proves, that while Spain was under the dominion of the Romans, they enjoyed security and tranquillity; yet we have no accounts of the Hebrew Philosophers, Mathematicians, Astronomers, Historians, Grammarians, Physicians, Theologians, Jurists and Poets of that period; their names are unknown, but the germs must have existed, that produced so many who in after ages illustrated the Peninsula, and rendered it so famed for learning. At the time that the rest of Europe was veiled in superstition and ignorance, and when it could boast of no other literature than Monkish legends that were unknown beyond the cloisters where they were penned, Jewish Rabbins occupied the highest chairs of Philosophy and Mathematics in the renowned Moorish Schools of Cordova and Toledo. Even in England the first school where experimental Philosophy, Geometry, Algebra and Logic were taught, was that of the Jews at Oxford, in the reign of Henry I.

[1] Semach David.

It has yet the record of its ancient teachers in the Hebrew names of Moses' Hall, and Jacob's Hall.

By them was the philosophy of the ancients made known to Europe. Accustomed from the earliest times, in the clear unclouded Oriental sky, to watch and observe the courses of the planetary system, their attention was incessantly directed to all the secret mysteries of nature; and they may be classed amongst the earliest astronomers.

In medicine they excelled. Various causes combined to give them this pre-eminence, their industry had rendered them masters of commerce. They travelled more than other people; and their knowledge of foreign languages led them to seek in Greece and the ruins of the Roman Empire for ancient manuscripts. They knew where the choicest drugs were to be found, and how best to preserve them. Their close connection with the East (for every doubtful legal question was sent to the famous Oriental schools for solution), and with Spain, which had become the centre of Arabian medicine, made them the chosen physicians of kings, princes, popes, and nobles, in preference to others. The Arabian medicine was the offspring of the Jewish; yet some historians have unjustly confounded them, giving to the former the honor that belongs to the latter. The Spanish Hebrews educated at Cordova, Toledo, and Zara, furnished masters to the celebrated schools of Montpelier and Salerno.

Europe has scarcely acknowledged, much less repaid, the debt she owes to the illustrious Hebrew schools of Spain.

They appear, in that country, not only to have been cultivators and possessors of the soil; but numerous, wealthy, respected and honored by its other inhabitants. Unimpeded, they observed their religion as when in the Holy Land; but as early as in 304, we find the Catholic Clergy, fearing the connection of the inhabitants with the Jews might prove obstructive to the propagation of Christianity, enacted at the Council of Elvira the following Canons against the descendants of Israel.[2]

"CANON 16.—The daughters of Catholics shall not be given in marriage to heretics, unless they submit themselves to the Catholic Church; the same is also ordained for Jews and schismatics. Parents who transgress this order shall be excommunicated for five years."

Jews were not then, as in later periods, considered heretics, or they would not have been particularly named.

"CANON 49.—Landholders are to be admonished not to permit the produce they thankfully receive from God to be blessed by the Jews, lest our benediction be rendered invalid and unprofitable. Should any person presume to do so after this interdiction, let him be entirely ejected from the church."

This shews that the bishops of that synod feared that the Hebrew benediction would be held in higher estimation than that of the Catholic Church; and that the inhabitants, from the example of the Jews, had learnt to praise and thank the Omnipotent Creator, who had bountifully supplied their wants.

"CANON 50.—If any person, whether clerical or one of the faithful, shall take food with Jews, he is to abstain from our communion, that he may learn to amend."

This proves the happy social state that existed before intolerance and bigotry broke the fraternal bond. The clergy as well as others partook of the hospitable meal, and joined the festive board of their Jewish neighbours.

[2] Aguirre, Col. Max.-

"CANON 78.—If one of the faithful, having a wife, commit adultery with a Jewess or Pagan, he is to be ejected from our communion."

This would almost lead to the supposition, that the Church permitted other adulteries. The Talmud, which has since been considered as inducing the Jews to be hostile to Christianity, was not then written.

Years elapsed without the annals of Spain recording any event that affected the Hebrew race.

In 410, the hordes of barbarians from the North, like a desolating torrent, inundated the Peninsula, and drove the Roman Eagles from the Northern provinces. While its conquerors professed Arianism, the Jews lived undisturbed under the new rulers of the land. Kings assumed the regal power only to be assassinated by their more fortunate rivals.

In 418, the Catholic bishop of Minorca persecuted them, and took away one of their two synagogues at Mahon, where the Jewish population was three hundred families. They were also numerous at Palma. Five hundred and forty are said voluntarily to have become converts; which is not probable, as we learn they returned to Judaism on the Moors conquering the islands.

Euric, the ninth sovereign, laid the foundation of the Fuero Juzgo, the Visigothic code, which was subsequently enlarged. His son Recared abjured Arianism, and was the first Catholic Visigoth king of Spain. Zeal for his new faith induced him, in the fourth year of his reign, anno 589, to convene the Third Council of Toledo. Amongst its canons the two following respecting the Jews were enacted.[a]

"CANON 14.—In conformity with the opinion of the Council, our glorious king has ordered to be inserted among the canons, that Jews shall not be permitted to have Christian wives or concubines.

[a] Aguirre.

All children born from such union are to be brought to baptism; nor shall they be permitted to purchase Christian slaves to serve them. If Christian slaves are circumcised, they shall be liberated without ransom, and they shall revert to the Christian religion. Nor shall they hold any public office whereby they can inflict any punishment on Christians."

Although they might not buy slaves to serve them, they were not prohibited a commerce which then was carried on to a great extent in Spain. From the latter enactment, it appears Jews previously held judicial offices.

"CANON 24.—It is decreed, that Jews, in carrying their dead, shall not be permitted to sing Psalms; but they are to observe their ancient custom of bearing and interring their dead. The penalty for transgressing this decree is six ounces of gold to be paid to the count of the city."

This seems to be an infringement on a custom then prevalent, and probably considered a religious duty.

Sizebut, the twenty-fourth sovereign in two centuries, being raised to the Gothic throne in 612 after the assassination of his three predecessors, took from the Romans many cities they yet possessed in Andalusia and the South. Seeking to secure his conquests, he sent an ambassador to the Emperor Heraclius at Constantinople to negociate a peace. The emperor, who had been foretold by an astrologer that Christendom would be in great danger from a circumcised people, considered it was the Jews, whose bravery he had experienced in his Eastern expedition, and whom he knew to be numerous in Spain, made it an article of the treaty, that Sizebut should compel them to renounce Judaism and be baptised, or quit the kingdom. That monarch made no difficulty to accept it, notwithstanding the remonstrances of some bishops who represented it as being contrary to Christianity; for

Gregory I. who then filled the papal see, desired that the concessions that had been granted to the Jews should be faithfully observed. Nevertheless Sizebut imprisoned many of the most wealthy, and sanctioned the murder of those who would not embrace Christianity. Numbers abandoned all they possessed to preserve their faith, and emigrated to that part of Gaul occupied by the Franks. Others passed over to Africa; yet a Spanish historian asserts that 90,000 received baptism, more to escape the horrors that awaited the refusal of those who were steadfast to the religion of their ancestors, than with sincerity. The severity of this barbarous chieftain, who is otherwise represented as governing mildly, can only be accounted for by the supposition, that he feared the immense number of the Jewish population in his dominions might fulfil the prediction made to Heraclius. On his death in 621, many of the converts, who had dissembled to accommodate themselves to the times, returned and openly professed Judaism.

The Jews seem to have had some respite from persecution, during the short reigns of Recared II. and Suintila, whom Sisenand, with the assistance of Dagobert, king of the Franks, deposed. He immediately convoked the Fourth Toledan Council, to secure himself the usurped Crown; for although Councils were originally established to regulate ecclesiastical matters, to suppress the scandalous irregularity and misconduct of the clergy, and to reform Church discipline, those of Spain, a few days after assembling, invited some nobles to join in their deliberations, thus constituting themselves a legislative assembly, and enacting canons that were to be the law of the land.

At this council held in 633, St. Isidor, the bishop of Seville, presided; and the following canons were enacted regarding the Jews.[4]

"CANON 57.—In respect to Jews, this holy synod has resolved, that in future no one shall be compelled to receive our faith; for God hath mercy on whom he will have mercy, and whom he will he hardeneth; as such persons are not saved unwillingly, but by consent, that the attribute of justice be preserved entire. For as man perished by his own free will in submitting to the serpent, so when the grace of God calleth, every man is saved by believing, by the conversion of his own mind. Therefore they are not to be constrained, but persuaded into conversion, by the free agency of the will. As to those already forced into Christianity, as was done in the time of the most devout prince Sizebut, since it is evident they have partaken of the holy sacrament, have received the grace of baptism, have been anointed with the chrism, and received the body and blood of our Lord; it is right they should be obliged to retain the faith they have undertaken, although under compulsion and necessity, lest the name of God be blasphemed, and the faith they have assumed be considered worthless and despicable."

Jews were no longer to be forced against their will to adopt the Catholic faith; but the cruelty of the other enactments of this Council were such, as a bigoted clergy would, in their thirst for domination in those dark ages of Gothic ignorance and superstition, devise against those who would not submit to their religious creed; and, as might be expected, would be sanctioned by Sovereigns, who raised to the throne in general, on the blood of their predecessors, required the powerful aid of the clergy to maintain on their heads the crown they had usurped.

"CANON 58.—The avarice of some persons is so great, that, as the Apostle saith, through covetousness they have erred from the faith. Many ecclesiastics and laymen have, by accepting presents from the Jews, bestowed their protection on infidelity; such persons are deservedly to be held as belonging to Antichrist, who thus act contrary to Christ. Therefore, whoever henceforth, whether bishop

[4] Aguirre.

ecclesiastic, or layman, shall afford them his protection for reward or favor, to the disparagement of the Christian faith, let him become an alien from the Catholic Church and the kingdom of God, as a truly profane and sacrilegious person; for it is right that he should be severed from the body of Christ, who makes himself a patron of Christ's enemies."

This shews that even the highest clergy could not resist a tempting bribe; and, notwithstanding their pretended zeal for the Catholic faith, Jewish money could purchase their protection.

"CANON 59.—Many who have formerly been elevated to the Christian faith, are now known, in contempt of Christ, not only to practise Jewish ceremonies, but have even dared to practise the abomination of circumcision. By the advice of our most pious and religious prince, Sisenand the king, this holy Synod hath decreed that such transgressors, being apprehended on the authority of the prelates, shall be recalled to the true worship, according to Christian doctrine, so that those who will not amend of their own accord, may be compelled by sacerdotal correction. Should such persons as they may have circumcised, be children of the above, they shall be taken from the society of their parents; and if slaves, they shall be liberated in compensation for the injury."

This proves that the forced converts returned as soon as possible to the religion of their fathers, and practised its earliest sacred rite. The sacerdotal correction of those who would not again be persuaded to follow Catholicism is not stated. Whatever it might have been, this is certain, priests became executioners.

"CANON 60.—We decree, that the sons and daughters of Jews are to be separated from their parents, lest they be involved in their errors. They are to be placed in monasteries, or with Christian men and women who fear God, that by their society they may learn the worship of the true faith, that, being thus better instructed, they may improve in morals and belief."

In the present age, it is hardly possible to believe that men, considered as ministers of God, could have enacted so barbarous and unnatural a decree, as to separate children from their parents. How discordant to the religion they preached!

"CANON 61.—If Jews that have been baptised, afterwards renounce Christianity, and thus become liable to any penalty, their believing children shall not be excluded inheriting their property; for it is written, The son shall not bear the iniquity of the father."

Policy may have dictated this, as fear of losing their portion of their father's property might have operated on children who had been converted, and induced them to renounce their newly-adopted creed, for the religion of their forefathers.

"CANON 62.—The company of the wicked frequently corrupteth the good, how much more that of the viciously inclined. Therefore, there is to be no communion between Jews that have been converted to the Christian faith, and those who adhere to their ancient rites, lest by associating with them they be perverted. Therefore, any that have been baptized, that do not avoid the society of unbelievers, shall be given over to Christians, and the former be publicly scourged."

By another barbarous enactment worthy of that age, a convert speaking to a Jew became a slave, and the Jew he spoke to was to be publicly scourged. On what a fragile reed must that faith then have rested, when two individuals conversing together became dangerous to it. The severity of this law is a proof how easily the newly made converts returned to their duty to their God.

"CANON 63.—Jews who have Christian wives are to be advised by the bishop of their diocese, that if they wish to live with them they must become Christians; and if, after being so admonished, they refuse to obey, they are to be separated, as an unbeliever cannot remain in wedlock with a woman who has become a Christian. The children are to brought up in the faith of their mother; and those born of unbelieving mothers and believing fathers, are to follow the Christian religion, and not the Jewish superstitions."

Separating husband and wife never was Christian

doctrine, this law enabled a faithless wife, by the act of embracing Christianity, to divorce herself without further ceremony from her injured husband; if such there were, could the Christian faith gain by the acquisition of such proselytes?

"CANON. 64.—He who is faithless to God cannot be true to man. Therefore Jews who were formerly Christians, but now deny the faith in Christ, are not to be admitted as witnesses, although they declare themselves to be Christians. For if suspected in respect to their faith in Christ, their testimony on human affairs is unsafe. No confidence can be placed in the testimony of those brought up in falsehood; nor is credit due to those that reject the true faith."

Persons suspected of having no religion might justly be excluded from giving evidence; but hereby Jews who continued faithful to their religion are not prevented being witnesses.

"CANON. 65.—By command of the most excellent Lord and King Sisenand, this holy council has decreed that Jews and their descendants are not to hold public employments, as scandal would thereby be given to Christians; therefore, provincial judges, together with ecclesiastics, are to prevent their fraudulently obtaining such employments, and their succeeding therein. Should any judge tolerate such proceedings, he is to be excommunicated the same as for sacrilege, and the person that obtains the office shall be publicly scourged."

This interdict shews that Jews at that period held public offices, and is opposed to their conversion; for no benefit could accrue therefrom, since even their descendants were precluded from holding public employments; yet the severity of the enactment against the judge who clandestinely permitted it, indicates they were in the habit of conniving at it.

"CANON. 66.—By the decree of the most glorious prince, this council has resolved, that no Jew shall have Christian servants, nor purchase Christian slaves, nor retain such by gift of any person. As it is shameful that the members of Christ should serve the ministers of Antichrist. Henceforward, should any Jew dare to keep Christian slaves of either sex, they shall be liberated, and restored to their freedom."

This was an infringement on their trade, which former Councils had not interfered with, the Third Toledan Council had only prohibited their keeping Christian slaves as servants, which it would appear had not been attended to, or they would not have found it necessary to repeat the injunction.

## CHAPTER III.

*Sixth, Eighth, Ninth, Tenth, Twelfth, and Sixteenth Councils of Toledo.—Settlements in Africa.— Seventeenth Council of Toledo.*

CHINTILLA having been raised to the throne on the demise of Sisenand, who had in 635, the last year of his reign, convoked the Fifth Council of Toledo, which probably, considering the preceding one had done sufficient against the Jews, makes no mention of them. But the Sixth, assembled by Chintilla, in 638, confirmed all former enactments against that innocent people; for we find no crime on record imputed to them individually or collectively, except their adherence to the law their forefathers had received at Mount Sinai, could be so deemed.

This Council less liberal than that St. Isidor had presided over, enacted by.[1]

"CANON. 3.—The inflexible treachery of the Jews has by piety and divine grace been overcome; for inspired by the Most High God, our most excellent and Christian prince, inflamed with ardour for the faith, together with the clergy of his kingdom, has resolved

[1] Aguirre, Coll. Max.

to destroy their prevarication and superstition to the utmost, by not permitting the residence of any person in the land who is not a Catholic. For which zeal we give thanks to the Almighty King of Heaven, that He has created so illustrious a soul, and endued it with His wisdom. May he grant him a long life in this world, and everlasting glory in the future.

"We therefore now decree, and confirm what has hitherto been enacted in general synod respecting the Jews, seeing that all requisite for their salvation has been done with circumspection. We now declare all such edicts to be valid." In addition to which they added: "We hereby deliberately resolve, that whoever in future shall obtain the sovereignty, shall not ascend the throne before he has sworn not to permit the Jews to infringe this holy faith, and in no wise to be seduced, either through neglect or cupidity to favor their perfidy."

The latter part of this Canon shews, that the Clergy suspected that even these intolerant Visigothic kings, might be bribed not to enforce the execution of the conciliary decrees; and is the first instance of their assuming in Spain to dictate laws to their Sovereign.

It might be supposed this rigorous decree would have struck a mortal blow to the Hebrew nation in the Peninsula; but the frequent revolutions of the throne, the instability of the royal authority, and the troubles that accompanied each election and accession to the crown, added to the ignorance of the administrators of the law and the clergy, who in general could neither read or write, were causes that prevented the strict execution of the decrees of the Councils, and rendered them ineffective. An extraordinary fact is, that these laws neither effected the conversion, nor extirpation of the Jews; but there were Christians who embraced Judaism. Attached to their domestic hearths, the productive returns of the soil they industriously cultivated, their extensive commerce, and the graves of their dearest ties, they yet remained; aware that their wealth and the venality even of the Clergy could secure them protection in time of need.

They do not appear to have been molested during the short reign of his son Tulga, nor in the succeeding one of Chindasvinto who had deposed him; although, to legalise his usurpation and obtain the support of the clergy, he took the prescribed oath. Contrary to the fundamental laws of the kingdom and the rights of the nobles, the crown being elective, he associated with him in the regal power his son Recesvinthus, who ascended the throne on the death of his father in 649.

At the Eighth Council of Toledo, he presented a memorial recorded by Aguirre, and embodied in the Fuero Juzgo,[2] said to be from the newly converted Jews of Toledo, who feared a threatened enquiry into their conduct as good Catholics. This seems to be a spurious document, and probably was some forgery imposed upon him; for it can scarcely be believed to have emanated from persons who had professed Judaism; that they would abrogate its most sacred rites, and break off all connection with their Jewish relatives, solely under condition that they should not be forced to eat pork.

We find no further mention made of them during his reign; if we except the twentieth canon of the Ninth Toledan Council held two years after, which enjoined all baptised Jews strictly to observe all the festivals of the New Testament, and to attend all solemnities of the Church, under pain of being sentenced to fast, or to be scourged.

[2] Vide infra, Chap. IV. law xvi

Notwithstanding the decrees of Councils, the Clergy sold their slaves to Jews; and the trade was so openly carried on, that the Tenth Council of Toledo, held in 656, found it necessary to enact a Canon against such traffic. On the death of Recesvinthus in 672, Wamba, against his will, was forced by the Nobles and Clergy to accept the Crown. He found his Jewish subjects numerous; for during the tranquillity they had enjoyed for some years, they had greatly increased, to which their early marriages and active life mainly contributed. As the new king was obliged to take the prescribed oath, and to order all unconverted Jews to be expelled from the kingdom, the decree was rigidly executed. Some went to Africa; and numbers who would not submit to baptism, passed the Pyrenees, and sought an asylum in Narbonne and Gascony, where they were kindly received. During his reign, the Saracens made their first attempt against Spain, but this attack his bravery defeated. Recovering from the effects of poison administered at the instigation of Ervig who, dazzled by the brilliancy of a diadem, sought his death, he retired to a monastery in 680, abdicating with pleasure to his ambitious rival a throne he had been forced to occupy.

To secure his ill-acquired dignity, Ervig, in 681, assembled the Twelfth Council of Toledo, when the following was enacted:[3]

"CANON 9.—.We have read with careful attention the laws lately promulgated by our most glorious prince, in various divisions, upon the execrable perfidy of the Jews. With due consideration, we likewise have approved all those regulations; and, as they have been justly ordained and approved by synodal examination, they shall henceforward be held as an irrevocable course in judicial proceedings against the transgressors of them."

[3] Aguirre.

"The laws in repetition of former laws against Jewish transgressions, and the late ratification of the same."

"That Jews shall not abstain themselves, nor withhold their children or slaves from baptism."

"That Jews shall not celebrate the Passover as accustomed, nor practise circumcision, nor dissuade any one from the Christian faith."

"That Jews shall not presume to observe the Sabbath, or any festival of their religion."

"That Jews shall not work on the Lord's day nor on other specified days."

"That Jews shall make no distinction in food."

"That Jews shall no longer marry near relations."

"That Jews shall not dare to defend their religion to the disparagement of ours, nor flee anywhere to avoid the faith; nor shall any person harbour such."

"That no Christian accept any gift whatever to the prejudice of the Christian faith."

"That Jews shall not read books abhorred by the Christian faith."

"That no Christian slave shall belong to Jews."

"If a Jew declares himself to be a Christian, and on that account refuses to give up a slave."

"Every Jew on embracing the faith to deliver his profession in writing."

"The conditions Jews are to swear to, on renouncing Judaism for the faith."

"Concerning Christian slaves of Jews not declared to be Christians, and respecting those who shall denounce them."

"No Jew shall dare to govern, strike, or arrest any Christian in virtue of any authority, except by royal ordinance."

"That unconverted slaves of Jews receiving the Christian faith, shall receive their freedom."

"That Jews shall not presume on the authority of land proprietors or others, to govern a Christian family, and the penalties to be inflicted on those that give them such authority."

"That a Jew arriving from any other province or territory of our dominions, shall without delay present himself before the bishop or priest of the place, and what is proper he should observe."

"The manner in which bishops are to muster Jews at stated times."

"Any person having a Jew in his service, shall deliver him up on the demand of any priest."

"That the duty of distinguishing Jews belongs solely to priests."

"On the penalties priests and magistrates incur for delay in executing the laws against the Jews."

"That magistrates shall not presume without the sanction of the priest, to decide any matter of Jewish transgression."

"That bishops are exempt from penalties when their presbyters have not sent for their abjudication, what they have failed to correct."

"The prerogative of mercy towards those who are truly converted to the Christian faith is reserved to princes."

"Every bishop shall furnish the Jews of his diocese with a book written against their errors, and shall store in the archives of his cathedral, their professions and conditions."

"The promulgation of all these laws as approved by synodal decision, by our unanimous consent, shall be enforced against those that transgress them."

These elaborate laws as will be seen could not be carried into effect. Probably the severity and prolixity of their enactments, rendered them as fruitless, as all other anterior decrees of councils had proved.

Ervig having named as his successor Egica, the nephew of Wamba, he was succeeded by him on his death in 687. The year after his accession, Egica convoked the Fifteenth Council, but nothing was said or done respecting the Jews. At the Sixteenth, held in 693, as he found the oppressive laws of his predecessors had proved ineffective, he sought by rewards to keep the converts to their newly assumed faith.

His patent for its convocation contains the following;[4] "In conformity to our late proclamation, none of those Jews who persevere in their obstinacy, shall approach the tribunal of justice on any subject whatever, nor shall presume to transact any business with Christians. Nevertheless, if any of the said Hebrews, their wives or children, shall hereafter sincerely embrace the Catholic faith, renouncing all prevaricating

[4] Aguirre.

errors and the ceremonies of their former religion, let him be free from every subjection he was under while in his state of error, and was accustomed to contribute to the public service." The council enacted :—

"CANON 1.—Notwithstanding many writers of the ancient fathers, and promulgated laws extant, condemning the false belief of the Jews, yet, as the prophetic record declares, 'the sin of Judah is written with a pen of iron, and with the point of a diamond,' they still persevere in the blindness of their obstinacy on a yet harder rock. It is too plain that the walls of the Catholic Church are often attacked by the engines of their infidelity. Therefore they must be unwillingly corrected, or awfully crushed while perishing for ever under the judgment of God.

"It is the laudable practice of skilful physicians to press the art of healing on those who suffer various diseases, until they accept the wholesome remedy. Then, as the earnest desire and ready devotion of our glorious and Christ-loving king, Egica, are willing to provide the virtue of this admirable medicine for them, that either they be converted to the faith, or if adhering to their infidelity be more severely treated, by his command and exhortation our council has unanimously resolved:—

"That all provisions contained in the decrees and laws of our predecessors in the Catholic faith, for the destruction of their perfidy, shall be more strictly enforced by all ecclesiastics and magistrates; and what we now ordain shall be equally zealously observed. Namely,

"That all those who shall be sincerely converted, and without subterfuge faithfully keep the Catholic faith, shall remain secure in their possessions and property, and exempt from every tax they have been accustomed to pay to our sacred treasury; but such as continue in their infidelity shall pay the full amount of their customary taxation for the public benefit.

"Those who have abandoned their errors, shall only pay to the revenue the same as other freemen, and be at full liberty to carry on business, and equally with Christians, shall discharge any public duty they may be appointed to by the king; for the rule of faith requires that every one adorned with the faith of Christ, should be held as noble and honorable among men.

"We fully confirm the said law, which, as above stated, has been promulgated by our lord the king, Egica, for the suppresssion of contumacy, and by this decree of our constitution, declare it to be of immoveable stability."

But Egica did not succeed, in his purpose; for although some few, allured by becoming nobles and being relieved from heavy imposts, may have abjured the religion of their fathers, they remained firm in their faith; and they appear to have been numerous. In the early part of his reign, instead of prosecuting, he was favorable to his Hebrew subjects. He annulled the capital punishments they were liable to, and substituted banishment or scourging, which was not even inflicted. They were at first tolerated, and then owned lands, houses, and slaves; for we find a colony of Jews at this period existed in the Pyrenees. Repeated emigrations had led them to form settlements on the opposite coasts of Africa, and naturally a mutual sympathy for absent friends and mercantile enterprise led to a constant correspondence and communication between the opposite shores of the Mediterranean, as Jews were located in most of the seaports, for the benefit of their commerce.

Although history is silent as to the Saracens making any attempt against Spain since their defeat by Wamba; it may yet be supposed the design was not abandoned. Egica suspected the Hebrews of the two shores had combined to assist them in the conquest of the Peninsula, a suspicion founded on the idea that they would gladly embrace the opportunity of avenging the wrongs and persecutions they had suffered since Catholic Visigoth sovereigns had wielded the Iberian sceptre. Proofs he had none, or he would have laid them before the Seventeenth Council of

Toledo, held the following year, 694, instead of the vague accusation, "that he had recently learnt by open avowal, that the Hebrews had plotted with others beyond the sea to effect the ruin of Christendom." That Council enacted;—

"CANON 8.—By command of our most pious king, Egica, who, inflamed with zeal for the Lord, and impelled by ardour for the holy faith, not only wishes to avenge the insult offered to Christ's cross, but to prevent by severity the ruin they had savagely engaged to bring on his country and people, that the perjurers themselves and their posterity be deprived of all their property and possessions, the same being confiscated to the national treasury, that they be deprived of their homes in all the provinces of Spain, and be subjected to perpetual slavery under those he may assign them to; and so remain for ever. Nor shall any opportunity by connivance be afforded them of recovering their liberty, while they continue obstinate in their unbelief, for they are branded with numberless transgressions.

"We likewise ordain, that certain Christian slaves that belong to such Jews, as shall be selected at the king's will, shall either receive from their owner's property as much as the king by his authority shall grant, or written letters of manumission; and the duties hitherto performed for the public by those Jews, are to be performed to the full extent, without diminution by the said slaves whom our said prince may have selected.

"Finally, the persons to whom the said Jews shall have been appropriated by our said Lord the king, shall sign a bond on their honor, not to permit them to perform their worship, or celebrate their rites, or in any way to follow the perfidy of their ancestors.

"We further decree that their children of both sexes of seven years old and upwards, are not to reside or associate with their parents, but their owners shall give them to be brought up by faithful Christians, keeping in view that the males are to be united in marriage with Christian women, and the females married to Christian men.

"And as before said, permission shall not be given either to the parents or children, to observe the ceremonies of Jewish superstition, nor opportunity be afforded them of again walking in the paths of their unbelief."

The foregoing demonstrates how inefficient all former decrees had been to eradicate Judaism from the Hebrew breast. Taught from their earliest infancy to acknowledge the unity of God, the Creator of heaven and earth, by " Hear, O Israel, the Lord is our God, the Lord is One!"[s] it remains indelibly imprinted on their souls, and with their last expiring breath, they repeat the sacred verse. Nor could anterior enactments be carried into effect, from causes before stated; to which probably may be added, the reluctance of the inhabitants to oppress a people with whom they had lived in friendly intercourse for centuries before the Gothic conquest.

Notwithstanding former interdicts, they yet were possessed of slaves, and served the State; and the latter part of the Canon corroborates the assertion of Llorente, that many of the present grandees and nobles of Spain are descended from Jewish ancestors.

This, like preceding conciliary decrees tended only to the involuntary apostasy of a few, and the emigration of many; for as Aguirre says, "Many edicts were in vain made by the Gothic kings against the Jews." The Fuero Juzgo was first compiled in 634; but by the following translation it will be seen that many later laws are added to it, and that those regarding Jews were more specially directed against converts.

[s] Deut. vi, 4.

## CHAPTER IV.

**The Fuero Juzgo** *or " Visigothic Code."*

BOOK xii.   TITLE 2.

LAWS ON HERETICS AND JEWS.

IV.—No Jew is in any manner to revile or abandon the holy Christian faith which the saints received by baptism. No person shall impugn it by word or deed, nor attack it either secretly or overtly. No one shall hide himself to avoid receiving it, nor shall any person secrete one that he may escape. No Jew shall in future think to return to his errors and excommunicated religion; no one shall imagine, utter, or by any act publish the deceitful religion of the Jews, which is contrary to that of Christians. No one shall attempt by force to infringe or to murmur against the Christian establishments. No person shall harbour any one acquainted with the said prohibitions, nor delay giving information against the person who hides one, and the place where he is secreted. Whoever transgresses what we here ordain, shall receive the punishment the law enacts.—*The King Don Recesvinthus.*

V.—No Jew shall celebrate his passover on the fourteenth day of any month, nor make holidays on the days they have been accustomed to, nor observe any of the great or minor festivals conformable to their former error. No one shall in future observe the festivals, sabbaths, or other feasts, nor

[1] Madrid Edit. 1600.

shall any one presume to respect or keep them hereafter. If any person is found to do it he shall receive the punishment specially established.—*Ibid.*

VI.—No Jew shall presume to marry or commit adultery, or incest with a relative within the sixth degree, nor make marriage feasts unless according to Christian custom: any person that does so shall be punished and fined.—*Ibid.*

VII.—No Jew shall circumcise himself, nor permit another person to do it to a freeman, slave, or one who has been liberated, whether a native or foreigner; he is neither thus to mutilate his flesh, nor that of any other person; and any one who does, or permits another to do it, shall receive the punishment established by law.—*Ibid.*

VIII.—The apostle St. Paul saith, that all things are pure to men who are pure in faith, but that nothing is pure to those that are defiled by not being of the faithful; therefore it is right that the impurity which is the greatest of impurities ought to be removed and rejected from among Christians; therefore we establish that no Jew shall make a distinction between one meat and another, according to their custom and the usages of their religion. No one shall abstain from eating such things as he ought, and that from their nature seem good. No person is to eat one food and refuse another, except such as Christian custom ordains, and should it be proved that any person transgresses this law he shall be punished accordingly.—*Ibid.*

IX.—We specially command by this decree, that no Jew in any cause can be a witness against a Christian, although the Christian be a slave; nor can he in any trial have a Christian put to the torture, nor can he be received as the accuser; that the faith of an infidel may not be more valued than that of the faithful, and the members of Christ be rendered subservient to their enemies; but Jews may give testimony in causes between each other or against their slaves. According to law they may plead, and bring them to judgment before Christian judges.—*Ibid.*

X.—A liar to man is disgraced, and ought to be punished, how much more so should those who are proved to act deceitfully against the law of God, such persons ought not to be admitted as witnesses against Christians; we therefore forbid Jews whether baptised or not, being received as witnesses against Christians; but their descendants may give testimony together with Christians, provided their good conduct and sincere faith is proved to the priest, king, or judge.—*Ibid.*

XI.—This law is made to punish the perfidy of the Jews, more severely than enacted by former laws, therefore we ordain, that every Jew who transgresses the enactments and prohibitions contained in the aforesaid laws, and refuses to observe and maintain them as they have engaged, is to be put to death by their hands, and to be stoned or burnt. If the prince desires to spare the life of any person convicted of such crime, he shall make him a slave to whomever he chooses, and his property shall be given to other Jews, in such manner that it never again come into his possession, nor shall he ever be released from slavery.—*Ibid.*

XII.—We order that no Jew shall purchase or accept as a gift a Christian slave; and if he buy or receive one as a gift, (and circumcise him, he is to lose the sum he paid, and the slave is to be manumitted) whether male or female. All the property of a Jew who circumcises a Christian slave shall be confiscated to the king.—*Sizebut.*

XIII.—Whereas the law made long since by our ancestor King Recared, that Christian slaves should not be in the possession of a Jew, would have sufficed had the Jews not subsequently beguiled the hearts of princes to benefit them contrary to justice; and whereas we have made laws against them and in various ways opposed their deceit; as in former times they have transgressed the law made by the said prince, our ancestor, we therefore by this law ordain, that any Christian slaves that were in the possession of Jews when the said law was made, whether liberated or not, are to have the rights of Roman citizens, and according to law are to be free. And if any of the slaves liberated in consequence of that ordinance of the king have been sold, or by deed or otherwise placed in the hands of another person, such bond is invalid, and such sale annulled. The slave is to be free, the seller receiving the value established by law, and he is to live in freedom by his labour, the same as other working people; and in proportion to the wages he earns, he shall be bound to pay a part to his former master. And if they have obtained any slaves since the law of the said prince was made, we command that they sell or liberate them by the calends of July. Christians who have been circumcised by Jews, and observe their customs, shall be punished according to law. Those who again become slaves to Jews, or that according to law ought to be free, and are yet held by them in slavery, shall receive amends for it according to law, the same as a free man would. Jews that are converted to the holy Christian faith, shall have their portion of their father's slaves, but neither the father or son shall make the apportionment in the sale of slaves; it shall be done by the purchaser solely. And Jews who have craftily obtained any concessions from our predecessors, the same are cancelled and devolve again to the king. Slaves of Jews that have had themselves baptised, or are found desirous to do so, and are in the possession of their masters, are to be immediately liberated; they are to pay the amount on receiving their freedom, and not having the means, and being unable to do it, they are to serve him at the same wages as a freeman, until the amount is paid.—*Ibid.*

XIV.—We give health to the poor of our kingdom when we relieve the faithful to God from the power of infidels; for the faith of Christians is much exalted when the craft of the Jews exercises no power over them: then the power of God can walk in the love of Christ. Therefore by this law which is to be valid hereafter for ever, in presence of all the barons of our court, we enact, that from the first year of our reign, no Jew shall have under him any Christian freeman, slave, or youth, nor have them to serve him gratuitously; nor do we permit him in any manner to exercise authority over such, but we permit him to sell his slave with his earnings and property to a Christian in our dominions. And we order that no person shall have the power to sell his slave out of the kingdom, but only in the places where they reside. And we order that if the slave has no property of his own, the vendor shall give the purchaser sufficient to clothe and maintain him; this we order, that it may not appear that the seller throws him on the wide world. And if a Jew wishes to liberate his slave, and he turn Christian, he is to do it according to the usage of Roman citizens, in such manner that he shall not be bound to serve any Jew, but may if he chooses, live away from them and their society. And if a Jew fraudulently liberate or sell a slave, and such sale or release cause injury to the person he had previously sold him to, if a freeman discovers the fraud, the Jew shall make good the loss, and if the Christian who assisted in committing the fraud have no property, he shall be given as a slave to whomsoever the king pleases; and should it be a person of rank half his property is to be confiscated, and he is to be degraded for ever. And if a slave discover it, he shall be liberated and released by his owner, which freedom is valid for his whole life, and he is to receive a pound of gold from those who committed the fraud, and the king shall give another slave to the owner in lieu of the one liberated. And if a Jew circumcises a Christian, or converts a Christian woman to his religion, he is to be beheaded, and his property is to be confiscated to the king, and the informer is to be rewarded.

Slaves born from the connection of Christians with Jews are by our order to be Christians. If they will not consent, they are to be publicly scourged and branded, and by order of the king shall be given to some Christian as slaves. If such connections are clandestinely carried on in our kingdom, the Jew may, if he chooses, become a Christian; but if he will not, the connection is to be broken off, and he is to be banished from our kingdom for ever. To the above we add, that if a Jew wishes to turn to the Christian faith, and receive the holy baptism, he shall retain unmolested all the property he then possesses. And we command that this law, and all we have ordered herein, is to be carried into full effect by the calends of July, and if after the said time until the calends of July next following, any Jew should be found possessing a Christian slave, half his property shall be confiscated to the king, and the slave will be free; nor may the Jew demand any payment for his person, nor anything from his future earnings. And this law, which we make from the love of mercy and religion, for the preservation of our people, we order with God's help is to be for ever in force.

Jesus Christ who conquers, will make all the kings our successors, who observe the enactments of this law, conquerors; and prolong the reign of those who shall be inclined to keep it; and although we do not believe, that the enactments of this law will ever be violated, yet should any one infringe or not observe it, let him in that age be degraded more than other men, and his life be destroyed at the time he thinks of acting contrary thereto; may the load of his sins for transgressing this law and its enactments be so heavy, that, on the awful day on which he is to come for judgment and our Lord is to appear, he be separated from the faithful flock of Christ, and placed with Jews on the left hand, and burnt in flames of fire with the devil for his companion. And we declare this, that the punishment of those who violate this law may be severe, and that those who enforce its provisions be well rewarded.

XV.—In the execution of the foregoing laws, which we and our ancestors have made to eradicate the perfidy of the Jews, we have been pleased, in confirmation and to enforce the same, to add the following: for where we have given shelter to the enemies of the faith, and established guards against all the deceptions of infidels, it is right that we should confirm what has been done, and that we respect those that have been confirmed; for inasmuch as the architect only demonstrates the ingenuity of art, while the work remains firm and is most respected, then, that the deceit of the Jews, which we have always in every way endeavoured to suppress, and to prevent the formation of their communicated establishments, we therefore by this law enact:—

That no person of any religion, or of any rank or quality, or attached to our court, either great or small, or any person of any people, or of any note, or of princes or grandees, shall endeavour or devise to assist Jews who will not be baptised, to remain in their faith and customs; nor those that have been baptized to return to their perfidy and bad customs. No person, from being powerful, shall presume to defend them to remain in their wickedness; no one shall endeavour by word or deed to aid them therein, as it is opposed to the holy Christian faith. Nor shall any one attempt to prove, say, or do, either privately or publicly, any thing against it, should any one dare to do it, whether he is a bishop, ecclesiastic, or layman, of whom it be proved, he shall be separated from the society of Christians, and excommunicated by the Church. A fourth part of his property shall be confiscated to the king; as it is just, that those who go in opposition to the love of Christ and the truth, in favour of its enemies, should be separated from the society of the faithful, and lose their property.

Whoever transgresses this law, shall receive the sentence promulgated in the preceding of King Sizebut.

XVI.—The abjuration and protest made by the Jews against their religion in the time of king Rescesvinthus:—

To our Lord the most merciful and much honored king, Rescesvinthus.

We, all the Jews of Toledo who have signed, and put our usual signatures hereto, salute you.

We remember that in former times by command of king Chintila, that we truly and justly promised and engaged by writings, that we all would receive and observe the Christian faith; but as the errors of our fathers prevent our sincerely believing in our Lord Jesus Christ, and firmly to practise the Christian faith; we therefore now of our free will and accord, answer to your highness for ourselves, our wives and children, that henceforward we will not practise any Jewish custom.

We will in no way associate with Jews that will not be baptised.

We will not marry with any relative within the sixth degree, nor commit incest with any female of our family; and hereafter, we, our sons, and descendants both male and female, will marry Christians.

We will not have our flesh circumcised, nor keep the passover, sabbaths, or the other festivals ; nor refrain from meats according to Jewish custom; nor live or perform anything as they do: but we all will with sincere faith, great devotion, and willing accord, believe in Christ, the son of the living God, as is ordained by the evangelists and apostles whom we acknowledge and reverence. All will sincerely profess the holy Christian faith, in the observance of the festivals, marriages, food, and every other custom, without hesitation, reservation, or any reason on our part against fulfilling all we here promise. In regard to swine's flesh, we promise, that although from not being accustomed to it we cannot eat it, yet, without objection or scruple, we will eat anything seasoned or cooked with it.

And should any of us be accused of transgressing the least of the aforesaid, or do anything contrary to the Christian faith, either by word or deed, or delay performing what we have promised, we swear by the said Father, Son and Holy Ghost, which are one God in Trinity, that we will stone and burn any of those who are reported to have transgressed anything of the above.

And should you in your mercy wish to preserve his life, he shall immediately become a slave ; and you may give him with all his property to whomsoever you please, and do with his person and property whatever you think fit, not only from the power you possess as king, but by this our act and deed we willingly sanction, under date of the 12th of the calends of March, in the sixth year of your reign (655).

XVII.—As Christians necessarily complain of the evil that arises from those opposed to the Christian faith, on that account they are not to pardon those that abandon the best promise and turn to the worst; and, in proportion as the presumption is more cruel and surprising, so ought the punishment to be more severe and cruel.

We therefore by this law enact, that any Christian, particularly those so born, whether man or woman, that should hereafter be found to be circumcised, or that practise Jewish customs, which, God forbid, shall suffer the severest punishment, and be put to death by us and Christians, to know how detestable and excommunicated is the crime he has committed, and all his property shall be confiscated to the king, that neither his heirs nor relations derive benefit from such error.

## CHAPTER V.

*The Jews recalled by Witiza—Invasion of the Moors—Jews protected by them — Capitulation of Toledo — Pelage forms a Christian Monarchy—Manuscripts of Granada burnt — Muley Hassan's Library at Tunis destroyed — Change of Moorish dynasty — The Persian Schools closed—R. Moses clad in Sackcloth—Heroic Conduct of his Wife—Talmud translated into Arabic.*

ON Witiza, who had for some years previously shared with his father Egica the regal power, becoming, in 701, sole sovereign of Spain, brighter prospects opened for the Peninsula. He sought to heal the wounds tyranny and persecution had inflicted on it during nearly three centuries. He reduced the taxes; he recalled those whom his father had banished; he reinstated them in their honors and offices and restored their property. That no remembrance of the accusations against them might remain, he ordered the proceedings to be burnt; and permitted the Jews who had forcibly been baptised, to return to the religion they had involuntarily abjured. Thousands returned to their abandoned homes and a country endeared to them by long residence, so that when a few years after, Granada was taken by the Moors, they found it a Jewish town. But so sudden a transition from the warlike habits of his people, to the enjoyment of peace, raised many enemies against him, the intolerant clergy was not among the most backward.

The monkish chroniclers of the time assert, that he assassinated the duke of Cantabria, and had the eyes of Theodofred, the brother of Rescesvinthus, pulled out. A rebellion broke out in Andalusia; Roderic, the son of Theodofred, was elected king in 709. By the assistance of the Romans, he defeated the army of Witiza, whom he took prisoner, and after depriving him of sight, sent him to Cordova, where he died in confinement.

Three centuries in a delicious southern climate had enervated the Northern warriors. They had degenerated into an effeminate, licentious, and dissolute people. The court became a scene of debauchery; the newly elected king, Roderic, gave the rein to his passions and violated the beautiful Florinda, daughter of Count Julian, governor of the Gothic possessions in Mauritania. On learning the insult and dishonor offered to his noble family, the enraged father conspired to deliver the southern promontory of Spain, where he commanded, to the Moors, who were anxious to avenge the defeat they had experienced from Wamba.

Muza, the lieutenant of the Caliph Walid the First, who then ruled over the immense Arabian empire, and resided at Damascus, dispatched his freedman Tarik with a small force for the coast of Spain. He landed at the foot of the rock Calpe, the present Gibraltar, in April 711, and was shortly after joined by Muza. Roderic had wielded the sceptre but two years, when the Mahometan arms came to arouse him from his stupor and licentious pleasures. He hastily assembled an army to check the victorious African chieftains. The forces met at Xeres de la Frontere: a bloody battle, which furiously raged for eight days, ensued. The combatants on both sides performed most valorous and chivalrous deeds; but the crescent was triumphant. The Visigothic empire was annihilated; and the banners of Muza and Tarik flew from one extremity of the Iberian peninsula to the other. Town after town surrendered to their indomitable arms; they garisoned the principal cities of Seville, Cordova, Granada, etc., with Mahometans and Jews, secure in their fidelity. They had been quiet spectators of the dreadful conflicts; but the injuries they had suffered under their persecutors must have induced them inwardly to pray for the success of the invaders, and to hail them as their deliverers from worse than Egyptian bondage.

Notwithstanding the assertion of some historians, that the Jews opened the gates of Toledo to the Mahometan forces, the capitulation proves it to be groundless. The Saracens had for some time besieged the capital of the Visigothic empire, and had been repulsed in various assaults, when bigotry caused its fall. On Palm Sunday a grand procession, attended by the major part of the inhabitants and the principal officers, proceeded to Sta. Leocadia without the walls. The Moors were watching an opportunity to render themselves masters of the city, and seized that moment to attack it. The commanders, finding their remaining forces inadequate for its defence, surrendered on the following terms, which, in mildness and tolerance, were not less honorable to the conquered than to the conquerors.

All who wished to quit were at liberty to do so in perfect safety, with their property; those who preferred to remain, were to have the free exercise of their religion. Seven churches were appropriated to the Christians; the remainder were converted into mosques. No new churches were to be erected. Taxation to continue the same as under the Gothic sovereigns. Christians and Jews were to have justice administered by their own magistrates, according to their own laws.

At Cordova and Seville, they had been equally tolerant, and the Jew in his synagogue, the Christian in his church, and the Moslem in his mosque, might be seen at the same time worshipping the Creator of all. Can it be supposed if the Jews had acted as traitoriously as archbishop Rodrigo asserts, that the Christian governors would have provided for them in the capitulation. What a contrast between the conduct of Mahometans and Christians towards nonconformists to their faith.

As soon as the Moors were settled in their conquests, the conformity of manners, opinions, sentiment, and even similarity of language, brought numbers of Jews to the Peninsula to partake of their prosperity and science; they were freely allowed to practise that worship, their Christian rulers had imputed to them as a crime. Attached to their new governors, their only rivalry was in learning; both united in the dissemination of knowledge. Foreigners flocked from all parts to receive instruction at the renowned Hebrew and Arabian schools of Cordova; for both flourished greatly under the protection of the Moors.

A few of the Visigoths had escaped the carnage of the bloody field of Xeres, they fled to the mountainous fastnesses of the Asturias, where, under Pelage, a scion of the royal race, they formed a small Christian sovereignty, the capital of which was Oviedo; and their successors, after seven centuries of constant warfare, regained inch by inch the land the Saracens had taken from them. The Gothic prince and his handful of adherents, compelled to devote their whole attention and study to the war against the Moors, were ignorant of commerce, and unaccustomed to industrial pursuits. They required the enterprising genius of the Jews to furnish them the means of existence; they therefore left them unmolested; and, though less fortunate than their brethren in the South, they lived in tranquillity, and ultimately became valuable assistants to the Castilian crown. The followers of Pelage required the aid of the Hebrew people; for they could not maintain themselves. War was their noblest occupation, their supreme necessity. They regarded with the utmost contempt, and considered unworthy their valour every art unconnected with warfare. The husbandman scarcely cultivated the land, the cavalier only knew to unsheath the sword, or brandish the lance. The gains of war and the field were in the end insufficient to supply the wants of life. The elements of cultivation were in the hands of the Jews, and they became indispensable to the Christians. The odium, although never extinguished, was diminished. The services they rendered were paid with contempt and regarded with mistrust; but at least their industry served to satisfy the caprices of some young magnates. The secret of the sciences they cultivated, from not being understood, were believed to be necromancy and witchcraft, for which many in 845 were burnt alive in various towns, for they had been admitted in all the cities retaken from the Moors. The descendants of the Goths, with few exceptions, regarded with contempt any literature but Catholic scholastic theology and legends of saints they themselves had canonized.

This continued in after-ages; for the destruction carried by Ferdinand and Isabella to Granada, extended to its valuable library of five thousand manuscripts. Cardinal Ximenes issued the barbarous decree, that deprived the lovers of the sciences of those precious volumes. He ordered all to be burnt except about three hundred on philosophy and medicine, which he sent to his college at Alcala, "without permitting (as his historian states) that the gold and pearl clasps and bindings should be taken from them, although they intreated, and would have paid the 10,000 ducats at which they had been valued; he did not permit it, because they had been instruments of that accursed race."[1]

Even when Tunis was sacked and pillaged by the troops of Charles V. in 1535, an immense number of valuable Oriental and Arabic books, that were in the library of the Bey, Muley Hassan, and where it is supposed the remains of the famous Alexandrian library of the Ptolemies existed, were destroyed and reduced to ashes. There were works on the human sciences and liberal arts, many on the Alcoran and on the history of the sovereigns of his family. The historian of the emperor, not being endowed with sufficient feeling to regret properly such a loss, although accustomed to unrol the mouldy parchments of barbarious ages in his Benedictine monastery, says, "What Muley Hassan felt most, as I have read, was the loss of his large and valuable library; the bindings

[1] Quintanilla y Mendoza.

and illuminations in blue and gold were worth an immense sum."[2] The historian, Jovius, who was present on that horrible day, heard Muley Hassan say, "that for the whole city of Tunis, he would not have lost such a library." Where such fanatic fury raged in those more enlightened times, it is matter of surprise that so many learned Hebrew and Arabic works have been preserved; numbers must have been destroyed in the continual warfare between the Christians and Moors; for under their reigns, Cordova, Seville, Toledo, Valencia, and other cities, were proud of their rich and valuable libraries.

The revolution that took place at Damascus in 750 to which nearly the whole of the Omeyade dynasty fell victims, and which raised Abul Abbas to the Caliphate, could not fail being felt in the West. Yusef Alphezi, then emir of Spain, declared himself in favor of the usurper, while the Moorish chiefs, desirous of independence, espoused the cause of the deposed family. They resolved to revolt against the Abbasides, and erect a Moorish Caliphate in Spain. But there was a difficulty as to whom they could place for sovereign of the new kingdom; this was obviated by the discovery that Abderachman ben Moaviah, a branch of the Omeyade family who had escaped the slaughter that had extirpated most of his relatives in Syria, was living concealed on the coast of Barbary. The discontented chiefs invited him to Spain. He crossed with a few followers; but soon found himself at the head of a numerous army, with which he defeated Yusef and the partizans of the Abbasides, and seated himself on the throne, assuming the title of Caliph of Cordova, in gratitude for the zeal which

[2] Sandoval.

that city had displayed in his cause; and to declare the independence of himself and his kingdom of the Eastern Caliphate.

Under the wise government of Abderachman, Spain became a place of refuge for the persecuted friends of the Omeyades. Civil dissensions had materially reduced the population; but the immigration of numerous agricultural and industrious Moors and Jews, soon, under his mild and paternal sway, restored it to its former prosperous state. The Omeyade Emirs had founded schools for their own people, and encouraged those of the Jews, which had been established at Cordova, Toledo, Granada, Barcelona, etc., and they could proudly boast there was not a Jew in Spain that could not read the Bible. The appreciation in which the talents of the Hebrews was held, by their enlightened and liberal Moorish sovereigns, cannot be better exemplified than by the fact, that Abderachman II., the third Caliph of Cordova, appointed R. Hasdai ben Isaac, who was his physician, and an able astronomer, to be his prime minister. He placed the utmost confidence in him; and, on the arrival of ambassadors from Germany, desired him to receive and give them the requisite information, before their presentation at Court.

In the East, they had long been known as useful subjects. Omar the second Caliph, and his successor Abdul Meleck, confided the important duty of the coinage to a Jew.

While the famed Oriental academies of Persia and Pumbedita existed, the Jews of Spain respected them as the head of the Hebrew nation, and referred every weighty point, or legal difference to their decision.

Notwithstanding the distance and the dangers of the voyage, they sent their sons to them for the study of the law and education. This may account for the paucity of Spanish Jewish writers in Spain, before the Eastern colleges were closed by the Persian Sovereigns. The only work that has been handed down to us, is the biblical dictionary of R. Menahem ben Saruch, written in 836, he therein arranges in alphabetical order all the Hebrew words in the Bible, with their meanings and derivations. Cordova, under the Moors, became the centre of civilisation, literature, and the arts and sciences. The Jews enjoying equal rights and privileges, rivalled their masters in wealth, splendour, and cultivation. Their superior intelligence gave them a large share in the high ministerial and confidential offices of the court; and they industriously pursued their commerce with success.

After the Persian dynasty had gained the Caliphate, it commenced persecuting the Israelites. Without regard to the flourishing state literature had attained in those Oriental Academies, they expelled the Jews from Babylon, closed their renowned Colleges, and dispersed their illustrious teachers. Four of these learned men were captured by a corsair, despatched by Abderachman from Cordova to cruise in the sea of the Grecian Archipelago. He sold R. Shemaria at Alexandria, who became head of the Jews in Egypt. R. Hoshiel he sold on the coast of Africa, whence he went to Alkirohan, at that time the most powerful of the Mahometan Western provinces, where he became Chief Rabbi. The other two, R. Moses, and his son R. Hanoch, he carried to Cordova. During the voyage he became enamoured of the handsome wife of R. Moses, and endeavoured to force her to his wishes.

She asked her husband in Hebrew, if those drowned at sea would be resuscitated at the resurrection; he answered her with the verse, "The Lord said, I will bring again from Bashan, I will bring again from the depths of the sea,"[3] on hearing which, to save her honor, she plunged into the sea and perished. On the vessel's arrival, the Jews of Cordova redeemed the two captives, although their abilities were not at the time known. One day, R. Moses, habited in sackcloth, with his son entered the college over which R. Nathan presided. The discussion was on a difficult passage of the treatise Joma:[4] after listening for some time, he explained it so satisfactorily to all the students present, that R. Nathan rose from his seat and said, "The stranger in sackcloth is my master, and I am his scholar;" and turning to those learned in the law, continued, "Do you make him judge of the congregation of Cordova," which they immediately did, paying him great honor, and giving him sumptuous apparel and a carriage: this occurred in 980.[5] On the captain discovering the worth of his late captives, he wanted to cancel the sale; but the Caliph would not permit it. R. Moses allied himself to the highest family of the congregation of Cordova, by the marriage of his son R. Hanoch, with a daughter of the house of Peliag, which was so wealthy, that when they went to Zahara, the pleasure seat of the Caliph, they had a retinue of seven hundred Israelites, in carriages, richly drest in the Moorish style. Although this may be considered an exaggeration of the Hebrew historian,[6] still, when the immense wealth of the Cordovese at this period is considered, it may be perfectly correct.[7]

[3] Ps. lxviii. 22.     [4] Day of Atonement.     [5] Juchasin
[6] Ibid.     [7] Appendix, No. 1.

The fame of R. Moses' learning spread through all Spain and the West. Numbers flocked from all parts to receive instruction from him. Among his disciples was R. Joseph ben Isaac Shatnesh, who by desire of the Caliph Hakim, translated the Talmud into Arabic. R. Moses wished in his latter days to return to his native land; but was dissuaded by the Caliph, who was pleased at the opportunity afforded to his Jewish subjects, of being able to receive instruction in their law, without having recourse to the East, then in the possession of his enemies, the Abbasides.

R. Hanoch, on the death of his father, succeeded to the post he had held with so much honor, and in which he had raised the academy of Cordova to the greatest renown. R. Joseph, who felt sorely aggrieved that R. Hanoch should have been chosen president in preference to himself, caused a great disturbance in the congregation, and was so violent, that they excommunicated him. He complained to the Caliph, in the hope that the monarch would have protected him; but the Caliph gave his support to the community, and said to him, "Had the Mahometans spurned me as the Jews have you, I would flee from them, and advise you to do the same;" upon which he quitted Spain, and, after wandering about, died at Damascus.[a]

A heavy tribute having been imposed on the people in 997, the authorities sent Amram ben Isaac to remonstrate against it. He was a philosopher, physician and astronomer of Toledo. The Governor of Seville, offended at the boldness of his representations, put him to death.

[a] Juchasin.

## CHAPTER VI.

*Abderachman III. his remarkable Opinion — Saracens form petty States — The Kingdoms of Navarre Aragon, and Portugal commence — Rabbinical establishments in Spain — R. Samuel a Levi, the Prince — R. Joseph his son succeeds him — Assassinated — Sufferings at Granada — Council at Coyaca — Learned Men — R. Solomon ben Gabriol, comparison of his writings with Rousseau — Five Isaacs — Anecdote of Alfez.*

THE Jews settled in every part of Spain. Under the counts of Barcelona they were numerous Pope Silvester II., in 1002, assigned those of Gerona to the bishop; for the Pontiffs had assumed the power of disposing of them as they pleased.

Moorish Spain, under the wise government of the Omeyade Caliphs, had arrived at the highest degree of civilisation, through their toleration and the protection afforded to the arts and sciences, agriculture, and commerce; the Eastern magnificence of their alcazars and mosques was beyond conception. Their description, and that of Cordova their capital, can only be equalled by those of the Arabian nights.[1]

Israel was at its zenith in the time of Solomon; so were the Mahometans of Spain under Abderachman, III. Like the wise king of Israel, he knew the vanity of mundane glory; for at his death, among his papers, was found this remarkable memorandum

[1] Appendix No. 1.

written by himself. "I have reigned fifty years in victory and peace, beloved by my subjects, feared by my enemies, and esteemed by my allies. Riches, honor and pleasure await my call, nor does any earthly blessing appear wanting to complete my felicity. In this situation, I have carefully reckoned the days of perfect happiness that have fallen to my lot: they amount to fourteen! Man, appreciate hence the value of splendour, worldly enjoyments, and even of life itself: place not thy dependence on this world."

Dissensions that daily increased among the Saracens, led to the dissolution and final overthrow of their empire. Almeria, Saragossa, Valencia, Toledo, Seville, and many other cities, became independent and separate sovereignties. The smaller were soon overpowered by their more powerful neighbours, or conquered by the Christian monarchs.

Navarre had been erected by Don Garcia Ximenes, a Spanish noble, into an independent kingdom separate from Leon in 850. Ramirez in 1035 placed the crown of Aragon on his head. Castille first became united to Asturias and Leon, in 1037. Portugal declared its independence in 1139.

The Jews took no part in the unceasing struggle for power between the Christian monarchs and the Saracen chieftains. Their utility as peaceable subjects, their talents and industry were acknowledged by all, and made useful to both Christian and Mahometan Governments.

On the death of R. Hanoch in 1015, one of the most distinguished of his disciples, R. Samuel a Levi, succeeded to the Chief Rabbinate of Spain, with the title of prince (Nagid), from which it may be reckoned that the government of the Jews was transferred from the banks of the Euphrates to the Iberian soil. Owing to the intestine wars between the two rival Moorish chiefs for supremacy, many of the inhabitants quitted Cordova. Some went to Saragossa, others to Toledo, and R. Samuel a Levi to Malaga, where he kept a druggist's shop. His profound knowledge of Arabian literature, and his beautiful writing, brought him to the notice of Algnarif, prime minister of Habuz of Granada, who made him his secretary, and on his death-bed recommmended his sovereign to be guided by him. In 1020, he was raised to that high post, and in 1027, secured the crown to Baarim, the eldest son of the deceased king, although the grandees had sought to place Balkin, the younger son on the throne of his father. R. Samuel a Levi, conferred great benefits on the Hebrew nation: his charity was not confined to Spain, but extended to his brethren in Africa, Egypt, and the Holy Land. Being exceedingly wealthy, he purchased many copies of the Talmud, Mishna, and other religious works, which, to disseminate learning, he distributed gratuitously. His fame and renown attracted many Jews to Granada from all parts of Spain. His son, R. Joseph succeeded to all his titles and posts of honor; but, unlike his father, whose mildness of disposition and humility had gained him universal esteem, R. Joseph was haughty and proud, and although he was very charitable, he raised himself many enemies among the grandees, who were jealous of his wealth, power, and ostentation. A conspiracy was formed against him, and at the same time a fanatical zealot sought to convert the Mahometans. This assisted the conspirators; for, although the madman was hanged and R. Joseph assassinated, the enraged population, in December 1068, murdered 1,500 families, who, by enjoying tranquillity under the Saracens for upwards of three centuries and a-half, had become immensely wealthy. Plunder probably had, in the Moorish breast, as much influence as religion, in the barbarous act of immolating men, women, and children. The Jews feared it might have extended to all the Moorish dominions; but it went not beyond Granada. Although at this time, by the laws of Spain, it was death for a Jew to commit adultery with a Christian woman, it was only punished by confiscation or scourging. The charter of Barcelona of 1024 records the confiscation of an estate at the foot of Mont Juich, belonging to a Jew named Isaac, convicted of adultery with a Christian woman.

The various Christian states were torn by civil wars. Disputed successions were constant causes for bloodshed; and the nobles had become so powerful, as in many instances to dictate to their sovereigns. The wealth and industry of the Jews became necessary to all; they were intendants of their households and domains, and were protected by all. The power of the bigoted clergy had lost much of its influence; but it yet exercised some authority with mildness. At a council held at Coyaca in the Asturias, it was enacted[2]—

"CANON. 6.—That no Christian shall reside in the same house with Jews, nor partake of their food; whoever transgresses this decree shall perform penance for seven days, or refusing to do it, if a person of rank, he shall be excommunicated for a year; if of an inferior degree, he shall receive 100 lashes."

[2] Aguirre.

Don Sancho Ramirez having, in 1070, peopled Estella, many Jews settled there, and had their Synagogue and separate quarter.

Although Cordova was the focus of Hebrew learning, it was not confined to that city of the arts and sciences. Many distinguished men were to be found in various cities of the Peninsula, who flourished at nearly the same period; among whom may be enumerated:—

R. SAMUEL COPHNI A COHEN—a renowned philosopher and jurist of Cordova, where he died in 1034. He wrote "Expositions on the Law," and a treatise on buying and selling according to the Talmudical Canons.

R. SOLOMON BEN GABRIOL—a native of Malaga, and resident at Saragossa; a poet of great repute, an excellent philosopher, astronomer, musician, and linguist. He wrote the "Azaroth," the 613 precepts in verse; a "Collection of Rubies," a moral work containing the sentences of the ancient Greek and Arabian philosophers, and some other moral works. He died in 1070. His beautiful (and probably the first) astronomical epic poem, entitled "The Royal Crown," based on the Ptolemaic system, was closely imitated by a celebrated French author seven centuries after, as the following extracts will shew. That of R. Solomon loses much of its beauty by being rendered in prose.

R. SOLOMON BEN GABRIOL.

Man, from his existence, is distressed, needy, mortified, and afflicted; from his beginning he is chaff that the wind blows away. From the time he came from his mother's womb, his night is sorrow, his day sadness. To day he is elevated, to morrow he breeds worms; a straw makes him draw back, a thorn wounds him. If in abundance he becomes wicked; if hungry, a loaf of bread renders him criminal. He comes into the world, but knows not whence; he rejoices, but knows not why; he lives, but

J. J. ROUSSEAU.

Que l'homme est durant la vie
  Un parfait miroir de douleurs,
Dès qu'il respire, il pleure, il crie,
  Et semble prévoir ses malheurs.

Dans l'enfance toujours des pleurs,
  Un pédant porteur de tristesse,
Des livres de toutes couleurs,
  Des châtimens de toute espèce.

L'ardente et joyeuse jeunesse
  Se met encore en pire état,
Des créanciers, une maîtresse
  Le tourmentent, comme un forçat.

knows not how long. In his youth he walks in his depravity. When reason begins to give strength to his mind, he diligently seeks to accumulate wealth. He is constantly liable to trouble and the endless changes of events, subject to evil occurrences that happen every moment, until his life becomes a burden to him; in his honey he finds the venom of vipers. As the infirmities of age increase, his intellectual powers diminish; youths mock him, they rule him; he becomes a burden to those who sprung from his loins, and all his acquaintance are estranged from him.

Dans l'âge mur, autre combat,
L'ambition le solicite;
Richesses, dignités, éclat,
Soins de famille, tout l'agite.

Vieux, on le méprise, ou l'évite,
Mauvaise humour, infirmités,
Toux, gravelle, goutte, pituite
Assiègent sa caducité.

Pour comble de calamité,
Un directeur se rend le maître;
Il meurt enfin peu regretté,
C'étoit bien la peine de naître.

Oxford possesses a MS. copy of Gabriol's poetical works.

R. ABRAHAM BEN HIYA—surnamed the Prince, born in 1070, was much esteemed for his proficiency in astronomy. His works are held in high estimation: they are,—1. A description of the form of the earth, the arrangement of the firmament, and revolutions of the planets.—2. A highly moral work entitled, "Meditations of a Penitent Soul, on reaching the Gates of Repentance."—3. A work on arithmetic, and the intercalation.—4. Another on the planets, the two spheres, and the Greek, Roman, and Mahometan kalendars.—5. A work on geometry, with an explanation of spherical triangles, and the conversion of angles and circles.—6. A Treatise on Music.

ABEN ZOAR—born at Penaflor in 1070, was a great observer of nature, profoundly versed in the Hebrew, Arabic, and Syriac languages; his talents were equal for either poetry or prose. Youseph, the Almovaride chief of Morocco, made him his physician, and was so attached to him, that the prince one day having entered his study, and found among his papers some verses regretting his separation from his family, which had remained in Spain, he secretly had them brought to Morocco, settled them in a fine house, and then enjoyed the agreeable surprise of his physician. Zoar died in 1161.

At this period, Cordova boasted of five sages, all having the name of Isaac.

R. Isaac ben Giath — a famous Greek scholar, and an excellent poet. He was the instructor of R. Azariah, son of the unfortunate R. Joseph a Levi, and gave him a home, in gratitude for the kindness he had received from his father and grandfather.

R. Isaac ben Jacob ben Baruch Alcalia — of a noble Jewish family that settled at Merida after the destruction by Titus. His father removed to Cordova, where he was born; his profound knowledge of Hebrew, Latin and Greek, caused him, at the age of thirty-four, to be appointed head of the famous college of his native city. From his proficiency in mathematics, he was invited by Abdallah, King of Granada, a great admirer of that science, to instruct him; and he made him chief of his household. He died there in 1094, aged fifty-nine.

R. Isaac ben Moses — who, to his knowledge of the law and learning, added the talents of a first-rate poet. He was complete master of all the Greek authors.

R. Isaac ben Reuben — of Barcelona, where he was born in 1073, was also a poet, and wrote in verse the 613 precepts; a commentary on the Talmudical treatise, "On Marriage Contracts;" and translated from the Arabic into Hebrew, a work of R. Hay Aaron, " On Buying and Selling."

R. Isaac al Fez — so denominated from being a native of that kingdom. Persecution and jealousy induced him, at the advanced age of seventy-five, to quit his native country for Cordova. Joining its academy, he taught and lectured on the Talmud. He formed an abridgment of it, omitting those laws that were only obligatory in the Holy Land. It is much esteemed, and termed the Little Talmud; it is frequently consulted at the present day. After being chief of the Synagogue for some years, he retired to Lucena, where he died at the age of ninety in 1103. A severe quarrel had taken place between him and R. Isaac ben Giath, who died in 1089. The latter on his death-bed, when his voice was scarcely audible, called his son R. Baruch, and said to him, "Go to R. Isaac al Fez, and tell him, I am leaving this world for the next, and sincerely forgive him all the harsh expressions, whether by writing or verbally, that he has made use of against me, and beg he will also pardon me. He will instruct thee. Remain with him; for I know he will do thee much good, and teach thee with all his heart. After my funeral, go to Lucena, and tell him all I have desired thee." When R. Isaac al Fez heard this, he rent his garments and wept. After being consoled, he said to him, "As thy father (blessed be his memory), is dead, I will be a father to thee, and thou shalt be my son; remain in my house until I have taught thee the whole Talmud."[3]

R. Joseph ben Meir a Levi ben Megas — a native of Seville, born in 1077, received his instructions from R. al Fez, whom he succeeded in the Presidency of the College of Cordova, which post he held for thirty-eight years, and was the instructor of Maimonides. He is highly eulogised by Aboab.[4]

R. Moses aben Ezra — of Granada, celebrated for his great ability in poetry and music. He composed a ritual for the Spanish Jews, by whom many of his poems are recited on the New Year and Day of Atonement. He also wrote some excellent moral works, and died in 1100.

Moses Cohen — a native of Huesca, physician to Alphonso VI., became a convert to Christianity. At the age of forty-four he was baptized in the Cathedral of his native city in 1106, on St. Peter's day; and, in honour of the saint, and his godfather the king, he took the name of Peter Alphonso.

[3] Juchasin.    [4] Nomologia, Par. 2, Ch. 23.

## CHAPTER VII.

*Ferdinand I.—Persecutions prevented.—Jews protected by Alphonso VI.—Capitulation of Toledo—Claim of Exemption from Capitation Tax.—Peter of Aragon—Nicholas de Valencia. Physician of Alphonso interferes with the Marriage of the Princess Urraca—assists in the Attack on Burgos.—Learned Men—R. Judah a Levi, extracts from some of his Writings. — Maimonides, his Opinions of Aben Ezra. — Anecdote of Saladin—His Opinion of the Deity compared with Voltaire's.*

THE religious chivalry of the age led many Christian warriors to join the banner raised by Ferdinand I. to humble the Saracenic power. His bigoted Queen, Donna Sancha, thinking to sanctify his war against the Moorish sovereigns, instigated him to extirpate the Jews; the bishops arrested his zeal; and their conduct was highly commended by Gregory, who then filled the papal chair. The revolution of the Moors in Africa in 1080 so distressed his successor, Alphonso VI., that he found himself obliged to befriend and favor the Jews. In order to make their purses and assistance serviceable to him, they were promoted to considerable posts, and obtained such privileges that Pope Gregory VII. disapproved of his conduct; but his censures were disregarded. Alphonso would not retract what he had done, nor withdraw his protection from them. Alphonso sought refuge from his brothers at Toledo. The reigning monarch Almamen kindly received and hospitably entertained him. In return he promised him his friendship and assistance against a meditated attack of the Caliph at Cordova. But after the death of Almamen and his son Hussein, Alphonso, considering himself relieved from his promise, laid siege to the ancient Visigothic capital, which resisted his forces during three years. At length, in 1085, Toledo capitulated. A large number of Israelites resided in the city and the surrounding country, and they suffered severely from the desolating warfare. The capitulation secured both to Moors and Jews undisturbed residence, the free exercise of their religious rites, and permission to be judged by their own laws; but, although respected by the monarch in their religious ceremonies, the Hebrews were not treated with that consideration the laws of nations demanded—a right ill-defined and worse understood at that period. After the surrender they demanded exemption from the capitation tax of thirty deniers, levied on all Jews in Castile, above sixteen years of age, on the plea, that their ancestors resided there at the time of the crucifixion, and therefore were not accessories to it.

Peter, king of Aragon, was preparing, in 1096, to join the crusade. Nicholas de Valencia endeavoured to dissuade him from it, representing that he need not go so far in search of foes, for he had too many dangerous enemies in his kingdom, alluding to the Jews, who he falsely asserted hated the Christians so much, that they never met them without ejaculating curses on their heads; thus pretending that the bigotry and intolerance of the Jews, was equal to those qualities inherent in the breasts of Dominican friars. But the king, averse to persecution, turned a deaf ear to his advice, and protected them from the massacres they suffered in other Christian states.

In Castile under Alphonso the Jews exercised great influence at Court; for, notwithstanding the ancient prohibitions of Christians holding intercourse with or consulting them in case of illness, his physician was a Jew named Isaac, the author of a learned work on fevers, which a modern medical writer of note, says, " is worthy of being printed at the present day."[1] He was requested by the Castilian nobles, who were averse to the marriage of the princess Urraca with a foreign prince, and wished her to be married to the Count de Candespina, the most powerful and wealthy grandee of Spain, to represent to the king the wishes of the nation, and to dissuade him from giving his daughter to the king of Aragon, fearing, from his impetuous temper, to address him themselves. Alphonso, irritated at the assumption of so much authority on their part, as to wish to control the marriage of the princess, dismissed his physician for conveying to him their representations, and hastened the nuptials, which took place at Toledo in 1106 with extraordinary pomp. His treasurer, a Jew, was sent with a guard of cavalry to demand the payment of tribute from Abenabed, king of Seville, and the restoration of some towns said to belong to the kingdom of Toledo. The envoy had his eyes put out, and his escort was cut to pieces.

In 1123, the castle of Burgos, which had been seized by the king of Navarre, was invested. The Jews of the city and the neighbouring Castilian towns, desirous of signalizing themselves in the service of their

[1] Morejon.

legitimate sovereign, raised a large force to assist in the siege. Their division attacked the place so vigorously, that the Governor, Don Sancho Azna, fearing an assault in that quarter, hastened to the spot with his troops, and was shot by an arrow of the besiegers. On his death the castle immediately surrendered.[2]

Spain, about this time, gave birth to many eminent men among the Jews; they were the ornaments of their age, and cast an imperishable lustre on Hebrew literature.

R. JOSEPH ABEN SACHAL—raised in 1113, to be judge of Cordova, possessed a refined taste for poetry, and was a profound philosopher. He wrote an "Exposition of the Precepts of the Decalogue;" and a philosophic work under the title of "The Small World."

R. BARUCH BEN ISAAC—also of Cordova, died in 1123, his great erudition obtained him the title of אבא "father"; he finished, "The Merchant's Chest, or Hebrew Jurisprudence," begun by his father R. Isaac.

R. ABRAHAM ABEN EZRA—born at Toledo in 1119, emphatically termed the Sage. He was an excellent philosopher, astronomer, physician, grammarian, arithmetician, poet, and cabalist; to which he added a complete knowledge of Greek and Arabic. To him the world is indebted for the Equator to the celestial globe. His thirst for knowledge induced him to travel into Italy, England, and Greece; during his travels, he wrote his numerous works, as his "Epistle on the Sabbath," written in London, testifies. He wrote commentaries on the whole Scripture, which adhere strictly to the literality of the text. They are highly esteemed, and were recommended by Maimonides to his son as the best. The following is an enumeration of most of his works:—
1. "The Secrets of the Law," written at Rome.—2. "On the Tetragrammaton."—3. "On the Mysterious Form of the Letters." —4. "An Enigma," on the four quiescent letters אהוי.—

[2] Sandoval, Hist. de los Reyes de Castilla.

5. "The Pure Speech," on the servile letters.—6. "The Garden of Wisdom."—7. "The Elegance of the Language." —8. "Acuteness of Thought," on Pronunciation.—9. "The House of Customs," on Moral Philosophy.—10. "The Book of Logic."—11. "The Book of Lights."—"The Book of Fractions," on Geometry and Algebra.—13. "The Value of Numbers."—14. "The Gate of Heaven," on Astronomy.—15. "The Book of Chance," on Astrology; with various other works, and a number of poems, among which is one on "Chess." His knowledge of Arabic enabled him to throw considerable light on the book of Job; he died at the age of seventy-five, at Rhodes.

R. ABRAHAM A LEVI BEN DAOR—born at Toledo, in 1120, one of the most renowned Talmudists of his time, highly esteemed for his historical knowledge. His work, "The Order of the World," shews the uninterrupted transmission of the Oral Law. He wrote "Chronicles of Rome," from its foundation, until the Mahometan Empire; "Chronicles of the Kings of Israel during the Second Temple." In Arabic an answer to Abu Alpharage, and under the title of "Exalted Faith," on the elements of nature, and how faith is attainable through them; and on medicine for the soul.

R. JONAH BEN GANACH—of Cordova, born in 1121, a celebrated physician and grammarian; the learned Aben Ezra styled him the most perfect master of language, and every ingenious argument. Pococke terms him the Prince of Grammarians; he wrote a Hebrew Dictionary, Lexicon, and Grammar in Arabic.

R. JUDAH A LEVI BEN SAUL—a celebrated poet and philosopher; many of his sublime poems are in the Synagogue service of the New Year and the day of Atonement. Although much of the beauty and elegance of poetry is lost by a translation in prose; yet, centuries later, his stands the test, and is not surpassed, as is shewn by the following extracts:—

"Reflect and consider the secret of thy soul, what thou art, and whence thy existence; who hath framed thee, and endued thee with understanding, and by whose power thou hast self-motion. Attentively consider the mighty powers of God; awake thy soul; scrutinize his works, but beware that thou attempt not to investigate the nature of his Divine Essence, where thou art contemplating the beginning and end of things, and into the wonderful and occult causes thereof."—*R. Judah a Levi.*

> A ta faible raison gardes-toi de te rendre;
> Dieu t'a fait pour l'aimer, and non pas pour le comprendre,
> Invisible à tes yeux, qu'il règne dans ton cœur:
> Il confond l'injustice, il pardonne à l'erreur:
> Mais il punit aussi toute erreur volontaire.
> Mortel, ouvre les yeux quand son soleil t'éclaire.
> *La Henriade*, Chant 7.

Some that were inedited have lately been given to the admirers of Hebrew poetry, by the learned Dr. Sam D. Luzato, of Padua, under the title of the "Maid of Judah." His philosophical, theological, philological, and cabalistical work, "The Cuzari," translated from the Arabic into Hebrew, by the celebrated linguist and scholar, R. Judah aben Sibon, has since appeared in most modern languages. In his latter days he went to the Holy Land, and was trampled to death by a troop of lawless Arabs.

R. BEHAYE (the elder) BEN R. JOSEPH PEKUDA—The exact time of his birth is not known; but from his famed work "The Duties of the Heart," having been translated into Hebrew from the Arabic (in which it was written), by R. Judah aben Tibon, is supposed to be about this time; he was a native of Barcelona, and judge of the Jews of that city. It proves the existence of a God to the most obstinate atheist, and by illustrations carries conviction to the most ignorant.

R. MOSES BEN MAIMON—more generally known by the name of Maimonides, was born at Cordova, in 1131, where his father R. Maimon was judge. His talents far eclipse the long line of sages he descended from. In his boyhood he was indolent, and so disinclined to study that his father sent him at an early age from his paternal roof. During his absence from home he was unremitting in his studies. An elegant oration made by him at the age of fourteen, reconciled father and son. Acquainted with all the writings of the ancient philosophers, he became the most eminent of his age. He was an able mathematician and metaphysician. When only twenty-three years of age, he began his imperishable work, "The Powerful Hand," which is a complete digest of Hebrew jurisprudence, customs, and religion; he completed it in the short space of seven years. About this period, he pretended to embrace Islamism, the Ahmohad monarch, Abdulmumen, having decreed that all Jews and Christians should become Mahometans. The Jews were particularly persecuted, in consequence of the rich coffin that contained the embalmed body of Mahomet at Mecca, having been robbed of many diamonds and valuable jewels, by a band of Arabs, aided by some accomplices in the town. The guards, to screen their negligence, accused the Jews that had come from Toledo of the act, saying, they had been sent by the other Jews of Spain to commit it. The report being believed, many were put to death, forty Synagogues were burnt, and this decree issued.[5] Maimonides escaped from Spain, and settled in Egypt (from which he is frequently called R. Moses, of Egypt), where he maintained his family at Cairo, by the sale of precious stones and goods he had brought with him. He declared himself to be a Jew, and opened an academy of philosophy and Hebrew, to which many scholars repaired; he joined the Medical School of that city. His talents brought him to the notice of Alphadel Abdelrahim ben Ali Abaisan, who greatly befriended him, and on becoming minister, appointed him physician to the court with a yearly salary. The estimation of his medical abilities is shewn, by the following letter to his friend, R. Samuel aben Tibon (son of R. Judah, and like him a profound scholar in the Arabic and Hebrew language), who wished to visit him.

"Come and welcome," says he, "when you like; for I shall have the greatest pleasure in seeing and talking with you; but I regret you should take the trouble of crossing the sea; and I advise you not to expose yourself to any danger, under the idea of deriving any benefit in literature from me, for, from my constant occupation, not a single hour will you enjoy of being alone with me. I reside at Cairo, the capital

[5] Usque Consoloçaos as Tribulaçoens de Ysrael.

of Egypt, and enjoy the greatest intimacy with the Sultan. In fulfilment of my duty, I visit him every morning and evening. When he or any of his wives or children are indisposed, I do not leave the palace the whole day. I am also engaged to attend the governors in their illnesses. Every morning I go to court; and, if nothing new occurs, at noon I return to my house, which I find full of Jews and Gentiles, nobles and plebeians, magistrates and merchants, friends and those who are not, waiting for me. As soon as I get home I salute them civilly, and beg them to permit me to take some food. Immediately on leaving table I go to learn their complaints, and prescribe what I consider requisite. Numbers have to wait until night; for so many apply, that they occupy me through the whole afternoon; and sometimes, being exhausted, sleep so overpowers me that I remain transfixed in the conversation, unable to utter a word."

His medical aphorisms are considered not inferior to those of Hippocrates. He made an abridgment of Galen, which a modern physician of note writes, " is a most useful work, and merits the highest eulogium, by forming a methodical and learned extract and compendium of the clinical and hygeian spirit of the Greek, Hebrew, and Arabic works. It was a beneficial and glorious undertaking."[6] He had perfected himself in the Æsculapian art under the celebrated Averroes; and, while physician to the famous Saladin, was invited to attend Richard Cœur de Lion during his illness, an honour he declined. He instructed the first-named sovereign in philosophy and humility, and he proved a worthy disciple of so great a master; for, at his death, he ordered his corpse to be interred without pomp, and that the banner carried before it should be a piece of linen the size of his shroud; the bearer loudly proclaiming, " Behold the trophies of Saladin, Sultan of Egypt, Caliph of Cairo, King of Damascus, and the conqueror of Jerusalem."

His " Sanctification of the Months," proves his proficiency in astronomy. As a philosopher, the following extract from his preface to the Mishna may not prove unacceptable. " Know," says Maimonedes," that every thing under the Lunar sphere is

[6] Morejon.

created for the use of man. If there are animals and plants, the utility of which is not apparent, it is because our ignorance has not been able to discover it. The proof is that every age makes discoveries of the utility of certain animals and plants; objects that to us seem poisonous possess their salutary qualities: we have an evident proof in vipers, which, although noxious reptiles, have been rendered useful to man. Then since man is the end of all the creation, we must examine for what purpose he exists, for what end he is created. We see every object of the creation produce the effect for which it is created; the palm yields its dates, the spider weaves its cobwebs. All their qualities render the animal or plant proper to attain their purpose. Then what is that of man? It cannot be to eat, drink, propagate, build walls, or to command; for these occupations are separate from him and add not to his essence, and he possesses nearly the whole of them in common with other animals. It is then intelligence only that augments his being, and elevates him from a lowly condition to a sublime state. It is but by reason that man distinguishes himself from the other animals; he himself is but a rational animal. By reason, I mean the understanding of comprehensible subjects, and above all of the unity of God, all other knowledge tends to conduct him to that; but to arrive at it he must avoid luxury, for too much care bestowed on the body destroys the soul. The man who abandons himself to his passions, who renders his understanding subservient to his corporal desires, does not demonstrate the divine power that lies within him, that is to say reason, which is a matter floating in the ocean of space.

"It results from what has been said, that the purpose of our world, and the objects contained therein, is man endowed with knowledge and goodness. For a man to be perfect, he must combine in himself science and actions, that is, the knowledge of truth with the practice of virtue. This is what not only our prophets, but the ancient philosophers taught us, and it will be found more detailed in my exposition of the "Ethics of the Fathers." Throughout the law you find this precept "Learn and then practise." It inculcates that knowledge precedes action, for knowledge leads to actions, while they do not lead to knowledge. This is the reason why our sages have said that 'learning begets practice.' But, probably, some persons will say, if the purpose of man is to acquire knowledge and perform good actions, why do we see the major part of mankind deficient in knowledge and even despising it; giving reins to their passions, and devoting themselves to mundane occupations? To this I answer: Man has many material wants; it requires the labour of a multitude to satisfy them. The length of Methusalem's life would not suffice were every one obliged to exercise all the arts necessary to supply his physical wants. The study of philosophy can only be the portion of a small number. Were every one to apply himself to that study, in a short time the human race would become extinct."

Maimonides had advanced in knowledge far beyond his time; and he who was and still is considered the greatest man, not only of his nation but of his age, came to be treated as a heretic by the bigoted French Talmudists, and some few of the Spanish Rabbins, for his invaluable work "The Guide to the Doubtful," written in Arabic, and translated into Hebrew by his friend, R. Samuel ben Tibon. They excommunicated him and caused the work to be burnt; but the more enlightened Spanish schools not only supported it, but placed under anathema his French antagonists. R. David Kimchi endeavoured in vain to reconcile this schism. At length the determined conduct of the Spanish Rabbins effected it after his death; and a deputation was sent in 1232, to his grave at Saphet, to ask pardon of his ashes. He is now acknowledged by all Jews to have been the greatest man among them since Moses; for they say, "From Moses until Moses there was not a Moses." His death, which took place in 1204, was considered a national misfortune by the Egyptians as well as the Jews; they observed a general mourning for three days, and called it the lamentable year.[7] At Jerusalem a fast was observed, and the section of the law read on the occasion was: "If ye walk in my statutes, and keep my commandments, and do them,"

[7] Juchasin.

etc.[8] And from the prophets, "And the word of Samuel came to all Israel," etc.[9]

In addition to the above mentioned works he wrote

"The Book of the Precepts." "The Book of Logic." "On the Resurrection, an Epistle against the prevalent opinion of Astrology." Another to the Jews of the South, exhorting them to remain firm to their religion. "On the Preservation of Health." "The Garden of Health." "On Natural History." "The Knowledge of God through his Creatures." "On Dreams." "On the Soul—solutions to various questions on religious points." "A Commentary on Avicenna." "Another on a part of the Guemara." "Sermons." "The Thirteen Articles of Faith," and various other treatises too numerous to detail. Many of his writings are in Arabic; those in Hebrew are in the purest style. His works are universally admired. An eminent English divine says—"The memory of Maimonides has flourished, and will flourish for ever."[10]

## CHAPTER VIII.

*Learned Men.—Nachmanides, his Conference with Fr. Paul.—Riot at Toledo.—Synagogue at Estella taken from them.—Privileges in Aragon.—Alphonso II. of Aragon has two Christians executed for the murder of a Jew.—Letter of Innocent III.—Fuero Viejo.—Caraites.—Alphonso IX. opposed to their Innovations.—Fuero Real.*

THIS may be considered the brightest period, the golden age of Hebrew Literature; for many other

[8] Lev. xxvi. 3.   [9] 1 Sam. iv. 1—11.
[10] Dr. Clavering, Bishop of Peterborough.

learned men flourished cotemporaneously with those noticed in the preceding chapter, among whom may be reckoned:—

R. Moses ben Tibon Marimon—a native of Granada, born in 1134, who even excelled his talented relatives, R. Judah and R. Samuel. His proficiency in the Hebrew and Arabic languages enabled him to translate from the latter into the former, the most classical works on Jurisprudence, Philosophy, Astronomy and Medicine; and those of Maimonides, Averroes, Aristotle, Alphagran, and Euclid's Elements. He obtained for his abilities the title of "The Father of Translators." He wrote in Hebrew a philosophical work, solving the problem why the sea and waters do not inundate the earth.

R. Benjamin ben Jonah—of Tudela, in Navarre, celebrated for his travels in the East, which he commenced in 1160, and continued for fifteen years. His itinerary has been translated into various languages. M. Asher, of Berlin, has lately made it familiar to the English reader with valuable notes.

R. Moses Giguatilla—born at Cordova in 1148, was a poet of great repute; he translated Job and various Hebrew writings into Arabic, and composed a Hebrew vocabulary.

R. Joseph Kimchi—was born at Narbonne, in 1160, but styled himself a Spaniard; much esteemed for his knowledge of sacred and profane literature, and particularly grammar and poetry. He wrote various controversial works against Christianity; " A Commentary on Jeremiah;" " The Holy Shekels;" a collection of poems; and " The Book of Memory," a grammatical work. His son—

R. Moses Kimchi—born in 1190, was also an excellent grammarian. Exclusive of his grammar, he wrote various works on it, having the titles of " The Entrance to the Road of Knowledge;" " The Paths of the Holy Tongue;" " The Gate of my Words;" " Good Understanding;" " The Book that heals." He also commented on Proverbs and Ezra, and wrote a moral philosophical work, entitled "The Delight of the Soul." But the greatest of this talented family which had furnished Rabbins to various congregations of Spain was his brother —

R. DAVID KIMCHI — born in 1192, denominated, from his excellent Hebrew dictionary and Grammar, "The Prince of Grammarians." His "Commentaries on Scripture" are highly esteemed; and considered necessary for the perfect understanding of the holy writings. He endeavoured, in vain, to effect a reconciliation between the French and Spanish schools on the subject of Maimonides' Guide.

R. ABRAHAM BEN HASDAI — Chief Rabbi of Barcelona, contemporary with R. David Kimchi, was a moral philosopher of note and a profound scholar. Under the title of "The Apple," he translated from the Arabic into Hebrew, a work containing numerous moral sayings and sentences of philosophers; "The Just Balances," a moral work of Algazali; and wrote a moral work entitled, "Directions for the Soul," and "The King's Son and the Nazarene;" also "Arguments on the Fear of God."

R. MOSES BEN NACHMAN — more commonly known by the name of Nachmanides, was a native of Gerona, from which he is sometimes called R. Moses of Gerona, born in 1198. From his great erudition, he obtained the title of "The Father of Knowledge." He was a profound philosopher, cabalist, and physician; and particularly famed for his abilities in the obstetric art. His reputation as a learned doctor in the law, led to his being nominated on the part of the Jews, to the public disputation with Fr. Paul Christiani, by the decree of James I., king of Aragon (to which kingdom Catalonia belonged), to put a stop to the daily disputes that took place between the Jews and Dominican friars who had studied Hebrew and Arabic. This decree induced the adverse parties to select their ablest advocates, and the above named were chosen. The conference took place in the presence of the king and court; the two orators defended their respective causes with great erudition and eloquence. As usual in similar cases, each party claimed the victory. R. Moses drew up an account of the proceedings, and proved that his arguments were answered only by sophisms. The king was so pleased with his conduct and talents, that he presented him with 300 crowns. In his latter days he quitted Spain, and retired to the Holy Land, where he built a handsome college, and died in 1260. He left a number of learned scholars, and the following learned works:—

"The Garden of Desire," and a dozen other Cabalistic works. Epistles on the "Sanctity of Marriage;" on moral subjects, addressed to his son; and one in defence of Maimonides; "An Exposition of the Law;" "A Commentary on Job;" another on some "Treatises of the Talmud;" "On the Works of Maimonides;" "The Law of Man"— directions how to conduct himself in Sickness, Trouble, Death, and the Hope of a Future Life; "On the Coming of the Messiah;" his sermon on the Excellence of the Law, preached before the king of Castile; "On the Redemption from Captivity;" a lament on the "Destruction of the Temple;" and his "Conference with Friar Paul."

Toledo had offered hospitality to the learned Hebrew strangers, who, emulating the thirst of glory and science which the sectarians of Mahomet had cultivated, contributed on their part to inoculate the Spanish people with it; but they, exclusively attached to the art of war, little heeded such pursuits. The favour shewn by the king to the Jews incensed the people against them. In 1108, a riot took place at Toledo, probably instigated by the fanatics then about joining the crusade, the archbishop, Bernard, having taken the cross. The populace, under pretence of the hatred they bore towards their religion, murdered numbers; the streets of Toledo streamed with Jewish blood. Fire consumed immense wealth; plunder and violence left every where the trace of desolation. This fatal example was a precedent for the many massacres that are indelible stains on the history of the Spanish nation. In vain did King Alphonso, animated by humanity, attempt to punish the perpetrators of the horrid attack. The mob, irritated at the privileges granted to the Jews, plundered the synagogues, and immolated the Rabbins at the foot of their altars; nothing had been respected. The laws were disregarded, or were too impotent; and the people carried their thirst for blood to the utmost excess. The Hebrew people, amidst the troubles of which they were the victims, sought protection from the king and church, by large contributions, exclusive of their ordinary taxation and capitation. The latter was frequently assigned to grandees for some signal action, or in exchange for some privilege, in lieu of a pension on the royal revenues.

The king of Navarre, Don Garcia the Monk, so called from having been bishop of Burgos and Pamplona, in 1135 assigned them to the citizens of Estella, for the services rendered him; and with the Catholic feeling of the time, deprived them of their principal synagogue, and gave it to his successor in the latter see, who dedicated it to the mother of God and all saints.[1]

The Jews had, in 1170, obtained many privileges at Nagera. King Sancho, the Wise, extended them to those of Tudela, to induce them to settle in Castile, and for their protection; they are thus detailed in the archives of Navarre (Dr. Asso y Rodrigues, the compiler of the ancient Spanish Laws, could not discover them complete):—

[1] Lezaun, MS. Mem. of Estella.

"The power of selling the houses they quitted within their barrier.

"To pay no tax, under condition that, with the exception of the principal tower, they should keep the castle in repair.

"That should they be attacked in Castile, and kill any person, they should not be punished for murder.

"That in taking oath on the demand of Christians, they should answer: 'I swear' ten times; and 'Amen,' ten times.

"The king will appoint a Christian judge to whom Christians are to apply in complaints against Jews.

"In trials between Moors and Jews, they are to be proved by Jews and Moors only; the same as is done between Christians, Jews, and Moors.

"Finally, he granted them land for a Cemetery."

Charles II. confirmed all the above in 1355.[2]

In the following year he granted the same to the Jews of Fumes.[3] Jews were not to pay tithes on what they inherited from their progenitors, but only on what they acquired from Christians.[4]

During the constant warfare carried on in Castile, Navarre, and Aragon, from disputed successions and the differences among the Moorish sovereigns, the services of the Jews were required by all the belligerents, and they were employed in the highest offices of state, both by Christians and Moors.

Alphonso VIII., who at an early age had been married to Eleanor, daughter of Henry II. of England, proved a second Marc Anthony. In 1171, he became enamoured of a beautiful Jewess, named Fermosa; neglected his queen, abandoned public affairs, and for seven years confined himself to his capital with his inamorata; although after his defeat at Alarcos, his states were menaced by the kings of

[2] Arch. Nav. Case 1, No. 34–53.   [3] Ibid. No. 36.
[4] Fuero de Sobarbe, No. 220.

Aragon, Leon, and Seville. The superstitious people attributed the disasters that befell the kingdom, to the impious love of the prince. They did not hesitate to sacrifice the mistress of the king to what they considered the welfare of the nation. A riot broke out at the residence of the king; the rebels entered his palace, and under his eyes assassinated the handsome Jewess, to whose influence they attributed all the public calamities. Alphonso, seeing the fury of the people, dared not punish any of the assassins, from fear of experiencing the fate of his favourite; but, aroused from his lethargy on the plains of Tolosa, he repaired the disgrace of Alarcos.

Alphonso II. of Aragon had two Christians executed for the murder of a Jew. As he owed 100 marabotins to one of the assassins, he is accused of having done it, not as an act of justice, but to rid himself of an importunate creditor.

Through the mediation of Henry II. of England, peace was concluded between Castile and Aragon; by which the revenues from the Jews of Estella and Euvenes were ceded to the former.[5]

Alphonso IX., whose reign began 1188, was particularly favourable to Jews and Moors. The favour shewn them by this liberal monarch, induced Pope Innocent III. to address him on the subject in 1205. He accused him of elevating the synagogue and mosque at the expense of the church; that he exonerated Jews and Moors from paying tithes, and permitted them to acquire landed property as they liked. That the slave of a Jew becoming a Christian, by that conversion became free, and instead of paying the owner the amount fixed by ecclesiastical canons,

[5] MS. Mem. of Estella.

the Jew was permitted to claim what indemnity he chose; that, latterly, the bishop of Burgos was compelled to pay 200 pieces of gold for a girl not worth ten sous, as the pope says. This latter part shews that the letter had been written through the influence of the Spanish clergy at the court of Rome. R. Hay, a native of Granada, was physician to the king. Finding the laws so inoperative, Alphonso, in 1212, revised the Fuero Viejo of Castile, a code formed by Sancho Garcia, count of Castile, between 995 and 1000, but which Dr. Asso y Rodrigues, who has preserved the revised code, could not discover. The following are the only ones wherein Jews are mentioned, and which place them on an equality with his other subjects: —

### Fuero Viejo of Castile.—Book III. Title 2.
### On Proofs.

If a Christian or Jew demand a debt from another Christian, which the latter denies, and the creditor asserts he can prove it, arbitrators shall be named in presence of the Alcalde (magistrate), whose decision after the examination of witnesses shall be binding; but if arbitrators are not appointed, the case remains undecided, and the parties may commence the suit *de novo*.

### Title IV.—On Debts.

§ 1.—If a knight is indebted to a Jew or Christian, and the debt is recognised and acknowledged, the debtor, if he possesses moveables, must deliver them to his creditor, and they are to be sold to pay him within nine days; but if immoveable property is deposited for the payment, the debtor is to keep possession, and enjoy it until the debt is paid; and should he incur any expense on it, he is to reimburse himself before the debtor receives anything from it; but if he will not uphold the property, he is to retain it in its depreciated state; but he may not sell it to another person.

§ 3.—If any person is indebted to a Jew, and has given a bond engaging all his property for the payment, he may dispose or mortgage a part of it before the Jew is in possession; but if he, or the sheriff in his behalf, is in possession of it, he may neither sell nor mortgage it to any other person until the Jew is paid.

§ 18.—If a Jew sues a man of the town, and he appears before the Alcalde, if he wishes to make terms with the Jew, the Alcalde shall fix the time at ten days.

§ 19.—If a Jew demands a bond debt, and the debtor denies it, the Alcalde is to take the bond; if the Jew proves it according to law, he must have his debt, and the person who denied it must pay a fine of sixty sous to the judge; if the Jew cannot prove it according to law, the bond is to be cancelled, and the Jew is to be fined sixty sous. If a Jew demands a bond which is proved to have been paid, the Alcalde shall tear the bond, and fine the Jew sixty sous; but the Christian who gave the bond must prove the payment by another Christian or a Jew, as his testimony alone is not sufficient.

## Title V.—On Pledges.

§ 3.—If a person pledges wearing apparel, bedding, plate, or other articles to Jews or Christians, and the holder claims a sum that the other disputes, and the holder declares the amount he advanced, and offers to prove they were pledged for that amount; if he cannot prove it, the other is to pay no more than he acknowledges, and is to receive his pledge. If the pledges are deposited with a Jew, as the Jew is to be secured for the sum he claims, the Christian must pay it, and fifty per cent. per annum for profit, unless he can prove he has not received as much.

§ 4.—If a Jew takes pledges of apparel, bedding, furniture, or plate, from a Christian, on interest, and another person claims them as having been lost or stolen from him, and demands their restitution: if the Jew declares that he took the articles in pledge, but does not know the person that pledged them, the Jew must swear in the synagogue that he does not know the person, nor has any understanding with him to return them, and also the amount he advanced, if the Christian wishes to redeem them. If they do not in right belong to the Jew, he must pay the amount advanced, and the Jew is to give them up without interest.

Many foreigners, for such they termed the Navarrese and Aragonese that had joined Alphonso against the Moors, being encamped in the vicinity of Toledo, with pretended zeal ill-treated the Jews and killed some. The nobles and Toledans took arms in their defence against the strangers; but it required all the authority and prudence of the king to quell the riot and secure the Jews from injury; and many quitted Spain at the time and settled in Barbary. During this reign, the Caraites made their appearance in Spain, and caused so much disturbance from their difference with the tenets of the Spanish Jews that the king was obliged to interpose his authority. At Burgos, they attempted to overthrow the customs and usages that had been practised for ages. The king sided with the majority; he prohibited the Caraites from practising their rites, and enjoined them to conform to the religion of the mass of the Hebrew people; which they either did or quitted the country, for no further mention is made of them in Spanish history. He protected the Jews in the free exercise of their religion, and prevented apostasy, as is seen by the subjoined extract from the code of laws which he added to his revision of the Fuero Viejo, for the government of his kingdom.

## Fuero Real (Royal Statute) of Alphonso IX.
### Book IV. Title 2.—On Jews.

I.—We forbid any Jew reading or keeping concealed books opposed to his religion, or that would invalidate it; any one possessing or finding such is to burn them publicly at the synagogue gates. We further prohibit their reading, or knowingly possessing any books that speak against our religion, or in disparagement of it. But we permit them to read and possess all books on their religion, as those given by Moses and the other prophets; and should a person read or keep any book contrary to this our prohibition, his person and property shall be at the mercy of the king.

II.—We strictly forbid any Jew to induce any Christian to turn from his religion, or circumcise him. Whoever does, shall die for it, and his property be confiscated to the king.

III.—If a Jew utters anything reviling against God, the holy Maria or other saints, he shall be fined ten maravedis for each offence, and the king shall order one hundred lashes to be given to him.

IV.—No Jew or Jewess shall presume to rear the child of a Christian, nor give his or her child to be brought up by a Christian. Any person so doing shall pay a fine of one hundred maravedis to the king.

V.—No Jew is to advance money at interest, or otherwise, on the person of a Christian. Whoever does shall lose whatever he may have lent, and the Christian can go free whenever he chooses. No law-suit or sentence to prevent him is valid.

VI.—No Jew shall lend at a higher rate of interest than thirty-three and a third per cent per annum. If he lends at a higher rate, it is void; and if he receives more, he shall pay double the amount he received to the person who paid it; and any law-suit instituted contrary hereto shall be of no avail. Furthermore we order, that no one shall presume to use any pledge he may have taken, or lend it to any other person: whoever does shall be fined half its value for the owner; nor shall any suit he may enter to use it be admissible, unless the pledge be free of interest during the time. We further forbid any further interest to be charged after the interest amounts to as much as the capital; nor is the bond to be renewed until the year is completed. Should any suit be craftily instituted to obtain more, it shall be void. And if in any way he receives more than the law permits, he shall refund it as said before. This law is for Jews, Moors, and Christians, or any one who lends on interest.

VII.—We do not prevent Jews observing their sabbaths, and the holidays enjoined by their religion. They may practise whatever the holy church and kings have permitted; and no person shall oppose or obstruct them. No one shall compel them to appear before a tribunal, nor condemn them, nor seize nor arrest their persons on those days, that they may not do anything contrary to their religion. Neither may they summon any other person to justice on those days.

## CHAPTER IX.

*Learned Men.—Poignard of Faith.—Christian Conquest.—Moorish Dissensions.—Cortes of Barcelona —of Saragossa.—Capitulation of Cordova.—Valencia surrendered.—Rescript at Gerona. — Ordinance of Lerida.—Seville reduced.—Kindness of Ferdinand. —College of Cordova transferred to Toledo.—Reported Crucifixion of a Chorister.—Alphonso X. the Wise, succeeds his Father.—Astronomers employed by him.—Jealousy of the Catalans.—A Duty levied on Foreign Jews and Moors.—Protected by Alphonso— his ordinance respecting Pledges. — Charter of Alcala — of Salamanca — of Sahagun. — Bull of Alexander IV.*

PERHAPS there are none in the present century whose fame is so great as that of those of the preceding one; but Spain yet could boast of many learned Hebrew writers, who do honour to its literature. Barcelona in 1200 gave birth to—

R. JOSEPH CASPI—a renowned philologist and grammarian. On the latter subject, his works yet extant are, " The Treasure of the Holy Tongue," explaining all the words in scripture. His dictionary, entitled " Silver Chains," contains the roots of all Hebrew words. He wrote an exposition of the precepts, with the title of, " The Book of Mystery." He also commented on Lamentations; the Guide of Maimonides; the Ten Predicaments of Aristotle; Plato's Government of State; and the Commentary of Aben Ezra.

R. JONAH OF GERONA — was born about this period. He wrote on the "Ordinances of Women;" "The Gates of Repentance," shewing its necessity; another work on lawful and prohibited things. The fame of his great piety and morality brought him to the notice of James I., of Aragon, who commanded him to write a work to instruct man in the duties of religion and piety; which he did, under the title of, "On the Fear of God." He died and was buried at Seville in 1264.

It is affirmed of this prince that he so highly respected the learned rabbins, that he claimed their assistance for instruction on moral subjects, and also borrowed their prayer-books for his private devotions; so that, although hated by the populace and the ignorant among the clergy, the great and learned not only protected, but admired and encouraged them. Although this prince persecuted the Albigenses, he treated the Jews kindly; his confessor, Raymond de Pennaforte, having recommended mild measures as the most effectual means of converting them. Pennaforte is by some supposed to be the author of "The Poignard of Faith," a violent attack on the Jews; but from its not appearing until three centuries later, it is far more probably the production of the envenomed pen of another less humane Dominican friar, named Raymond. This monarch would not permit a Spanish translation of the Bible in his dominions, probably from that of R. David Kimchi (from which the Ferara edition is supposed to have been printed) being the only one then known.

R. JACOB ANTOLI — a native of Granada, born in 1210, was a profound mathematician, linguist, and expositor. He translated into Hebrew Maimonides' Compendium of Logic; the

Isagoge of Porphyrus; the Book of Aristotle on the Interpretation; the First and Second Book on Syllogisms, with the Commentary of Averroes, and the Arabic of Alphragan on the Celestial Revolutions. He wrote a philosophical exposition of the Pentateuch in Hebrew, bearing the title of "The Instructor of Scholars."

R. JACOB BEN MACHIR TIBON—born at Cordova in 1215, resident at Seville, was a mathematician, astronomer and philosopher of high repute. He wrote on the Astrolabe, under the title of " The Quadrant of Israel;" another astronomical work; a commentary on the Pentateuch; and translated Averroes' Arabic comment on Aristotle, and Euclid's Elements, into Hebrew.

R. ISAAC ABEN LATIPH — was also highly esteemed as a philosopher, astronomer, geographer, and physician. He wrote a theological philosophical work, entitled, "The Gate of Heaven;" "The King's Treasury," or questions on philosophical subjects; "The Form of the Universe," on the terrestrial and celestial globes, and some theological works.

R. MOSES MICOZZI, of an Italian family, but a native of Toledo, was a famed preacher of great repute and eloquence. He severely reprobated a custom, then prevalent, of marrying strange women; he travelled much in Spain, and taught the law in his native city. His learned commentary on the precepts is highly esteemed.

R. JOSEPH BEN SHOSHAN—must have held an important office under the Moorish king of Seville, for, among some tombstones found at Seville, where he died in 1233, his epitaph expresses, that "he was mighty in the law, a prince in government, and that all the nobles of the king bowed their heads to him."[1]

R. JOSEPH BEN DAOUD—is another proof of the high consideration the Moorish sovereigns entertained for their able Jewish subjects. Although no mention is made of him in history, his epitaph states, that "the Arabian kings conferred honour and power on him." He died at Seville in 1240.[2]

[1] Appendix, No. 2.     [2] Appendix, No. 3.

R. MEIR BEN TODROS—a native of Burgos, taught the law at Toledo, where he died in 1244; he wrote various cabalistical works; a letter against Maimonides; and a treatise on the Masorah, entitled "The Fence of the Law."

R. ABRAHAM BEN JUDAH—of Barcelona, born in 1230, was a superior Theologian and Jurist; he wrote, under the title of, "The Four Orders," an excellent work on the existence of God, Divine Providence, the final cause of the law of Moses, and the purport of its precepts.

R. PEREZ A COHEN—a Jurist of high repute, a great cabalist, and celebrated physician, was born about 1241, at Gerona; his work, "The Dispositions of the Divinity," is much esteemed.

R. GERSHON BEN SOLOMON—also a native of Catalonia; his work, "The Gate of Heaven," treats on natural objects, astronomy according to the systems of Ptolemy, Alphragan, and Averroes, and on theological subjects.

The victorious arms of the Christian princes achieved conquests from the Moors, notwithstanding they bravely defended the possessions which the indomitable courage of their ancestors had wrested from the Visigothic monarchs five centuries before. By their subdivision into numerous petty states, for almost every town of note had declared its independence, the extensive Cordovese empire had become eight separate kingdoms; Toledo, Seville, Cordova, Jaen, Granada, Murcia, Valencia, and Badajoz, each had its sovereign. Their mutual jealousies, and the hope of retaining their small dominions, often led them to join their forces to those of the Christian princes; and the banner of the crescent might frequently be seen, with that of the cross, unfurled on the field of battle against their more powerful Moorish neighbour.

The six catholic kingdoms of Castile, Leon, Asturias, Aragon, Navarre, and Portugal, had by intermarriages, notwithstanding their frequent quarrels, become more united against the Saracens. These causes led to the gradual waning of the crescent, destined no longer to cast its refulgent light over the fertile fields of Andalusia; and a few years later it set for ever on the most fruitful portion of Europe.

In 1224, Ferdinand III. commenced the conquest of Andalusia, by taking Baeza; upon which all the neighbouring towns of that small state surrendered.

The cortes held in 1228 at Barcelona, deprived the Jews of a privilege they had long enjoyed in Catalonia; it decreed, if there was no document proving a debt, that the oath of a Jew was not alone sufficient for the recovery of it.

James I., in 1230, added Majorca to the crown of Aragon, and held a cortes at Tarragona in 1233; among other laws are found[3]:—

§ 15.—We also enact, that Jews are not to lend at a higher rate than twenty per cent. either in Aragon or Catalonia, nor is the interest to exceed the capital.

§ 20.—Jews are not to become Mahometans, nor are Moors to embrace Judaism.

In the following year, he issued another, entitled[4]—

" Regulations against the Avarice of the Jews, and the Cruelty of Usury." The preamble states, that Christians had almost renounced usury; but that the insatiable avarice of Israelite usurers had reached the point of overthrowing fortunes, and knew no bounds, particularly by the accumulations on the capital. The intention of government is not to prevent Jews lending money; for those transactions are useful to Christians. But to stop abuses, it is ordained that all Jews in town or

[3] Marca Hispanica, App. 515.     [4] Idem, 51.

country, that would lend on interest, are to swear in presence of a notary, that they conform to the law. The oath is not to be taken in the synagogue or a private place, but in a court of justice, or the place where oaths are administered to Christians. They shall swear on the law of Moses and the Decalogue, and add all the ceremonies and curses as practised by the Jews of Barcelona. The notaries shall register their oath, and draw up no acts for Jews that are not registered and sworn to. The interest, whatever may be the term of the loan or quality of the security, in no case shall exceed four deniers on a livre per month. No Jew is permitted to add the interest to the capital, and charge compound interest; nor may he demand a larger amount of interest than the capital. All contracts and demands that are not conformable to these statutes shall be void; and the Jew who lends on illegal terms shall lose the amount of the loan, half to be for the informer, and half for the king's lieutenant. Notaries who draw up such contracts are to be deprived of office for ever. Christian borrowers shall make oath before the notary, that the capital and interest are really the amounts expressed in the bond.

In Navarre, it appears no distinction was made between Christians and Jews; for, in 1234, Pope Gregory IX. ordered the king, Thibaut I., to compel the Jews to dress differently to Christians, as established by a general council, which he was informed was not enforced in Navarre.[5] By the Fuero of Sobarbe, Jews were permitted to marry as many wives as they could (*gobernar*)[6] maintain, but might not leave one without divorcing all. If a Jew cohabited with a Christian woman both were to be burnt.[7]

After an obstinate resistance, Cordova, the capital and seat of the Spanish caliphs, surrendered to the victorious forces of Ferdinand in 1236; the inhabit-

[5] Arch. Nav. Case 2, No. 12.   [6] Query—To govern?
[7] Arch. Nav. Case 2. Fuero de Sobarbe, 76.

ants, by capitulation, were allowed to retire with their property. Many Jews, with regret, quitted a city that had become dear to them, from the tranquillity they had for centuries enjoyed under the Moslem sovereigns, and the reminiscence of the glory shed by their schools on the literary character of the Hebrew nation.

Two years after, a similar fate attended the city of Valencia. It surrendered, after a prolonged siege, to the army of James, who, by his many conquests during a long successful reign, had greatly enlarged the kingdom of Aragon. Upwards of 50,000 Moors are said to have quitted those (to them) Elysian fields, among whom were many Jews; the inhabitants being permitted to carry away their gold, silver, and other property.

In 1240, James issued a rescript at Gerona,[8] ordaining that on doubts arising in a court of law between a Christian borrower and a Jew lender, they were to be decided in favour of the former; and that a Christian might prove a debt against a Jew by Christian witnesses only; thus abrogating the privilege that no debt could be proved against them without a Jew witness. In Valencia, it was necessary that all debts above five sous should be proved by Christian witnesses or writing. Although kindly disposed towards the Jews, he wished for their conversion; and to encourage those who became Catholics, he issued an ordinance in 1242 from Lerida, authorising it unconditionally, and securing to them their property of whatever nature it might be, and that the children or relatives of the convert should claim no part of it during his life-time, but on his death might inherit such

[8] Mar. His. 513.

portion as though he apostatised to Judaism or Paganism. This decree also included Moors.

In 1244, Ferdinand compelled Granada to become tributary; and, after an obstinate resistance, his son Alphonso, in 1248, forced Seville to capitulate: 400,000 persons of all ages and sexes, fearing new persecutions, are said to have quitted the Andalusian capital, among whom were a number of Jews. Many retired to Africa; others, to various parts of Spain; from whence many afterwards returned, which may be attributed to the conduct of the prince, who, desirous of the Jews remaining in the conquered city, shewed them particular favour. In dividing Seville, he appropriated the three parishes of Santa Maria la Blanca, St. Bartholomew and Santa Cruz, to them for a Jewry. He also gave them three mosques, situated within those parishes, for synagogues; and for their protection surrounded it with a wall, extending from the Alcazar to the gate of Carmona, of which vestiges are yet remaining, as well as some mutilated Hebrew inscriptions in a synagogue they built in the parish of St. Bartholomew. Within the Jewry they had their exchanges, markets, courts of justice, and slaughter-houses; and in an adjacent field their cemetery. The liberality of Alphonso, his son, the Infante who headed the army, went farther; he granted the rights of inheritance to those who had dwelt there under the Moorish sovereigns, as well as to all those that might be attracted to it by its immense population. Ferdinand, who was afterwards canonised, protected learning, and with it the Hebrew scholars; for under his auspices the famous college of Cordova was in 1249 transferred to Toledo, which became the principal seat of Jewish literature, although Seville, Barcelona, and other cities possessed schools of high repute and many learned men. His physician was Solomon ben David, and he had many Israelites in his service as receivers and auditors, who administered the royal revenues. In the general division, on the conquest of Seville, he rewarded those Jews who had accompanied him, by giving them lands in the Loza, afterwards called the Paternilla of the Jews. In seeking to ameliorate their condition, he not only attended to the voice of humanity, but likewise to the progress and diffusion of the elements of civilisation; and established professorships of Hebrew at Toledo, Seville, and other important cities of his dominions. In gratitude for these favours, on his public entry into Seville, the Jews presented him a key of most curious and elaborate workmanship, bearing in Hebrew and Spanish the inscription, " God will open, the king shall enter." It is yet preserved in the cathedral. To the protection of St. Ferdinand may be attributed, that the Jews were not persecuted from the false report that they had stolen and crucified a young chorister of the cathedral of Saragossa, named Dominic, whose murder it is said was discovered by a miraculous light appearing over his grave, from which he was disinterred and sainted. This attempt of the clergy by whom it was concocted, only exposed the Jews to the insults and hatred of the populace; but they suffered no violence from it.

The tolerant spirit of this prince is demonstrated by the liberal code of laws under the title of " Las Siete Partidas," which he left nearly completed at his death; for in those superstitious times, it was no easy task to protect the Jews and conciliate the clergy. The laws that appear severe against them, are only conformable to papal and conciliary decrees, which could not, from the influence of the clergy, be abrogated, either with safety to the sovereign or those they wished to protect. He was succeeded in 1252 by his son Alphonso X., surnamed the Wise. This illustrious prince was much attached to astronomy and mathematics. At an early age he sought the aid of the many Jewish proficients in those sciences, and in the Arabic language. At his desire, before his ascension to the throne, his physician R. Judah Mosca, translated a curious ancient Arabic manuscript into Spanish, which had originally been written in Chaldee. It treats on 360 stones, their colour, virtues, where found, and the figure of the celestial sign from which each derives its strength; thus combining mineralogy with the superstition of the day—astrology: the work, yet in the library of the Escurial, is elaborately illuminated. He also translated, by the king's desire, the astronomical work of Ali ben Ragil, of which another translation was made by R. Judah a Cohen, who, by order of his sovereign, translated the astronomical treatise of Avicenna on 1022 stars; and wrote a work on the forty-eight constellations formed by the 1252 stars which he reckoned in the firmament, contrary to the general opinion of Avicenna and cotemporary astronomers.

R. Zag, of Sujurmenza, by command of this learned prince, wrote on the various astrolabes then in use, and gave rules for making dials.

R. Isaac ben Said, the reader of the Synagogue of Toledo, where he was born in 1242, was also employed by him to assist in forming the famed Alphonsine tables; he was one of the profoundest mathematicians of the age.

The protection afforded by this learned monarch, greatly increased the Hebrew population of Castile. As many as 12,000 students are said to have resided then at Toledo. Although astronomy was his favourite study, the learned and scientific were equally protected and patronised by him; but, notwithstanding his liberality, he could not attract all the Hebrew scholars Spain then could boast of. Exclusive of these Castilian subjects, Aragon and the principality of Catalonia possessed many learned Jews; although the Hebrew population was not as numerous as in Castile, owing to the jealousy of the Catalans, who had sought to place their commerce on the same system as Genoa and Pisa. The privileges Barcelona had obtained from the kings of Aragon, had rendered it a vast emporium. They no longer required the aid of foreigners, and obtained permission from the king to expel the Lombards, Pisans, and Florentines; nor were foreigners permitted to establish banks at Barcelona. The native Jews were tolerated; but Moors and Jews coming from foreign parts were subject to an import duty, and figured in the tariff among silks, saffron, soap, and other merchandise.

The Jews had claim to the benevolence of the Castilian monarch; their doctors of the law possessed the arts and sciences in the highest perfection; and it was impossible for a king who devoted to their study the moments of leisure that state affairs left him, not to feel a lively sympathy towards their most renowned cultivators. Alphonso used all the means within his power that did not place him in direct opposition to his vassals, to protect the Jews; as thereby he protected the advancement of human knowledge: giving thus an impulse to Spanish civilisation.

The removal of the Cordovese schools to the ancient capital of the Visigoths was of the utmost importance at the time. The learned Rabbins who had competed with the Arabian Ulemas, made their voices heard in the Jewry of Toledo; and when the star of Arabian civilisation became eclipsed in the capital of the Western Caliphs, the learning of the descendants of Judah seemed to shine with more brilliancy in the first metropolis of Christian Spain.

The reason is not given; but some cause must have induced Alphonso to issue the following ordinance respecting pledges to the Jews.

"We ordain that Jews may lend to the amount of eight maravedis on pledges, without being bound to swear or requiring disinterested witnesses; and should an article, pledged without witnesses for a sum not exceeding eight maravedis, be afterwards claimed from the Jew as having been lost or stolen, the Jew shall be bound to disclose who was the person that pledged it; but if he does not know him, or the person is not known, he shall swear in the prescribed form on the book of the law in the synagogue, that he does not know the person; that it was deposited with him by a respectable person, and that it is not done as a cover. If then the claimant wishes to redeem it, he shall pay the amount to the Jew, who shall not be liable to any penalty. We further ordain, that if a Jew lend more than eight maravedis on a pledge, he must receive it in presence of witnesses, and take the prescribed oath before the notary who draws up the agreement; that he is not to receive more than thirty-three and a third per cent. and that he lends it on those terms. And should an article pledged for more than eight maravedis be claimed, as having been robbed or stolen, and the person who pledged it is known, but denies it, if the Jew cannot prove or will not denounce the person, he shall deliver up the pledge to the claimant without being paid, but shall incur no further penalty."

Almost every city of Spain enjoyed its particular Fuero or Charter, which charters were granted by different sovereigns. In most, certain privileges were given to the Jews. In that of Alcala we find the following—

"Any Christian inhabitant that wounds or kills a Jew, shall pay the same fine as a Christian would for a similar act to another.

"A Jew that wounds or kills a Christian, shall be fined the same as if it were committed by a Christian.

"Jews that wish to reside and settle in Alcala, may do so in full security."

In that of Salamanca,—

"Jews have the same rights as Christians, and any person that kills or wounds them is to suffer for such crime, the same as if it were committed on a Christian, or on an inhabitant of Salamanca.

"Jews and their heirs are to be treated the same as if they were inhabitants of Salamanca; and their sentences are to be signed by two Jews and a Christian, or two Christians and a Jew."

In the charter given by Alphonso to the town of Sahagun, is the following:—

"We order that the Jews of San Fagund shall enjoy the same privileges as the Jews of Carion. They shall be judged by the chiefs appointed by the Rabbins of Burgos; and the chiefs so nominated, shall, in presence of the abbot, swear to act justly and impartially; and should they object to the decisions of the said chiefs on points of their law, they are to appeal to the said Rabbins.

"In disputes between Christian and Jew, or Jew and Christian, they shall be tried by the Alcalde of San Fagund, and they may appeal, in conformity to the charter of the town.

"All claims between Christians and Jews must be proved by two witnesses, a Christian and a Jew, or two Christians if there is no Jew, or two Jews if there is no Christian.

"A person who kills a Jew shall pay 500 sous to the abbot: this and all other fines shall be given to the town, or according to their law, in conformity to the charter."

Don Moses Levi Abulaphia practised medicine at Seville with great celebrity. He died 1255; he had been physician to the last Moorish king.

By letters patent, dated Segovia, 16th September 1256, addressed to the High Alcaldes, Rodrigo Estevan and Gonzales Vincente, the king granted to the metropolitan church of Seville, a tax of thirty deniers, which all other bishoprics received from every Jew above ten years of age within their diocese.

A bull of Alexander IV., in this year, empowered the king of Navarre not only to prevent the usury of Jews, but to deprive them of the property they had so acquired, and to return it to its owners, or appropriate it to charitable purposes.

In 1261, Alphonso completed the Code of Las Siete Partidas. They exhibit the protection afforded by these enlightened monarchs to the persons and property of the Jews, and the free exercise of their religion. The laws made under the influence of the clergy do not appear to have been enforced.

## CHAPTER X.

**Las Siete Partidas,** *or "Seven Codes."*[1]

### ON THE SACRAMENTS OF THE CHURCH.[2]

LAW 63.—*What Jews and Moors are to do on meeting the Host.*—It sometimes happens that Jews and Moors meet the Host, when being carried to administer the sacrament to some sick person, as stated in the preceding law. We therefore say, that if any person not of our faith, and who does not believe it, should meet the Host, he will do right to kneel the same as Christians, that being nothing more than true religion. But if he does not wish to kneel, we order that he withdraw from the street, that the clergyman may pass without interruption; if it should be proved of any person that he would not, the judge of the place where it occurs shall commit him to prison for three days. And should he act thus again, we order the punishment to be double, and that he be imprisoned six days. If thereby he is not warned, but a third time should act contrary hereto, we order that he be arrested and taken before the king, who shall inflict the punishment he may think proper for such act. Should the king be far from the place, the person so acting shall be properly secured until he be informed thereof, that he may order the punishment such person deserves. We order this for two reasons:—First,—That Jews and Moors may not say that we injure or wrong them in our dominions. Secondly,—That the judges and those charged with the execution hereof, perform it without being induced to condemn them from envy of their property, nor the pleasure of personally injuring them from any ill-will they may bear against them. The aforesaid punishment is to be understood only for those Moors and Jews who are inhabitants of places within our dominions; but if they are

---

[1] Mad. Edit. 1711.   [2] Code i. Title 4.

strangers that come from foreign parts and are unacquainted herewith, we consider it just that they should not be liable thereto, as such persons do not deserve punishment, unless knowingly and maliciously they act contrarily.

### On Lawyers.[3]

LAW 5.—Furthermore, we say that no Jew or Moor may act as advocate for a Christian; nevertheless he may act as such for himself, or any person of his religion.

### On Oaths.[4]

LAW 11.—Jews having to make oath, must do it in the following form:—The person who demands that a Jew be sworn, must accompany him to the synagogue, to witness his swearing in presence of Christians and Jews. The Jew that is to be sworn must place his hand on the book of the law from which they read; and the person who administers the oath shall conjure him as follows:—You A. B., a Jew, swear by that God who is Omnipotent, who created heaven, earth, and all other things, and who said, Swear not falsely by my name: by that God, who made Adam, the first man, placed him in Paradise, and commanded him not to eat the fruit which he forbade him; and because he ate thereof, drove him from Paradise: by that God who accepted the offering of Abel and refused that of Cain; who at the time of the Flood saved Noah, his wife, his sons, their wives and all living things in the ark, that they might afterwards people the earth: by that God who saved Lot and his daughters from the destruction of Sodom and Gomorrah: by that God who said unto Abraham, that in his seed all the nations of the earth should be blessed, and commanded that all people proceeding from him should be circumcised, and chose for himself his son Isaac and Jacob as patriarchs: who saved Joseph from the hands of his brethren, that they did not kill him, and gave him favour with Pharaoh, that his family might not perish during the famine: who preserved Moses from perishing when cast into the

---

[3] Code iii. Title 6.   [4] Code iii. Title 11, extract.

river, and afterwards appeared to him in the similitude of fire: who inflicted ten plagues on Egypt, because Pharaoh would not let the children of Israel go to sacrifice in the desert; and made a path in the sea that they might pass on dry land, and drowned Pharaoh and his host that pursued them therein: who gave the law to Moses at Mount Sinai, and wrote it with His finger on tables of stone: who made Aaron his priest, and destroyed his sons for sacrificing with strange fire, and caused the earth to swallow Dathan, Abiram, and their companions alive: who gave the Jews manna to eat in the wilderness, and made the water that came from the rock sweet that they might drink, and sustained them during forty years in the desert, that their clothes neither became old nor broken; and when the children of Israel fought with the people of Amalek, made Moses to raise his hand so that they conquered; and commanded Moses to ascend the mount, and he was not afterwards seen; and, except Joshua and Caleb, would not permit any of those that came out of Egypt, for their disobedience, to enter the promised land; and turning the waters upwards, made them cross the Jordan dry: who cast down the walls of Jericho, that Joshua might take it the sooner; and further, made the sun stand still at noon, until Joshua had conquered his enemies: who chose Saul for the first king of His people Israel, and after him made David reign, and put the spirit of prophecy upon him and the other prophets; guarded him from many dangers, and said he should be called a man after his own heart: who took Elijah up to heaven in a chariot of fire, and performed many wonders and miracles among the Jewish people: and you further swear by the Ten Commandments that God gave to Moses: to all which he must answer "I swear." The person who receives the oath must then tell him that as he has sworn, if he knows the truth and denies or conceals, and does not avow it, may all the plagues that came on the Egyptians, and all the curses denounced in the law upon those who despise the commandments of God, come upon him. This being said to him, he must answer, "Amen."

### On Relationship in Marriages.[5]

Law 6.—A Moor or Jew, being married according to their religion to a relative or sister-in-law, and afterwards becoming a Christian, the marriage of such as have been so married, is not on that account to be annulled, notwithstanding they are related within the fourth degree.

### On Divorce.[6]

Law 7.—A person who becomes a Heretic, Moor, or Jew, cannot accuse his wife of adultery, because he has committed spiritual adultery. And whereas, the person who carnally commits adultery, may, on its being proved, be ejected; much more may it be done to those who commit it spiritually, by changing their belief, and persisting in their wickedness. In another case, a wife may not be accused of adultery; which is, if a Jew, having been married and separated from his wife, by giving her a bill of divorce according to the Jewish law, should afterwards become a Christian, and she should marry another Jew. And if it so happen, that after being married to the second husband, she becomes a Christian, and claims for her husband, the man who had turned Christian, to whom she was formerly married, before he has married another, she may do it; he must receive her, and cannot accuse her of adultery, nor may he, on account of her second marriage, eject or refuse to receive her again.

### On Slaves.[7]

Law 8.—No Jew, Moor, Heretic, or other person, not of our religion, can possess any Christian slave. Persons acting contrary hereto, and knowingly possessing a Christian as a slave, shall suffer death, and their property be confiscated to the king. We furthermore declare, if any of the aforesaid persons possess a slave who is not of our religion; if the said slave becomes a Christian, as soon as he has been baptised, and

---

[5] Code iv. tit 6, extract.   [6] Code iii. tit. 6, extract.
[7] Code iv. tit. 21.

received our faith, he must be liberated, and is not bound to pay anything to the master he belonged to before his conversion. And, even if his former master subsequently should become a Christian, he has no right or claim on the slave that became a Christian before him.

This is to be understood, when the Jew, or Moor, has bought the slave, who has thus turned Christian, for the purpose of serving him, and not as merchandise for sale: but if he purchase him for sale, he must dispose of him within three months. And if, before the expiration of three months, while the owner is endeavouring to dispose of him, he should turn Christian; the Jew, or Moor, ought not to lose the entire sum they may have paid for him. On the contrary, we ordain, that the slave himself, or the person who induced him to turn Christian, shall be bound to pay the sum of twelve maravedis, current money of the place, to the owner. Should he not have the means of paying that amount, he must serve, not as a slave but as a free man, until he has earned it. And if the slave has not been sold within the term of the three months, although the master afterwards turns Christian, he has no right to, or claim upon him.

## On Moors.[s]

LAW 10.—*The Punishments to be inflicted on Moors and Christians that cohabit together.*—If a Moor cohabit with a Christian woman, he shall be stoned for it; and for the first time she shall lose half her property, and her father, mother, or grandfather, shall have it, and, in default of such relatives, it shall go to the king. And for the second time, she is to lose the whole, and the aforenamed are to have it, or, in default, the king; and she shall suffer death. We further command, that the same shall be done with a widow. And if he should be connected with a married woman, she shall be delivered into the hands of her husband, that he may burn, acquit, or do what he chooses with her. And if he cohabit with a prostitute, for the first time both shall be scourged together through the town; and for the second offence they shall suffer death.

[s] Code vii. Tit. 21.

## On Jews.[9]

Jews are a description of people that will not believe in the faith of our Lord Jesus Christ; but Christian potentates have always permitted them to reside among them. Whereas, in the preceding title, we treated on diviners, and other persons who assert that they are acquainted with events that are to happen, which in a measure is a contempt of God, pretending to render themselves equal to him, by knowing his acts and secrets, we shall here treat of the Jews, who contradict and deny his name, and the miraculous and holy deed he performed when he sent His Son, our Lord Jesus Christ, into the world to save sinners. We shall shew:—

The meaning of Jew, and whence the name is derived;— the reason why the Church and Potentates allowed their residing among them; the mode of life they must lead among Christians; what they may not practise or do according to our religion; the Judges who are to pass sentence on them for any crime they commit, or for debts they may owe; that Jews who become Christians are not to be molested; the advantages Jews who become Christians have over those who are not converted; the punishment to be inflicted on those who injure and insult converts; the punishment Christians are to receive who become Jews; and, on Jews who make Moorish slaves belonging to them turn to their religion.

LAW 1.—*The meaning of Jew, and whence the name is derived.*—Those are termed Jews who believe the Law of Moses, following it to the letter, who practise circumcision, and perform other ceremonies enjoined by their religion. The name is derived from the tribe of Judah, which was the noblest, and braver than the other tribes; it also had another pre-eminence, the king of the Jews was to be elected from it; besides, in battle that tribe was the foremost. The reason the Church, emperors, kings and princes, permitted Jews to live by themselves among Christians, is, that they might always live as in captivity, and that they may ever be a memorial to mankind,

[9] Code vii. Tit. 24.

that they are from the genealogy of those who crucified our Lord Jesus Christ.

LAW 2.—*The way Jews must live among Christians, what they may not practise nor do according to our religion, and the punishment of those who act contrary.*—Jews residing among Christians must live humbly, and without evil intention, observing their religion, and not speak ill of the faith of our Lord Jesus Christ, which Christians observe. They must be careful not to preach, praising their religion, and disparaging ours, nor to convert any Christian that he turn Jew, any person so doing shall suffer death, and all his property be confiscated. And whereas, we are informed, that some Jews, by way of derision on Good Friday, in commemoration of the passion of our Lord Jesus Christ, steal children and crucify them, or make images which they crucify, when they cannot procure children. We order, that if it can be proved that such act is committed in any place of our dominions, all persons concerned therein are to be arrested, imprisoned, and taken before the king; and, when the king has ascertained the fact to be true, he must order all the parties concerned therein to be executed immediately. Furthermore, we forbid any Jew leaving his house, or going without their barrier on Good Friday, they shall be confined to the Jewry until Saturday morning; should they act contrary, no reparation is to be made for any insult or ill-treatment they may receive from Christians.

LAW 3.—*No Jew to hold any public office or post, enabling him to pass sentence on Christians.*—The Jews were formerly highly honored, and possessed greater privileges than all other nations. They only, were called the people of God. But as they would not recognise him who had honored and benefitted them; and instead of rendering him honor, they disgraced and put him to death on the cross, it was just and proper that for such an enormous crime and wickedness as they committed, they should be deprived of the honor and privileges they enjoyed; and ever since the day they crucified our Lord Jesus

Christ, they have not had a king or priest of their own, as they had before. The emperors, who were formerly masters of the whole world, considered it just and right, that for the treason committed in putting their Lord to death, they should lose the honors and prerogatives they formerly enjoyed, so that no Jew should ever hold a post of honor, or public office, by virtue of which he would have to pass sentence on Christians.

LAW 4.—*How Jews may have Synagogues among Christians.* —A Synagogue is a place where Jews perform their devotions. In no part of our dominions without our permission, may any new one be erected; but should those they have fall into decay, they may rebuild and repair them on the same site, and in the same manner as before; but they may not enlarge, elevate, or beautify them. The Synagogue that is otherwise constructed is to be taken from them, and to be given to the principal church of the place where it is erected. As a Synagogue is a building where the name of God is praised, we forbid any Christian presuming to destroy or to take anything from it, except a criminal who has sought refuge therein. Such may be lawfully seized by force and brought to justice. We further forbid Christians putting animals in or near them, or causing any molestation to Jews, while engaged at their prayers, according to their religion.

LAW 5.—*Jews not to have sentence passed on them on Saturdays; and what Judges are to pass sentence on them.*— Saturday is a day whereon Jews observe their Sabbath, and are tranquil in their homes; they neither work, trade, nor carry on lawsuits thereon. And as they are bound by their religion to observe this day, no person may summon them, or bring them to judgment thereon. We therefore order, that no judge shall condemn or arrest Jews on Saturdays, or bring them to judgment for debt, or seize, or do them any hurt on that day. There are other days of the week sufficient to arrest and demand what may justly be demanded from them; and Jews shall not be compelled to answer any summons made them on that day; and we further command, that any sentence passed on them on that day shall be null and void. But should Jews wound, kill, rob, steal, or commit any similar crime, for which they ought to receive corporal punishment, in such cases Judges may have guilty persons arrested on Saturday. We further command, that all demands Christians may have against Jews, or Jews against Christians, shall be heard and determined by our Judges and not by their elders. And as we forbid Christians punishing Jews or bringing them to judgment on Saturday, we also declare, that Jews neither personally nor by their representatives may have Christians tried or punished on that day. Furthermore, we forbid any Christian to dare to seize or do any injury to the person or property of a Jew; but if he has any demand against him, he is to bring it before our Judges; and should any person presume to steal, or forcibly take anything from a Jew, he shall be compelled to return double the value.

LAW. 6.—*Jews not to be compelled to turn Christians; the advantage granted to Converts, and the punishment of Jews that injure them.*—No force or compulsion is to be used to make Jews turn Christians, but by good example, kindness, and the maxims of the Holy Scriptures, should they be converted to the faith of our Lord Jesus Christ, for he neither requires nor desires compulsory service. Furthermore, should any Jew or Jewess hereafter wish to become a Christian, other Jews are in no manner whatever to prevent them, and should any of them stone, wound, or kill those that wish to become Christians, or that have been baptized, if proved, we order, that the murderers and advisers of such outrage are to be burned. And if they should not kill, but should strike or illtreat them, we command the Judges of the place where it occurs to have reparation made, and inflict such punishment, as they consider the persons who committed the offence deserve. We furthermore order, that all persons in our kingdom are to respect Jews that become Christians, and no one insultingly shall reproach them or their descendants with having been Jews. And they shall keep possession of their property and all belonging to them, sharing with their brothers, and inheriting from their fathers, mothers, and other relations, the same as if they were Jews; and they are to be eligible to every honour, post, and employment held by other Christians.

LAW 7.—*The punishment of a Christian turning Jew.*—Such evil results from Christians turning Jews, that we order, that any Christian who does shall suffer death, the same as if he had become a heretic. We furthermore ordain, that his property is to be treated in the same manner as we have ordained that of heretics to be treated.

LAW 8.—*Christians not to live with Jews.*—We forbid Jews presuming to have Christian slaves in their houses; but they may employ them as labourers and cultivators of their outdoor possessions, and to guard them when travelling on a road considered unsafe. We furthermore forbid Christians to invite any Jew or Jewess, or to accept an invitation to eat and drink wine with them, or to drink wine made by Jews. Further, we order, that no Jew is to presume to bathe in the same bath with Christians. We also prohibit Christians receiving any medicine or purges made up by Jews, nevertheless they may take it on the advice of an experienced person, provided it be compounded by Christians, who know and understand the ingredients of which it is composed.

LAW 9.—*The punishment of a Jew cohabiting with a Christian Woman.*—It is highly disrespectful and insolent for Jews to cohabit with Christian women. We therefore order, that if it be proved of any Jew, that he has committed such an offence he shall suffer death for it. For where a Christian deserves death who commits adultery with a married woman, Jews that cohabit with Christian women deserve it much more; as spiritually, by reason of faith, and the baptism received in his name, they are spouses of our Lord Jesus Christ; and we consider it right that a Christian woman guilty of such a crime should not go unpunished; we therefore order, whether she be a virgin, married woman, widow, or prostitute, she shall suffer the same punishment, as enacted for a Christian woman who cohabits with a Moor.[10]

[10] Vide page 96.

Law 10.—*The punishment Jews incur for possessing Christian slaves.*—Jews may not purchase or possess Christian slaves, either male or female. And if any one should act contrary, the Christian shall be restored to freedom without repaying any part of the cost price; unless when the Jew made the purchase he did not know he was a Christian. But, if the Jew knew it when he bought him, and afterwards treats him as a slave, the Jew ought to suffer death for it. Furthermore, we forbid any Jew presuming to make his slave a Jew or Jewess, although they are Moors or other Barbarians.[11] Should any one act contrary hereto, we order that the slave who has become a Jew or Jewess, shall in consequence be free, and released from the power of the person he or she belonged to. And if, perchance, a Moor who was a slave to a Jew should turn Christian, he must immediately be liberated.

Law 11.—*Jews to wear a distinctive mark or sign.*—Many mistakes and injurious occurrences take place between Christians and Jews and Jewesses, and Christian women, from their living and residing together in towns and dressing alike. Therefore, to avoid the errors and evils that may thereby happen, we order that every Jew and Jewess residing in our dominions shall wear a particular sign on their heads, that people may publicly know who are Jews and Jewesses. And we order that any Jew who appears in public without it, shall be fined, for each time, ten maravedis of gold; and if he has not the means to pay the fine, he shall publicly receive ten lashes.

[11] Natives of Barbary.

## CHAPTER XI.

*Jews accused of Murder at Ossuna. — Discovery of the Plot.—Sahudano, Minister to James II.— Clement IV. wishes James to expel the Jews and Moors. —An additional Tax laid on them.—Join the Authorities to preserve Estella for Donna Johanna.—Orders respecting Debts due to them in Navarre. — Their Petition to the Cortes of Barcelona. — Alphonso's conduct to Don Zag de la Malea.—Cortes of Palencia. — Hebrew Population in Castile and Murcia. — Assessment. — Physician to Don Sancho. — His Treatment of Fever.—Learned Men.—Cortes of Valladolid.*

THE protection afforded by the laws and this monarch to the Hebrew people, inflamed the zeal of the bigots against them; for about this period many were massacred at Ossuna, in Andalusia, from the following circumstance. Three villains threw a corpse into the house of a Jew and accused him of the murder; the calumny spreading through the town, the populace massacred every Jew they met. Many sought refuge in the houses of their Christian friends, who readily granted them an asylum; but they suffered great privation, for, being the week of passover, they would not eat the leavened bread of their hospitable protectors. Many from the same cause were killed at Palma. The Jews, to prevent the extension of the massacres, found it necessary to send a deputation to claim the protection of the king. The envoys, R. Joseph, the Chief Rabbi, R. Samuel ben Shoshan, and R. Abraham Benevista, travelled through bye-roads to avoid their persecutors, who, thereby, were enabled to make their accusation before the Jewish deputies arrived. R. Joseph pleaded his cause so powerfully and eloquently, that he was admired by the whole court, and the Jews were acquitted of the crime. Their innocence was subsequently proved. Owing to a reward offered by the king, it was discovered that one Juan de la Vera, to avoid payment of a debt he owed to the Jew into whose house it had been thrown, had with the assistance of some friends exhumed the corpse, and the empty grave was found. The accusers wanted the Jew to be put to the torture; but the king refused, as a few years previously two brothers, Judah and Samuel Ankoah, had, while on the rack, confessed having stolen two of the royal golden goblets. Three days after their execution, the goblets were found in the possession of one of his servants. The horrid sufferings of the torture frequently induced the innocent victims of this barbarous punishment to acknowledge themselves guilty of the crimes they were accused of, seeking in death relief from their cruel persecutors.

The king recommended the deputation, at their departure, to advise their people to suppress their usury, the costliness of their dress, and their public display of state and grandeur, as those things tended to excite the rage and hatred of Christians.

On the marriage of the Infanta Constance with Don Pedro, the Infante of Navarre, in 1262, the town of Gerona, and the Jews residing in it, were assigned for her dowry. James of Aragon in 1263, sent out a fleet to protect the coasts of his kingdom against the Moors of Barbary, who had come to assist the Castilian revolters. His minister and treasurer, a Jew named Sahudano, to whom he entrusted the chief business of state, furnished him the means for its equipment, as well as to garrison the city of Valencia; he was a man of such probity and honor, that the writer of the "Annales de Aragon" only regrets that he was a Jew.[1]

Alphonso being at Seville in 1263, the Alcalde of Burgos applied to him for instruction on various doubtful points. The following is found among the answers:—"When a Christian has borrowed money from a Jew, and a time is fixed for the payment, if the Christian wants to acquit his bond and pay the amount, with the interest for the time he had the money, and the Jew will not receive it, then I order what you are to do. I say that when such a case happens, act rightly and justly towards the borrower. On the Christian paying the capital and the interest then due, the Jew must receive it."

After the disputation between Fr. Christiani and Nachmanides, Pope Clement IV. wished James to punish the Rabbins, and drive the Jews and Moors from his states as dangerous to the faithful; but the only thing he did was to levy an additional tax on them, to defray the expenses of Christiani, who went in 1265 to the principal cities, with power to assemble the Jews to hold conferences wherever he chose, and to make them exhibit their books. Aided by a number of monks, he willingly undertook the mission; the censorship was so inconsiderately executed, that

[1] Zurita.

the Jews complained to the court of the inquisitorial proceeding; upon which they were ordered to take them to Barcelona to be examined. Foreseeing that they would not be treated better by the clergy of that city, than they had been by the missionaries, they only took a few, and secreted a large number.

The Jews were not only numerous in Navarre, but so wealthy and powerful, that on the death of Henry in 1274, they were invited by Don Juan Sanchez de Montagueda, governor of the castle of Estella, to join the civil and military authorities in an oath to maintain and defend the castle, city and Jewry, for his infant daughter and successor Donna Johanna (which they did on the book of the law), until she was twelve years of age. The document, dated 14th November, is yet preserved in the archives of Estella. In consequence of many pretenders for her hand, this oath was again confirmed by the same parties three years after, when Philip III. of France, as guardian of the infant queen, ordered that the Jews should wait eight years for the payment of debts due to them, receiving an eighth part annually.[2]

In 1276, Don Meir and Don Joseph, sons of the high treasurer, Don Zag, farmed the royal taxes of Castile, for 500,000 maravedis, of the coinage of the Algerine war.[3] Alphonso in 1280, being in want of money for his expenses, in paying a visit to the king of France at Bayonne, taking example from the sovereigns of England and France, issued an order from Valladolid, to seize all the Jews on one Saturday, and thus extorted from them 2,000 maravedis a day until his return.[4]

[2] Arch. Estella. [3] Arch. Aguilar del Campo. [4] Chron. Alph. 10.

In consequence of the delay granted by Philip, for the payment of debts due to Jews, the inhabitants of other towns in Navarre applied to him; in 1280 he ordered the Viceroy to attend to the remonstrances of the inhabitants of Ribaforada, who were indebted to the Jews of Tudela, and not permit them to molest Christians for usury due to them on loans; and that the Hebrews of Buñuel should only be repaid the capital without interest.[5]

From the conflicting claims to jurisdiction over them in Catalonia, at the cortes of Barcelona, in 1283, they petitioned that the laws which attached them to the lord of the soil, or the fortified places where they had their domiciles, might be observed. The cortes confirmed those ancient laws subject to the privileges and special agreements that may have been stipulated. They yet possessed in Aragon the right to own slaves; but that right became almost illusory by the ordinance of Peter II., which liberated the slaves of Moors and Jews when they embraced Christianity; thus they had only to be baptised to become free.

Alphonso could not forget the unfortunate result of the siege of Algesiras in 1281. He knew that the Infante, Don Sancho, had been the cause of the irreparable injury; but not daring to vent his anger on his son, he had the receiver-general, a powerful Hebrew, Don Zag de la Malea arrested, for having delivered to Don Sancho the money destined for the expedition (who, by its misappropriation in giving it to the Queen Violante, had caused the disaster), which he could not resist; and for not informing him in time to enable him to remedy the mischief.

[5] Arch. Nav. Let. ii. 170.

However specious the charge, the sole object of the king was to sacrifice a victim to his resentment; and what was at most an inconsiderate act, became an enormous crime; and he condemned him to death. The king, desirous of shewing his anger towards the most guilty party, ordered that Don Zag should be dragged to the place of execution, in front of the Infante's residence. Don Sancho wished to descend to rescue him, but was prevented by his brothers; he swore to avenge a death so insulting to himself, and rebelled against his father. Another cause of his rebellion was, that Alphonso had named his grandson, the son of his eldest son Don Ferdinand, deceased, to be his successor. Sancho, his second son, considered himself more entitled to the crown; the discontented grandees joined him, and in a cortes held at Valladolid, they declared him king. He continued in arms against his father until a short time before his death, when, by nominating him for his successor, they were reconciled, and he succeeded to the throne in 1284. To regulate the administration of justice in the kingdom of Leon, a cortes was held at Palencia in 1286, when, at the request of the representatives, the first infringement of their ancient privileges took place. The sixteenth ordinance runs thus:—

I consider it right that the Jews should not have separate and particular Alcaldes, as hitherto; but that one of the judges to whom the justice of the city is entrusted shall be appointed to try their causes. That both Christians and Jews may have their rights, and no delay is to take place, through the neglect of the proper authorities, in passing sentence that my taxes be not withheld.

This applied only to the Jewish inhabitants of that

kingdom, in which, by the following assessment, there appears to have been upwards of 70,000 above sixteen years of age, as they paid a tax of three maravedis a head; and in Castile and Murcia 630,000; together, upwards of 700,000 in the three kingdoms of Don Sancho. A satire written against the king, for the protection of the Hebrew population, states it to be upwards of a million and a-half.[6]

The following is the division made at Huete (that is the city of Huete), among the Jewries of the Jews, by command of Don Sancho the brave, in the month of September, 1290 (era 1328).[7]

### La Frontera.

At the meeting of the deputies they agreed that the appointment should be made by Don Jacob Hayon, Don Zag Abenasor of Niebla and Xeres, and Don Abraham Abenfar, from Cordova, and the person chosen by the representatives of the bishopric. They are to apportion it in such manner that no right of the king be injured; and if these do not agree, they shall apply to Don David Abudarham the elder, and the Jewry of the Jews of Toledo, to divide among themselves 191,898 maravedis.

### The Kingdom of Leon.

By agreement made with the other Jewries, that in the kingdom of Leon among themselves, in such manner as not to reduce any of the king's rights in that amount.   218,500
The kingdom of Murcia   -   -   -   -   22,414

*Tierra Rasa.*

|  | Maravedis. |  | Maravedis. |
|---|---|---|---|
| Villareal | 2,468 | Madrid | 10,605 |
| Toledo, together with the places hitherto taxed with it | 216,505 | Alcala | 6,800 |
|  |  | Azeda | 2,841 |
|  |  | Salamanca | 1,014 |

[6] Appendix 5.
[7] Asso y Rodrigues' Discurso sobre los Judios de Espana.

## ASSESSMENT IN 1290.

|   | Maravedis. |   | Maravedis. |
|---|---|---|---|
| Buytrage | 6,044 | Sariega | 2,030 |
| Guadalajara | 16,986 | Dueñas | 1,827 |
| Almoquera | 400,588 | Penafiel | 6,597 |
| Fita | 13,588 | Cia | 4,923 |
| Dorita | 6,833 | | |
| Briviega | 24,471 | | 236,845 |
| Baguer | 11,162 | | |
| Alcaraz | 12,771 | | |
| Montiel | 1,522 | | |

*Bishopric of Burgos.*

| Burgos | 87,560 |
|---|---|
| Castiella | 4,002 |
| Pancorvo | 23,850 |

758,216

*Bishopric of Calahora.*

| Calahora | 11,697 |
|---|---|
| Vitoria | 8,521 |
| Villabrea | 12,850 |
| the king allowed half to be paid as they had been robbed, and hereafter | 21,780 |
| Miranda | 3,312 |
| Alfaro | 3,256 |
| Najara | 19,318 |
| Logrono | 15,008 |
| Alueda and Alfacel | 15,110 |
| Azuedo | 3,617 |

114,469

| Muño and Lerma de Pezuelo | 7,850 |
|---|---|
| Buesca[9] | 11,700 |
| Villadiego | 13,770 |
| Aguilar | 8,060 |
| Bilforado | 8,500 |
| Medina de Guzman Oña and Frias | 12,042 |

177,334

*Bishopric of Segovia.*

| Segovia | 40,806 |
|---|---|
| Pedraza | 3,653 |
| Coa | 892 |
| Sepulveda | 18,912 |
| Fuente Dueña | 3,413 |
| Cuellar | 933 |

68,609

*Bishopric of Cuença.*

| Cuença | 70,882 |
|---|---|
| Ucles | 28,514 |
| —— con Alcouz | 46,680 |

146,076

*Bishopric of Palencia.*

| Palencia | 33,280 |
|---|---|
| Valladolid[8] | 69,520 |
| San Fagund | 23,203 |
| Carion, and the villages taxed with it | 53,480 |
| Paredes de Nava and Cisneros | 41,985 |

*Bishopric of Siguença.*

| Siguença and Medina Celi | 25,835 |
|---|---|
| Atienza | 42,434 |
| Almaran | 25,083 |
| Berlanga | 3,347 |
| Cifuentes | 2,029 |
| Aillon | 6,564 |

105,292

[8] The bishop granted a deduction to it, and the villages taxed with it.
[9] The king issued an order for them to contribute to the tax of Castile which together was 12,050.

|  | Maravedis. |  | Maravedis. |
|---|---|---|---|
| *Bishopric of Avila.* |  | Trugillo - - - - | 3,763 |
| Avila - - - - - | 59,592 | Medellin - - - - | 3,348 |
| Piedratita, Bongilla, and Valle de Corneja | 21,026 |  | 26,785 |
| Medina del Campo - - | 44,064 | *Bishopric of Osma.* |  |
| Olmedo - - - - - | 31,659 | Osma - - - - - | 14,510 |
| Azevalo - - - - - | 12,327 | Sant Estevan - - - | 16,841 |
|  |  | Aza - - - - - | 2,529 |
|  | 168,718 | Soria - - - - - | 31,351 |
|  |  | Roa - - - - - | 6,085 |
| *Bishopric of Plasencia.* |  | Agreda and Cervera - | 3,549 |
| Plasencia - - - - - | 16,244 |  |  |
| Bejar - - - - - | 3,430 |  | 74,865 |

Grand Total - - - - - - - - 2,310,021 maravedis.

The above amount is what we have assessed this year, and have set our names to this act, and signed the same in a meeting of 220 persons appointed by the bishop.

In the reign of Don Sancho, an eminent physician practised at Toledo. His reputation must have stood very high; by being called to attend the infant prince Ferdinand, whose life he saved, as is collected from his valuable manuscript in the Escurial, which Morejon says, is the first work in Europe on local medicine and medical topography. Piquer regrets it has not been translated from the Hebrew into Spanish. In treating on fevers, he says, " I witnessed this in my time, in the case of the young Don Ferdinand, son of the king, Don Sancho, who had been attacked with a violent fever. I was sent for at midnight, and found him with a burning fever, accompanied with headache, delirium, want of sleep, restlessness and pains. From the combination of these symptoms, there could not be a doubt but that the fever had a tendency to inflammation of the brain. I learnt they had given him all that day old Orihuela white wine to drink.

Considering his heated temperament, I resolved he should drink large quantities of very cold snow-water. After having drank it, the restlessness and pains subsided. He had a sound sleep, and in the morning had scarcely any fever. I continued this regimen, and on the third day he was completely cured." The name of this physician is unknown, as it is not affixed to the manuscript. Another Hebrew of great celebrity also flourished at Toledo at this time.

R. ISAAC ISRAELI — born at Toledo in 1262, was considered the most able mathematician and astronomer of his age; his astronomical works and tables are highly esteemed. "The Gate of Heaven" is on the planetary system, according to Ptolemy." "The Foundation of the World," is considered a first-rate work.

Among the many learned Jews in Spain at this period may be mentioned:—

R. SOLOMON BEN ADERET — a native of Barcelona, deeply versed in philosophy and jurisprudence; he was in 1280 acknowledged Chief Rabbi of all the Jews in Spain. He wrote a cabalistical treatise on "The Service of the Passover Eve;" "A Commentary on the Allegories of the Talmud;" a work entitled "The Law of the House;" on Domestic Duties; "The Holy Service," on Various Ceremonies, and a number of Answers to Judicial Inquiries. In conjunction with R. Asher, he prohibited the study of Grecian philosophy until after twenty-five years of age.

R. JACOB SAHOLA — a celebrated orator and poet, died in 1268; under the title of "Ancient Proverbs," he has left us a pleasing volume of moral fables and apologues.

R. JEDIDIAH HAPENINI BEN ABRAHAM BADRASI — born at Barcelona in 1250, more generally known by the designation of Anbonet Abram. His celebrated work, "An Examination of the World," on its vanities, is translated into every European language; he addressed a letter to Aderet, on

"The Prohibition of Philosophical Studies." He wrote a Commentary on Psalms, notes on various treatises of the Talmud. A Comment on Aben Ezra's "Exposition of the Pentateuch;" a hymn, each line beginning with a ל, and another with a מ; answers to some philosophical questions; a collection from the Grecian and Arabic sages, and a work on the game of chess; which he says he did to arrest the pernicious vice of gambling with cards and dice then prevalent; thus proving that they were invented long previously to what is generally supposed. From his eloquence, his co-religionists called him the Orator; and Christians, the Hebrew Cicero.

R. DON JOSEPH BEN JACHIA—of a noble Portuguese family, born at Barcelona, where he succeeded Aderet as head of its Hebrew college, he ranked high as a poet, grammarian, and theologian. All his learned works were burnt by Fr. Vincent Ferrer, except some Talmudic decisions, an elegy on Aderet, and some poetry.

R. MOSES BEN SHEMTOB—a philosopher, poet and theologian of repute, was born at Leon; his "Weight of Wisdom" contains the sayings of various philosophers, which he ably criticises. He also wrote "The Soul of Wisdom" and some cabalistical works.

ABNER—a convert from Judaism, was born at Burgos, and practised medicine at Saragossa with great repute. Before his apostasy he wrote in favour of the Jewish religion; after being sacristan of the cathedral of Saragossa, he wrote under his baptismal name of Alphonso of Burgos, in favour of Christianity.

R. BEHAYE BEN MOSES—a native of Saragossa and prefect of the synagogue of that city. His defence of Maimonides' "Guide" against the French Schools, exhibits his great literary abilities.

R. HAIM BEN SAMUEL—a cabalist philosopher and poet of Tudela, where he was born. He wrote a work entitled, "The Bundle of Life;" "A Commentary on Part of the Doctrine of Cabala," and "The Bundle of Silver;" a work in verse on moral philosophy.

At a Cortes held at Valladolid, in 1293, complaint was made that the Jews and Moors received interest at a higher rate than thirty-three and a third per cent.[10]

Don Sancho confirmed that to be the legal interest, adding, as the Jews were suspected of receiving more (for no proof was adduced),—

That the notary should insert in the bond the names and residences of the debtor and security. That the debtor should only be responsible to the person who lends the money, or who presents the bond, as no Jew can recover a bond debt in the name of another. No bond debt to be exacted after six years; and if payment is not demanded within thirty days of the bond becoming due, the interest to cease.

On the subject of pledges, the king ordered that the ordinance of his father should be observed:—

We order that Jews and Moors who lend on pledges upwards of eight maravedis, are to receive them in presence of witnesses, and the parties are to swear before the notary: the Christian, that he is to pay but four for three (or thirty-three and a third per cent.); and the Jew, that he does not lend at a higher rate.

Representations were made to this cortes against the Jews being permitted to purchase landed property at will, as it would appear their lands were not as heavily taxed as those of Christians. The king had no hesitation in ordaining:—[11]

That, hereafter, they should not acquire, either by purchase or grant, any landed property from Christians; as those acquisitions were injurious to the royal revenue. That within the term of a year they should sell the properties so acquired, and

[10] Petition 21.  [11] Ibid. 22.

only keep possession of estates mortgaged to them, from the debtor not being able otherwise to pay for want of a purchaser, under condition that they dispose of them within the said term of one year.

This law neither affected their hereditary property nor such as they might acquire from Moors; but seems to have been enacted to prevent their accumulating extensive landed property from Christian landowners, and hereby injuring the royal revenue. This cortes established in Castile the law respecting particular magistrates, that had been enacted in 1286 by the cortes of Palencia for the Jews of the kingdom of Leon.[12]

James II., who had succeeded in 1291 to the throne of Aragon, equally desirous as James I. for the conversion of the Jews and Moors, confirmed the ordinance of 1242, and threatened severe punishment to persons who should insult a convert by calling him renegade, turncoat, apostate, etc. He at the same time ordered the Dominican friars to preach, argue, and explain the Christian faith to Jews and Moors, who should be compelled to attend their summonses, and listen attentively to their discourses; and to avoid their suppressing the conviction of the truth they should answer the questions and objections of the said brethren. They were also to be compelled, when ordered, to give free access to their books for the investigation of any subject. And if any new convert should refuse, or fail to attend the summons and admonitions of the said brethren, the magistrates, or other officers present, were to inflict corporal or any other punishment the said brethren sentence the offending party to.

[12] Petition 23.

Ferdinand was only nine years of age on the death of Don Sancho in 1295. By his will, Donna Maria de Padilla, mother of the infant king, was appointed regent. To her wise administration in conciliating the turbulent grandees he was indebted for the preservation of the crown.

A Cortes was held at Valladolid in 1299. The answers given to petitions against the Jews, shew that the regent, acting in the name of the king, respected and adhered to existing laws, and would not infringe on the privileges the Hebrews enjoyed. A petition[13] was presented against their having separate magistrates. The ordinance of 1293 was continued; and if there were no magistrates, the judge was to act instead. Another[14] required that Jews might not be permitted to receive from the royal chancery letters of appeal against Christians, as they were not granted to Christians against them. The answer was: "I order the same to be done, as was customary in the time of my grandfather, Don Alphonso, and my great grandfather, Don Ferdinand." A petition[15] to reduce the period for the recovery of bonds due by Christians to Jews to three years, was refused, and the law of Don Sancho limiting it to six was confirmed. In 1299, Philip le Bel, as regent of Navarre, ordered, that the ordinance of St. Louis, king of France, respecting the usury of the Jews, should be observed in Navarre, and that only the sum lent should be repaid.[16]

[13] Petition 11.  [14] Ibid. 12.  [15] Ibid. 13.  [16] Arch. Nav. Let. ii. p. 170.

## CHAPTER XII.

*Privileges enjoyed in Castile. — State of Society. — Ordinance respecting the Capitation Tax at Segovia. — Cortes of Medina del Campo. — Ferdinand's attachment to them. — Council at Zamora. — Cortes of Carrion. — The Shepherds — the Infante Alphonso, and the Jews repulse them. — Riot at Barcelona. — Council of Salamanca. — Relative Population of the towns of Aragon.*

BEFORE entering on the gradual deprivation of the rights and privileges the Jews enjoyed under the Spanish sovereigns, which commenced about this period, it may be necessary to take a review of the state of society in Spain.

While persecuted in every other part of Christendom, their worth had been learnt from the Moorish conquerors of the western parts of Europe; and for many succeeding ages they were protected by the monarchs of Spain, who, although strictly adhering to Catholicism, acted towards the descendants of Israel more in accordance with the tenets of Christianity than the sovereigns who wielded the sceptres of Germany, France, and England.

The Visigothic code, too barbarous ever to be enforced, was by the victorious arms of the sectarians of Mahomet driven, with the last of the Goths, from the

Iberian soil. This epoch was the commencement of the great influence the Jews subsequently attained.

The Spaniards, conquered by the Moors, for many years had no other object in view than to regain their independence. Occupied solely in military expeditions, they could not apply themselves to the cultivation of letters; nor were they able to carry on and extend their commerce, even had they known its benefits.

The Jews were the only people acquainted with trade, for the Lombards only learned it from them after their expulsion from France by Philip Augustus; they were, consequently, quick calculators, able and dexterous in conducting a mercantile enterprise, and above all excellent in the administration of the royal finances. These circumstances gave them great advantages; for, although the clergy instilled into the people a hatred against them on account of their religion, their services became indispensably necessary for many branches of the civil government. They were the intendants, major-domos, stewards, physicians, and apothecaries of the court and grandees. These employments acquired for them the highest favour and confidence of the king. The direction and administration of the royal revenues were constantly under the management of Jews, who either administered them for the state, or farmed them according to the value, with the titles of almoxarifs, treasurers, farmers-general, receivers-general, etc.

They not only enjoyed the same rights as other citizens, but particular privileges were conceded to them; some placing them on an equality with the highest of the land. Their religion was not simply tolerated, but they were protected by the laws of the country;

their sabbaths were inviolably respected, their ceremonies and observances performed without molestation; every thing held sacred in the Hebrew's breast freely practised. This endeared Spain to the descendants of Israel. Whilst driven as culprits from breathing even the same air inhaled by bigoted benighted Europeans; or, from dread of polluting by their tread the Christian soil, and ignominiously exiled from Germany, France, and England, Spain not only offered them an asylum and a resting-place "*for the sole of their feet*," but granted them extraordinary immunities. They formed an *imperium in imperio*.

The trial of all causes, whether civil or criminal, was by their own chiefs, from whose sentence an appeal might be made to the Rabbi, and from his decision to the king; but in criminal cases, the king had the power to order an enquiry, and that his Alcaldes should assist at the trial.

Like nobles, except for king's dues, they could not be arrested for debt.

They could acquire and hold landed property.

For recovering loans made to Christians, the oath of the Jew was sufficient, unless the debtor and creditor disagreed on the nature of the debt, and the Jew sought to prove it was not usurious; then the proof was to be remitted to the oath of the Christian also, or disinterested witnesses.

They were not bound to divulge the names of persons who deposited pledges with them for as much as eight maravedis; but above that sum they were. And on swearing that he did not know the person who pledged it, the Jew was to receive his money, although the article had been stolen.

But they paid a capitation tax of thirty deniers or three maravedis, as before stated. And when the kings of Castile entered a town that had its Jewry, it paid for every book of the law it possessed twelve maravedis to the king's body guards, to protect them from insult and injury, requiring the safeguard of the king to defend them from a lawless soldiery.

Such was the state of the Jews when those dark clouds began to eclipse their glory, and disturb the prosperity and tranquillity by storms they had been unaccustomed to for centuries in the Iberian Peninsula.

The Moors enjoyed similar privileges to those of the Hebrew people.

The Christian vassals of the Castilian crown may be divided into the following classes.

1.—The high nobility which exercised an unbounded authority over their vassals, and frequently were in arms against their sovereign. Jealous of the influence the Jews had acquired at court, they were constantly endeavouring to supplant them, although they protected them on their immense estates; and as a means of ensuring their revenues, employed them as intendants, collectors, and in every other confidential post.

2.— The inferior nobility, proud of their noble descent, but too indolent to attend to their affairs, were always in want of money to supply their extravagant expenditure. They had recourse to the Jews, who by industry and frugality had become wealthy, and were able to lend to the necessitous Hidalgo. The legal interest was thirty-three and a third per cent. per annum. In three years the debt became doubled; it daily was more inconvenient, and often impossible to pay. Then a cry was raised against the usury of the Jews, and the murder of the too confiding dependant on Castilian honour, was found to be an easy mode of cancelling the obligation.

3.— The priesthood, with some exceptions, proved to be their most determined enemies, and their most inveterate foes. An infatuated bigotry was sometimes the apparent cause, but without reason. The Jews of Spain had never acted hostilely against Christianity; it was only at its commencement in the East that religious fanaticism led to those horrid scenes, alike repugnant to the Mosaic and Christian religion, that soil with bloody stains the pages of history, when the followers of each respective creed, inflamed by an intemperate zeal, sought to crush the other. Under the pretext that Judaism was inimical to Christianity, thousands were immolated. Priests whose duty it was to preach the peaceable doctrines of the gospel, by their harangues from the pulpit, instigated and then led on an infuriated populace to murder the harmless unarmed descendants of Israel. They accused the Jews of making converts—an accusation never proved or made against them in the many persecutions suffered by the Hebrew people in every part of Europe. Their religion is opposed to it; but many who had forcibly been compelled to abjure the faith of their fathers, probably returned to that which, only for the moment, they had apparently abandoned; this may have led to the fallacious assertion. They forbade the people employing Jews as physicians, apothecaries, and surgeons, under pretence that from the hatred they bore to Christians, they would seek to kill them; but it was in reality to monopolise the practice to themselves. Except the Jews, monks only practised the healing art; they gleaned from the barbarous Latin of their scholastic theology an insight into the works on medicine; yet the Castilian monarchs preferred confiding the health of their bodies to Jewish practitioners, rather than to cloistered quacks. Their chief object was to increase the wealth of their convents; by constant attendance on the sick, when *in extremis*, they worked on their fears, and deprived many an heir of his rightful property to enrich their various monastic orders. Endeavouring to remove the Jewish physician from the death-bed of the dying Christian, suited their interested purpose; for chiefly thus was acquired the immense property the cortes have within the last few years taken from the clergy for the benefit of the state. Another cause also aroused the jealousy and envy of the clergy: they, likewise, were borrowers; and, although they at times accused the Jews of desecrating the Host, yet they pledged the church plate to them to raise money for unholy purposes.

4.—The small landholders, whose scanty means and improvidence prevented them from cultivating their land without borrowing from their more wealthy neighbours. Their loans were not confined to money; for the law established that if they borrowed three *fanegas* of corn, four was the most that was to be returned. They were equally glad to be relieved from importunate creditors.

5. The people who, through a bigoted veneration for the priesthood, were led to believe the Jews the authors of every public calamity, were always

ready to wreak their vengeance by attacking the Jewries, plundering the houses, butchering the inmates, and enriching themselves at the expense of the wealth and lives of the Hebrew people.

With such inflammable materials as the Spanish population thus consisted of, the smallest spark readily ignited a flame not easily extinguished. The law was often too powerless to afford protection to the objects of popular fury, and the assailants too numerous to be punished; nevertheless, on many occasions, the instigators and ringleaders met from the sovereign the punishment due to their crime; but the injury was irreparable—life could not be restored to the murdered victims of fanaticism and envy.

But to resume; shortly after Ferdinand assumed the reins of government, the bishop and chapter of Segovia complained to him that the Jews defrauded them, by not paying the capitation-tax of thirty deniers, whereupon he issued the following:[1]—

We, Ferdinand, by the grace of God, king of Castile, etc., etc. To the Jews of the Jewry of Segovia, and all other Jewries of the towns and places within the said diocese, to whom this my order or a copy of it signed by the Notary Public, cometh, health and grace. Know ye, that the bishop and dean have complained to me, and say, that you will not pay nor account with them, nor to their order, the thirty deniers each of you have to give in memorial of the death of our Lord Jesus Christ, when the Jews crucified him, and intreat me to order what I deem right. You are bound to pay the same in gold, and I consider it just that you pay the amount in the current coin.

Therefore I command that you give and pay the same, and annually make payment thereof to the bishop, dean, and chapter, aforesaid, or any of them, or the persons that receive

[1] Colmenares, Hist. Segovia.

for them, thirty deniers of the current coin, each of you well and truly, in such manner that there be no deduction therefrom. And should they require assistance for the fulfilment hereof, I command the councillors, magistrates, alcaldes, judges, and all other officers, or any of them, to whom this my order, or a copy of it duly authenticated, cometh, to accompany and assist them in such manner that what I command be fulfilled.

Given at Palencia, 29th August, 1304.

Ferdinand was particularly attached to the master of his household, Don Samuel, who is represented to have been a man of great talents and trust; possessing great power, he is said to have used it despotically. Whether from that cause or jealousy, an assassin, who was not discovered, entered his house at Seville, after the king had left for Badajoz in 1305, and stabbed him.[2] Ferdinand had acted very ungratefully to his mother; and as the enemies of Don Samuel represented that he had been the cause, she was not afterwards kindly disposed towards the Jews.

Although the name of the Hebrew who succeeded Don Samuel is not mentioned, there can be little doubt but the new treasurer was an Israelite; for a league was formed by the grandees, clergy, and people, against these wealthy and powerful financiers. Jealousy, from their rigid administration of the royal finances, was the cause (and to which, probably, a haughtiness in their high office contributed) that led to a petition against them,[3] in the cortes of Medina del Campo in that same year; whereupon it was ordered that they should not be collectors nor sub-collectors of taxes.

Ferdinand's attachment to the Jews led him to invite Don Guedalia Jachia, who was physician to

---

[2] Chron. Ferd. IV., ch. 18-19.     [3] Pet. 8.

Dennis, king of Portugal, to come and reside in Castile, and appointed him to be his physician.

In the following year, a petition was presented to the cortes of Valladolid, to deprive the Jews of separate judges in Castile; but the king ordered that what had been done in the reigns of his grandfather and father, should be followed.

On the sudden death of Ferdinand in 1312, his son, Alphonso, a child of a few months old, was acknowledged as king; different parties claimed the regency, and intestine quarrels caused the renewal of those scenes that had taken place during the minority of his father. To calm dissensions, and guard the crown for her grandson, Donna Maria de Padilla came from her retreat; and in conjunction with Don Pedro, uncle of the infant monarch, took the helm of state; but the civil wars of the regency belong to Spanish history more than to that of the Jews.

Pope Clement V., who had removed the papal see from Rome to Avignon, in 1311, summoned the council of Vienne. The intolerant spirit that pervaded that assembly communicated itself to Don Rodrigo, archbishop of Saint Iago, who, taking advantage of the disturbed state of the kingdom, held a provincial council at Zamora in 1313, which exercised so much influence, that public opinion and ideas became changed; the people openly declared against the Jews, and began to regard them with a species of horror. At almost every cortes after, petitions poured in, either against them, or demanding that some privilege they enjoyed should be taken from them. But the legislators of Castile had far different views; successive monarchs continued their protection, and the effect of the following constitutions of that council was only to awaken the ill-will and hatred of the populace to their Israelite fellow-subjects and citizens; for, it will be seen, the sovereigns heeded neither its imprecations nor enactments.

CONSTITUTION 1.— Thirty days are allowed to all Jews[4] that now do or hereafter may reside in our province, for the execution hereof.

That in criminal, civil, and all other causes, they shall not oppose nor defend themselves by the privilege they have; saying, that as no Jew was summoned against them in the cause, they cannot be condemned; nor may they claim that or any other privilege to the prejudice of the Christian faith, nor presume to obtain such or similar privileges.

Therefore we ordain, that in criminal, and all other causes, the testimony of Jews against Jews shall be valid as heretofore; but not of a Jew against a Christian, nor, as is proper or just, shall his testimony be received. Those persons that desire to place Jews above Christians, and do not observe these and all other constitutions made against the Jews, whether they be ecclesiastic, layman, or secularised clergy; may the curse of Almighty God, of St. Peter and St. Paul, whose constitutions they are inclined to break, and the curse of St. Iago come upon them. The ordinary prelates shall compel and oblige them to observe this. Those persons who act contrary shall receive from the holy church the punishment the sin deserves.

2.— Henceforth Jews shall hold no post or dignity from kings, or any secular prince; and within the aforesaid time they shall resign those they now hold.

3.— They are not to be admitted into frequent association with Christians, lest from the intimacy, they adopt their errors which they do not understand.

4.— That they do not serve as witnesses against Christians, nor claim as hitherto the benefit of the laws.

5.— That no Christian women, either temporarily or otherwise, act as wet nurses, or rear their children.

[4] Aguirre.

6.— They are not to appear in public, from the Wednesday of Passion Week until Saturday; and on Good Friday are to close their doors and windows the whole day, not to mock the sorrow of Christians for the passion.

7.— That Jews and Jewesses wear an ostensible sign, that they may be distinguished and separate among Christians, which is right, and practised in other states.

8.— Notwithstanding their learning and reputation, they are not to practise medicine with Christians.

9.— They are not to invite Christians to their feasts, that Christians do not eat with Jews; in particular they are not to eat their meat or drink their wine.

10.— They are annually to pay tithes on their landed property, and the houses they occupy, the same as Christians did before they belonged to Jews.

11.— Synagogues that have been newly erected or enlarged, shall be restored to their former state between this date, and the next great festival of the resurrection; this term is peremptorily fixed, and if at its expiration the Jews have not executed it, the judges, alcaldes, communities, and universities of the cities, towns, and places where synagogues have been recently erected and elevated, are to fulfil and have this ordinance executed, in virtue of holy obedience under the penalty of Constitution 1.

12.— They are not to practise usury, nor exact, nor take any interest from Christians, as is prohibited by the constitutions of Pope Clement V., enacted at the council of Vienne; and any person who acts contrary, or attempts to hide it, incurs the penalties ordained by the said council.

13.— On Sundays and other Christian holidays, they are not to work publicly for themselves or other persons.

In 1315, a cortes to regulate the affairs of the kingdom, was held at Burgos; among its ordinances are the following:—

4.— Henceforward no Jew or Moor shall be called by Christian names; any that may be, are to be tried as heretics.

5.--Christians are not to live with Jews or Moors, or rear their children; the judges of towns and places where it occurs, are to make examples of those persons that do it, the same as on those who break their religion.

26.—We consider it just, and order, that Christians indebted to Jews from past times, shall pay them as heretofore.

27.—We order that no debtor shall avail himself of any bull, papal decree, or any other reason; not to pay according to this ordinance.

28.—We consider it right, that henceforward no Jew shall presume to lend on usury, or at a higher rate than thirty-three and a third per cent. according to the ordinances King Alphonso and King Sancho enacted on that subject; and if it be proved and verified that any Jew has lent at a higher rate, his person and property shall be confiscated to the king.

30.—In places where Jews have an officer who recovers their debts, if the Christian debtor possesses moveables, he must secure the property until the cause is determined by law; if landed property it may not be sold during the suit; nor may it be ill-used, nor any injury be done to it, that no wrong may be suffered by the Jew.

However prejudiced Donna Maria might have been against the Jews, the foregoing shews that she protected their property from injury, and acted towards them with justice. It is also proved that she employed them in posts of high trust, for a petition was presented to the cortes held at Carrion, "That those persons who had not rendered their accounts to the receivers-general, Don Juan Garcia and Rabbi Don Moses, might not be punished for it; and that all proceedings in consequence might be staid,"[5] which she granted; as also, "That noblemen, ecclesiastics, or Jews, should not farm any king's dues or taxes; and that no punishment should be inflicted on those persons who had not attended to the summonses issued

[5] Petition, 7.

by them in the king's name."[6] In 1321, a rabble band of fanatics, who assumed the denomination of "the Shepherds," sprang up in Languedoc. Friends and foes were alike the objects for pillage and plunder; the Jews, in particular, from their wealth, were inhumanly butchered. One hundred and twenty synagogues are said to have been destroyed by them. The Pope issued bulls and excommunications against them, but they were disregarded. By order of the king of France, the nobles armed against them; the count of Toulouse made some prisoners, but they were released by the monks. Driven from France, they entered Navarre and Aragon. At Montreal the Jews themselves repulsed them. James II. sent an army under his son, the Infante Alphonso, against them; a number of Jews joined it. His master of horse killed the ringleader, and completely routed the remainder, which saved the Jews of Spain from the horrors their brethren had experienced in the south of France[7].

Donna Maria, queen of James II., being at Barcelona for the benefit of her health, a violent tumult took place on Easter Sunday between the Jews and her attendants, some of whom were severely handled, although no lives were lost. The queen was highly incensed that the civil authorities and the royal officers had not protected her servants. On the arrival of the king, he ordered the guilty parties to be severely punished. From Zurita not stating that it was the Jews that were punished, it may be presumed justice was impartially executed[8].

Councils respecting ecclesiastical discipline were

[6] Petition, 8.     [7] Seder Adoroth.     [8] Zurita.

held in various parts of Europe, but less frequently in Spain, although no clergy required it more; and until that of Zamora, the Jews had been unmolested; but that seems to have aroused the dormant hatred of the Spanish clergy towards the descendants of Israel; for although but a *brutum fulmen*, as they were disregarded even by monarchs, which history testifies, the Council of Salamanca, held in 1322, enacted the following canons[9]:—

1st. That infidels (Jews and Moors) be not permitted to be in churches during divine service, particularly while mass is performed. At its commencement, they were to be expelled, or locked up by the sacristan in some private place, until it was ended.

2nd. Christians who were present at the marriages or funerals of Jews or Moors, were to be excommunicated.

3rd. Prohibited the appointment of Jews or Moors to public offices.

4th. Christians were not to employ Jews as physicians, surgeons, or apothecaries, nor take their medicines, from the danger of death they incurred by so doing.

5th. Converts were to be provided for, by being admitted into monasteries, or other religious establishments. Those who were not of handicraft trades were to be taught them, and furnished with tools; but no relief was to be afforded to those who could gain their livelihood, or had sufficient personal property for their maintenance. Such as were desirous, and by their learning competent for the priesthood, were to be instructed for it, and the bishops were exhorted to provide them with churches; but caution was recommended in permitting them to preach to their former co-religionists. The customary laws of inheritance were to be observed.

When the kings of Castile or Aragon visited a town, a tax was imposed on the inhabitants to defray the expense and maintenance of their retinues, exclu-

[9] Aguirre.

sive of the ordinary taxes. The Jewries and Moorish Aljamas also had to contribute. By an account yet preserved, it appears, that from 1282 until 1336, the Jews and Moors of Aragon, including Catalonia, paid the following:[10]—

|  | Sous. |  | Sous. |  | Sous. |
|---|---|---|---|---|---|
| Tortosa, | 4000 | Saragossa, | 400 | Villafranca, | 200 |
| Barcelona, | 500 | Teruel, | 300 | Tarrazon, | 145 |
| Gerona, | 500 | Besalu, | 250 | and |  |
| Valencia, | 500 | Daroca, | 200 | Calatayud. | 50 |

which shews the relative population of the various towns.

## CHAPTER XIII.

*Alphonso XI.—Their Petitions to him.—Amount of their Debts reduced.—Protection afforded them.—Revolt at Valladolid against Don Joseph of Ecija.—Murders at Estella, the Instigator punished, and the City fined.—Cortes of Valladolid.—Ordinance respecting bonds at Vittoria.—Council of Salamanca.—Martinez's plan to destroy them—his end.—Cortes of Alcala.—The Plague.—Massacre of the Jews.—Rabenu Asher.—Suicide of his son.—Ordinance respecting Usury.—Riot at Barcelona.—Physicians and men of note.*

THE Cortes of Valladolid, in 1325, declared Alphonso of age. He had, on the representation of his uncle, the Infante Don Philip,[1] learned that, in Castile, Jews

[10] Capmany, Com. de Barcelona.      [1] Chron. Alph. XI.

had long held the post of Almoxarif in the king's household. At his recommendation, he appointed Don Joseph of Ecija to the office, being a man of great talents; from the favour he received from the court, he exercised great authority over the kingdom. One of the first acts of Alphonso, on assuming the regal power, was to do justice to the Jews. Christians had sought to defraud them of the debts they owed to them. His attention was called to it by their petition,[2] and he issued the following ordinance:—

Whereas the Jews have complained to me, that many persons of my dominions, as well clergy as laymen, have asked and obtained bulls and prelates' letters, excommunicating those persons that enforce debts due to Jews: I consider it just, and command that my officers of cities and towns arrest all persons who exhibit such bulls and letters, who are not to be released even under security, until they give them up, and they are immediately to be forwarded to me.

At the same cortes, petitions[3] were presented against the Jews. Complaints were made of their usuries; and the king was requested to cancel a third of the debts due by Christians, and to make the balance payable one-half in eight months, and the other ten months after. But the king, probably under the advice of Don Joseph, who knew that the Jews would willingly make some sacrifice to get their money, ordered—

That debts due by Christians to Jews on bonds or pledges, shall have the interest at the rate of thirty-three and a third per cent. added to the capital, and from the total amount, one quarter should be deducted, and the three-fourths should be payable in equal payments without further interest, in four, eight, and twelve months, so that the whole be paid within a year. And those persons who did not pay at the specified terms, were to lose the benefit of this ordinance.

[2] Pet. 16.     [3] Pet. 14.

The Jews having represented to him that since the death of his father, Don Ferdinand, many obstructions and delays had been caused them in the recovery of their debts, he ordered—

That all delays, general or special, that had been granted during his minority, whether instituted by councils, prelates, knights, or otherwise, to prevent the recovery of their debts, should be examined into; and that the six years and thirty days, formerly allowed them, should not be reckoned in such delays.

Furthermore, Jews who may have gone to reside in other kingdoms, and come to live in mine, where they become taxpayers, I command that the councils, and persons in office, are to assist and protect them from injury.

In answer to a petition that they might be permitted to acquire landed property, the king limited it to the value of twenty thousand maravedis north of the Douro, and thirty thousand south of it—a right they retained until the expulsion. The king placed the utmost confidence in his councillors, Garcilaso de la Vega, Count Alvar Nunes Osorio, and Don Joseph.[4] The latter had a large retinue of knights and squires for his guard. From the trust the king placed in him, he sent him to Valladolid to bring his sister, Donna Leonora, to Toledo; and ordered her chancellor, the bishop of Burgos, to accompany her. Her duenna, Donna Sancha, told the chiefs of the city, in secresy, that they wanted to take away the Infanta to marry her to Count Alvar Nunes, who, being powerful, and possessor of many fortresses and castles, would afterwards do what he chose with the king's person; but she was not generally believed. The Infanta, ignorant of the report, prepared for her journey; when on her mule, a mob, instigated by those in the plot, riotously

[4] Chro. Alph. XI.

wanted to kill Don Joseph and his attendants; upon which she returned with him into the house, which was immediately surrounded. Donna Sancha pretended to be much grieved at the occurrence; but privately encouraged them to enter the house and kill Don Joseph. The mob procured ladders to scale the walls. When the Infanta learnt this, she requested that four of the principal men should come to speak with her. She asked them to permit her to go to the Alcazar of the city, and to protect Don Joseph in accompanying her, when she would give him up. The mob, on learning this, withdrew and dispersed. When the Infanta perceived this, she mounted her mule, and the Jew walked by her side holding her skirt. Some attempts were made on his life. On their arrival at the Alcazar, the princess ordered the gates to be shut, and would not deliver him up to the rioters.

As soon as the king learned this, he summoned a council, and would have proceeded to Valladolid to take summary steps against them; but was dissuaded by Alvar Nunes, who advised him to continue the siege of Escalona, and to notify his displeasure to them.

The Jews, finding the king, from his friendship to Don Joseph, so well-disposed towards the Hebrew people, made many complaints of the excesses committed against them, which he carefully looked into, and redressed, as the following shews.

In 1327, the Jewries of Seville begged that the dean and chapter should not exact more from them than the thirty deniers imposed by Alphonso X. at the conquest of the city. The king, desirous of doing justice, entrusted the investigation of the facts to

Ferran Martinez of Valladolid, chief notary of Castile, who, on the 10th of November, pronounced a final sentence in the cause, ordering all Jews, without exception, from sixteen years of age, to pay three maravedis of ten deniers each, making the thirty to which only they were liable.

The many complaints made to the cortes of Valladolid against Don Joseph, induced the king to order an examination of his accounts, which was a prelude to depriving him of office. He dismissed him from the council and the post of Almoxarif; and ordered, that none but Christians should in future hold that office, with the title of Treasurer instead of Almoxarif. Although Spanish historians attribute his dismissal to a deficiency in his accounts, it is far more likely the king did it to quiet his rebellious subjects, who were daily in arms against him. At Soria, while at his devotions, they assassinated Garcilaso de la Vega, another of his particular friends; for Don Joseph, as will be seen, notwithstanding his dismissal from office, retained the friendship of his sovereign. The Jews of Estella complained (to Juan Pasta, dean of Chartres, Hugo de Visac, and Ferri de Piqueni, knights, who had been ordered by Charles le Bel, to remedy abuses in Navarre) against Juan Garcia, the collector, for exacting, during some time, fifty sous a day from them for collecting the king's taxes, and placing double guards at their expense, almost ruining them. The knights, desirous of preserving the property of the king, and of the Jews who belonged to him as his own, ordered, that Juan Garcia should no longer be the collector of taxes from them, but that their bailiff should receive them as formerly customary.[5]

[5] Arch. Nav. Case 6. No. 45.

following constitutions of that council was only to awaken the ill-will and hatred of the populace to their Israelite fellow-subjects and citizens; for, it will be seen, the sovereigns heeded neither its imprecations nor enactments.

CONSTITUTION 1.— Thirty days are allowed to all Jews[4] that now do or hereafter may reside in our province, for the execution hereof.

That in criminal, civil, and all other causes, they shall not oppose nor defend themselves by the privilege they have; saying, that as no Jew was summoned against them in the cause, they cannot be condemned; nor may they claim that or any other privilege to the prejudice of the Christian faith, nor presume to obtain such or similar privileges.

Therefore we ordain, that in criminal, and all other causes, the testimony of Jews against Jews shall be valid as heretofore; but not of a Jew against a Christian, nor, as is proper or just, shall his testimony be received. Those persons that desire to place Jews above Christians, and do not observe these and all other constitutions made against the Jews, whether they be ecclesiastic, layman, or secularised clergy; may the curse of Almighty God, of St. Peter and St. Paul, whose constitutions they are inclined to break, and the curse of St. Iago come upon them. The ordinary prelates shall compel and oblige them to observe this. Those persons who act contrary shall receive from the holy church the punishment the sin deserves.

2.— Henceforth Jews shall hold no post or dignity from kings, or any secular prince; and within the aforesaid time they shall resign those they now hold.

3.— They are not to be admitted into frequent association with Christians, lest from the intimacy, they adopt their errors which they do not understand.

4.— That they do not serve as witnesses against Christians, nor claim as hitherto the benefit of the laws.

5.— That no Christian women, either temporarily or otherwise, act as wet nurses, or rear their children.

[4] Aguirre.

6.— They are not to appear in public, from the Wednesday of Passion Week until Saturday; and on Good Friday are to close their doors and windows the whole day, not to mock the sorrow of Christians for the passion.

7.— That Jews and Jewesses wear an ostensible sign, that they may be distinguished and separate among Christians, which is right, and practised in other states.

8.— Notwithstanding their learning and reputation, they are not to practise medicine with Christians.

9.— They are not to invite Christians to their feasts, that Christians do not eat with Jews; in particular they are not to eat their meat or drink their wine.

10.— They are annually to pay tithes on their landed property, and the houses they occupy, the same as Christians did before they belonged to Jews.

11.— Synagogues that have been newly erected or enlarged, shall be restored to their former state between this date, and the next great festival of the resurrection; this term is peremptorily fixed, and if at its expiration the Jews have not executed it, the judges, alcaldes, communities, and universities of the cities, towns, and places where synagogues have been recently erected and elevated, are to fulfil and have this ordinance executed, in virtue of holy obedience under the penalty of Constitution 1.

12.— They are not to practise usury, nor exact, nor take any interest from Christians, as is prohibited by the constitutions of Pope Clement V., enacted at the council of Vienne; and any person who acts contrary, or attempts to hide it, incurs the penalties ordained by the said council.

13.— On Sundays and other Christian holidays, they are not to work publicly for themselves or other persons.

In 1315, a cortes to regulate the affairs of the kingdom, was held at Burgos; among its ordinances are the following:—

4.— Henceforward no Jew or Moor shall be called by Christian names; any that may be, are to be tried as heretics.

Through the friendship and favor of the king, Don Samuel also farmed, at a low value, the frontier duties. The following curious document is yet preserved in the archives of Vittoria.

Don Alphonso, by the grace of God, king of Castile, &c. &c. to the Alcaldes and Magistrates of Vittoria, health and grace.—Know ye, that the Council of Vittoria has sent to complain to me, and say, that from a long time they have had the usage and custom, which has been preserved until now, that Jews residing in the city or elsewhere did not make bonds for debts on the Christian inhabitants; but latterly, that the Jews, or some of them, do make Christians give bond for debts; and if it be permitted, great injury will result herefrom; that the said city would become depopulated, and that it would tend to my disservice; they send to beg the favor of me to order what I consider right.—Therefore I command you, at sight of this my order, that if they have had the usage and custom for a long time, and have retained it until now, as is asserted, that henceforward you do not permit the said Jews, or any of them, to make bonds for debts on any of the Christian inhabitants of the said city; and if they do, they shall be null and void. Therefore you are not to do it under the penalty of 100 maravedis of the annual new coinage. And that you fulfil this my order on its being shewn to you, I command every Notary Public who may be called for the purpose, to give a certificate, under his hand, to the person who exhibits it to you, that I may know how you execute this my order.[16]— Given at Burgos, 28th April, 1332, (era 1370).

Don Joseph, who had formerly been of the king's council, and his friend, seeing the great profit Don Samuel made by his contracts, particularly from the export duty paid by the Moors, from jealousy and thinking to regain the king's favor, outbid Don Samuel for the frontier custom duties, by which he obtained them. Don Samuel, out of revenge to injure

[16] Arch. Vit. Case B. No. 17.

him, privately advised the king to stop the exportation by the Moors, so that he might not derive benefit. The king considering the advice given him to be for his interest, regardless of his treaties with the Moors, adopted it. In 1335, the Council of Salamanca[17] endeavoured to destroy the medical practice of the Jews among Christians, asserting—

That under the pretext of surgery and medicine, they craftily insinuated themselves with the people, to the injury of the faithful.— It prohibited Christian women giving suck or nursing the children of unbelievers. All correspondence, in writing, with them was interdicted to the faithful. The penalty for any of these acts was excommunication. The Jews in every town were to reside in a separate quarter, to be called the Jewry; they were not to live in the vicinity of a church or cemetery; Christians who leased houses to them in such situations, incurred excommunication.

A war with the Moors soon followed the infringement of treaties. Gonsalez Martinez, a brave man, who had served under Don Joseph, and had by him been appointed to some command, became master of Calatrava; envious of the favor his former benefactor enjoyed from his sovereign, and jealous that the Jews should enjoy so much power, he proposed to buy from the king ten of the principal Jews, for which he would pay into his exhausted treasury 800lbs. of silver. As the king needed money to repel the Saracen invaders, he consented; upon which Gonsalez seized Don Joseph, the physician, who died under torture ; Don Samuel, whom he put in irons, and who died of grief; and eight others of the wealthiest Jews with their families; by which he got a large sum in gold, silver, and money. The king, distressed for means to oppose the forces

---

[17] Aguirre.

from Morocco under Abomelique, which Gonsalez (plotting against Don Samuel Benayes and R. Moses Abudiel) perceiving, advised the king to expel the Jews from his kingdom; for while the king was engaged in fighting, they were eating and drinking peaceably; and he would give 400,000 ducats, and the people as much more towards the expenses of the war. The king listened and was silent; the grandees reproved Gonsalez, and said the advice he had given was not good. Don Gil de Albornoz, archbishop of Toledo, said to him, " Who has made you an enemy to the king, by giving advice that is degrading to his house, for the Jews are the king's treasure, and you want to destroy them, and for him to do what his ancestors never did?" so his purpose was not effected. The Moors collected a large force; the king joined his army, and made Gonsalez general of it; and he gained a complete victory. Becoming haughtier than before, he thought the king would fulfil his wish of destroying the Jews; but some accusations being made to the king against him, he sent an officer to arrest him. Gonsalez retired to a fortress, and from the tower sent an insolent answer, whereupon his brothers were arrested, thrown into prison, and their property confiscated to the royal treasury. The king sent to seize him; but he had fortified himself in the castle, from which he shot the envoy. The king ordered fire to be set to it: Gonsalez was taken, tried, found guilty of the crimes imputed to him, beheaded, and his corpse burnt.[18] Christian writers say he was accused of many crimes, and summoned to Madrid to exculpate himself before the king. He would not appear, and went over to the Moorish king of Granada. At length,

[18] Shebet Jehudah.

being taken as a traitor, he was beheaded and burnt.[19] This happened about 1340.

Salhadin of Angleura, being governor of Navarre in 1336, ordered the land which had been appropriated for the Jewry of Pamplona by King Charles, to be rebuilt. It had been destroyed by the French army that devastated the whole of Navarre in 1277. The new Jewry was to be enclosed and secured from injury; the Jews were to be obliged to build their houses within, and not to be permitted to reside in other parts of the city among Christians.[20]

In 1344, the Jews were so numerous and wealthy at Palma, that the Bishop Villanova fined them 150,000 florins for sheltering two German Christians who had embraced Judaism.[21]

At the Cortes of Alcala de Herrures, in 1345, a petition was presented to grant time, and to cancel the interest on debts due to Jews. The king answered,

> I consider it right to grant the delay of one year, for the payment of debts due to Jews, during which no interest is to be charged, but if any delay has been previously granted, it is to be included in the said year.[22]

The Jews and Moors having complained of being arrested for debts due to Christians, the following ordinance was issued in 1347, by the Cortes of Segovia.

> Many complaints having been made to me that Jews and Moors, indebted to Christians on bonds and otherwise, have been arrested, where the debt is not for our taxes and dues, contrary to the privileges granted by the Kings from whom we descend, and ourselves; whereby the Jewries of the Jews and Aljamas of the Moors are wronged and injured; and as the Jews and Moors residing in our dominions are separately ours, we order

---

[19] Chron. Alph. XI.    [20] Arch. Nav. Case 7, No. 67.
[21] Anonym. Hist. of Mallorca.    [22] Pet. 4.

that in future no Jew, Jewess, Moor, or Morisca, shall be arrested for any debt or obligation they may have given, to any person of whatever rank or condition they may be, except the debt is for our taxes and dues; nor shall any Christian be arrested for bonds due to Jews or Moors.

Notwithstanding the protection afforded by the king to the Jews, he had been compelled to sign an order for their banishment, on account of an indignity pretended to have been offered to the Host by a Jewish boy, as it was carried through the streets. A council was immediately summoned to deliberate, whether they should be massacred or banished; the latter advice was adopted. But the edict was not issued, owing to the prince having obtained a revision of the proceeding, when it was discovered that curiosity to see the procession, had brought a young Christian to the window, who accidentally overturned a vessel of water over the chalice. The king upon this revoked the order, to the mortification of the zealots, who reported that the Christian had been bribed to depose in favor of their enemies; nor did it prevent the populace murdering the Jews in another city on the same excuse; and the persecution would have extended much farther, had the King not have had ten of the ringleaders hanged.

R. Joseph Levi Abulaphia, who died in 1351, appears to have been a great favourite with Alphonso, as his tombstone testifies, in saying, " The man whom the king delighteth to honour; and he put a chain of gold on his neck." [28]

The Jews had scarcely escaped the danger just recorded, when in 1348-49 a devastating plague spread from Germany to the Peninsula; and they were accused

[28] Appendix 4.

of having caused it by poisoning the waters of the Tagus. The infuriated populace massacred them without mercy, particularly at Toledo, where the York tragedy was repeated. One of the sons of the famed Rabenu Asher (who, owing to the persecution in Germany, had in 1303, quitted his native land with his eight sons for Spain, where his great learning obtained for him the high post of Chief Rabbi of all the Jews in Spain, which he held until his death), perceiving the murderers breaking his doors, with the intention of massacreing them, became so frantic and desperate, that he stabbed his wife and all the family that had taken shelter under his roof, and then himself, to avoid the barbarous cruelties practised by the populace, under whose murderous weapons 15,000 innocent victims are said to have been immolated, for a crime which reason demonstrates to be impracticable and impossible.

Alphonso, who was then besieging Gibraltar, was unable to suppress the outrages that were being committed. The plague was making dreadful ravage among his troops; to arrest which his whole care was directed.

Whereas, usury is said to be a great sin, forbidden both by the laws of nature and by scripture and grace—a thing that weighs heavy with God, which brings trouble and misfortunes on the country where it is practised; and to permit, order, adjudge to pay or receive the same is a great sin; and, besides, it brings destruction and ruin on the properties of some persons, and the inhabitants of the country where it is allowed. And, whereas, it has hitherto been permitted, and not condemned as it should have been; we, to follow God and preserve our souls as we ought, to prevent the injuries that thereby accrue to our people and country, consider it right to order and prohibit all persons, Jews or Moors, henceforward, for themselves or others, to lend usuriously. And all charters, privileges, and immunities, that have hitherto been granted, authorising the same in certain modes; and to have magistrates and receivers thereof, we cancel, revoke, and by the council of our court declare to be null and void. And we hold it right that hereafter they shall be of no value, the same as those that may not be granted, nor are they to be maintained, being, as before said, contrary to religion. We command all judges, magistrates, and officers, of whatsoever rank they may be, in all our kingdoms and dominions, that, hereafter, they do not concede or grant any charter or license for usury. And further, we request and desire all prelates of our dominions, to excommunicate all persons who act contrary, and to denounce them as transgressors. And it is our will that Jews be maintained in our dominions and to purchase landed property as enacted; for, as Holy Church declares, they are to turn to our faith and be saved, according to the prophets.

Whether religious motives were the sole cause of the decree or not, the king manifests the desire that the Jews should continue to reside in Spain.

Peter IV. of Aragon, in that year, held a cortes at Barcelona, while there at the dedication of St. Maria de las Nieves. A large mob assembled, and notwithstanding the royal presence, with great daring and insolence attacked the Jews; and it was not without difficulty that the riot was suppressed.[24]

It will be seen, that in this reign many Jews held high offices; besides whom the following may be named as conferring honour on the Hebrew name.

DON ABRAHAM BEN MACHIR—had been physician to Alphonso before Don Samuel; he died in 1322 at Seville.

DON SAMUEL BENVENASTE—taught medicine with great repute at Saragossa; he was a profound grammarian. He translated the "Consolation of Boetius," and Maimonides'

---

[24] Zurita, Ann. Aragon.

Treatise and Cure of the Asthma" into Hebrew, in 1323, at Taraçon.

Don David Jachia—son of Don Guedaliah, the physician of Ferdinand IV., wrote two works on " Customs and Ceremonies." He probably held some post at court, for on his tombstone, dated Seville, 1325, we read " He stood in the presence of kings."[5]

R. Solomon ben David—about this time wrote a general treatise on " Theoretical and Practical Medicine," according to Avicenna and Averroes.

R. David Abudarham—born at Seville in 1300, was one of the most learned Rabbis of that city, and an excellent astronomer; he wrote on the Intercalation, the Solstices, the Equinoxes, and a most valuable commentary on the " Ritual of the Year."

R. Joseph Ben Abraham ben Shoshan—an eminent physician and astronomer of Seville, died in 1336. This family appears to have made medicine their study; for Don Meir, who was one of the royal physicians, died in the plague of 1348, together with his son Don Isaac, at the age of twenty-five.

R. Elhazar a Cohen ben Ardot—a native of Majorca, was famed as a professor of logic and medicine in 1330.

R. Abraham ben David Caslari—of Besalu, wrote four medical works, among which is an unedited treatise on " Contagious and Pestilential Fevers." In the preface he says, he wrote it on witnessing the dreadful plague that ravaged Spain in 1349.

R. Baruch a Rophe—was another famed practitioner at Besalu.

R. Kreskas Vidal ben Keslad.—in 1327 translated into Hebrew the Latin medical work of Bernabe de Villanueva, under the title of " The Regimen of Health." His

לפני מלכים יתיצב [5]

family produced many learned men, who were Rabbis at Barcelona and Saragossa.

R. SOLOMON ABEN ZARSAL—was a celebrated physician at Seville, where his tombstone is yet to be seen; it bears date 1345. His father, R. Abraham, had also practised medicine with great repute. The number and fame of the Spanish Hebrew practitioners, led foreign princes to seek their aid. The count of Poitou, brother of the king of France, sent to Aragon for an oculist who cured him.

R. JUDAH BEN ASHER—died at Toledo in 1349, and did not commit suicide, as asserted by Rodrigues de Castro, as his tombstone proves. He was author of "The Ordinances of the Law," and the "Ordinances of Heaven." His brother, R. Jacob, compiled the whole of the Jewish laws, under the title of "The Four Orders."

R. JOSEPH OF TOLEDO—where he was born about 1304, wrote under the title of the "Ruler of the World," the origin and reason of all the Judaical rites.

## CHAPTER XIV.

*Peter the Cruel.—Samuel Levi.—New Synagogue at Toledo.—Murderers executed at Miranda del Ebro.—Sentences of the Jew Magistrates in Navarre, to be executed by the Bailiff.—Abu Said beheaded.—Henry, Count of Trastemar, crowned at Burgos.—Cortes of Burgos.—Gallant Defence of Briviesca, Toledo, and Burgos.—Protection offered to Jews of Castile on settling in Navarre.—Cortes of Toro.—Massacre at Granada.—Cortes of Burgos.—Learned Men.*

PETER, surnamed the Cruel, was only sixteen years of age when he succeeded his father in 1350. At the recommendation of Don Juan Alphonso de Albuquerque, he appointed Don Samuel Levi to be his high treasurer. He became a great favourite with the king, who particularly favoured the Jews. The Christians, not satisfied with having deprived them of their particular judges, attempted to deprive them of a privilege they had long enjoyed, of having in every city, town, and place, where they had Jewries, a separate Alcalde appointed to try their causes. A petition[1] was presented to the cortes of Valladolid in 1351, requesting the sovereign to order—

That the Jews should not have a separate Alcalde, but that suits between them and Christians should be remitted to the ordinary Alcaldes. (The king answered), That as the Jews

[1] Pet. 7.

were a weak people that required protection, by appearing before all the Alcaldes their causes would be greatly prejudiced and attended with heavy expense, because Christians would injure them by the delays they would cause, and the demands they would make against them; therefore I consider it right that the Jews should appoint one of the ordinary Alcaldes of each city or town, as they have been accustomed to try and decide their civil causes. Besides, not generally being persons acquainted with the laws and charters, and not being powerful, Christians frequently presume to bring vexatious and frivolous defences against their claims, putting in malicious pleadings which they ought not.

The object of the sovereign, by this reply, was to prevent the injustice so frequently committed against them, for he acknowledges them to be a weak and injured people, who at times could not recover their debts, as the officers did not render them strict and impartial justice.

In 1355, the king being at play at Morales, said all the money he possessed was twenty thousand doblas. In the evening, Don Samuel observed to the king, that he considered the remark he had made was a reflection on his conduct as high treasurer; but if he would appoint two fortresses where he might put the money in safety, he should soon have much more. Whereupon the king gave him the Alcazar of Trugillo, and the castle of Hita; and appointed Don Juan Alphonso de Albuquerque, governor of the former, and Don Juan de Illescas, of the latter, both noblemen on whom he could depend. He then demanded from all the receivers-general their accounts, and drew bills for their balances. When the persons who had the bills returned, he put them on oath to declare what they had received. Some out of forty thousand maravedis

THE SYNAGOGUE OF TOLEDO,
built in 1357.

received only twenty thousand, the remainder being given in bribes, etc. If the receiver could not prove he had paid the full amount in cash, Don Samuel made him pay the amount he had paid short; one half of which he gave to the holder of the bill, who considering the whole to be lost gladly accepted it. The other half he put into the king's treasury; by these means, in the course of a year, a large sum was deposited in the fortifications of Trugillo and Hita, and was the commencement of the treasure Don Pedro amassed.[2]

About this time, Don Samuel obtained permission to build another synagogue at Toledo, which he erected at his private expense, and furnished it with many gold and silver ornaments. It was completed in 1357. It is unrivalled in the world, and is considered one of the finest architectural monuments of that age in Spain. The Hebrew, Gothic, and Moorish art combine to render it matchless. The beams of the roof are of cedar from Lebanon. Immediately under it is a green band, having the eighty-fourth psalm in large Hebrew characters, in white cement, running round it. Beneath that is a wide band of beautiful arabesque work, interspersed with flowers and fruit, the vine predominating; its broad foliage and tendrils being here and there lost, then again appearing, running through the whole, excites admiration at the fine taste and infinite labour of the artist. Below this again are Hebrew inscriptions in relief.[3] Pieces have fallen off some of the letters, otherwise it is in tolerable good preservation. On each side of a recess at the east end, where the books of the law were kept,

---

[2] Chron. Don Pedro.   [3] Appendix, No. 8.

are six lines of Hebrew, surmounted with a beautiful arabesque.

The conduct of Don Samuel towards the receivers-general, and the power he had from the favour of the king, raised him many enemies. In 1360, they succeeded in persuading the king to arrest him for malversation, and to seize his property, which he confiscated, and obtained 170,000 doblas, 4000 marcs of silver, 125 boxes of gold and silver stuffs, a large amount in jewels, and 80 Moorish slaves, besides 700,000 doblas from his relations, all of whom he arrested, and confiscated their property. Don Samuel was sent to prison at Seville. To discover if he had more property, he was put to the torture, and he died under it[4].

In this year, the king went to Miranda del Ebro, where the Jews had been pillaged and murdered. He had eight of the ringleaders executed, and savagely had one roasted alive, and another boiled in a cauldron. While he was thus cruelly punishing the murderers at Miranda, the Infantes, his brothers, put all the Jews they found on taking Najera to death[5].

The Jews of Tudela entreated the Infante Luis, the viceroy of Navarre, " That he would be pleased to order, and that we practise the Jewish law as our ancestors have hitherto; that is, when a Jew or Jewess commits a sin, on our magistrates applying to the bailiff and notifying to him the sin committed, and the punishment it deserves according to Jewish law, the bailiff shall execute it, and enforce the sentence of our said magistrates, whether of condemnation or acquittal; or of any demand from one Jew to another, as we have been accustomed, not affecting the rights of

[4] Chron. Don Pedro. [5] Ibid.

our lord the king." The prince finding this to be correct, ordered Don Marce de Soterel, abbot of Tiebar, and bailiff of Tudela, to execute it[e].

When Abu Said, the usurper of Granada, came in 1362, with valuable presents, to seek the protection of Don Pedro, he and his attendants were lodged in the Jewry at Seville. During a banquet on the third day the Castilians seized them, and all were beheaded the next morning; but the Jews were not molested. Alphonso XI., besides his legitimate son, Don Pedro, had nine children by Donna Leonora, the beautiful young widow of Don Juan de Velasco. Some died young, others fell victims to the suspicious fears and cruelty of the king. Henry, count of Trastemar, the eldest of those that escaped the fury of his brother, Don Pedro, became a rallying point for the numerous discontented nobles. One of the most sanguinary civil wars that ever devastated a country ensued. Henry had, in 1366, been declared king by his partisans; but the principal cities preserved their loyalty to their legitimate sovereign. Thus Castile had two kings, for Henry had been crowned at Burgos. When Don Pedro found he could not defend it, he relieved the inhabitants from their allegiance, and Henry was acknowledged; on which occasion the Jews made him considerable presents, for which he was not ungrateful. At a cortes he held in that city in 1367, the following petitions were presented against them:—

That all cities, towns, and places of the kingdom, consider that all the evils, misfortunes, murders, and banishments, that have happened in past times, were from the advice of Jews, who until now have been favourites and officers of former kings, because they wished harm and injury to Christians, they

[e] Arch. Nav. Case 13, No. 144.

therefore beg that we may be pleased to order, that no Jew be physician, officer, or hold any post in our household, nor in the queen's my wife, nor in the Infantes', my children[8].

The king would not grant it, but answered,—

We consider it right to grant what is asked in reason, but such a request was never made to any other king of Castile. And although there are some Jews employed in our court, we shall not appoint them to our council, nor give such power to them, as that any injury can result to the country.

The Jews had farmed the arrears of taxes, against which a petition[9] was presented; and the answer returned was—

I would have farmed them for less to Christians, but none wanted or applied for them.

It was also sought to deprive them of the privilege of not being arrested for debt; but the king replied—

The same is to be done as in the time of my father.

A petition from the Jews[10], for permission to rebuild the walls of Jaen, Lorca, and Medina Celi, which had been much injured, and liable to attack from being frontier towns, was granted.

The rival brothers continued the war with alternate success. Henry was first driven from Spain. He sought and obtained assistance from France and Aragon, by which he compelled Pedro to quit Castile. He went to Portugal, but not being well received, repaired to Bayonne, and formed an alliance with the English, who sent an army under the Black Prince to assist him. On recovering nearly the whole of the kingdom, his conduct made his allies abandon him, and leave him to fight his own battles.

The Jews, who by duty and gratitude owed allegi-

[8] Pet. 10.   [9] Pet. 12.   [10] Pet. 18.

ance to Don Pedro, fought bravely in his cause, and in defence of the cities that remained faithful to him. At Briviesca, jointly with the Moors, they had possession of the castle, and repulsed the French assailants led by Du Guesclin, by throwing boiling water on them. It was ultimately taken by storm, and every soul put to the sword. Two hundred Jewish families are said to have perished.

Later, streams of Jewish blood flowed in the streets of Toledo. It sustained a long siege. When taken by assault, twelve thousand Jews are said to have perished by fire and sword. In the ancient capital of the Visigoths, their shops were plundered, and the Jewries horribly sacked by the allies and partisans of Don Henry. The descendants of Israel, as loyal subjects, rallied round the banners of their legitimate sovereign, and great numbers fell fighting in defence of their king and country. One-third of his army, in his last battle near Toledo, consisted of Jews and Moors. Pedro, in 1369, at Montreal, fell under the fratricidal dagger of Don Henry, who proceeded to Burgos. The Jews offered an obstinate resistance, saying, they would only deliver up the city to their lawful sovereign. On being informed of the death of Don Pedro, they obtained favourable terms from Don Henry, contrary to the opinion of his allies, who would have put all to the sword; but he observed, that such devoted loyal subjects ought to be cherished and protected. The people had hoped the Jews would have been severely treated by the new sovereign, as their fidelity to Don Pedro had been highly prejudicial to his success; but Henry knew the value of such subjects, and sought to conciliate them by kind treatment, and by acting justly, cause them to be as faithful to him, as they had been to his brother[11].

The queen of Navarre, Donna Juana, in 1370, ordered that all Jews coming from Calahora, or Castile, should be protected. Rich and poor were to pay two florins per annum; and, except the excise on meat and wine, were not to be compelled to contribute, with the Jewries of the kingdom, the same as other Jews; and were not to be subject to excommunication or outrage[12].

The representations made against the Jews by the deputies to the cortes of Toro, held in 1371, is a proof of the ill-will of the people towards the Hebrew people:—

As to the favour they intreat, that from the insolence and authority of the enemies of the faith, particularly the Jews, in all our kingdoms, as well in our household as in those of noblemen, estateholders, knights and squires, from the high offices and honours they hold, all Christians have to obey, fear, and show them the greatest respect; so that all the councils of cities, towns, and places of our kingdoms, and every individual, are slaves, afraid and subjected to the Jews: first, from the high offices they see them hold in our household and in the houses of the grandees of our kingdoms, besides, from the incomes and posts they have, the said Jews, as a wicked and daring people, the enemies of God and all Christendom, with great insolence commit many wrongs and extortions in such manner that every one in our kingdoms, or the greater part of them are ruined and driven to despair by the said Jews, which they do in contempt of Christians and our Catholic faith. And since it is our will that this evil company may live in our kingdoms, and our pleasure was, that they, as well as Moors, should wear a distinguishing badge, that they may live marked and apart from Christians, as God commands, and justice and the laws ordain; besides, that they should

[11] Nomologia.   [20] Arch. Nav. Case 36, No. 12.

not hold any post in our household, nor in those of the grandees, knights and squires of our kingdoms., nor wear as good and respectable apparel as they, nor ride on mules, that they may be known among Christians, nor presume to use Christian names.

The king answered—

We consider it right that they should continue the same, as in the time of the kings our predecessors, and our father Don Alphonso.[13]

This proves that the government considered the Jews as useful subjects, and wished to preserve them in the kingdom, and to defend and protect them from violence, and that the demands of the people were unjust; yet he was the first Castilian monarch that obliged them to wear a badge, although Popes had ordered it long before.

On a petition[14] to admit Christian evidence against them, he answered,

That the evidence of Christians shall in no manner be received against them without the testimony of a Jew, in regard to debts Christians may owe them; but in all other civil or criminal cases that happen between Christians and Jews, the evidence of Christians, if persons of good repute is to be valid.

In answer to a petition respecting pledges,[15] the king replied,—

As to what you say, that some Jews in our kingdoms, when they were favourites in the royal household, obtained from former sovereigns the privilege that if they held any thing in pledge or as security, they were not bound to tell the name of the person they received it from to the owner, who was bound to pay the Jew the amount he swore he had advanced on it, which gives rise to many robberies and thefts, as property pledged could not be recovered until what the Jew swore he had advanced was paid; we order, that the

[13] Pet. 2.   [14] Pet. 18.   [15] Pet. 19.

Jew shall be put on his oath, and give up the name of the person he had received it from.

The Jews by their commerce and industry had become possessors of almost all the wealth of the kingdom. The Castilians had pride and a bigoted devotion; the Hebrews, talents and money. The Christians, in their necessities, were compelled to have recourse to them; although by their offers they had induced the Jews to transgress the laws, they applied to these Cortes [16] to reduce the amount of their debts, on which the following order was issued.

Within three days after the return of the representatives to the cities, towns, and places, it shall be published in the principal places of the archbishoprics, bishoprics, etc., that all persons indebted to Jews, shall, within fifteen days, pay two-thirds of the amount; and those persons who do not, shall have no deduction, but shall pay the full amount.

The debts of Christians had so accumulated in the reign of Alphonso, that probably the Jews were glad to lose a third on receiving the balance immediately, without further trouble. Where the legal interest was thirty-three and a third per cent, it may be supposed commerce was in a miserable state, and that the Castilians possessed neither capital, speculative energy, nor financial resources.

The Jews had lived unmolested, as will have been seen, under the Moorish sovereigns of Spain. From a chance event, many were killed at Granada in 1375. Two men quarrelling obstructed the street; and a bystander, in the name of Mahomet, begged them to desist, but they continued their noise. Isaac Amoni, the king's physician, passing just then in his carriage, again requested them to cease, and

---

[16] Pet. 30.

the tumult was immediately hushed. The Moors, considering their religion insulted by more respect being shown to Amoni than the name of the prophet, fell upon the Jews, and murdered a number. Many sought an asylum in the Alhambra, where they were protected.[17]

The Jewry of Pamplona paid monthly to the king of Navarre, fls. 261 : 4 : 11; that of Estella, fls. 119 : 1 : 9; and that of Tudela fls. 521 : 7 : 2, in the year 1375.[18]

A petition[19] against the usury of the Jews was again presented to the Cortes of Burgos in 1377, it was ordered,—

That the ordinance of Alphonso should be observed; but to prevent their usury, no bonds were to be given by Christians to Jews, except for the royal taxes and duties.

The latter part shews, that although their names are not recorded, they administered the royal revenues.

Complaint being made that some knights, squires, and men of rank, bring Jews to live with them, who, by their authority, collect the crops, to the great injury of the people, and requesting that it might not be permitted.[20] It was ordained,—

That in future no Jew could be their almoxarifs, majordomos, or hold any offices under them; but we consider it right that they may live with them.

In these reigns many Jews of note were either born, or flourished:—

DON JOSEPH BEN MACHIR—was physican to Don Pedro. He died in 1362.

R. MENAHEN BEN ZARACH—of Estella, where all his family were massacred in 1328; severely wounded, he was left for dead. At night a soldier, in passing, heard his groans, bound up his wounds, and had him cured. R. Menahen then

[7] Shebet Judah.  [18] Arch. Nav. Case 33, No. 8.  [19] Pet. 2.  [20] Pet. 10.

went to Toledo, and from thence to Alcala, where, on the death of R. Jacob Abalesh, he became Chief Rabbi. Having lost all his property during the civil war, Don Samuel Abarbanel of Seville, liberally supplied him during the remainder of his life, which he spent at Toledo, where he died in 1374. He dedicated his work "Provisions for the Way," on Jewish rites and ceremonies, to his benefactor.

R. DAVID — of Estella, born about 1306, was an eminent teacher and expounder of the law, and an eloquent preacher. His sermons are published under the title of "The Tower of David." He also wrote "The House of God," an exposition of the precepts; and "The City Book," an explanation of the Jewish ritual institutions.

R. ABRAHAM BEN ALNAKOVA — who died at Seville in 1360, was a person of great wealth and consequence; for by his epitaph, we learn "he associated with kings and the councillors of the land, and gave lodging and board to all travellers that would accept his hospitality"[21].

DON SANTO DE CARRION — a moral philosopher, and one of the most celebrated troubadours in the reign of Don Pedro. In his old age he abjured Judaism.

R. MEIR ALDABI — of Toledo, flourished in 1360. He wrote an esteemed work, entitled "The Paths of Faith," treating on the creation, the formation of man, his faculties, faith in the law, future rewards and punishments, the resurrection, and the redemption of Israel. He is supposed by some writers to be the R. Meir alluded to in the inscription of the famed synagogue of Toledo; but, judging from his epitaph, it is more probable it alluded to R. Meir, the father of Don Samuel.

R. DAVID COHEN — of Seville, born in 1356, much esteemed for his knowledge of Hebrew, Latin, Greek, and Arabic. He composed an Arabic Dictionary in Hebrew characters, arranging it in the Hebrew alphabetical order, and translated from the

---

[21] Appendix, No. 6.

Hebrew into Spanish, "The Book of Fear" of R. Jonah of Gerona.

R. NISIM BEN REUBEN — of Gerona, and chief rabbi of Barcelona, wrote on the Talmud, and the works of Al Fez. His rabbinical decisions are dated 1349 to 1374; he also practised medicine.

R. VIDAL — of Tolosa, wrote a work impugning some passages of Al Fez and Maimonides, a commentary on Job, and remarks on the book of logic of Abu Achmet Alguzali. He died in 1375.

R. MOSES A COHEN — of Tordesillas, flourished in 1375. He wrote a famed controversial work against Christianity, under the title of " The Help of Faith."

R. MATHIAS HAIZARI — born at Saragossa about 1370, was chief of the Jews in Aragon. He wrote an esteemed commentary on the 119th psalm.

R. SHEM TOB BEN ISAAC SPROT — born at Tudela in 1374, was a celebrated philosopher, physician, and talmudist; under the title of the Touchstone, he wrote a polemical work against Christianity; " The Garden of Pomegranates," explaining the allegories of the Talmud; and translated the book of medicine of Almanzor.

## CHAPTER XV.

*John I.—Joseph Pico.—Prevented leaving Navarre.— Cortes of Soria.—John of Castile claims the Crown of Portugal.—David Negro saves the King by his timely notice.—Cortes of Segovia.—Cortes of Saragossa.—Laws at Briviesca.—Council of Salamanca. —Cortes of Palencia.—Representation of Seville against the Archdeacon of Niebla.*

In 1379, John succeeded his father. He held a cortes at Burgos; and in the regulations he there made for the royal officers and attendants, he raised the tax of twelve maravedis, paid by the Jews on each book of the law to the life-guards, on the first visit of the king to a town, as established by Alphonso X., of four reals of plate.

Petitions[1] similar to No. 18 and 19, presented to the cortes of Toro in 1371, were again presented to this, to which the king returned the same answer as his father. While the king was at Burgos, the Jews artfully obtained from him an order for the execution of Joseph Pico, who was receiver-general of the Alcavales, and high treasurer of the kingdom. He was opulent, and a person of consideration among his people. From the posts he held, he exercised great authority and influence. Historians record no crime of him, but attribute it to the envy and jealousy of the chief men of his nation. Joseph was tranquilly at

[1] Pet. 23, 24.

home, secure from such an event, when he was seized, led to execution, and his house destroyed. From the haste with which the royal executioner performed his office, he is supposed to have been deceived or bribed. The king discovering that he had been imposed on, had the guilty parties punished, and deprived the Jews of the privilege they enjoyed of taking cognisance of criminal causes where they might inflict the punishment of death.

Charles II., of Navarre, imposed a tax of five sous per livre, on all landed property that had been sold or mortgaged to Christians by Jews, within the last fifty years, according to the ordinance.

Inasmuch as, long since, it was ordained, prohibited, and forbidden, for any Christian or Moor to presume to purchase, or accept as a gift or alienation, any landed property whatever from Jews without license of the king.[2]

The king gave as a reason for it, that many Jews had quitted his kingdom, by which the revenue had fallen off, and the taxes diminished daily.[3] It is to be inferred from this, that the reason for prohibiting the purchase of landed property from them, was to prevent their quitting the country.

Pedro Alphonso a convert from Judaism had falsely asserted that the Jews, in their prayers, daily invoked maledictions on Christians; which induced the king— although he always calls them " ours and belonging to us," and ordered that they should be guarded and protected, as in time of his predecessor—to issue the following decree, at the cortes of Soria, in 1380.

1.— Whereas we have been informed, that the Jews are commanded by their books and other writings of the Talmud,

[3] Arch. Nav. Case 37, No. 27.  [4] Ibid., No. 28.

daily to say the prayer against heretics, which is said standing, wherein they curse Christians and churches, we strictly command and forbid any of them, hereafter, to say it, or have it written in their rituals or any other books; and those that have it written in the said books, are to erase and cancel it in such manner as not to be legible, which is to be done within two months after the publication hereof; and any one who says or responds to it, shall publicly receive one hundred lashes. And if it be found in his breviary or other book, he is to be fined one thousand maravedis; and if he cannot pay the fine, one hundred lashes are to be given to him. And furthermore, be it known, we shall proceed severely against them, the same as against persons that curse the Christian religion.

2.—Furthermore, as the Jews have been accustomed to choose their Rabbis and other judges among themselves, empowering them to decide all causes that come before them, whether civil or criminal, which it is a great sin to authorise and permit; for according to the words of the prophets they were deprived of all power and liberty on the coming of our Lord Jesus Christ. And as many injuries and much harm accrue to our kingdoms, and to all Christians of our dominions and the commonalty therefrom, by their Jewries generally and in particular. For this reason we ordain and command that henceforward it shall not be permitted for any Jews of our kingdoms, whether rabbis, elders, chiefs, or any other persons that now are, or shall be hereafter, to interfere to judge any criminal cause to which death, loss of limb, or banishment is attached; but they may decide all civil causes that appertain to them according to their religion. Criminal cases shall be tried by one of the Alcaldes, chosen by the Jews in the towns and places of their respective jurisdictions. But, whereas the said Jews are ours, it is our pleasure that the appeals of said criminals, whether belonging to the Seigniories or any other places whatever, shall be brought before our court. This is to be understood for those criminal cases that have hitherto been tried by the said Jews. And if any cause has been decided contrary hereto, we order that the sentence be null, and that no alcalde, judge, or other person, undertake to execute it, under the penalty of six thousand maravedis each. And if any act or ordinance contain anything contrary hereto, we command that it be not executed, nor is it to be valid. And if, thereby, any penalty or fine is inflicted, we order that it be annulled.

3.—Furthermore, whereas we are informed, that the Jews make some persons as well as Moors, Tartars, and other sects converts to Judaism, by circumcising them, and by other ceremonies; all of which is a disparagement and contempt of our religion. Therefore we ordain, command, and forbid that it be done hereafter, in any manner. And should any Jew or Jewess do it, they shall become our slaves; and those persons who are converted from any other religion to theirs, shall be treated as we may be pleased to order.

On a petition[4] that Christians might not be permitted to nurse the children of Jews or Moors, nor reside with them; the King decreed:—

That any Christian nursing the child of a Jew or Moor should be fined six hundred maravedis to the Exchequer; but they may live with them, that they may have people to cultivate their land, and to accompany them from one place to another; otherwise they might be ill treated or murdered.

After the assassination of Peter the Cruel, by Henry of Trastemar, Ferdinand of Portugal, as a legitimate descendant of Sancho IV., laid claim to the crown of Castile, in preference to the bastard of Alphonso XI. A coalition of the Spanish sovereigns was formed, but broken by the politic Henry, and Ferdinand was left alone to assert his right; through the mediation of Pope Urban VI., a peace was ultimately concluded. By the treaty, Donna Beatrice, daughter of Ferdinand, was engaged to the second son of Henry. John, losing

[4] Pet. 11.

his queen, offered his hand to Donna Beatrice, as the tender age of Ferdinand would have delayed her marriage for many years. By this treaty, if the king of Portugal died without male issue, his eldest daughter, Donna Beatrice, was to succeed him, and her husband, the king of Castile, might style himself king of Portugal; but the government was to be vested in the Dowager Queen Donna Leonora, during her lifetime; or until Donna Beatrice and her husband had a child fourteen years of age, who should then leave his parents and assume the government and title of king of Portugal. On the death of Ferdinand shortly after, in 1383, John laid claim to it in right of his wife, and his views were favoured by the widowed Donna Leonora. He marched an army into Portugal to enforce it, for the Portuguese always bore a hatred to Castilian dominion, and had raised John, master of the order of Avis, a bastard brother of their deceased sovereign, to the vacant throne: he was John I. of Portugal. This digression was necessary, from the two kings having the same names and designations.

John of Castile was with his army at Santarem, when the chief rabbi of Portugal died. Donna Leonora hastened to meet him, to ask for the place, which was a post of the highest honour and gave unbounded power over the Jews, for her friend Don Judah, a wealthy and highly respected man, who had been high treasurer to her husband Don Ferdinand. The king excused himself and gave it to his queen Donna Beatrice for Don David Negro, also a friend to the late king. Donna Leonora, a proud imperious woman, considered herself insulted at being refused the first favour she asked from the king, for whom she had done so much; and to her subsequent conduct in a great measure may be attributed his loss of the crown of Portugal.[5]

A monk in the city of Coimbra, where the king then was, who was a great friend of Don David and who carried messages between the disaffected and the insurgents, wrote confidentially to him to retire within the city with his family, and he would find a mode to place him out of danger. The monk afterwards called on him, when he enquired the meaning of the note. He told him some disturbance might take place when the city was given up; and he learnt from him that on a certain night when Count Gonsalez sent to say they were ready, a trumpet was to be blown in the city, as a signal that the count was without with the people. Don David informed the king of the whole plan: he could scarcely believe it, but the Queen did; by this timely notice it was frustrated and rendered abortive.[6]

The produce of the tax of five sous per livre, on landed property, sold by Jews and Moors to Christians, or by Jews to Moors, after the great mortality by the plague, in the towns of Tudela, Cortes, Bruñel, Monteagudo, Cascante, Corella, Cinteonigo, Fustinani, and Cabanillas, amounted in 1384 to fls.2221:0:4.

In that year, John framed some new laws at Segovia. The three following concerned the Jews and Moors:—

Jews and Moors shall not be permitted publicly to work, or sell anything, or cultivate their lands, on Sundays and Christian holidays; but in their houses they may, provided it is done without noise, and not exposed to view.[7]

That Jews and Moors are not to live or associate with Christians.[8]

[5] Chron. Joao 1.  [6] Idem.  [7] Law 2.  [8] Law 5.

That one-third is to be deducted from debts due to Jews and Moors, and the balance is to be paid half at Midsummer, and half at Christmas, 1385: those overdue are to be paid half in nine months, and half six months after. Persons not paying at the periods fixed, are not to have the benefit of this law.[9]

The next cortes met at Saragossa in 1385. A number of petitions were presented against them. The following will shew their tenor:—

We answer, that Christians do right not to live with Jews or Moors, either for hire or otherwise; nor shall Christians nurse their children. Persons that transgress this ordinance, shall be publicly whipped in the place where it happens. Any person may give information. And we order our justices to make enquiry, should no one inform, and inflict the punishment.[10]

We answer that, it is our pleasure, that the ordinances made at Soria, by which no Jew or Moor should be Almoxarif to us, our queen, the infantas, our brothers, or to any person holding office in our household. Now to please our subjects, we consider it just to observe and fulfil the same, as they request. And should any Jew or Moor act contrary, their property shall be confiscated, and they shall receive such corporal punishment as we may think fit.[11]

That, as we cancelled one-third of debts due to Jews and Moors in the cortes of Segovia, and granted time for the payment of the two-thirds, which will be highly prejudicial to them, it would be against our interest and receipts to go further; but where usury can be proved against them, they shall refund it to the owner.[12]

That Jews and Moors lend on pledges; and when the owner wishes to redeem them they demand more than the amount lent, with the interest due, and refuse to restore the pledge. To our great injury, they are believed on their oath; for, although there is no truth in them, they get what they demand. We therefore ask, that two or three Christian witnesses shall be believed on their oaths.[13]

[9] Law 19.  [10] Pet. 3.  [11] Pet. 9.  [12] Pet. 10.  [13] Pet. 11.

That Jews have privileges on bonds drawn up between Christians and Jews by notaries; but if there should not be the testimony of a Jew against the Jew, the contract is void. We therefore beg, that, should there be no Jew witness, the testimony of three Christian witnesses shall be sufficient.[14]

To these two petitions, we answer, that, as the kings, our predecessors, suspected, that, from the enmity Christians bore against Jews and Moors, they would not give true testimony against them for debts, or in civil cases, they granted them the privilege, that oaths of Christians should not be believed against them, without the corroborative testimony of a Jew or Moor. We intend to continue to observe the same.

That Jews and Moors have the privilege, that if an article, stolen from a Christian, be found in their possession, they are not bound to give up the person they received it from. We beg, that in such cases, they shall be subject to the same penalties as receivers of stolen goods.[15]

It is our pleasure, that the said privilege be rescinded; and that Jews and Moors be liable to the same as Christians.

As Jews and Moors claim payment from Christians of bonds from ten to twelve years' date, which are cancelled from the length of time, and the chiefs of places order them to be paid, we beg that they be declared null and void.[16]

The ordinance made at Alcala by our grandfather, Don Alphonso, is to be observed.

That Jews and Moors be not permitted to have separate collectors for the recovery of their debts, as they charge ten per cent.; but that the collection be remitted to the ordinary tribunals.[17]

There is no harm in Jews and Moors having separate collectors; but they shall not charge more than six per cent., as was usual and customary; and in places where the charge has been less, that only is to be paid.

That Jews and Moors be not permitted to have separate Alcaldes.[18]

It is our pleasure that the same be practised as hitherto.

[14] Pet. 12.  [15] Pet. 13.  [16] Pet. 14.  [17] Pet. 15.  [18] Pet. 17.

The number of taxpayers at Tudela in 1386, being reduced from five hundred to less than two hundred, from their general poverty, Charles II. of Navarre remitted the sum of four hundred and eighty-one livres they owed for taxes.[19]

At Briviesca, in 1387, some laws were established. The two following were the only ones that concerned the Jews and Moors.

No work is to be performed on Sundays, under the penalty of thirty maravedis: one-third to the informer, and one-third to the church, and one-third to the king; but Jews and Moors may quietly work in their houses.[20]

None of our subjects shall presume to keep Jews or Moors that are not slaves in their houses; for they are not to have authority over Christians; nor is association with them permitted, according to law, except medical men, when required. Persons of whatever rank or condition who act contrary, shall be fined six thousand maravedis to the Exchequer, a third of which shall be given to the informer. And we forbid Jews and Moors to have Christian servants to live with them, under the penalty that their persons and property be at our disposal; a third of the latter to be for the informer.[21]

The large fine shews they were generally employed by the nobles and grandees, in high posts in their households.

The council that assembled at Palencia in 1388, confirmed the act of the council of Salamanca—

Respecting the Jews living in Jewries; but permitted Jews and Moors, who were merchants, traders, or mechanics, to have shops, warehouses, booths, stalls, and workshops in the streets and public places of the cities and towns where they resided; provided the domiciles for their wives and families were within the Jewry, to which they were to retire at night. Christians were not to dwell within the quarters assigned to

---

[19] Arch. Nav. Case 52, No. 10.  [20] Law 7.  [21] Law 17.

Jews and Moors; and those that resided within them, were to remove therefrom within two months after the publication of this decree in the cathedral; and if they did not, were to be compelled by ecclesiastical censure.[22]

The reason the council assigns for it is—

Because we know many injuries to the bodies, and dangers to the souls of Christians, have resulted from their intercourse with Jews.

A cortes was also held the same year at Palencia, to which a petition[23] was again presented against their usuries, to which the following answer was returned—

They inform us, that they have suffered such great injury from being heavily taxed, that they have daily borrowed money from the Jews, and given bonds for twice and thrice the amount, and beg to repay the principal only.

The answer of the king was—

When it can be proved to have been usurious, the capital only is to be repaid as requested; but if the Jew can prove the correctness of the transaction, the full amount is to be paid; but if no proof can be adduced, it is our will that one third be deducted, and time be given for the payment of the balance, until Midsummer, 1389. If not then paid, the benefit of this law is forfeited; which is only for debts, contracts, and bonds made with Jews from 1387 to the present date.

To the honour of the town council of Seville, it complained to the king of the conduct of Fernandez Martinez, the archdeacon of Niebla, who, with more zeal than prudence, by his sermons incited the people against the Jews. The laws made for their protection had not provided against such attacks; probably imagining that, however great the rancour churchmen bore towards the descendants of Israel, the pulpit was not the place whence their hatred should be

---

[22] Aguirre.     [23] Pet. 6.

preached to the tumultuous and sanguinary populace. The king had not sufficient courage to repress it. His answer to the judicious representation of the council was, "that he would send to see; for, although the archdeacon's zeal was holy and good, he should be careful not to excite the people by his sermons and discourses."

Deeds afterwards proved the "*sanctity and goodness*" of the archdeacon's intemperate zeal. Want of energy on the part of the king, and his remaining passive in the prospect of the horrors and butcheries about to be perpetrated, emboldened the unchristianlike churchman in a short time, by his sermons, to raise the populace to dye their hands in the blood of the unfortunate Jews. The king did not live to see the dire effects of his pusillanimity; he was thrown from his horse, and killed in October, 1390. In this year, R. Solomon Levi, a native of Burgos, at the age of forty abjured Judaism. After being archdeacon of Triveno, and bishop of Carthagena, he became bishop of Burgos, and is commonly known by the name of Paul of Burgos. He proved an inveterate enemy to the Hebrew people. He states, that the Jews held the principal posts in the palaces of kings, and the households of grandees; that in consequence vassals, however Christian they might be, shewed them the greatest respect and veneration, which was injurious to simple souls, as they readily adopted the errors of their superiors and persons in power.[24]

[24] Scrut. Scrip. par. 2, ch. 26.

## CHAPTER XVI.

*Henry III.—Riot at Seville. — Massacre at Palma. — Jewries of Cordova, Toledo, Burgos, Valencia, Barcelona, etc. attacked and plundered. — The consequences.—Anecdote of Queen Leonora, of Henry.— His Physicians. — State of the Jews in Spain at the end of the 15th Century.*

HENRY III. was only eleven years of age at the death of his father; six noblemen had been named by him as guardians of his son and regents of the kingdom; they summoned a cortes to Madrid. The Jews who had repaired to that capital to farm the royal revenues, of which the laws were unable to deprive them, complained to it of the sufferings of their brethren at Seville.

The archdeacon, encouraged by the conduct of the late king, and the dissensions among the regents, who were attending solely to their private interests, descended from the pulpit of the cathedral to preach his inflammatory sermons in the streets of the Andalusian capital. His themes were the obstinate adherence of the descendants of Israel to the religion of their forefathers, and the injury done to the state by their usuries and commerce; he harangued with so much force, that the enraged populace, giving vent first to invectives, then carried their hatred against them to the utmost excess. The cause of this attack had been previously arranged, the combustible matter only required the lighted torch to be applied to raise an unquenchable flame. The town council, which had complained of the archdeacon's intemperate conduct, had not taken a single precautionary measure to prevent the horrible scenes of carnage that ensued. The opposition of the ecclesiastical chapter served to raise more and more the indiscreet zeal of the fanatic priest. At the commencement, the people had listened to his sermons with indifference; but finding it was sought to favour the Jews, they took part in the question: they applauded the intolerant preacher; they assembled in the public squares, and then spread themselves through the city, heaping insults and menaces on the Jews, who were soon obliged to shut themselves within their Jewries; but neither there were they respected. Justice in the meanwhile sought to quell the riot. The Count de Niebla and Don Alvar Perez de Guzman, the high constable of the city, hastened to where the greatest tumult prevailed. They seized two of the most furious, and had them publicly whipped as a warning and example to the rest. Far from appeasing, the punishment irritated more the ungovernable mob; the arms tinged with Jewish blood were turned against the count and his assistants; their lives were exposed to the greatest danger; they saved themselves only by releasing the prisoners, and abandoning the unequal contest. This happened on Ash Wednesday, 1391. The rioters, having rescued their friends, seemed pacified; and for a time the city enjoyed that calm which is the presage of a storm.

The 6th June dawned, crowds were seen hastening in a continual torrent towards the Jewries, which were attacked in all quarters; the exterminating steel spared neither age nor sex; those that implored mercy, or that sought to escape, were alike murdered; 4,000 Israelites perished in that dreadful slaughter. Amidst the yells of the savage mob and the groans of the dying, was heard the voice of the archdeacon, encouraging them in those horrible scenes of carnage and extermination.

These were the complaints made by the farmers of the royal revenues to the national representatives, in the name of the violated laws, the outrages the council of government was called on to suppress, created by a king whose indifference had been the principal cause of them. The Cortes of Castile, less prejudiced than the multitude, and more desirous of justice than the late king had been, heard with horror the relation of such sanguinary deeds. Duty to the world and their own consciences, imposed on them the obligation to apply promptly the desired remedy to so many evils. They despatched judges with the titles of *Priors*, a title then having great authority, to proceed to Seville and the other towns of that kingdom, where the flame of insurrection had spread, to punish severely the seditious and abettors of those crimes. But, notwithstanding the researches made, the integrity and rectitude of the judges, and the strict orders of government, they gained no information, but imprisoned and punished the archdeacon, as an example and warning to others not to cause riots under the colour of piety.

Two of the synagogues within the Jewry of Seville were converted into parochial churches, under the names of Santa Cruz and Santa Maria la Blanca. The Jews were now reduced to a single Jewry, known at present by the name of St. Bartholomew's. It required great perseverance and resignation in those that escaped with life, and all the energy and industry they were susceptible of, to replace in some measure the severe losses they had sustained. The Christians, on the contrary, rich with plunder, and flushed with their double victory, considering they had performed a meritorious act, increased their wealth.

At Palma, the civil authorities and nobles endeavoured in vain to repress the violence of the bigoted infuriated mob. Many were murdered by the islanders, who vied with their continental brethren in enriching themselves by the plunder of the unfortunate Israelites[1].

This fatal impunity had, and necessarily would have, the most deplorable consequences. Little more than a year had elapsed. On the 5th August, the Jewries of Cordova, Toledo, Burgos, and Valencia were attacked by the populace, plundering and sacking the numerous houses and shops, and killing all who offered the least resistance. It is thus described by Dr. Lozano:—

The people went so riotously and resolutely to each of these places, so eager for plunder, so prepossessed by the voice of the archdeacon, that they might conscientiously rob and kill that people, without respect to the laws, or fear of judges or ministers, plundering, robbing, and murdering, that it was horrifying. Every city was that day a Troy. The shrieks, lamentations, and groans of those who saw themselves ruined and destroyed without a crime being much pitied by those not concerned in the deed, the rage and cruelty increased. They only acted mercifully, and spared the lives and properties of those who desired to become Christians, and cried out for baptism, a wrong determination, under the cloak of religion.

[1] Hist. de Malorca.

It was the cause of innumerable errors; for many Jews, seeing that they could escape by being baptised, asked for it, while their predilection was always for their sect, so that apparently Christians they daily Judaised. Finally, notwithstanding the judges proceeded to institute inquiries, and punish, it was useless, for it seemed highly improper to chastise or destroy a city, or a whole town, to restore and save a Jewry, and the more so, where the riot was caused under the pretext of religion, and maintained by the archdeacon as being rightly done[2].

In their mad rage, they wanted, in like manner, to attack the Moors, but were restrained, by the fear of the Christians in their hands meeting a similar fate from their Saracen masters.

At Barcelona, and in many towns of Aragon, they experienced the same fate. The duke of Montblanc was at Valencia, preparing the expedition for Sicily, but was unable to prevent the riot. Eleven thousand Jews are said to have received baptism in that city, and as many as two hundred thousand in the kingdoms of Castile and Aragon. This dreadful persecution led a number of the Hebrew people to quit Spain. As no part of Europe offered a secure asylum for them, many emigrated to Africa. At this period, the first settlement of the Jews at Algiers took place. The Jewries were completely ruined. Justice had been defied, and all rights had been trampled on. The Christian people, who had been goaded to unmerciful rage against the Jews, perceived not, that in destroying their industry and overturning the means of fully developing it, they brought on themselves the charges that had previously been divided between them, and suffocated in blood the germs of prosperity and success. What became of the numerous looms of Toledo and Seville? Where were the extensive and rich markets in which the

[2] Reyes Nuevos de Toledo.

Hebrews warehoused all the valuable productions of the East and West; where the silks of Persia and Damascus, the skins of Morocco, and the Arabian jewellery competed? They burnt their well-stocked shops in the bazaars of Valencia, Toledo, Burgos, and Seville. Their streets became desolate and deserted. The revenues of the king and church suffered greatly, as is shewn by the history of the celebrated chapel of the Reyes Nuevos of the ancient Gothic capital. When Henry II. raised that sumptuous mausoleum for himself and family, he had endowed the chaplains with part of the contributions paid by the Hebrews of Toledo. The almost total ruin of that Jewry had caused the hopes of its founder to vanish. His perfect reliance on the exactitude of the Jews, and the security of the payments, had induced him to provide its revenue out of the Jewry; but by this destruction, Henry III. was deprived of the means of supporting the royal chapel.

The Jews, nevertheless, collected the remains of the dreadful wreck. Resigning themselves to their misfortune, they thought only of reconstructing the shattered vessel, ever exposed to destruction, and to be agitated by furious storms. In the great and continual wants of the Spanish monarchs, when the Moorish wars drained their treasuries, and the taxes and contributions were inadequate to the expense, the coffers of the Jews were ever open to them; yet among the means they considered advisable to remedy the sad catastrophe, was to appeal to the generosity and clemency of the grandees, promising further taxes and tribute to secure their protection.

The Queen Donna Leonora, the first wife of Henry III., was much praised for her charitable acts; with her own hands she distributed a large portion of her income to the needy. From the protecting hand she extended to the Christian poor, she inspired so much respect and confidence in the Jews, that to enable her to continue her benevolence and to gain her protection, they offered her a sum from the Jewries, which she refused, saying, "she never would ask a supply from them, lest they might privately curse her."

The guardians and regents, by dilapidation and rapacity, had so impoverished the treasury, that the following anecdote is related of the king.

Henry, not to burden his vassals, practised the utmost frugality and most rigid economy. Returning home one evening without having any thing to eat, nor money, jewels, or credit to purchase the meanest food, while the grandees were prodigally spending their ill-acquired wealth in sumptuous entertainments, he had to dispose of his cloak to procure a miserable meal. On that same night a supper was prepared at the archbishop of Toledo's, where every delicacy and luxury was in the greatest profusion. Henry being informed of it, but not believing all he heard, resolved to witness it. In disguise he went to the festive hall, and mixing with the numerous attendants, he noticed there had been no exaggeration, and he was struck with the audacity of the guests, boasting of the wealth they had amassed by their peculation. The next day he summoned them to appear before him. On their being assembled, he entered completely armed, with his drawn sword. Addressing himself to the archbishop, he asked him how many kings he had raised in Spain. "Sire," answered the prelate, "your grandfather, your father, and yourself." "Although so young," replied the king, "I have known twenty where there should only be one; it is time that I should be sole, and all the others perish." He then made a signal, on which the soldiers he had prepared appeared, together with the executioners, block, axe, and ropes. The grandees alarmed, threw themselves at his feet, imploring his clemency, and placing their persons and property at his disposal. Henry generously granted them their lives, but exacted a strict account of their administration of the public treasury during his minority, forcing them to refund the sums they had appropriated to themselves; to give up for the benefit of the royal patrimony the enormous pensions they had received; and to surrender the castles and fortresses they had taken possession of.[1]

It is not surprising after this, that, notwithstanding the laws and the decrees of councils, the kings of Castile employed Jews in offices of trust in preference to Christians. They found the former possessed, from their commercial habits, of more talent for the administration of finance; and although they might enrich themselves by the lucrative posts they held, they had not the ambition of the latter, who sought to aggrandize themselves at the expence of the people and of the crown, against which they were frequently in open rebellion.

Henry farmed the royal revenues to Jews. His chief physician was the unfortunate R. Meir Algudes, who was chief rabbi of the Jews of Castile, a man of great learning and experience, and a great favourite with the king: he translated the ethics and maxims into Hebrew. R. Meir Benshushan, an eminent physician of Toledo, also attended him, as well as R. Moses

[1] Anquetila, His Universal.

Zarzal, a fragment of whose tombstone was discovered a few years back, at Carmona. Henry is termed " The Sickly " in Spanish history, for, from his infancy he never enjoyed good health, which accounts for the number of his physicians. The clergy incited the people against the Jews; and, in consequence of a sermon preached in the cathedral of Seville on the subject of the new synagogues they were permitted to build to replace some of those destroyed or taken from them of late years, there were riots in various parts of Spain. Many Jews fell victims to the popular fury; others, to avoid this persecution, were baptized.

Previous to detailing the persecutions the descendants of Israel experienced in the fifteenth century in Spain, to which the horrid scenes perpetrated at the instigation of the archdeacon of Ecija had been the prelude, it may be necessary to review the state of the Hebrew people and their adversaries at this period. Constant complaints were made of the usury of the Jews; but the Castilians were so accustomed to apply to them when they wanted money, that they were the first to infringe the laws and ordinances. They could neither equip themselves for war, nor sow or cultivate their land without pecuniary advances. Government, continually occupied with wars, was incapable of providing for agriculture. It shewed itself indulgent while that class ruined itself by borrowing. The Jews became rich and wealthy, while the people became impoverished. In revenge, they incessantly sought to excite the king against the Hebrews, and under the most false pretexts to draw persecution on them.

When the judges coolly examined the case, the

imposture of their accusers was sometimes discovered, and the innocence of the Jews clearly established; but they were not always fortunate in meeting with magistrates free from popular prejudices; and judges frequently allowed themselves to be influenced by the clamours of an infuriated mob. What tended also to exasperate the people against them was, the ostentation of their wealth, in their rich dresses, and the jewels and gold their wives and daughters displayed, while their Christian neighbours could only clothe themselves in the coarsest materials. This naturally created jealousy and envy. This odium was increased by the fanaticism, bigotry, and intemperate zeal of some of the clergy, but more particularly of the Dominican friars, an institution that from its origin seemed to have been formed for the destruction of the Hebrew people, for its monks demonstrated on every occasion their hatred against the descendants of Israel.

There was another class of men that did them the greatest injury and were their bitterest foes. These were the Jews who having apostatised from the religion of their fathers, and having obtained power by ecclesiastical dignities, were despised by their former brethren. They repaid this contempt by the grossest falsehoods, representing their ancient rites (although instituted centuries previous) as inimical to Christianity, and their observers as the avowed enemies of Christians. It is not then surprising that an ignorant populace, accustomed to warfare, should be found ever ready to imbrue their hands in Jewish blood, where plunder was the reward, and the hard-earned wealth of their murdered victims was indiscriminately appropriated to themselves, under the sanction of those whose duty it was, to preach "peace and goodwill to all mankind."

But the sovereigns of Spain found their talents so useful and indispensable, that, notwithstanding the decrees of councils and the laws they themselves enacted to meet the demands of the people, they employed them as collectors and receivers of the revenues and taxes, as physicians, and in every important office of trust and responsibility.

The monarchs, from their continual wars with their neighbours and the Moors, were ever in want of means for prosecuting them. The Jews alone, of all their subjects, could assist their wants by farming certain portions of the taxes and revenue.

Such was the state of the Jews at the commencement of the last century, in which they were permitted to reside within the Spanish dominions.

## CHAPTER XVII.

*Cortes of Madrid.— Regency of John II.— Ordinance of the Regent.— Vincent Ferrer.— The ancient Synagogue of Toledo converted into a Church. — False Accusation against Don Meir Algudes. — Another False Accusation at Segovia.— Learned Men and celebrated Physicians.*

In 1401, R. Joseph Ora Buena, chief Rabbi of the Jews of Navarre, was appointed physician to Charles III.

The synagogue of Tudela requiring repair, the king contributed towards it 120 livres, which sum the Jewry was indebted for taxes.[1]

Henry III., as before stated, had been obliged to make use of their services; but he was not inclined to be friendly towards the Jews, as is demonstrated by the laws enacted at the Cortes of Madrid in 1405, in answer to petitions.

From the representations made to us, that Jews, availing themselves of privileges formerly granted them, lend on usury, contrary to the laws of Don Alphonso, my great-grandfather, and Don Henry, my grandfather, by the advice of our council, from this day we hereby annul and revoke the same; and order that no judge or other officer in all our kingdoms and dominions, permit any contract or bond to be given or granted that bears interest, as it is represented to us as being contrary to the law of God; and prelates are to excommunicate all persons giving them.

But that Jews may be enabled to maintain themselves in our dominions, and have the means of living comfortably as holy church orders,—for, according to the prophets, they are to turn to our holy faith and be saved,—they may possess and purchase for themselves and their heirs, landed property within the boundaries of all the cities, towns, and places in our royal domains, to the value of 30,000 maravedis to the northward, or 20,000 to the southward of the Douro; and they may have houses of their own, in addition to those they may now possess; they may also purchase to the same amount within the jurisdiction of the abbacies, lordships, and seigniories, with the permission of the proprietors of the same.

And whereas Jews and Moors charge more than they lend, they are not to draw bills, or take bonds from Christians, councils, or corporations, for money, bread, wine, or oil, either as a loan, purchase, sale, or deposit; but in all sales and purchases, the price of the article sold or bought, for which the contract or bond would be made, is to be paid for immediately; and if,

[1] Arch. Nav. p. 6, No. 24, 30.

in contravention hereof, any bond or obligation is given, it is of itself void; and no judge, magistrate, archer, or other dignitary, shall recognise the same or have them paid or enforced.

And any notary of our kingdoms who shall presume to draw up, or order such contract or bond to be drawn up, by the act forfeits his office; and such documents, bonds, etc., are null and void.

But if a Jew or Moor sell any moveable or immoveable property to a Christian, and the same is to be received and paid for as before said, should the Jew or Moor require a document in testimony thereof, to secure the contract, and in proof of said sale or purchase, it may be made, provided it contains no obligation to pay at any future fixed period.

We order and command this ordinance to be fully observed, except towards those Jews and Moors who farm our revenues. They may make and receive bonds and obligations as hitherto in respect to our revenues, and may receive and give receipts for whatever they may so receive or pay.

As regards this ordinance, no Jew or Moor shall presume to make, either for himself or other persons, any obligatory bond or bill on any Christian, council, or corporation, for any debt, whether for money, bread, wine, oil, wax, or any other article, although the same be executed in the presence of witnesses.

And whereas the Jews and Moors, fraudulently and in violation of the laws, seek in various modes to lend at usury, and not only obtain bonds from Christians made in the presence of a notary-public and witnesses, but even induce them to assume and acknowledge sums they never received; and then, on such acknowledgment being made, they demand sentences from judges, for which no provision is made by the laws; it is my will, and I order, that should any Christian acknowledge before an authorised magistrate what is due to the said Jew or Moor, in gold, silver, money, or any other article, in whatever way it may be, except for any revenues or taxes as aforesaid, and the said Jew or Moor pray the judge or magistrate to condemn the Christian in the amount he acknowledges, such acknowledgment is to be considered null and void; magistrates, judges, and other officers are not to pass sentence thereon; and should they act in violation of this law, I order from henceforth that the same be invalid, and considered null and void.

Jews and Moors are bound to give the names of persons who have deposited or pledged anything with them, on the same being claimed by any Christian, notwithstanding any law or privilege to the contrary.

Only one-half of unpaid debts is to be paid, on the presumption that the other half is interest, as Jews and Moors generally take bonds for double the amount they lend to Christians; unless the Jew proves by credible Christian witnesses, or it is a recently made bond, that the whole he demands is for principal only, then the Christian shall pay the full amount acknowledged, or which the Jew or Moor proves; but if the Christian produce a receipt, or a sufficient reason for not paying the whole, or any part of the bond, and if the person should persist, but cannot produce a receipt, or adduce a valid reason, he must pay one-half the amount of the bond as before said.

And it is my pleasure to release Christians from all penalties they may have incurred for the non-payment of their Jewish or Moorish creditors at the time agreed; and they shall pay half the amount as aforesaid, in two payments, half at Midsummer, 1406, and half at Christmas, 1407; and those who do not pay at the said dates, are to lose the benefit of this act.

And it is my pleasure, that no person shall condemn or exact from any Jew or Moor, such penalties as they may have incurred for having lent on usury to the present date.[2]

It is my will and pleasure, that in all civil and criminal cases, Christians may and can be witnesses against Jews and Moors, the same as against Christians, without the testimony of a Jew or Moor being required, provided the Christians are reputable persons.[3]

Jews and Moors are to wear an ostensible sign or badge, and if found without it, or placed out of sight, they are to forfeit the clothes; but, to avoid being hurt by Christians, they need not wear it while travelling, but on their arrival at their destination they are, as well as within ten days after the publication

---

[2] Pet. 1.  [3] Pet. 2.

of this ordinance in the capital, and within thirty days after it is published in the capital of each diocese; nor are they to wear slashed hose, or flowing robes. All privileges and laws to the contrary I hereby revoke and annul.[4]

Shortly after the death of Henry, their implacable enemies, the Dominican friars, obtained from his queen an order for expelling them the kingdom; but it being represented to her that it would be highly impolitic to root up so productive a vine, she is said to have relinquished it by receiving 50,000 crowns.

Henry was succeeded, in 1406, by his infant son, John II., a child only twenty-two months old. He had nominated the queen and his brother, Don Ferdinand, to be regents. Some disaffected nobles offered to the infante the crown of Castile, which his disinterested zeal for the benefit of his innocent nephew and ward made him refuse. Yet his conduct could not conciliate the queen-mother. The intrigues of the clergy and courtiers that surrounded her, and by whom she was completely guided, led to such disunion, that each guardian acted independently and despotically in the portions of the kingdoms each held. The country could not do otherwise than feel the sad effects of this divided authority. The Jews naturally suffered most. The queen, encouraged by the clergy (who swayed her councils), in her hatred of the descendants of Israel, hastened to oppress them by the most unjust and cruel ordinances.

Don Ferdinand found himself obliged to follow her persecuting system, in order to please and gratify the popular jealousy and hatred against the Jews. Being shortly after raised to the throne of Aragon, he left them unmolested in his new kingdom; it may there-

[4] Pet. 3.

fore be supposed, that his conduct towards the Israelites of Castile was more the effect of circumstance than inclination.

The regents were not slow in their aggressions against the Hebrew people, for in 1408, from Valladolid, they issued jointly, in the name of the infant monarch, the following decree:—

Don John, by the grace of God, king of Castile, etc. etc. to all officers (here detailed), health and grace.

Know ye, that whereas by the laws of the Partidas, it is a privilege that authority be not given to Jews to decide over Christians, to receive the tolls, and constitute them collectors and receivers of other dues Christians have to pay to the lords of the soil, and to farm them to them, whereby they assume great authority over Christians; and it affords them the opportunity, in various modes, of doing many wrongs and grievances, from which accrue great dis-service to God and me, and great injury to the inhabitants of my kingdoms. Therefore, desirous to provide a remedy thereof, and understanding that for my service and the welfare of my kingdoms, the said laws of the Partidas, and others ordained on this matter, be observed; and as it is notorious, manifest, and appears by experience daily, that great injury results therefrom to those of our kingdom and to their public welfare;—

Therefore it is my pleasure, that henceforward no Jew, of whatever rank or condition he may be, shall presume in any manner to farm any toll, tax, or duty, which the subjects of my kingdoms have to pay, within a year from the date hereof, or hereafter annually, either the revenue of excise, coinage, tithes, tolls, or any other tax; nor be collectors nor receivers of the same; nor openly or privately be security for any persons concerned therein; nor farm themselves any tithes, or other temporal or spiritual dues, belonging to archbishops, bishops, or masters of the military orders, or any other lords, that now are, or may hereafter become due from their vassals or subjects. And if they farm, collect, receive, or publicly or privately in any manner bid, either at public sale, or otherwise, to farm, collect, or receive the same; or become security for any other persons therein, on the same being proved, they shall pay twice the amount of that revenue; and if their property is not worth that amount, the whole shall be confiscated; and, besides, they shall publicly receive fifty lashes. And it is my pleasure, that the proof against such Jew shall be on the testimony of two Jews, a Jew and a Christian, two Christians, or the confession of the Jew himself.

Furthermore, it is my pleasure, that should any Christian give a share in the said receipts to any Jew, or make him receiver of them, or should treat, or advise, or in any way consent that the said Jews farm, receive, or collect the same by sale or otherwise, or become security for the said Jews therein, it being proved against such Christian by two Christians, or on his own confession, he shall pay twice the value of the said receipts; and should his property not be worth as much, the whole shall be confiscated, and he shall be condemned to serve for a year in such of the frontier fortresses as the court that condemns him may appoint.

And the aforesaid penalties shall be, one-third for the accuser of the said Jews or Christians, who transgress this my ordinance; one-third for the court that condemns them; and one-third for my treasury.

And for the better and immediate performance and execution hereof, I command the queen, Donna Catalina, my mother, and my uncle, the Infante Don Ferdinand, my guardians and regents of my kingdoms, that they have this ordinance observed and fulfilled, in all their cities, towns, and places.

And I order you, the said magistrates, councils, officers, and all other persons above-mentioned, and each of you, in your places and jurisdictions, that you observe and fulfil, and have all, and every part hereof, observed and executed; and that you do not farm to, nor permit any Jews, either by sale or otherwise, to farm any receipts, taxes, dues, tolls, or any other imposts, dues, or taxes, that the persons of my kingdoms have to pay, or that in any manner belong to me, under the aforesaid penalties herein contained; and that immediately you have the whole hereof publicly proclaimed in the customary squares and market-places of each of the said cities, towns, and places, that every one may know it, and no person be able to plead ignorance.

But it is my pleasure, that as in the present year the said Jews have farmed some revenues, and are the collectors and receivers thereof, were this my order and all contained therein observed and executed, it might cause a diminution in my revenue, in respect to them, you are to have it observed and executed from the day the contract of the receipts and revenues the said Jews now have expires.

And in no manner are either of you to act or do otherwise, under pain of my displeasure, a fine of ten thousand maravedis to my treasury, and the afore-mentioned penalties.

Given at Valladolid, 25th October, 1408.

This ordinance, like all similar ones, proved ineffectual. The constant quarrels between the four Christian kingdoms of Castile, Aragon, Navarre, and Portugal,—the continual warfare with the Moorish state of Granada,—and the turbulence of the powerful grandees,—rendered the wealth of the Hebrews absolutely necessary to the Spanish sovereigns, to meet the exigencies of the state. Whatever policy might have dictated such laws, the Jews were aware of their futility, and continued to act in all the interdicted offices, knowing they had nothing to fear where the sovereigns themselves were the first to violate their own ordinances.

A greater misfortune for the Hebrew people commenced at this period and continued for some years, during which time 100,000 families are said to have resided in Castile. It was the appearance of Fr. Vincent Ferrer, a Dominican friar, as an itinerant preacher, for which he possessed all the qualifications,—a persuasive eloquence, indefatigable ardour, an unbounded devotedness to the church, and extraordinary energy; his austerity of manners caused him to be considered as a saint by the populace, who were pleased with his presence: even kings consulted and employed him in state affairs. This missionary, revered as a saint by Christians, was dreaded by the Jews as an inveterate enemy. The exaggerated picture he drew of the passion, exasperated the people against the descendants of Israel; and each sermon of the preacher acted as a goad to the ignorant multitude. Many Jews became converts when they saw their synagogues destroyed. Many were abandoned and converted into churches; among the latter was the ancient one of Toledo, which was dedicated to Sta. Maria la Blanca. The French, in 1808, turned it into a military depot; since which it has remained in the dilapidated state shown in the frontispiece. The beams are cedar from Lebanon, which harbours no insects, so that not a cobweb is to be seen; and it is said the ground was earth brought from Mount Zion. But this, as well as the assertion that it was built on the arrival of the Jews in Spain, may be doubted; for, from its being in the Moorish style of architecture of the eighth century, it is more likely to have been built about that period, when the Moors were in quiet possession of Castile. But Ferrer's success was most in Aragon, owing to the protection and favour he received from Ferdinand, in return for being one of the twelve that voted for his being elected king, and his activity in securing the crown for him. He went from town to town with a crucifix in one hand and a book of the law in the other, loudly calling on the Jews to rally under the cross. He was followed by an armed multitude, who attacked and killed those that refused; many abandoned every thing, and to save their lives emigrated to Barbary. The largest number of converts that he made (if pretending to embrace Christianity, in order to save their lives, can be considered conversion), was of the Jews of Aragon, Valencia, Majorca, Barcelona, and Lerida, and a lesser number in Castile. Desirous of extending his missionary labours, he wished to enter Portugal, where there was a large population of Jews; but he first sent to ask the king's permission, which was immediately granted, under condition that he should previously put on a crown of red hot iron. Not liking so warm a reception, he retired to a cooler field for action. Many of the converts, who were now designated New Christians, from fear of the persecutions and death that awaited them, quitted Spain; some went to Portugal and other Christian states where Jews resided, but the greater part retired to the Saracen kingdoms of Africa, and returned to the religion of their forefathers. Those whom neither force nor threats could induce even apparently to abjure their faith, who remained in Spain, became subject to many vexatious laws and restrictions, as will be seen hereafter.

When Ferrer was at Perpignan with the Emperor Sigismund, the kings of France and Aragon, and the antipope Benedict XIII., the Jews were compelled to attend his public sermons; but notwithstanding the presence of the sovereigns, they could not suppress their indignation at his false quotations and misrepresentations, and exclaimed, that he quoted falsely and misinterpreted; but probably considering the imprudence and danger of opposing a monk who was supported by the whole town and the crowned heads there assembled, many afterwards submitted to baptism.

Wherever the monk appeared, many Jews apparently embraced Christianity. Many abandoned every thing, and retired to Portugal and to the Moors of Andalusia and Africa. He is said to have converted 35,000 Jews and 8,000 Moors: a Hebrew writer[*] states the number to have been 200,000; but that must have included those who became converts after the conference ordered by Benedict XIII. What tended to increase the number, was their exemption from taxes, and every civil honourable post and ecclesiastical dignity being opened to them. The number of Jews that became converts at Palencia was so great, that being large landholders, and thus relieved from tithes and other taxes, the revenue of the bishop, Don Sancho de Roxas, was so reduced, that he was forced to apply to the king, saying, "that the triumph of the church had been a temporal misfortune for him;" and he obtained compensation from the royal treasury. But the major part of these converts dissembled only as long as they saw a necessity, and to avoid severe treatment. They conformed in outward appearance, but secretly lived like Jews, circumcised their children, observed the passover, and every other Jewish rite.

Don Meir, the physician of Henry III., had, from the favour he received from his sovereign and his abilities, raised many enemies against him, who implicated him in the following improbable accusation:—

[*] Juchasin.

Some Jews are stated to have bought a Host from the sacristan of the cathedral of Segovia, and having thrown it into a cauldron of boiling water, it rose to the surface. The Jews at sight of the miracle became alarmed, wrapt it in a cloth and secretly gave it to the prior of the Dominican convent, relating the circumstance to him. He told it to the bishop, who had Don Meir and the other Jews arrested and put to the torture. To terminate their cruel sufferings, they acknowledged themselves guilty, and a confession was extorted from Don Meir that he had poisoned the king, his friend and benefactor. They were drawn and quartered at Segovia, in 1406; but the injustice committed being soon after discovered, the only sufferers were the innocent accused.

From another false accusation made about the same time, the Jewish people were not so fortunate as to escape. Many were plundered and massacred; many abandoned all they possessed and quitted Segovia. This persecution arose from the inveterate hatred a nobleman bore to the bishop. Fearing to assassinate him, yet resolved on his death, he sought to satiate his revenge in a way not to be suspected. To effect which he bribed the bishop's cook to poison him. Every thing was prepared, when it was discovered. The cook was arrested, and thrown into prison, and put to the rack, but no confession could be got from him, as to who was the person that had instigated him to so atrocious an act. Notwithstanding the torture he suffered, he would not discover the name of the cowardly assassin, although his life was offered as the reward for the discovery. The nobleman, fearing his resolution might fail, advised him to inculpate the

Jews, by saying that from the hatred they bore the bishop, as being a Christian prelate, they had given him a large sum to commit the deed, his life was spared; but as he did not accuse any particular individual, numbers fell a sacrifice to his false confession.

The following proclamation was made at Alcala de Henares, 30th November, 1411, by order of Don Alphonso Fernandez de Cascalles, chief alcalde, and some of the king's council.

1.—Our lord the king orders and considers it right, that no Jew or Moor should be physician, surgeon, apothecary, accoucheur, or sick nurse, to great or small, or sell any eatables.

2.—That no Jews or Moors shall have Christians to serve them in their houses.

3.—That no Christian is to invite Jews or Moors, or accept invitations to eat or drink with them, or drink wine made by them; or eat any victuals or meat they may give or send them.

4.—That no Jew or Moor shall presume to bathe in the same bath with Christians.

5.—That no Christian eat their unleavened bread, or the meat they kill, or live in the same house with the said Jews or Moors.

6.—That Jews and Moors shall not be bakers, millers, or grinders of meal.

7.—It is further commanded and considered just, that any person who opposes, or acts contrary hereto, shall lose whatever property he may possess, half of which shall be to redeem captives, and half for the informer.

Notwithstanding these persecutions, the Jews were not regardless of study, and some men of superior talents shewed themselves amidst these troubles; viz.—

R. ISAAC CAMPANTON—born in 1360, was chief rabbi of all Spain, he lived to the extraordinary age of 103; his only work is "The Paths of the Talmud," in which he lays down general rules for understanding its style.

R. YOM TOB ASCIVILI—born at Seville in 1380, was a celebrated Jurist and Talmudist; he wrote "The Tower of Strength," a defence of Maimonides; "The Law of Judges," on the administration of justice, and some expositions.

R. JOSEPH ALBO—a native of Soria and inhabitant of Saragossa, one of the disputants in the conference with Jerome de Santa Fé. After which he wrote "The Book of Principles," on the existence of God, the divine origin of the law of Moses, and on the future reward and punishment of human actions, a work highly appreciated.

R. VIDAL BENVENISTA—a celebrated Talmudist and orator. From his proficiency in Latin, his associates appointed him to open the discussion with Jerome of Santa Fé. He wrote a work on the Heathen Mythology.

R. JUDAH ALCOPHNI—a philosopher, physician, and poet of great repute. Master of the Arabic, he translated Maimonides' "Guide;" his "Introduction to the Mishna;" "The Orchard of Pomegranates;" of R. Hasdai, Galen's work on the Soul; "The Maxims of Philosophers" of R. Hananiah; "Aristotle on Government;" and "The Poems of Abu de Borra" into Hebrew. His poetry is universally admired. He also wrote on physical health.

DON JUDAH BEN DON DAVID JACHIA—of Lisbon, held in high consideration from being deeply versed in philosophy, jurisprudence and poetry. He wrote "An Explanation of the Service of 9th Ab," and added a lamentation, which is read in the service for that day.

DON GUEDALIAH JACHIA—a brother of the preceding, was chief of the Hebrew College at Lisbon, where he practised medicine with great reputation. He has left in manuscript a philosophical work entitled "The Seven Eyes," treating on the seven liberal sciences.

R. SIMEON DURAN—of Majorca. Owing to the massacres

in 1391, he emigrated to Algiers, where, from his profound learning, he obtained the title of the Great. He wrote various works, some so violent against Christianity and Moslemism that they have very properly been suppressed by his coreligionists. The horrible persecutions his people had suffered, may have led to his inveteracy. He was famed for his medical abilities, and had practised with great reputation in Aragon. His profound erudition in rabbinical science, philosophy, and medicine, procured for him the esteem of the learned Israelites of his time. He died in 1444, aged 84. His learned solutions of upwards of 700 points of law, are consulted at the present day.

R. JOSEPH BEN BIBAS—of Lorca, in Murcia, where he practised medicine with great reputation. His grandfather, of the same name and place, was profoundly versed in philosophy, medicine, and Arabic, from which he translated into Hebrew " The Logic of Maimonides," and " The Canons of Avicenna;" he also wrote some learned philosophical and medical treatises.

R. PERIPOT DURAN—a celebrated grammarian and mathematician. He commented on " The Guide" of Maimonides, and wrote " The Work of the Breastplate," a profound Hebrew grammar; " The Band of the Breastplate," a geometrical work. He was considered one of the profoundest Talmudists of his age, and is supposed to have assisted at the conference at Tortosa, after which he quitted Spain and went to Egypt, where he wrote his famous letter to his son.

DON TODROS BEN DAOUD—of Calatayud, rendered himself celebrated by his medical attainments. He enjoyed from his cotemporaries a high consideration for his learning.

R. SHEMTOB BEN JACOB —a distinguished physician at Toledo, and a great cabalist. In 1415 he wrote a work on that science, and some others subsequently.

R. ISAAC BEN SOLYMAN—a physician of Guadalajara. This celebrated practitioner wrote in Arabic, in 1415, a treatise on the virtue of remedies.

R. Moses Abdalla—of Cordova, a physician of great repute. He wrote, in 1413, a medical work in Arabic, and commented on the Aphorisms of Hippocrates in Hebrew, whose writings he wished to render familiar to his brethren, exhibiting his taste in clinical medicine. His medical works consist of an anonymous treatise "*De Alimentis*," a compendium of medicine with the title of "*Galeni Paraphrasis Artis Medendi*," and some other books of Galen.

## CHAPTER XVIII.

*Ordinance of the Queen Regent at Valladolid—of Don Ferdinand, the other Regent, at Cifuentes.—Memorial of the Jews.—Continued in Public Offices.*

The prospects of the unfortunate descendants of Israel were particularly gloomy in 1412. Every thing was to be feared from the hatred of the bigoted queen-mother, supported by that inveterate enemy to the Jewish name, Fr. Vincent Ferrer. The year had scarcely commenced, when the following edict appeared in the name of the innocent infant monarch, then not eight years of age.

Don John, by the grace of God, king of Castile, etc. etc. etc. to all officers [here detailed]:—Laws respecting the Jews and Moors to be observed.

1.—That all Jews and Moors of my kingdoms and dominions, do dwell and live apart from Christians, in a separate part of the city, town, and place where they reside, surrounded by a wall, having a single gate for ingress and egress. All Jews and Moors are to reside within the said inclosure assigned to them, and in no other place or house without it. They are to separate themselves within eight days after places shall be assigned them; and any Jews or Moors residing without the said inclosure, after the said time, shall lose all their property, and be at my mercy, to receive such corporal punishment as I may please to order.

2.—Furthermore, no Jews or Moors shall be spice-dealers, apothecaries, surgeons, or physicians; or sell bread, wine, flour, oil, butter, or other provisions to Jews or Christians; or publicly nor privately keep warehouses, shops, or tables for selling. Any Jew or Moor who acts contrary hereto, shall incur the penalty of two thousand maravedis for each time, besides the corporal punishment my pleasure may inflict, that they learn to fulfil my orders.

3.—If any Jew or Moor, inspired by the Holy Ghost, wishes to be baptised, and turn to our holy Catholic faith, they shall not be prevented, or impeded by force or otherwise, from becoming converts, by Jews, Moors, or Christians, man or woman, although they be father, mother, brother, or any other person; and whoever opposes, or acts contrary hereto, proceedings are to be taken against them, for the civil and criminal penalties they justly incur.

4.—Jews and Moors are not to eat with Christians, nor Christians with Jews or Moors, either in or without their houses, in the towns where they reside, except in case of need, or in travelling, or at the king's court. If they find only taverns kept by Christians, and if there are no Jewries in places where fairs are held, although in such places they eat in Christians' houses, my pleasure is, that they shall incur no penalty for so doing.

5.—No Jews or Moors are to have Christian lacqueys or domestics, or any other persons to serve them, execute their orders, perform their household work, cook their victuals, or do any thing for them on Sabbaths, as lighting fires, carrying wine or similar articles; nor have Christians to nurse their children, nor to be their herdsmen, gardeners, or shepherds; nor are they to attend marriages, funerals, or *honras*, under the penalty of two thousand maravedis for each offence. No Jews or Moors are to be farmers, attorneys, collectors, stewards, or receivers of my revenues, or those of any Christian lord or lady, or exercise any of those offices for them or themselves, under the penalty of one thousand maravedis.

6.— Jews and Moors are not to have squares or markets, to buy or sell any thing to Christians to eat or drink, under the penalty of five hundred maravedis for each time; but they may have them within their inclosures, to trade among themselves.

7.— That the communities of Jews and Moors, in my kingdoms and dominions, shall not henceforth have among themselves, Jews or Moors for judges, to decide civil or criminal causes that may occur between Jews or Moors; and I revoke any power that I, or the kings, my predecessors, have granted, either as privileges or otherwise, and declare the same to be void. And I order that all causes, whether civil or criminal, shall be tried by the alcaldes of the cities, towns, and places where they reside; but my pleasure is, that in deciding civil causes, the said alcaldes shall observe the customs and regulations that have been observed among the said Jews and Moors, provided they appear authentic, and have long been sanctioned by them.

8.— No Aljama, or community of Jews or Moors, shall presume to levy any tax or contribution on themselves, or impose a duty on any article, without my permission or order, and of the queen my mother, and the Infante my uncle, my guardians and regents of my kingdoms; and if any authority has been given to the said Jews or Moors, whereby any duty has been imposed, either generally or on particular persons; or on meat, merchandise, or any other object, whether by their judges, or any of them, from holding privileges or charters from former kings, my predecessors, or myself, to that effect; henceforward they are not, nor shall they be bound to pay the said taxation, for I, by my royal authority of king, revoke any privilege that may have been given in respect of the same. And I order Jews and Moors not to exercise such power, under pain of corporal and other punishments; and I also command said Jews and Moors not to pay such contributions as may be thus levied, without, as before said, my licence and order being expressly given for the purpose.

9.—No Aljama or community of Jews or Moors shall presume to levy or apportion any tax without my permission and order; and where any tax is so levied for my service, they shall divide among them the amount I order and send for and no more; and if a larger sum is levied or apportioned, the persons who did or advised it, for the act, are to lose all their property and be executed by justice.

10.—No Jew or Moor shall presume to visit Christians in their illnesses, or give them medicines or draughts, or talk idly to them, or send them presents of dried herbs, spices, bread, wine, fish, game, fruit, or other articles of food. Any Jew or Moor acting contrary hereto, shall for each offence be fined three hundred maravedis.

11.—That no married or single Christian woman, kept mistress, or prostitute, may either by day or night enter within the enclosure where Jews or Moors reside; and any Christian married woman that does, for each time she enters, she shall pay a fine of three hundred maravedis; if unmarried or kept, she is to lose the clothes she has on; and if a prostitute, to receive from justice one hundred lashes, and be driven from the city, town or place where she resides.

12.—No Jew or Moor shall designedly be styled Don, either by writing or verbally; and if he permits himself to be so styled, he is to pay five hundred maravedis for each offence; but otherwise he incurs no penalty.

13.—All Jews and Moors are to wear long robes over their clothes as low as their feet, and are not to wear cloaks; and in all cities, towns and places, they are to wear their distinctive red badge. But it is my pleasure, that, to avoid the dangers they might otherwise incur in travelling, they may wear the clothes they now have, as well as in the places they may go to.

14.—That all Jewesses and Moriscas of our kingdoms and dominions, shall, within ten days from this date, wear long mantles, reaching to their feet, and cover their heads with the same. Those who act contrary, for so doing, are to forfeit all the clothes they may have on to their under garment.

15.—That no Jew or Moor, ten days after this date, shall wear cloth of which the entire suit costs upwards of thirty maravedis; those who act contrary shall, for the first offence, forfeit the apparel they have on to the shirt; for the second, lose all their clothes and receive a hundred lashes; and for the third, all their property shall be confiscated to my treasury. But it is my pleasure that, if they choose, they may make coats and cloaks of the clothes they now possess.

16.—No Jew or Moor shall remove from Valladolid, or any other place where they have their domicile, to any other part, under the penalty of losing all their property for the act; and their persons shall be at my disposal.

17.—No nobleman, knight, or squire, shall shelter in their towns or villages any Jew or Moor who resided, or belonged to another place; and if any person has sheltered any Jews or Moors of this city of Valladolid, or of any other city, town, or place, they shall send them back to the place where they resided, with whatever they brought with them; and if they do not, for the first offence they incur the penalty of fifty thousand maravedis; and for the second, lose the place where the said Jew or Moor has been sheltered.

18.—Henceforward Jews and Moors are not to shave their beards, or have them shaved with razors or scissors; nor trim nor cut the hairs, but are to wear them long as they grow naturally, as they were formerly accustomed. And any person who acts contrary hereto, shall receive a hundred lashes, besides paying a fine of a hundred maravedis for each time he transgresses.

19.—No Jews or Moors shall, by the day or otherwise, hire any Christian to cultivate or work on their lands, vineyards, houses, or other buildings. Whoever acts to the contrary shall receive a hundred lashes for the first offence; for the second, a hundred lashes and pay a fine of a hundred maravedis; and for the third time, forfeit all his property, and again receive a hundred lashes.

20.—That no Jews or Moors shall be smiths, carpenters, doublet-makers, tailors, clothworkers, shoemakers, butchers, curriers, or clothiers for Christians; or sell them shoes, doublets, breeches, or any other article of clothing: whoever acts contrary incurs the penalties of the preceding law.

21.—That no Jews or Moors of my kingdoms and dominions shall be carriers, or bring produce to sell to Christians, as oil, honey, rice, or provisions; any one acting contrary, incurs the penalties of the preceding law.

22.—One third of all the aforesaid penalties shall be given as a reward to the informer, whether he belong to the city, town, place, or territory where it occurs, or a stranger, and two-thirds to my treasury; but it is my pleasure, that no person shall arrest or take up any Jew or Moor until he has been summoned before a judge, heard, and lawfully condemned.

23.—All Jews and Moors departing from my kingdoms and dominions, and taken on the road or in any other place, shall lose whatever they have with them, and be my slaves for ever.

24.—None of the said civil or criminal penalties are to be remitted, excused, mitigated, dispensed with, reduced, or increased by any alcalde, magistrate, judge, governor, or any other person of the said cities, towns, and places, although they are noblemen possessing sole control, or joint authority therein, under pain of losing their seigniories, and all other offices and posts they may hold.—Given at Valladolid, 2nd January, 1412.

Although in the eighth law the name of the Infante appears, he was no party to this act, which was signed only by the queen; but he found himself obliged, six months after, to issue the following, which, notwithstanding its severe enactments, is rather more liberal and mild than the preceding.

Don John, by the grace of God, king of Castile, etc. etc. etc. Whereas I am informed, that owing to the constant association and great intimacy that exists between Jews, Jewesses, and Christians, some things are done contrary to the service of God and the Catholic faith; and, as according to the established laws of my kingdoms, Jews and Jewesses may live among Christians, observing their religion, and not doing any thing against ours; but as from the aforesaid causes, tumults might arise against the Jews and Jewesses, which would be a contempt of my justice, which as king it behoves me to preserve, as being the chief privilege and duty of the government of the people, as thereby the affairs of state are properly maintained; and as it is my pleasure that the Jews and Jewesses be protected in my time, as they were in the times of the kings my ancestors, as they belong to me, and to avoid the dangers that might arise from the aforesaid causes, I therefore ordain and command—

1.—That all Jews of my kingdoms and dominions reside and live apart from Christians, in an inclosure in a part of the city, town or village, where they are resident; and the streets around it shall be closed with gates in such a manner, that all the gates lead to the enclosure; and that the said enclosure have one principal gate, and no more; and that the Jews and Jewesses reside within the said enclosure, and in no other part of the said place. I command that each city, town, and place nominate two discreet persons to be gate-keepers; and if the said Jews and Jewesses have a separate Jewry, I order that it be appropriated as a barrier, and that they commence to separate within one year from the day places are assigned to them, that time being allowed to build houses for their residences; but by my favour, if there should be houses already built within the said enclosure that they can hire to the satisfaction of the owners, and that the said term be fulfilled, then the said Jews and Jewesses are bound to reside within the said enclosure, and remove from the said Christians; and any Jews or Jewesses that should reside without the said limit, shall lose all their property, and their persons shall be at the mercy of the king, to inflict such corporal punishment as he may please to order.

2.—Furthermore, I ordain and command, that no Jews or Jewesses shall be spice dealers, apothecaries, surgeons, or physicians, or sell bread, wine, flour, oil, butter, or other eatables to Jews or Christians, or keep warehouses, shops, or tables for selling, either publicly or secretly, except for the disposal of grapes, live stock (that they have a license for), as well as fruit and vegetables, the produce of their own or hired gardens; the said articles they may sell within the barriers where they reside, or in the gardens and estates they own or rent, either to Christians, Jews, Moors, or any other persons, and in fairs, and on market days, placing the articles they have for sale in the said fairs and markets, in the squares, open courts, and shops, provided no Christian dwells in them; but it is my pleasure and will that they neither sleep nor dwell therein, except for the sale of the said goods; and it is also my pleasure, that in the said cities, towns, and places they may, carrying them in the hand, sell any article not prohibited herein; any Jews or Jewesses whomsoever who act contrary hereto, shall incur the penalty of 500 maravedis for each offence, besides the corporal punishment my pleasure may choose to inflict, that they may learn to perform my order.

3.—I also ordain and command, that if any Jews or Jewesses, inspired by the Holy Ghost, wish to be baptised and turn to the Holy Catholic faith, they shall not be impeded or prevented by force or otherwise from becoming converts by Jews or Christians, whether man or woman, although it be their father, mother, brother, or any other person; and proceedings are to be taken against those persons who oppose or act contrary hereto, for the civil and criminal penalties they justly incur.

4.—I likewise ordain and command, that Jews and Jewesses are not to eat with Christians, nor Christians among Jews and Jewesses, either in or out of their houses in the towns where they reside, except in case of need, or in travelling, or at the king's court, if they do not find taverns but in houses of Christians, and wherever fairs are held, if there is no Jewry; although if in such cases they eat in the houses of Christians, they incur no penalty for so doing.

5.—Furthermore I ordain and command, that no Jews or Jewesses shall have lacqueys or servants, either Moors, Christians, or other persons, to serve them, or execute their orders, or do their work, or cook their victuals, or do anything for them on Saturdays, as lighting their fires, or carrying wine, or any similar article; nor have Christian nurses to rear their children; nor attend or assist at marriages, funerals, or *honras*, under the penalty of 2,000 maravedis for each time they act contrary hereto, or any part thereof. But I consider it just, that the said Jews and Jewesses may employ Christian carpenters and other workmen to repair their houses, and cultivate their vineyards and lands, as day-labourers, engaging them, as is usual, in the public squares by the day; they may also have *jagers* and shepherds to tend their flocks, and gardeners to work in their gardens; but it is my will that, agreeably to the foregoing laws, they neither reside nor eat with them.

6.—Furthermore I ordain and command, and consider right, that the law ordaining that no Jews or Jewesses should be farmers, attorneys, bailiffs, stewards, or receivers of my revenues, or those of any lord or lady, or exercise those offices, or any of them for Christians or among themselves, that the said law, under the pains therein contained, may be fully observed as therein expressed.

7.—Furthermore I ordain and order, that no Jews or Jewesses shall be brokers, or bankers, or carry swords, daggers, or similar arms, in the cities, towns, and places of my kingdoms; but they may carry knives to cut food. Any Jew or Jewess who acts contrary hereto, or to any part hereof, shall be fined for each time so offending 500 maravedis.

8.—Whereas the king, Don John, my grandfather, of illustrious memory, to whom God grant Paradise, was informed that the Jews and Jewesses of his kingdom practise some things against our religion, and as it was not right to permit it, ordained certain laws, the tenor of which is as follows:—

The ordinances made at Soria in 1380 are here copied.

Which laws, and each of them, as they are highly advantageous and beneficial to the public welfare of our kingdoms, I therefore ordain, that the same be fully observed, under the penalties therein contained.

9.—Furthermore I ordain and command, that no Jew or Jewess shall presume to visit Christians in their illnesses, or give them medicines, or draughts, or talk idly to them, or send them presents of dried herbs, spices, bread, wine, fish, game, fruit, or other article of food: any Jew or Jewess acting contrary hereto, shall be fined 300 maravedis for each offence.

10.—Furthermore I ordain and command, and consider it right, that no married or single woman, kept-mistress or prostitute, either by day or night, enter the enclosure where Jews and Jewesses reside: any married Christian woman that does, shall pay a fine of 200 maravedis; if unmarried, or kept, she is to lose the clothes she has on; and if a prostitute, she is to receive from justice 100 lashes, and be banished from the city, town, or place where she resides.

11.—Furthermore I ordain and command, that no Jew or Jewess shall be styled, either in writing or verbally, Don or Donna: if by their consent they are so called, for each time they are to pay a fine of 500 maravedis, but otherwise they incur no penalty.

12.—Furthermore I ordain and command, that Jews shall not wear hoods with long tassels, but their caps shall be made a palm in length, shaped like a funnel, or horn, and sewed round to the point.

13.—Furthermore I ordain and command, that all Jews in my kingdoms shall wear over their clothes coats with skirts, and shall not wear cloaks; and in the cities, towns, and places where they reside, they shall wear the customary red sign or badge; but it is my pleasure, that in travelling, as well on the road as in the places they go to, they may wear the clothes they now have, to avoid the dangers they might otherwise encounter.

14.—Furthermore I ordain and command, that no Jew shall wear cloth, the entire dress of which would exceed in value sixty maravedis. Those who act contrary shall, for the first time, forfeit all their clothes to their body linen; for the second shall, in addition, receive one hundred lashes; and for the third, all their property shall be confiscated to my exchequer.

15.—Furthermore I ordain and command, that none of the Jews of my kingdoms and dominions shall shave, or have their beards shaved with razors; but they may cut them with scissors, provided they leave some hairs round the chin; but they may cut the hair of the head as they were formerly accustomed. Any person who is known to act contrary shall, for each offence, be fined five hundred maravedis.

16.—Furthermore I ordain and command, that no Jewesses of our kingdoms shall wear mantillas or veils with lace or trimmings; and the clothes they wear shall not be of a higher value than those worn by Jews; nor shall their head-dresses have gold ornaments. Any one who acts contrary hereto, each time shall lose all the clothes she has on to her body linen.

17.—Furthermore I ordain and command, that if any Jews or Jewesses wish to remove from one place to another, they may do it, and no person shall presume to stop them, or the persons they take with them, but they are to be allowed freely to go; and we order, that any person who acts contrary, shall be proceeded against as in justice and right.

18.—Furthermore I ordain and command, that all knights, squires, and all other persons that have separate places, seigniories, and jurisdictions of their own, shall rightly and fully observe, and have observed, every thing contained in these ordinances, and each of them, in their respective villages, cities, and towns; and any person that does otherwise, if he possesses lands or grants from me, for the first time shall lose the benefit of them for one year; and if he possesses no land or grant, he incurs the penalty of ten thousand maravedis to my exchequer; and for the second time, those who have lands or grants from me, the same shall be forfeited, and they shall have no others from me; and those who have not, shall pay a fine of one thousand Castilian doblas of gold to my exchequer; and for the said act a third time, they shall lose their possessions which shall belong to my crown.

19.—Furthermore I ordain and command, that no Jew is to be a tailor, or make dresses for any Christian woman, of whatever rank or condition she may be. If the contrary is done,

one hundred lashes shall be given to the Jew for each offence; and the Christian woman who gave the clothes to be made, shall pay one thousand maravedis to my exchequer.

20. Furthermore I ordain and command, that all the aforesaid penalties, or any of them that may be inflicted on any person, of whatever rank or condition soever, shall be one-third for the informer, and two-thirds to my exchequer, which it is my pleasure and will that no alcalde, judge, lord, or magistrate shall remit or excuse, under pain of losing the offices they hold from me.

But it is my pleasure that no individual shall arrest, or inflict the said penalties upon any Jew or Jewess whatever, until they shall have been taken before the judge, and duly condemned.

Given in the town of Cifuentes, 17th July, 1412.

A most virulent pamphlet against the Jews, by one Marcos Rodriguez, had been one of the causes that induced the Councils of the two Regents to issue these harsh decrees. The Jews refuted it in a memorial to the king, and named a number of Jews, who in various honourable posts and employments, had faithfully served the crown. They stated that they were allied to the principal houses of Castile, for, that from their property, wealth, and the protection of the Court, they were the most powerful body in the kingdom, and therefore, it was not surprising that many distinguished families sought their alliance.[b]

Such insensate decrees could only be the work of men unacquainted with the world and the state of society. They were not observed because they went too far. It was absurd to attempt to prevent hundreds of thousands of strangers quitting the country, and yet to isolate them. What is surprising is, that ordinances which extended to their dress and beards,

[b] Asso and Rodrigues.

contain not a word against usury, to which, could these laws have been carried into effect, they must have been driven, by depriving them of every other means of obtaining a livelihood. Although much has been said of their usury, not a single instance of it is recorded in Spanish history; therefore it is to be presumed the charge was only made when an impoverished or dishonest creditor wished to avoid payment, which the enormous legal interest rendered extremely onerous. The regency of John II. added to the misfortunes of the Israelites, without the least benefit to society, and tended to foster the prejudices of the vulgar against them.

Fortunately, the Jews had too much talent, credit, and money, to heed these intemperate prohibitions; they continued to practise medicine; and under the titles of stewards, treasurers, intendants, and administrators, to conduct the monetary concerns of the grandees and the state. It is probable that the greater part of the money then in circulation passed through their hands.

## CHAPTER XIX.

*Jerome of Santa Fé.—Disputation at Tortosa.—Benedict's Address to the Rabbins. — Termination of the Conference. — Bull of Benedict. — Riot at Toledo.— Council of Tortosa.—Cortes of Burgos.—Comparative Population in Aragon. — Alphonso de Spina. — Fortress of Faith. — Jews and Converts of Toledo plundered by Don Henry.*

FROM the persecutions suffered by the descendants of Israel in Castile, we must turn to the neighbouring kingdom of Aragon, where they also became the victims of religious fanaticism. On a vacancy occurring in the Papal see, three candidates appeared for the infallible post; each had his partizans — and each excommunicated the other. Pedro de Luna, of Tortosa, on assuming the pontifical dignity, took the name of Benedict XIII. At the instigation of his physician, Joshua Halorqui (of Lorca), an apostate from Judaism, who at his baptism had taken the name of Jerome of Santa Fé, a man of abilities, not only in his profession but also as an able Talmudist, the antipope convened an assembly of rabbins, to argue with this inveterate foe to his former coreligionists, on the following points:—

1. Those that Christians and Jews agree on respecting faith, and those on which they differ.
2. On the twenty-four attributes of the Messiah.

3. Whether the appointed time for the coming of the Messiah had not long expired.

4. Whether the Messiah had not been born, at the time of the destruction of Jerusalem.

5. Whether he had not been born, or his advent announced, when the destruction of the Temple was foretold.

6. That the Messiah had come in the year of the passion and death of the Saviour.

7. That the prophecies that speak of the acts of the Messiah, the restoration of the Temple, the reduction of Israel to one people, and the felicity of Jerusalem, are to be understood morally and not materially.

8. Twelve questions to be put to the Jews on the acts of the Messiah while on earth.

9. That the law of Moses is neither perfect nor everlasting.

10. On the sacrament of the Eucharist.

11. When and why the treatise known by the title of the Talmud was composed.

12. Whether Jews are obliged to believe the whole contents of the Talmud, or if it is permitted to deny any part of it.

13. What is to be understood by the article of the law, proving that it is not an article of the Jewish law, that the Messiah has not come?

14. What is faith, and what is Holy Scripture?

15. On the abominations, impure heresies, and vanities of the Talmud.

16. That the Jews suffer the present captivity, only for the sin of their gratuitous hate towards the true Messiah.

With such a programme, the Jews would willingly have declined the discussion; but they had not the power of refusing. Their only resource was to appoint their ablest theologians to defend their cause, although aware that nothing they could urge would satisfy their adversary the disciple of Vincent Ferrer, the antipope, or King Ferdinand, who, although raised to the throne of Aragon, continued to act as guardian to his nephew,

John II. of Castile, in which capacity he signed the decree of Cifuentes, although in his new kingdom he had hitherto left them unmolested. The Jews nominated the following. From—

Saragossa. . R. Zachariah Levi; R. Don Vidal Benvenista; R. Mathias Haizari, chief rabbi of Aragon; R. Samuel Levi; R. Moses ben Moses.
Huesca. . R. Todros.
Alcoy. . R. Don Meir Galigon; R. Joseph ben Aderet.
Daroca. . R. Asher a Levi.
Monreal. . R. Joseph Albo.
Monzon. . R. Joseph a Levi; R. Yom Tob Carcos.
Montalban. R. Abugarda.
Gerona. . R. Don Todros ben Jachia.
Velez. . . R. Joseph Abalegh, and R. Bongoza.

In all, sixteen profound talmudists, a proof that, notwithstanding persecution, the Jews did not neglect their studies. Benedict named as assistants to Jerome of Santa Fé, his almoner, Andrew Beltran, bishop of Barcelona, also a convert from Judaism, and Garcia Alvarez, of Alarçon, a profound Hebrew scholar, and probably another convert.

On the arrival of the rabbins at Tortosa, where Benedict held his court, they had an audience. He received them with great affability, and the assurance that nothing should be extorted from them. He encouraged them fearlessly and freely to reply to the arguments Jerome might adduce. Knowing by experience the result of similar conferences, they intreated to be excused from entering into the controversy, as they could not argue by sophistry and syllogisms. They had lodgings and provisions consistent with their rites, liberally supplied at the expense of the antipope.

Many were gratified at their kind reception; but the more experienced foresaw, that the termination of the discussion would prove disastrous.

At the first meeting, held the 7th February, 1413, there were seventy seats occupied by cardinals, bishops, prelates, and persons of the highest distinction. Benedict thus addressed them:—

Ye learned Hebrews, know that I have not come here to discuss which religion is true, yours or ours. I am certain mine is the truest. Your law was formerly the only true law; but it is now abrogated. You are convoked here solely by Jerome, who has engaged to prove to you that the Messiah has come, by the evidence of your Talmud, which was composed long since by rabbins far superior to yourselves in wisdom; therefore be careful of your arguments.

Sixty-nine meetings were held. When Benedict could not attend, the master of the palace presided. The Jews acted with the greatest respect and deference to the pope, but did not pay much to his physician; for at the fourth meeting, they plainly indicated their opinion, by stating that they were not ambitious to be made bishops. At the sixth meeting, Jerome having been forced against his will to concede an important point, which the Jews had contended for on the prophecy of Jacob, they wished to put an end to the discussion, and had gained over some of the prelates to persuade the pope to terminate it; but he considered Jerome was now bound to persist. The arguments frequently degenerated into insults, of which the Christian theologians, strong from their powerful support, were not sparing, nor in the expression of their contempt for their opponents. As in all similar disputations, each party claimed the victory.

Christian writers admit that the Hebrew disputants exhibited vast erudition in their replies to the attacks of their antagonists.

The Pope, at the sixty-eighth meeting, exercising his authority, abruptly announced an approaching persecution, the dread of which led many Jews to embrace Christianity. The historian of Aragon states, that in the summer of 1413, and the first six months of the following year, upwards of 200 Jews of the synagogues of Saragossa, Calatayud, and Alcaniz were baptised. Among those of Saragossa was Don Todros Benvenista, who was deeply versed in his religion, with others of his family. While the Pope was with his court at Tolosa, many of the most learned Jews of Calatayud, Daroca, Fraga, and Barbasto, to the number of 120 families, became converts, and were baptised; and all the Jewries of Alcaniz, Caspé, and Maella, were in general converted—upwards of 500 persons; and subsequently the Jewries of Lerida, Tamarit, and Alcolea, became converts. Altogether, in the Papal residence and other places, 3,000 were then converted, "apparently with sincerity." Such is the tale related by Zurita. Many undoubtedly did apostatise to secure their lives and properties; but that they were the most learned, we have only the assertion of the annalist of Aragon to prove.

Another consequence of this meeting was the following bull, issued by Benedict from Valencia, the 11th May, 1415:—

1.—To prohibit generally all persons, without distinction, publicly or privately, to hear, read, or teach the doctrines of the Talmud; ordering that within one month there be collected in the cathedral of every diocese, all copies that can be found of the Talmud, its glossaries, summaries, compendiums, notes, and every other writing that has directly or indirectly any relation to such doctrine; and the diocesans and inquisitors are to watch over the observance of this decree, visiting the Jews personally or by others, within their jurisdictions every two years, and punishing severely every delinquent.

2.—That no Jew be permitted to possess, read, or hear read, a book entitled "Mar Mar Jesu," it being full of blasphemies against our Redeemer Jesus Christ; nor any other book or writing that may be injurious to Christians, or that speaks against any of its dogmas, or the rights of the church, in any language in which it may be written: the contravener of this decree is to be punished as a blasphemer.

3.—That no Jew may make, repair, or under any pretence, have in his possession any crucifix, chalices, or sacred vessels, nor bind Christians' books in which the name of Jesus Christ or the most Holy Virgin Mary is written. Christians who give any of these articles to Jews, from any cause whatever, are to be excommunicated.

4.—No Jew may exercise the office of judge, even in causes that may occur among his people.

5.—All synagogues recently built or repaired, are to be closed. Where there is but one, it may remain, provided it is not sumptuous; and should there be two or more, one of the smallest only is to be left open; but should it be proved that any one of the said synagogues has at any time been a church, it is immediately to be closed.

6.—No Jew may be physician, surgeon, druggist, shopkeeper, provision dealer, or marriage maker, or hold any other office, whereby he has to interfere in Christians' affairs; nor may Jewesses be midwives, or have Christian nurses; nor Jews have Christians to serve them, or sell to, or buy provisions of them, or join them at any banquet, or bathe in the same bath, or be stewards or agents to Christians, or learn any science, art, or trade in their schools.

7.—That in every city, town, or village where there are Jews, barriers shall be appointed for their residence apart from Christians.

8.—That all Jews or Jewesses shall wear on their clothes a certain red and yellow sign, of the size and shape designated in the bull,—men on the breast of the outward garment, and women in front.

9.—That no Jew may trade, or make any contract; thus to avoid the frauds they practise, and the usuries they charge to Christians.

10.—That all Jews and Jewesses converted to the Catholic faith, and all Christians generally who are related by consanguinity to Jews, may inherit from their unconverted parents and relatives; declaring null any testament, codicil, last-will, or donation *inter vivo* they may make to prevent any of their property devolving to Christians.

11.—That in all cities, towns, and villages, where there may be the number of Jews the diocesan may deem sufficient, three public sermons are to be preached annually: one on the second Sunday in Advent; one on the festival of the Resurrection; and the other on the Sunday when the Gospel, "And Jesus approached Jerusalem," is chaunted. All Jews above twelve years of age shall be compelled to attend to hear these sermons. The subjects are to be—the first to shew them that the true Messiah has already come, quoting the passages of the Holy Scripture and the Talmud that were argued in the disputation of Jerome of Santa Fé; the second to make them see that the heresies, vanities and errors of the Talmud, prevent their knowing the truth; and the third, explaining to them the destruction of the Temple and the city of Jerusalem, and the perpetuity of their captivity, as our Lord Jesus Christ and the other prophets had prophesied. And at the end of these sermons this bull is to be read, that the Jews may not be ignorant of any of its decrees.[1]

Among those commissioned to carry the bull into effect, was Alphonso, bishop of Carthagena, son of Paul of Burgos, also a convert. The lucrative prelacies were the places sought after by the apostates

[1] Bibli Española, vol. i.

from Judaism, as best affording them the means of persecuting the descendants of Israel. Many ambitious men looked to the loaves and fishes of the Church for their reward; to obtain which, and prove their sincerity to the Catholic faith, they became the most inveterate persecutors of the Hebrew people.

The promulgation of this decree opened the cloisters of St. Dominic: there sallied from them a host of missionaries. Eloquent preachers, instructed controversialists, spread themselves to effect conversions. They laboured with unremitting fervour and extraordinary talents; and they adopted the most violent measures, provided they could injure the welfare of the Jews. No where were they safe from the incessant persecutions of these inimical monks. Fortunately for the Jewish people, the authority of Benedict did not extend beyond Aragon. Its short duration, and the death of Ferdinand a few months after the Valencian bull, rendered it nugatory; and the Hebrew people in that kingdom remained unmolested, to follow their industrious avocations, which the bull shews they pursued, and of which it sought to deprive them. Tranquillity enabled them to increase greatly; for, as will be seen, a few years after, their indefatigable industry led them to settle in almost every town of consequence in Aragon and Catalonia.

The exhausted state of the finances of Castile, from the quarrels and mal-administration of the regents, to which the constant feuds of the grandees greatly contributed, rendered fresh taxes indispensable. An insurrection, in 1419, at Toledo, was the consequence: the Jews, as usual, were the sufferers. The new converts, who had hoped that abjuring their faith would protect them from violence, found themselves deceived: they were equally plundered with those who had remained firm in their religion; and the populace demanded that converted Jews and all their descendants should be for ever excluded from every dignity and public employment. The Court, too weak to resist, was obliged to grant the demand. This, for a time, put a stop to conversions; for the new Christians found their only gain in renouncing the religion of their fathers, was the contempt of their former co-religionists. The ambitious saw their golden dreams vanish; mitres were no more to deck the brows even of the children of apostate Jews, while adherents to their faith were, notwithstanding the laws and decrees to the contrary, employed by the Spanish sovereigns as receivers, collectors, and physicians.

On the death of his mother, in 1420, John assumed the regal authority. He found Castile torn by intestine broils, and his kingdom threatened by Aragon and Navarre. While employed in restoring peace to his distracted country, the Jews appear to have been unmolested and even protected by him. The council of Tortosa, in 1429, intreated, that for divine mercy's sake, the king of Aragon, the barons, knights, prelates, and universities, would protect the Jews from violence, from which they would otherwise have suffered, although not recorded by Zurita.

The canons of former Councils against them were simply renewed, which shews that Judaism did not suffer from the bull of Benedict, from the number of Jews that distinguished themselves in the study of philosophy, medicine, poetry, and Hebrew literature. Complaints were incessantly made of their fortunate speculations and their wealth; the great profit they made from the Spaniards was always regarded with envy and jealousy.

At the Cortes of Burgos, in 1430, a petition was presented, begging the king to have enforced the laws of his father, and the Papal decrees against Jews and Moors holding any post giving them authority over Christians; so that they should neither hold them, nor evade the ordinance.

To which he answered,—

I will order to be seen what has been ordained by my father, and my favour, and the Papal bulls; and whatever is for the service of God, his divine law, my service and the welfare of my kingdoms, shall be observed, and neither be revoked nor derogated in respect to giving places to infidel Jews and Moors.

At the Cortes held at Segovia in 1433, the amount to be paid the lifeguards of Espinosa was reduced to two blancas, which was also ordered to be paid to the guards of Bavia.

And in the following year at those of Medina del Campo, on the representation of the inhabitants of Segovia against the usuries of the Jews, the ordinances of 1405, made at Madrid, were confirmed, and the penalty was raised to 10,000 maravedis. The Jews of Tudela, in 1435, had become so reduced in number and property, that the king, seeing they could not pay the contribution, and to induce those who had quitted to return to his kingdom, remitted during his pleasure, a further sum of 342 livres of the annual taxes.[2]

In 1435, the Jews of Palma were accused of crucifying one of their Moorish slaves, in mockery of the crucifixion. Four, under torture, acknowledged the crime, and were condemned to be burnt alive; but

[2] Arch. Nav. Case. 137, No. 3.

being promised, if they would receive baptism, they should be hanged first, they consented. They were R. Astruc, Sibili, Farrig, and Estelada, the principal men of the place,—for, by the bye, it was only the wealthy that were accused of this crime. Their lives were spared, as it was conceived their example might induce many others to abjure their religion. Two hundred are said to have received baptism, and many of their books were burnt.

The following account of what the Jewries of Aragon and Catalonia paid for the king's table, in 1438, will shew that the bull of Benedict XIII. had not had the desired effect of destroying the Hebrew people, which, in the course of a century, had greatly increased and extended. The large number formerly at Tortosa, the seat of the court of the antipope, had probably mostly removed, as it does not appear in the following list.

|  | Sous. |  | Sous. |  | Sous. |
|---|---|---|---|---|---|
| Saragossa, | 300 | Monzon, | 350 | Fraga, | 200 |
| Alagon, | 130 | Sariñena, | 50 | Ruesca, | 160 |
| Tarrazon, | 200 | Huesca, | 300 | Monclus, | 33 |
| Almuema, | 140 | Seros, | 100 |  | Sous Bar. |
| Calatayud, | 350 | Exéa, | 250 | Gerona, | 550 |
| Daroca, | 50 | Tauste, | 250 | Castellon, | 100 |
| Teruel, | 160 | Jaca, | 200 | Murviedro, | 100 |
| Albarracin, | 150 | Barbastro, | 400 | Burriana, | 30 |

This tax was called *cenes* (suppers) in Aragon, and in Castile, *yantares* (dinners).

A convert from Judaism, who had taken the name of Alphonso de Spina, from being a Franciscan friar, became rector of the University of Salamanca. He wrote the "Fortress of the Faith," against the Jews and Moors: it is full of the vilest calumnies and falsehoods. He depicts them as bad citizens, guilty of the most horrid crimes and the most detestable vices, deserving the harshest treatment. He complains of the favours, grants, and indulgences they obtained from the courts. He approves of all the persecutions and massacres they had suffered in various countries; and, under the mask of religion, this pretended zealous monk wished to provoke similar acts in Spain. Not satisfied with writing against his former co-religionists, he tendered his hateful services to various bishops, who employed him to persecute them in their dioceses. Those who fell into his merciless hands were to be pitied.

In 1441, the Infante, Don Henry, who was in arms against his father, being in want of money to pay his troops, was advised that the surest mode of obtaining it, would be to pillage the houses of the Jews and new converts of the city of Toledo. The advice pleased him; and he effected it without opposition from the chief alcalde, Pedro Lopes de Ayala. The populace followed the example, although the clergy and the respectable citizens endeavoured to prevent it; fear of being punished by the king for the crime confirmed that city in favour of the party of Don Henry.

## CHAPTER XX.

*Ordinance of John for the Protection of Jews and Moors.—Henry IV. succeeds his Father.—Abraham Benevista, negotiator between Castile and Aragon.— Cortes of Toledo.—Gaon sent to Biscay to raise the Pedido—Murdered.—Answer of the Basques to the King's Demand.*

VARIOUS cities and towns, taking advantage of the distracted state of the country, followed the example of Alcala de Henares, and framed laws against the Jews and Moors on their own authority, either to gratify the ill-will of the populace, or from the jealousy and envy their prosperity under all their sufferings caused. At length the king, finding the diminution of his revenue, and probably actuated by a feeling of humanity towards such useful subjects, put a stop to the usurped municipal power, and secured to his Jewish and Moorish subjects the means of industriously gaining their livelihood, by issuing the following decree:—

Don John, by the grace of God, king of Castile, etc., etc., to all persons in office [detailing the various titles and offices], health and grace.

Whereas, I have been informed that some persons, to the injury of my service, with great presumption and insolence have and do raise disturbances against the Jews and Moors of our cities, towns, and villages, desirous of injuring, hurting, and doing other wrongs to their persons and properties, without reason, right, or any cause; saying, they must neither buy, sell, partake, nor communicate with them, nor tend their flocks, nor till their lands. And that in some places, without my license or order, they have enacted severe statutes and ordinances against them; were the like permitted they would, without cause or crime, be deprived and interdicted from participation and communication with Christians; such privation and interdiction not being for objects or causes established by justice, for which, and for no others ought they to be interdicted from such participation and communication. All which has been unduly and unjustly done under color of the apostolic bull of our holy father, Eugenius IV., issued on the manner Jews and Moors should live in my kingdoms among Christians, which was published when I was at Toledo.

I am much surprised that such presumption and insolence should be practised; the truth being discovered, I intend to order that the same be punished and chastised, as a punishment for them and a warning to others not to do the like. And as, according to the said apostolical bull, canon rights, imperial and royal laws, Jews and Moors are to live peaceably and unmolested among Christians, observing certain things that are prohibited to them. But neither by the said bull, nor canon right, nor the laws of my kingdoms, is it permitted, allowed, or opportunity afforded, that any harm or injury be done to them, or any other wrong to their persons, or anything belonging to them; but, on the contrary, it is expressly permitted and tolerated, by common, canon, and civil right, and by the laws of my kingdoms, that they may quietly and peaceably live and reside among Christians as aforesaid; and by the said rights and laws it is expressly ordered and forbidden, that any person whatever shall dare to strike, wound, kill, seize or arrest them, or their property, without authority; or without right or reason, to do or cause to be done to them any harm or injury; and whoever acts contrary is to be chastised and punished.

Besides, by the said bull, the said Jews and Moors are prohibited exercising certain high offices among Christians, that are therein expressed and named, that is to say, they may not be judges, farmers, receivers, collectors, directors, or stewards of the revenues, taxes, dues, or contributions on the produce of estates and affairs of Christians; nor may they be their auditors, attornies, bailiffs, agents, or conductors of their business; or brokers, holders of deposits, contractors of marriages, or co-partners in any art or trade with Christians; nor may Jewesses or Moriscas be chambermaids to Christians.

It also prohibits them generally from holding any post, dignity, or public office, that may require to have honour paid to them, or by which they would have authority over, or to pass sentence on Christians; which is also prohibited by communal rights and the laws of my kingdoms.

It likewise forbids Christians, in illness or disease, to receive medicine, draughts, plasters, or any physic from Jews or Moors; or to eat with them, or accept their invitations to feasts, or live in the same house, or bathe in the same bath; nor may they have Christian nurses to rear their children; nor have regular Christian servants or attendants in their houses or on their lands. And that the said Jews and Moors should every where wear a mark and different dresses, that they may be known from Christians, and that Jews and Moors do not reside among Christians, but within barriers and enclosures apart.

But it does not follow therefrom, that they are prohibited to contract, buy, sell, or exchange any goods and wares among, and with Christians; nor are trades and useful handicrafts forbidden to them, as clothesmen, silversmiths, carpenters, barbers, shoemakers, tailors, clothiers, milliners, braziers, bridle-makers, saddlers, rope-makers, potters, curriers, basket-makers, money-changers, and all other similar trades, mechanical arts, and useful handicrafts, in which they use manual labour and work. Christians may serve them in such trades and handicrafts for just wages and hire, as no authority is thereby derived over them; nor are they in any way honoured thereby; nor can they assume power from such trades; nor can they thereby injure, molest, or condemn Christians; nor would it cause too much familiarity, nor constant company and association, provided the said Jews and Moors do not form partnerships with the said Christians in the said arts and trades, or become too familiar, or keep constant society with them. Nor are Christians forbidden to tend their flocks, or till their lands, or guard them from injury in travelling.

And as by the laws of my kingdoms, and the said bull, Christians are forbidden to receive medicines and aperients compounded by Jews or Moors, yet they may take advice from any learned Jew or Moor; but the said prescription is to be prepared by a Christian, who understands and is acquainted with the articles of which it is composed. Notwithstanding, in case of need, recourse may be had to Jewish and Moorish physicians, which in such cases is not prohibited or forbidden by the said bull, right, or the laws and ordinances of my kingdoms. On the contrary, it is permitted by them.

Therefore I command all and each of you to guard, defend, and assist the said Jews and Moors, their concerns and properties; and that you neither aid, nor permit any riot, tumult, or scandal against them; nor that any harm, injury, or wrong be done to them, without right or reason; for the said Jews are mine, and belong to my exchequer. And I take them under my safeguard, security, assistance, and royal protection, and which I order shall be duly observed. And that you, the said magistrates, have it published in all cities, towns, and places, by the public crier, in presence of a notary public, that all persons may know it. And should any person, after this publication, act contrary, you are to prevent it, and arrest their persons, sequestrate their property, and proceed against them and their property, for the highest civil and criminal penalties, which persons incur that violate the safeguard established by their sovereign and natural lord.

And that you make all and every person act accordingly, and fulfil and have the contents of this my order observed and executed, and that you do not act otherwise, or violate it, or permit it to be infringed and transgressed, or any part thereof, in any manner, now or at any time hereafter, but that you permit the peaceable residence, and proper association of Jews and

Moors among you without further molestation, in manner aforesaid, and in the exercise of the beforementioned rights that are not prohibited to them; and that you neither prevent nor interdict any of the aforesaid trades to them; and further, that you neither forbid nor prevent them to buy, sell, contract, or barter any of the aforesaid articles, since neither by right, the laws of my kingdoms, nor the said bull, are they prohibited to them; nor are the trades and objects aforesaid forbidden, save and except depriving them of the offices mentioned in the said bull, and any other public office, dignity, or post of honour they may hold, whereby they would be enabled to oppress Christians.

Yet that they may be known among Christians conformably to communal rights, and as the said bull exacts, Jews and Moors are to wear their signs agreeably to the ordinance of Don Henry, my father. And furthermore, I command that in all cities, towns, and places where they reside, they shall live and dwell in separate enclosures and barriers.

And in case they go to markets and public places to practise and exercise the said trades not prohibited to them by the said bull nor by right, or to contract, buy, sell, or barter any goods or merchandise as aforesaid, you shall allot them places; but they shall be bound to make their habitual residence within the said barriers, to which they are to return and assemble there to sleep, where they have their regular dwellings, and in no other house without the barrier of the city, town, and place where they reside. Besides, it is my pleasure, that, in all cities, towns and places where the said Jews and Moors have not separate barriers and appointed enclosures, such be appropriated to them in populous and suitable districts, where they can live and reside commodiously. And, for my information, the same is to be immediately notified to me, that I may order and assign a reasonable extent of ground, within which they can live and dwell. And should there not be in the city, town, or place, such populous district as can be conveniently, and without detriment to Christians, given to them, then some other suitable place shall be assigned, where they can comfortably build and construct their houses. And in every other respect you are to treat and act kindly to them, as justice and the laws of my kingdoms enact, since it is not opposed to the said bull. And as regards the pecuniary penalties, and other things therein contained beyond the foregoing, I intend to send to the holy father shortly, that they may be explained, and confined to the fulfilment of the service of God, mine, the welfare of my kingdoms, and the preservation of my rights. Furthermore I command, that henceforward you make no ordinances or statutes against the said Jews or Moors without my permission and order; and if any have been made, they are to be suspended and not executed, until you shew me cause for their enactment. I will and command that they be suspended, and not acted on, until I examine and order what is to be done as aforesaid. And you are not to act otherwise, under pain of my displeasure, deprivation of office, forfeiture of lands, favors, rations, grants, and every other benefit you hold from me, and confiscation of all other property to my exchequer. And further be assured, that should you act otherwise, or permit the contrary to be done, I will order that you be severely punished and chastised, so that no person presume to do the like.

Given at Arevalo, 6th April, 1443.

In 1445, a report was spread that the Jews had undermined the streets of Toledo, through which, on the festival of Corpus Christi, the procession of the Host was to pass, with the intention of setting fire to it at the time. The mob would have fallen on them, had not the authorities proved the report to be false, and prevented the massacre. But they were not so fortunate as to escape from the many false accusations propagated against them.

At the village of Tavora, a small place between Zamora and Benevente, a young man was condemned to death for some crime. His unhappy father, a blacksmith, on the melancholy fate of his only child, completely lost his senses. At night he would wander about the streets, knocking at people's doors. The inhabitants became so accustomed to his wanderings, that they took no notice of him, and he was known by all the town as "The Mad Jew." A party of Christian young men having been at some feast, as then customary in Spain, sallied out armed; they attacked and killed some Jews of the place. When the king heard of it, he ordered them to be arrested; but the people, to screen them from being treated as murderers, in exculpation testified to the king that the demented smith, in revenge for the execution of his son, when at home, was making hooks and cramps to fasten the doors, and caltrops to strew in the streets, intending to set fire to the place, when none could have escaped, which had induced them to commit the act. As all agreed in their story, the king and council considered they could not punish the whole population, and thus the guilty escaped.[1] Espina states, that the king prohibited Jews residing in Tavora, and that a magical brazen head kept in the castle, would exclaim when a Jew entered the town, "A Jew is in Tavora;" and, when he left, "The Jew is out of Tavora."

After this tale, it would be loss of time to discuss the credit due to Espina's stories. Another of his fabrications is, that being at Valladolid in 1454, a Genoese, son of an eminent Jew physician named Don Solomon, came to him to be baptised, who related to him, that at Pavia one Simon de Ancona, a physician, with other Jews, had killed a child for their sacrifices, but they had escaped from justice. He says that he also told him, that four years before, when at Savona, in the Genoese territory, his father took him to a house

[1] Usque.

where he met seven or eight Jews; they fastened the doors and killed a Christian child of two years old; its blood was caught in a basin; they mixed apples, pears, and pounded nuts with it, and all eat of it. The body was thrown into a privy.

Such were the calumnies propagated by this enemy of the Hebrew people, to inflame the minds of a bigoted populace against the descendants of Israel. While they were thus obtaining favours, distinctions, and even beatification, the diffusion of these falsehoods increased the misfortunes of the unfortunate Jews, the laws were too powerless to afford them protection, the tribunals composed of declared enemies, and their former brethren their most inveterate accusers.

Commerce and industry had perished under the numerous persecutions; and to satiate the revenge of the nobles, Jews had been deprived in 1453 of farming the royal revenues.

At Avila, the bishop of Cuença, the prior of Guadaloupe, and Friar Gonzales, of Illescias, who had been appointed governors, ordered the cities within their jurisdictions to receive and protect them.

Henry IV. succeeded his father in 1454. From his conduct to the Jews of Toledo in 1441, he was considered inimical to the Hebrew people. Advantage was immediately taken of that and the disturbed state of the kingdoms, to propagate the most unfounded calumnies against them. The following is said to have occurred in that year. In the lands of Don Luis de Almanzar, near Salamanca, the child of a rich merchant went out one holiday finely dressed with gold bands and tassels. Two thieves planned to rob him. They artfully enticed him away from the town, and stripped him. The boy, crying, was returning home. The thieves being natives of the place, fearing discovery, ran after, caught and murdered him, and buried the body in a private part of a field. On the child being missed, strict search was made, and rewards offered for his discovery or for information of him. A few days after, some shepherds, driving their flocks near the spot where the murder had been committed, their dogs scratching the ground discovered an arm, which they carried and laid at the feet of their masters. The shepherds, alarmed, repaired to the spot and found the body. The father, on learning this, went to the field with some friends, and recognised it to be the corpse of his child. Considering who could have committed so cruel an act on a young innocent unoffending child, they decided it could not be a Christian, but that it must have been done by some Moor, slave, or Jew. As soon as the latter was named, it was set down as certain, as in Germany and other parts of Christendom, they were accused of stealing children to sacrifice their blood. The report spreading that they had cooked the heart and eaten it, all the country was in arms, and prepared to wreak vengeance on the Jews. The king ordered a strict inquiry to be instituted, and through the goldsmith to whom the thieves had sold the stolen articles, the truth was discovered.[2] Espina says, a Jew with red hair was suspected, and on the rack confessed it; but that the Jews appealed against this extorted confession to the king, who appointed three judges to examine into the case. The Jew was acquitted, which he attributes to the king and judges having been bribed.

[2] Usque.

Such were the inventions of Alphonso de Espina, to bring persecution on the Jews. Many others might be adduced from his " Fortalitum Fidei," but the foregoing will be sufficient to shew in its proper light, the animus and falsehood of this apostate. Henry was fully occupied in endeavouring to suppress the rebellions of the nobles. His favourite minister, Abraham Benevista, was for two years the negotiator between the crowns of Castile and Aragon; and when taken prisoner at Tudela, was considered a prize of great importance. It was probably jealousy towards this Israelite, that led the grandees in 1460 to make it an absolute condition for laying down their arms, that the king should dismiss from his services Jews and Moors, " as they blemished religion and corrupted good conduct;" but this was only an excuse to impose laws on their sovereign, and to oppress the descendants of Israel by flattering the passions of the people; for it would be surprising that men who outraged both, should appear so zealous for religion and good conduct.[3]

While the king was at his favourite residence at Segovia, in 1461, a violent dispute arose between two friars on the treatment of the Jews. Coming from the pulpit of the church of Espirito Santo, it spread consternation in the court. One, with the bitterest acrimony, condemned the free communication held with them, prophesying innumerable evils on the whole kingdom that tolerated it. The other preached and proclaimed the maxims of the Gospel, and shielded by the canons and the laws of Castile, defended the unfortunate race. More than once had the partisans of the two monks nearly come to blows; and the

[3] Herrera.

former would have succeeded in his devices, had not the king espoused the side of his opponent, yet he adopted no measures to restrain the fire that was then spreading through all his dominions. This want of precaution was the cause that, in May of that year, the Jews of Medina del Campo suffered severely from the intemperate preaching of a fanatic monk, who, with a crucifix in hand, so inflamed his auditory, that they fell on the unfortunate Israelites, burnt some of them with their books, and pillaged their property. When the king learnt of this riot, he arrested its progress by punishing the ringleaders.

No legislation affecting the Jews is recorded until 1462, at the cortes of Toledo, when a petition was presented, the tenor of which will be seen by the king's reply:—

To this I answer, that I have ordered inquiry to be made respecting the contents of your petition, and it has been found that in most of the seigniories and abbacies of my kingdoms, the laws you mention regarding contracts and bonds between Christians and Jews are not observed, whereby some of the Jewries of the royal patrimony remove to live in the seigniories to my detriment and the injury of my revenue, taxes and dues. As many Jews live by buying and selling, and experience shows they cannot dispose of their goods and merchandise without giving credit, and that they trade and make contracts with each other, and that even oaths are administered in regard to their contracts, agreements, and decisions; although, were the laws observed in all the cities, towns and places in my kingdoms, and the seigniories, trading in goods and contracts that fairly and justly might be made between Christians and Jews, would in a great measure cease, whereby my revenues, taxes, and dues, would be diminished:—

And as I am informed that in the time of my father, Don John, whom I have succeeded, various grants and petitions were signed by him, and subsequently by me, and countersigned by some of his council and by mine, and by the auditors of my *audencias*, on the subject of your petition, some of whom order the said laws to be observed, and others direct them not to be enforced. And as from the severity of the law which enacts that Christians are not to burthen their consciences by paying heavy charges to Jews, and as lawful and fair contracts, proved to be such by public documents, witnesses, or their own acknowledgment, and which have not been fraudulently made to cover usury are not paid; desirous of remedying and providing for the same, as the holy fathers, Martin V., Eugenius IV., and their successors have issued and granted certain bulls, wherein they declare that without sin or charge against the said Jews, all descriptions of contracts, treaties, agreements, and arrangements, that are necessary for their legal transactions, may be made. Confirming and approving the penalties established by justice and the laws of our kingdoms against Christians, Jews, and Moors, that lend on usury, and further extending the ordinances, if necessary and requisite, it is my will and pleasure, that the said Jews and Jewesses, may freely receive from Christians and any other persons, without incurring penalties or fines, lawful contracts that are permitted by justice, and that are not usurious, nor dissembled and fraudulently made for usury, but for sales, payments, barters, agreements, and in any other manner. And they may receive written and verbal acknowledgments and judgments in the said legal and permitted cases; and such agreements, judgments and acknowledgments are valid, and shall have full force and efficacy in law, unless it be proved that they are usurious, or simulated, and fraudulently made to cover usury. It is my will and pleasure, and I will and command, that this be executed and fulfilled, notwithstanding the laws and ordinances of the said king, Don Henry my grandfather, and the kings my ancestors of glorious memory, and their presumptions and suppositions; which said laws, it is my will, shall have no force in justice, nor be entertained, contrary to this which I now make and ordain, and which henceforward shall be observed and executed. But I will, and it is my pleasure, that in contracts for loans the creditor shall be bound within two years to prove its contents, and if the debtor deny or object to the same on oath or otherwise, as not having been actually received or the amount given, this law may not in such case be renounced. This law which I now make, will, ordain, and command, shall be observed and fulfilled in all contracts, judgments, agreements and covenants hitherto made, or that hereafter may be made, provided they are not usurious, nor simulated, and fraudulently made for usury, that have not been brought before justice. All I desire is conformable to justice; and it is my will, pleasure, and command, that it be observed and fulfilled in manner aforesaid, notwithstanding the laws and ordinances of the kings my predecessors, or of any charters granted by them, me, my council, or the auditors of my *audencias;* nor shall such hereafter be granted. But it is my pleasure that bonds for loans that have or may be given to Jews, or other persons known as public usurers, are not to be enforced; but the laws and ordinances made by Don Henry my grandfather, and the kings my predecessors, are to be acted on, under the presumptions therein contained. Persons are to be considered as public usurers who are proved thrice, or oftener, to have lent on usury.

The following year Henry repaired to the frontiers to have an interview with Louis XI. The extravagance and splendour the Castilian monarch displayed required large supplies. From Fontarabia he despatched his finance minister Gaon, to levy the *pedido* (a tax so called from the king asking it of the Basque provinces, which at their pleasure they granted or refused). They termed themselves Hidalgos (noblemen), and ever declared their independence of royal authority, and only acknowledged the sovereign of Castile as lord of Biscay. As this was an infringement on their liberties and privileges, on the arrival of the Jew at Tolosa, the populace assassinated him. Henry, enraged, sent to demand the surrender of the murderers, which was refused, and the following answer returned by the Biscayans.

The Basques are the representatives of the Iberian nation. They lavished their blood against the Carthaginians, Romans, and Goths, for Spanish freedom. They restored Spain by expelling the Saracens who had conquered it from the barbarians. For upwards of six centuries the Basques struggled with the Caliphs of the West. The small state of Castile scarcely existed, when our nation living in the Pyrenees reckoned ages of glory and enterprise. In return for the services we have rendered Castile, we claim to be allowed peaceably to enjoy our lives and liberties, which our ancestors preserved to us at the cost of so much blood, and so many glorious deeds. If, however, the Castilians act ungratefully and unjustly towards us, they shall find to their cost, who were and still are their masters in the art of war, and their mountaineer liberators. As regards the *pedido* unjustly demanded of us, and the death of the Jew, know that the brave Guipuscoan who killed him, deserves well of his country. Tell this to King Henry. Return and bid him remember that one of our fundamental laws is " We ordain that any person, whether a native or foreigner, who shall coerce any man, woman, people, village, or town of Guipuscoa, by order of our Lord, the king of Castile, which has not been previously agreed to and sanctioned by the general assembly; or whoever violates our rights, laws, charters, and privileges, shall not be obeyed; and if he persists he shall be put to death."

The assassination of Gaon remained unpunished; for Henry was too weak to attempt any severe measures against those hardy mountaineers.

Although bonds given by Christians to Jews had been declared void, the law was not enforced; and that justice was done to them, is proved by a document yet existing, which states that Don Lope Lopez de Ayala, the ordinary Alcalde of Vittoria, sold, the 16th August of this year, by public auction,[4] the property of Don Beltran de Guevara, at the demand and suit of Don Abraham Algudia, for a bond of eight thousand maravedis due to him.

## CHAPTER XXI.

*Laws made at Medina del Campo.—Accused of crucifying a Child.—Persecution of Converts, the causes.—John II. of Aragon operated on for Cataract.—The Jewry of Pampluna ordered to be repaired.—Cortes of Ocana.—Mock Deposition of Henry.—Persecution in Andalusia.—Riot at Segovia.—Outrages in Sicily.—Assessment in Castile.—Isabella becomes Queen.—The Crowns of Castile and Aragon united.—Cortes of Toledo.—The Inquisition founded.*

HENRY, finding the laws to be ineffective, appointed the count of Palencia, the marquis de Villena, and some other noblemen, to revise them and form a new code, which they did. They are dated Medina del Campo, 16th January, 1465; but it was never carried into effect. The following, confirming former laws, respected only the Jews and Moors:—

Law 7.—Not to make Christians converts to their religions.

98.—Not to hold posts giving them authority over Christians. To reside in their own Jewries and Aljamas.

99.—Christians not to live within the Jewries or Moorish Aljamas.

[4] Accurdos Vic. vol. i., p. 54.

100.—To wear the distinguishing badge.
101.—Not to work in public on Sundays and Christian holidays.
102.—Christians not to live in their houses.
103.—Not to be collectors or farmers of taxes; nor for noblemen, church dignitaries, etc.
104.—Not to sell provisions to Christians.
105.—Not to leave their houses from Holy Thursday until Saturday.
106.—Not to be apothecaries or compounders of medicine for Christians.
107.—To give up the person from whom they had received any thing claimed as having been stolen.
108.—Not to possess Christian slaves.
109.—Not to build new synagogues or mosques.
110.—May possess landed property, as granted by Henry III.
111.—Not to take crucifixes or church-plate in pledge.
112.—The law respecting bonds confirmed.
113.—Bonds made in the names of Christians for their benefit to be null and void.
114.—Not to act as advocates for Christians.
115.—Penalties on magistrates not publishing these laws.
116.—Oaths of Christians to Jews or Moors not to be binding by law.
117.—Christians not to be copartners with them.
118.—Not to wear silk, gold, pearl, scarlet, or cloaks.
119.—Not to be allowed to quit the country.
146.—The ordinance of 1433 respecting the guards of Espinosa and Bania, confirmed.

In 1468 the Jews were again accused of murdering a child. The story is thus told. The Jews of Sepulveda, by the advice of their rabbi, Solomon Pichon, caught a child, and carried it to a retired spot, where, after cruelly illtreating, they crucified it. Don Juan Arias, bishop of Avila, then supreme judge of matters that concerned the faith, on hearing of it, had a number of Jews arrested and put to the torture, under which some acknowledged the crime, whereupon he sent sixteen to Segovia. Some were burnt, others were hung and quartered; yet these executions did not satisfy the inhabitants of Sepulveda, they swore to exterminate them. Animated by a desire for vengeance and a thirst for plunder, they attacked them in their houses, and immolated the major part to their fury; the remainder saved themselves by flight, seeking an asylum in other towns, in which they experienced great difficulty; for the report had spread, and in every place some similar tale was renewed.

Hitherto all the shafts of rage and cruelty had been directed against those who continued firm to their faith and the religion of their forefathers, even amidst riots and massacres; the lives and properties of those who had embraced Christianity had been respected. Persecution began to present another aspect; the mere fact of being a descendant of Judah was sufficient. Honours and favours had been heaped on those who had abjured Judaism; now, their sincerity becoming suspected, they were regarded with dislike and mistrust. This change of conduct towards the converts arose from various causes. Christians did not stand so much in need as formerly of the Hebrew people: their conquests within and without the Peninsula, and the study of ancient literature by the higher classes, had contributed to render them less dependent than they had hitherto been for the arts and sciences on Jewish rabbis. Old Christians, particularly the clergy, regarded with envy and jealousy the honours conferred on apostates, to their prejudice. Catholic domination could not tranquilly permit the descendants of Israel to partake the ascendancy they considered as belonging exclusively to themselves. The clergy of Spain at this period is represented by Mariana " to have been extremely ignorant, few understood Latin; they were generally addicted to gluttony and debauchery; their avarice corrupted every thing. The purchase of benefices had formerly been held to be simony, now it was considered a legitimate mode of amassing wealth." Probably it was by these means converts frequently obtained high ecclesiastical dignities. The new Christians had not with their religion abandoned their industrious habits. Their wealth and prosperity were inducements that avaricious people could not resist, and, instigated by many fanatic ecclesiastics, under the cloak of religion, their plunder and assassination was the consequence.

A deputation of Jews and converts from Valladolid, where they had suffered, went to the king at Segovia to ask his assistance and protection against the injuries they experienced from the partizans of his sister, Donna Isabella, to whom the disaffected nobles had repeatedly offered the crown. When she learned it, she hastened with her husband Don Ferdinand from Dueñas; but sought in vain to quiet the disturbance. Blood had been shed, the laws had been trampled on; but the converts obtained no satisfaction. Valladolid returned to its allegiance. Henry, pleased at the city returning to his authority, and the riot being quelled, remained satisfied, and feared to punish the guilty.

John II. of Aragon, in 1468, was successfully operated on for cataract in both eyes by an eminent Jew, surgeon and physician of Lerida, named Abiathar.

Donna Leonora, the princess of Navarre, for the preservation of the Jewry of Pampluna, ordered the auditors of accounts to oblige the Jews that resided without it to remove thereto, threatening punishment for non-compliance, and to compel the Jewry to repair the houses belonging to the royal patrimony.[1]

Henry held a cortes at Ocana in 1469, at which the following petition was presented:—[2]

Besides, most high Sir, your highness knows that the kings, your predecessors of glorious memory, by many laws enacted in cortes, prohibited Jews and Moors being farmers and receivers of your tributes and taxes, and that they should not be bailiffs and stewards to Christians, nor hold other posts in the household of grandees, under certain penalties imposed by the said laws, on those who should accept such offices; and we know the said kings had just cause for the said prohibition. But as we see that the said laws are not observed, and that the principal offices in the customs and the collection of your revenues, taxes, and duties, are held by Jews, and we believe were your revenues let at reasonable prices, Christians would farm them, and as the laws of the kingdoms enact, they ought to be let to them lower; but even worse is done in your kingdoms, for many prelates and other ecclesiastics farm to Jews and Moors the revenues and tithes that belong to them; and they enter churches to apportion the tithes among the contributors, to the great offence and injury of the church. And as by the said laws Jews and Moors are prohibited being collectors of the royal taxes and revenues, with greater reason ought they to be prohibited being farmers and collectors of tithes and other ecclesiastical revenues. Therefore we entreat your highness will be pleased to order that the laws of your kingdoms thereon be observed, and that your high auditors hereafter observe, and do not contrary to their tenor and form. And further, to order and forbid Jews and Moors henceforward to farm, collect, ask, or demand tithes, or any other revenues of the church, or of any other ecclesiastic, and to impose severe penalties for so doing.

To this no answer appears on record.

[1] Arch. Nav. Case 160, No 58.   [2] Pct. 20.

The king found many of the disaffected grandees desirous of deposing him; and a mock deposition was publicly performed at Avila. At the head of these rebellious nobles was the archbishop of Toledo, through whose intrigues the infanta, Donna Isabella, contrary to the wish of the king her brother, had been married to Ferdinand, heir to the crown of Aragon.

Andalusia was deluged with Jewish blood in 1473. The populace sought to exterminate the descendants of Israel. Plunder was their aim. The storm fell alike on those who had received baptism, and on those who remained firm to the religion of their ancestors. The tempest commenced at Cordova. The infuriated mob, without dread of punishment, attacked these miserable people. Those who kept from the tumult, said it was a punishment from God, as many of the converts forsook and apostatised from the Christian religion, which they had previously embraced. Other cities and towns followed the example of Cordova. The storm fell with the greatest violence on Jaen. The constable, Iranza, endeavoured to protect them from injury, and with his soldiery made head against their furious assailants. The mob, enraged at their attempt being frustrated, conspired against him, and assassinated the worthy magistrate while attending mass in the cathedral. Their thirst for revenge and their fury respected nothing; in the most solemn service of Catholic worship, a church was desecrated by murder. The protection afforded the Hebrews served to multiply victims. The laws in their favour tended only to increase conflicts. The Andalusian movement was soon followed by the Castilians. The disaffected and turbulent grandees seized this new pretence to gain their incessant pretensions, as the following event, in 1474, at Segovia, demonstrates.

Don Juan de Pacheco, thinking by intrigue to regain his former favour with Don Henry, planned to dispossess Don Andres de Cabrera (husband of Donna Beatrice de Bobadilla, lady to the Infanta Isabella, and who enjoyed the fullest confidence of the princess) of his command, as governor of the Alcazar of Segovia. To gain his purpose, he seduced many persons of distinction in the city, concerting with them that, under pretence of following the example of those that persecuted the converted Jews, they should shout and arm; and a riot being caused, he would fall on Don Andres, imprison him, and seize the Alcazar. The plan became known, but shortly before it was to take place; Cabrera scarcely had time to prepare himself, and repair to the defence of the converts and city. The rebellion broke out—Segovia was filled with armed men—the houses of the converts were attacked—every thing was destroyed—and every unfortunate descendant of Israel they met was murdered. The massacre would have been immense, had not the governor hastened with a body of troops to arrest the havoc and overawe the rioters. The parties met, the city was strewed with corpses. For a time victory appeared doubtful, but the king's troops fought with the greatest bravery and concert. The slaughter was dreadful. Wherever the conspirators and rioters showed themselves, they were defeated and dispersed; and for once Jewish blood was in a measure avenged, although Pacheco was not punished for causing the riot.

What is inconceivable is, that in the middle of the

fifteenth century, the age of the Marquis de Santillana, Juan de Mena, Jorge Manrique, and Don Henry of Aragon, there should be a Castilian nobleman who, by a cold calculation to suit his ambition and policy, would be ready to immolate numerous families who, by a solemn abjuration, had separated themselves from the Jewish flock; and who, living under the safeguard of the laws, never could have expected such attacks.

The storm was not confined to the Iberian continent. Sicily, which then belonged to the crown of Aragon, became the scene of similar attacks on the Jews. In many cities and towns without any known cause the armed populace like furies committed the most violent outrages; disregarding the orders of the viceroy Don Lope de Urrea, and heedless of the execution of some of the guilty, they murdered many and plundered the houses of this unfortunate people.

Notwithstanding the laws and bulls against Jews practising as physicians, or holding public offices, the following document shews the king continued to employ them:—

To the chief auditors of our lord the king, the apportionment that I, Rabbi Jacob aben Nunes, physician of our lord the king, his chief judge and apportioner of the taxes which the Jewries of his kingdoms and dominions are to pay annually, I make that the said Jews are to pay this year, 1474, for taxes to his highness, 450,000 maravedis. The Jewries of the bishopric of

| | | |
|---|---|---|
| Burgos . . . . 30,800 | Salamanca and Ciudad Rodrigo. . 12,700 |
| Calahora . . . 31,100 | Leon and Astorga . 31,700 |
| Palencia . . . . 54,500 | Zamora . . . . 9,600 |
| Osma . . . . . 19,600 | Plasencia . . . . 56,900 |
| Siguenza . . . 15,500 | Archbishopric of Toledo . . . 64,400 |
| Segovia . . . . 19,500 | The Jews of Andalusia . . . . 59,800 |
| Avila . . . . 39,590 | |

which together amount to 451,000 maravedis,[3] and which the said Jewries are to pay the said lord the king for the said taxes for this present year, 1474, in the manner stated, according to the details written on both sides of four sheets of paper, signed with my name. This appointment made in the city of Segovia. RABBI JACOB ABEN NUNES.

Was it that the Hebrews possessed more integrity, or that they were more exact in collecting the taxes, which induced Henry, in defiance of the laws, and the threats of the confederate representatives, not only to have Jew receivers and collectors of taxes, but likewise that they should style themselves his chief judges? The Jews were more attached to passive gains, more accustomed to bear the insults and odium attached to those offices, and they presented more satisfactory results to the state than the collectors of the cities. The administration of the Jews was to a certain point as necessary in the fifteenth century as it had been in former ages. Henry, notwithstanding his weakness and natural indolence, could not be unacquainted with the state of the public revenues, nor think of forming a new system when he had not time to avoid the persecutions of the turbulent grandees. Other reasons likewise existed why one of the Hebrew nation should apportion the contributions of the Jewries; it was not possible that Christians would have the requisite impartiality to make an equitable and just division. This would have been destroying them at one blow, and would deprive the state of the wealth that contributed to its support and aggrandizement. These two circumstances must have had great weight in the

---

[3] The figures do not agree with the amount stated, owing probably to some typographical error; the difference of 1000 maravedis, Rios supposes to be for the Rabbi or his secretary.

minds of the sovereigns, although sometimes the riots and disturbances compelled them to fail in doing justice, by leaving the massacres of the Jews unpunished. Referring to the apportionment, the great reduction of this contribution will be perceived. In former times it had produced large sums to the public treasury, and was the most certain, from not being subject to the votes of the Cortes, nor the fluctuation of an absurd and frequently contradictory policy, nor the eventual calamities of the country. This diminution may be attributed to the repeated persecutions which induced many to receive baptism, others to emigrate, and the ruin many celebrated Jewries had suffered. Castile at this period contained two hundred and seventeen Jewries. The value of money having more than doubled, the Hebrew population in that kingdom may be estimated from the amount of the tax at between 200,000 and 300,000 of sixteen years and upwards.

On the death of Henry, the cities and fortresses raised the royal standard, and declared in favour of his sister, Donna Isabella, excluding the daughter of his second queen, Donna Juana, Infanta of Portugal, who, from her mother's intimacy with Don Beltran de la Cueva, with the privity of the king, was considered illegitimate. In Henry's lifetime, some grandees, at his desire, swore allegiance to the young Donna Juana, from which they were now absolved by the pontifical legate. Although the Portuguese armed in support of Donna Juana's rights, their defeat at the battle of Toro confirmed the crown to Isabella; and, by the death of his father, Don Juan, in 1479, Ferdinand succeeded to the throne of Aragon, by which the two kingdoms became united under these sovereigns. The union of Castile and Aragon could not fail to produce the most favourable effects for the aggrandisement of Spain and the royal authority, which had hitherto been despised and disregarded. To secure her triumph, and strengthen her party, the queen had been obliged, on ascending the throne, to gratify the ambition of many grandees by honors and presents. The united sovereigns resolved to put an end to the restless feudal anarchy; and, well aware that for the tranquillity of the kingdoms, attacks on the Jews, like those which had taken place at Cordova, Jaen, Valladolid, and other towns, should not be repeated, their efforts were directed to the happiness of their vassals.

They held a cortes at Toledo in 1480, when many laws were enacted for the government of the joint kingdoms. The following regarded the Jews and Moors alone:—

LAW 63.—According to the ancient laws of the kingdoms, our guards of Espinosa were to charge the Jews that came to receive us, twelve maravedis; but, in consideration of the difference of money, it ought to be increased. We therefore ordain and command, that instead of twelve maravedis, they shall have for each book of the law, four reals of plate; and they shall not demand or charge more, under the penalty for those who act contrary, of ten days' imprisonment in irons, and paying twice the amount received, which shall be given to the poor; and if we enter a town twice in a year, this tax is only to be paid the first time.

§ 76.—As great injury and inconvenience results from the constant society of Jews and Moors living intermixed with Christians, we ordain and command, that all Jews and Moors of every city, town, and place in these our kingdoms, whether they are in the royal domains, the seigniories, lordships, abbacies, or belonging to military orders, shall have their distinct and separate Jewries and Moories by themselves, and not reside intermixed with Christians: nor have enclosures together with them; which order shall be executed and fulfilled within two years next following the day these our laws shall be published and proclaimed in our capital. To effect and fulfil which, we intend immediately to appoint trustworthy persons, to make the said separations, indicating the grounds, houses, and sites where they can conveniently reside, and carry on their business with the people. And if in the places so appointed, the Jews have not synagogues, nor the Moors mosques, we order the persons so deputed to appoint as many and as extensive grounds and houses within the said enclosures, whereon the said Jews may erect as many synagogues, and the Moors mosques, as they had in the places they quitted; and the synagogues and mosques they formerly had in those places, are no longer to be used as such. And we hereby give licence and authority to the said Jews and Moors to dispose of, or sell to whomsoever they choose, or pull down, and do what they please with the synagogues and mosques they leave; and to erect and build others of the same dimensions on the sites and grounds that shall be appointed for the purpose, which they may erect and build without hindrance or obstruction, and without incurring, or being liable to any penalty for so doing. And we order, that the persons appointed by our letters for the performance hereof, do compel and sentence the owners of such houses and grounds that may be designated for the erection and building of the said synagogues, mosques, and dwellings, to sell them to the said Jews and Moors at reasonable prices, to be fixed by two persons, one to be named by the Christian owner, and the other by the Jewries, for the grounds required by Jews, and that for Moors by their aljamas; under oath, that they will truly, faithfully, and impartially value them; and the better to effect which, they shall receive every information from the officers of the place if they require it; and if the two do not agree, the said deputy, or deputies, shall meet the parties so sworn, and determine together the value of the houses and grounds. And we order, that the aljamas of the said Jews and Moors use diligence and care, that within the said term of two years they have the houses in the enclosure finished, and dwell therein; and that hereafter they do not reside among Christians, nor any where without the enclosures and places assigned for the said Jewries and Moories, under pain that any Jew or Moor who resides without the said enclosure or barrier, by the act loses all his property, which shall be confiscated to our treasury, and their persons be at our disposal. And any judges may, within their jurisdiction, have them arrested, wherever found, and send them at their expense to our court, that we may order to be done to their persons and property what our pleasure wills. Bonds made in their favor are void. And we order noblemen and commanders of cities, towns, and places of the seigniories, military orders, abbacies, and lordships, that each within their respective places and commanderies, immediately appoint the grounds, houses, and sites for the synagogues, mosques, and dwellings that they may require, so that within the said term of two years the said separation be effected. And that each of the said Jews and Moors live and dwell within their enclosures, under the penalty of such noblemen or commanders forfeiting whatever sums they are in any manner entitled to on our books, or by our grants.

§ 117.—When the Jews come to receive the king, none but the person who carries the book of the law shall wear Taleth, or the cloth, over their clothes, nor in carrying a corpse for interment, are they to wear it, or chaunt in the streets.

In carrying into general effect former laws for confining Jews and Moors in Jewries, their ordinance was equitable and just towards those they had determined should be isolated from the Christian inhabitants. In some towns it was immediately attended to, for in the records of the Town Council of Vittoria, on the 21st February, 1481, mention is made of its extending from the King's bridge to the houses of

Don Solomon and Don Eliezer Tacon, shopkeeper, which had belonged to his father Don Gaon, and is now called the New Street.[4]

Shortly after, that dreaded tribunal, the Inquisition, commenced its sanguinary proceedings, from which may be dated the beginning of the desolation and depopulation of the most fertile and productive state of Europe.

## CHAPTER XXII.

*The Inquisition. — Opposition to its establishment. — Usque's picture of it. — Torquemada. — Llorente's observations on it.—Its Power.—Number of Victims. — Indications of Judaism of the New Christians.— Inscriptions on the Offices at Seville. — Inquisitors of Toledo.—Extracts of Llorente's History of it.*

ALTHOUGH many authors date the introduction of the Inquisition into Spain in the year 1481, it was first founded by a brief of Gregory IX. in 1233, against Heretics generally, but more particularly against the Albigenses; and its administration was entrusted to Dominican friars in Aragon. Jews and Moors were not subject to its jurisdiction, unless verbally or by their writings they induced Catholics to embrace their religion. But when the kingdom of Aragon became united to Castile, by the marriage of Ferdinand with Isabella, he transplanted to his new dominions what may be termed the modern Inquisition; but from the severity

---

[4] Acuerd de Vit. p. 44.

of its statutes and laws it was generally resisted, even by the Aragonese, who had patiently submitted to the yoke of the former. The major part of the officers of state in Aragon were descended from Israelites; they had daughters, sisters, nieces, and other relatives, who would become wives to the first nobles of the kingdom; so that actually they are the ancestors of many grandees of Spain of the present day. By their powerful influence, they engaged the representatives of the nation to appeal to the pope and the king against the introduction of the new Inquisitional code. The resistance of Saragossa where the chief inquisitor, Arbues, was assassinated in the cathedral, extended to nearly all the provinces of Aragon. At Teruel, violent popular tumults were only quelled by the extreme severity of the measures taken by Ferdinand. Similar riots took place at Valencia, and the same rigorous steps were adopted to put them down. In Catalonia, at Barcelona, Lerida, and many other cities, the establishment of the new Inquisition was obstinately opposed. But Ferdinand was bent on enforcing it in his states. It offered an easy mode of replenishing his treasury, by the confiscation of the immense wealth of the Jews, and the advantage of being assisted in the execution of his plan by the Pope. The only obstacle he had to overcome was the repugnance of Isabella to consent to what was proposed to be done in Castile. She would not sanction what was directly opposed to the natural mildness of her disposition; but he was certain of obtaining her consent by alarming her conscience, and making her believe that under the circumstances it was a religious duty; and by the representations of her councillors she was ultimately induced to permit its introduction; and the tribunal thus graphically described by Usque, became firmly established in Castile and Aragon.

They introduced from Rome a ferocious monster, of so strange and hideous a form, that at its name alone all Europe trembled. Its body, covered with scales harder than steel, is formed of rough iron and venomous matter. A thousand wings of black feathers raise it from the ground; it moves on a thousand distorted feet; its countenance partakes of the ferocity of the lion, and the horrid likeness of the serpent of the deserts of Africa. The size of its teeth is that of the strongest elephant. Its breath kills more speedily than the basilisk. Its mouth and eyes incessantly vomit devouring flames; it feeds only on human bodies. The velocity of its flight exceeds that of the eagle. However bright the sun may shine at the time, wherever it passes it causes a sad and fearful obscurity, and leaves in its track a darkness similar to that inflicted on the Egyptians as a plague. Wherever it takes an upward flight, every green thing it treads on, and every leafy tree whereon it rests its feet, it blights and withers. Like a cancerous worm, by its venom it destroys their roots, and leaves every thing within its range desolate as the arid sands of Syria.[1]

The plea for its introduction, was the pretended necessity for punishing the apostasy of the newly converted Spanish Jews; but Judaism was only the pretext for the establishment of the Inquisition by Ferdinand V. The real motive of this extraordinary measure, was to put in force a system of confiscation against the Jews, that would make all their wealth fall into the hands of government; while Sextus IV. had no other design, than to realise the project so cherished by the Roman See, of extending its authority.

The blood-thirsty Torquemada and his successors

[1] Consolaçaõ, etc.

rendered it a terror to all Spain. No one was safe from its baneful influence; for not only Jews, Moors, and converts from the Mosaic and Mahomedan creeds fell under its colossal power, but even their descendants were declared base and infamous. It will not appear less unjust than cruel, that a family should be deprived of the consideration it enjoys, merely because its ancestors were Jews. Yet Llorente asserts,

That the Arias Davila, counts of Pugnorostro, are among them in the male line, and nearly all the grandees of Spain from the female. The Spaniards only began to boast of not being of Jewish descent, when the policy of the Inquisition made it to be regarded as dangerous and humiliating to have such an origin. All Spaniards are descended either from idolatrous Pagans, Mahometan Moors, or Israelites. The least honourable of these origins is exactly that which the capriciousness of our ideas makes us prefer to the others. I allude to the former. Is it not known that idolators, not content with worshipping false divinities, despite of reason and humanity, offered human sacrifices to them, while Mahometans and Jews acknowledge an only God, the true Creator of the universe, and never degraded human nature, by immolating their fellow-creatures to false deities? It required an institution like the holy office, so completely to denaturalise the light of natural reason, the empire and action of which are of such incontestable utility for the government of human society.[2]

No one was beyond its reach. Royal princes, ministers of state, nobles, archbishops, bishops, and even persons subsequently canonised, were persecuted by it. The dead were not suffered to rest in peace. The bodies of those suspected of heresy were exhumed and burnt, for the purpose of robbing the heirs of the property, as unless they could prove the innocence of the accused, confiscation was the consequence.

[2] Preface.

Instances have occurred where men have been forced to refund the dowries received with their wives, from the father-in-law having been declared guilty of heresy before the marriage of the daughter; for it was difficult, if not impossible, to rebut secret accusations, the accused being informed neither who were the accusers, nor the act he was accused of. It was sufficient for a converted Jew to die rich, for them to endeavour to raise suspicions of his faith and religion, so great was the ill-will towards the descendants of Jews, and the wish of persecuting them, thereby to enrich themselves by their spoils, as one-third of the confiscated property went to the Inquisition, a third to defray the expenses of the trial, and a third to the king. Tortures of the most barbarous description often extorted the confession of crimes the innocent sufferers had not committed. The Castilians, although not as violent as the Aragonese, were equally as averse to the establishment of the Inquisition, for when the inquisitors arrived at Seville, and exhibited their commission and the king's orders, they could neither procure the small number of persons, nor any other assistance they required to commence their operations. The council of the sovereigns issued a new order from Medina del Campo to the authorities of Seville and the diocese of Cadiz, to assist the inquisitors to install themselves, and enter on their office, yet the order of the king was interpreted as only affecting the inhabitants of cities and towns belonging to the royal domains, whereupon many of the new Christians removed to those of the duke of Medina Sidonia, the marquis of Cadiz, the count d'Arcos, and other noblemen. This voluntary exile induced the inquisitors, ever thirsting for prey, to obtain an ordinance from the king against the emigrants. The new tribunal declared that the fact of their emigration almost convicted them of heresy, in seeking by flight to avoid the surveillance and authority of the Inquisition. The first act of its jurisdiction after its installation at the Dominican convent of St. Paul, at Seville, was to publish an edict, stating that from the information which they had received of the emigration of the new Christians, they ordered the marquis of Cadiz, the count d'Arcos, dukes, marquises, counts, knights, grandees of Spain, and other noblemen of the kingdom of Castile, to seize their persons within the term of fifteen days, and to send them under escort to Seville, and to sequestrate their property, under pain of excommunication of those who do not conform to the order, besides the other penalties they would in justice incur as abettors of heresy, particularly confiscation of their property, and the loss of their titles, offices, and rights as nobles; from which it will be seen, that it was no sooner installed than it commenced its encroachments on the civil and royal power.

During the eighteen years that Torquemada was inquisitor-general, the number of victims is stated by cotemporary historians to have been as follows:—

10,220 burnt alive.
6,860 burnt in effigy, persons who were dead or had escaped.
97,321 who were declared infamous, and excluded from public honourable offices, and punished by confiscation of their property and perpetual imprisonment.

114,401

Thus making more than a hundred thousand murdered and sacrificed under the cloak of religion. What profanation of the sacred name of that which is the consolation of every faith!

Exclusive of the victims, how many, from the ties of relationship or friendship, participated in the misfortunes of those condemned, when the following edict for the supposed apostasy of the new Christians was declared imperative on every Catholic, to denounce them to the holy office, under pain of incurring themselves the liability of an inquisitorial prosecution? Dread of so cruel a tribunal, and in many instances private animosity (as the accuser's name was always an inviolable secret), led to the butchery of numerous innocent individuals.

1. When a Jew who has been baptized, expects the Messiah, or says he has not come.

2. When having been regenerated by baptism, he again embraces Judaism.

3. If he says the law of Moses is as efficacious for salvation as Christianity.

4. If he put on better or cleaner clothes than usual on Saturdays, or a clean tablecloth on his table.

5. If he washes the blood from meat, or extracts the prohibited parts from it.

6. If he examines the knife before slaying an animal, or covers the blood.

7. If unnecessarily he eats meat during Lent, and believes he may do it without offending God.

8. If he observes the fast of atonement, a proof of which is, if he seeks and asks forgiveness of those he may have offended, or puts his hands on his children's heads to bless them, without making the sign of the cross.

9. If he observe the feast of Esther.

10. If he fasts on the 9th of Ab in commemoration of the destruction of the two Temples.

11. If he observes the feasts prescribed by the law of Moses.

12. If he celebrates the Passover by eating bitter herbs and lettuces.

13. If he observes the feast of Tabernacles by placing green boughs in his house, or sending or receiving presents of eatables from Jews.

14. If he lights extra lights at the feast of Dedication.

15. If he says grace after meals like the Jews.

16. If he had drunk wine made by Jews.

17. If he says grace before meals in the same manner as Jews.

18. If he uses meat slain by Jews.

19. If he eats the same meats as Jews, or has sat at their table.

20. If he recites the Psalms of David without saying " *Gloria patri*" at the end.

21. If a female fail going to church forty days after childbirth.

22. If he has had his son circumcised.

23. If he has given him a Hebrew name, such as Jews bear.

24. If, after baptising his children, the new Christian has the part of the head washed that received the holy unction.

25. If in marrying he observes the rites prescribed by the Mosaical law.

26. If he invites his relations and friends to a repast the day before undertaking a voyage.

27. If he carries about him certain names used by the Jews.

28. If when making bread he takes a piece of the dough and burns it in sign of an oblation.

29. If while dying he turns towards the wall, or any one places him so.

30. If he washes, or has a corpse washed with warm water.

31. If he pronounce praises or recites lamentations over the dead.

32. If in sign of mourning he eats fish and olives instead of meat.

33. If he empties vessels containing water in his house, or in the neighbourhood, where a death takes place.

34. If he has a corpse interred in virgin ground or the Jew's Cemetery.

It is no wonder, where such means were employed, that the prisons were soon found to be too small for the number of victims; we therefore find that in the first year of its establishment it was removed to the Chateau de Triana, when the following inscription in barbarous Latin was shortly after engraved.

The holy office of the inquisition established against the wickedness of heretics, commenced at Seville in the year 1481, under the Pontificate of Sextus IV., who granted, and in the reign of Ferdinand and Isabella, who had asked for it. The first Inquisitor-general was Friar Thomas de Torquemada, prior of the convent of Santa Cruz, of Segovia, of the order of the preaching brotherhood. God grant that for the propagation and maintenance of the faith it may last until the end of ages. "Arise, O Lord, be judge in thy cause. Catch the foxes for us."[3]

Not blushing at the horrors it committed in the name of a religion that preaches "peace and goodwill to all mankind," and to perpetuate the remembrance of them, the following inscription appeared on the magnificent palace of the Inquisition erected at Seville.

In the year of the Lord 1481, under the Pontificate of Sextus IV., and in the reign of Ferdinand V. and Isabella, sovereigns of the Spains, and the two Sicilies, the holy office of the inquisition against Judaising Heretics, commenced in this place for the exaltation of the faith; where, from the expulsion of the Jews and Moors until the year 1524, under the reign of Charles, emperor of the Romans, successor to those two sovereigns by maternal right, and the most reverend Don Alphonso Manrique, archbishop of Seville, being inquisitor-general, upwards of twenty-thousand heretics have abjured their criminal errors, and more than one thousand

[3] Zuniga's Ann of Seville.

persisting in heresy have been delivered to the flames, after having been tried according to law with the approbation and favour of Innocent VIII., Alexander VI., Pius III., Julius II., Leo. X., Adrian VI. (who was raised to the Pontificate, while cardinal governor of Spain, and inquisitor-general), and Clement VII. The Licentiate de la Cueva has had this inscription (which was composed by Diego de Cartagena, archdeacon of Seville) placed here by order, and at the expense of our master, the emperor, in the year of the Lord 1524.

In 1486, the inquisitors of Toledo compelled the rabbins of the synagogues to declare the converts that had returned to Judaism. They condemned 750 to walk barefoot, in their shirts, carrying a lighted taper, through an immense crowd; 1,700 were condemned to other penalties, and 27 were burned alive.[4]

The Inquisition soon attempted to defy the royal authority; for Torquemada, in 1488, issued a provisional order to the treasurer of the holy office, not to pay the royal orders until the salaries of its officers and the expenses of the tribunal were liquidated;[5] and had the insolence to write to Ferdinand to sanction it, which he refused.

The vacillating and avaricious conduct of the court of Rome greatly aggravated the sufferings of the converts: it sold them, at enormous prices, protection against the Inquisition; but on the representations of Ferdinand and Torquemada, they were no sooner given than they were revoked; but the expenses they had cost were not returned.

Llorente, who had been secretary to the Inquisition, and has published the best history of it extant, says,—

The conduct of the holy office will be acknowledged to have

[4] Llorente.     [5] Ibid.

been one of the principal causes that has reduced the population of Spain, by the expulsion of the Jews and Moors, forcing innumerable families, at all periods, to quit the kingdoms; immolating on its scaffolds, in the space of three centuries, upwards of 300,000 persons. Thus, by a blind zeal for religion, arresting the progress of the arts, of industry, and of commerce, which would have constituted the glory and happiness of the nation.[6]

Speaking of the Jews, he writes:—

I know not what confidence the proofs alleged of the crimes the Jews were accused of merit. But admitting that there was a foundation for believing them to be true, it was quite unnecessary to banish all the Jews from the kingdom. Religion and policy rendered it a duty to treat them with mildness, and to grant to their good conduct the esteem that was not refused to Christians; at the same time they might have punished those who were guilty, the same as Spaniards convicted of murder or any other crime. The contempt and bad treatment with which Christians loaded them, naturally would lead them to vengeance, and instil in them a deep hatred against their persecutors. In adopting a different policy towards the Jews, they would not have been long in making them new men, and like their descendants, at present established in the various states of Europe, have become useful, good, and peaceable citizens, by being neither debased nor persecuted.[7]

Notwithstanding, it appears that until the expulsion the Jews were not all molested by the Inquisition; for Abarbanel, who shortly after its establishment went to Castile, states, that he was astonished at the power of the Castilian Hebrews, and the grandeur of the law, and applied to them the verse of David; "There thrones of judgment are set, thrones for the house of David."[8]

[6] Llorente's Preface.  [7] Llorente, vol. i. p. 259.  [8] Psa. cxxii. 5.

## CHAPTER XXIII.

*Employed in Public Offices. — Town Council of Vittoria. — Appeal of the Jews. — Cortes of Tafalla. — Learned men. — Don Isaac Abarbanel and his sons. — Donna Leonora of Toledo, wife of Cosmo de Medici, educated by Benvenida Abarbanel.*

THE conjoint sovereigns, like their predecessors, continued to employ Jews to collect their taxes. It is on record that Ben Aroyo, the collector, asked and received from the town council of Vittoria, letters to the authorities for some business he had to transact at Soria,[1] the 9th November, 1481.

On the 22d May, 1482, a Jew named Barzelai being confined in the public prison of Vittoria, but it is not stated for what crime, the attorney general, Inigo Perez de Orosco, required the alcalde, Garcia Martinez de Estella, to try the cause without delay, to prevent any disturbance in the city. The council ordered him, under a fine, to decide it before the following Saturday; but neither the crime nor the sentence is recorded. At the same meeting, the council ordered him, under a similar fine, to publish that no Christian female should enter the Jewry, fixing various penalties for so doing.[2]

To prevent interruption to service, on the 28th August the town council ordered—

That no Jew or Jewess, during the performance of mass,

[1] Acuerdos de Vit. p. 69.   [2] Ibid. 81.

should presume to enter the monastery of San Francisco, its porticoes, or cloisters, under the penalty of 600 maravedis for each time, to be applied to the paving and repairing of the walls of the city of Vittoria; and ordered it to be publicly proclaimed in the said city.[3]

On the 3rd September is found the following record:

Eliezer Tello, a Jew, for himself and in behalf of Don Eleazer Chacon, and Moses Balid, each for their share as sequestrators and depositaries, of 14,900 maravedis, received by the collector of Trevino, Juan Martinez de Arratia, and 575 maravedis from Diego de Onateguy, which the receiver and the said Jews had received, bind themselves to deliver and refund to the council of the said city.

This shews that Christian receivers deposited what they received with Jews.

On the 23rd October, the alcaldes, aldermen, the attorney general, Juan Martinez de Alava, and the members of the council, resolved and ordered, that the following ordinances and proclamations should be published in the city and its Jewry:—

We resolve, ordain, and command, that no Christian woman or girl above ten years of age, is to enter or walk, either by day or night, in the Jewry of this city, without a male companion upwards of fourteen years old, under the penalty of 60 maravedis, half for the informer, and half for the justice of the city; and the culprit shall besides be imprisoned nine days.

Further, that no Christian female, whether accompanied or not, shall presume to light fires, or cook for Jews in their houses on Saturdays, or any other days, under pain of fifty lashes; and the Jew that permits it in his house shall be fined 200 maravedis for each time.[4]

As soon as it was published, the Jewry and individual Jews announced that they appealed to the

[3] Acuerdos de Vit. p. 87.   [4] Ibid. vol. i., p. 101.

deputation and the proper authorities against the ordinance respecting Saturdays. The result of the appeal is not stated.

The Cortes held at Tafalla, in Navarre, issued an ordinance in this year,—

That on holidays Jews should not quit the Jewries, nor walk in the streets among Christians, until after mass, except physicians and surgeons to visit the sick.

In the latter part of 1484, there appears on the records of the town council of Vittoria, the following, dated 5th November[5]:—

Resolved at this meeting, that whereas some persons desiring the welfare of Christians, state that some Christians, acting contrary to justice and the laws of these kingdoms, weary and injure themselves more in expenses, by empowering and authorising Jews to read the sentences of ecclesiastical courts, so as to make them charges, even without incurring expense, or pursuing the regular process, charging them expenses, and not following up the case: we order, that no Christian empower or give the said sentences to Jews to read; nor are the said Jews to accept such charge, under pain of such Christian paying a fine of 1000 maravedis; and such Jew incurs the penalty of 2000 maravedis for each time, and loses the costs he would thereby derive, and all the expenses he may have incurred, which we order to be published in the court and Jewry of this city.

On the 26th November and 10th December, Don Eleazar Chacon, Don Samuel Aben Nunez, and Eliezer Tello, appealed to the town council to appoint judges, to try the suits they had instituted against Guizon de Vetonez; which, according to law, they did.[6]

On the 26th June, 1485, the council ordered the following to be published in the city:—

[5] Arch. Nav. Case 164, No. 128.   [6] Acuerdos de Vit. vol. 1, p. 162.

That no person shall presume to enter the streets of the Jewry to sell fruit, vegetables, or any eatable, grass, or green barley; but they may carry them to the gate of the Jewry, but are not to enter within it, under pain of losing what they so carry for sale, and further incur a fine of 24 maravedis, half to be for the informer, and half for the paving of the city.

Furthermore, no woman or girl shall presume to enter the streets of the said Jewry for anything they may require, without a man accompanying her, until she leaves the street, under the same penalty and three days' imprisonment; and no Jew is otherwise to admit her into his house, under the penalty of five hundred maravedis, besides being imprisoned for nine days.

Furthermore, no Christian women or girls are to hire themselves by the day, to any Jew or Jewess, under the said penalty of twenty-four maravedis and three days' imprisonment.

On the day these ordinances were published in the city, David Chacon, in the name of the Jewry demanded a copy, that they might appeal against them to the deputation: it was ordered to be furnished to him.[7]

From this it would appear, that the former ordinance respecting females not entering the Jewry had not been attended to. The appeal, in this instance, would lead to the supposition that the former had been successful.

These acts, probably, are those alluded to by Pulgar (the private secretary of the queen), in a letter to the cardinal of Spain, intimating that the queen was displeased at certain municipal ordinances against the Jews in Guipuscoa.

At a meeting held 20th July, there is a notice (but without stating the cause), that Jacob Tello had been condemned to the loss of half his property[8] and;

---

[7] Acuerdos de Vit. vol. i., p. 2076.   [8] Ibid. p. 182.

a record of 16th September, that Dr. Abraham, the physician of the city, gave notice that he abandoned the law-suit he had pending with Martin Gonsalez.[9]

The Jews of Spain, notwithstanding these vexations and the persecutions they had suffered, continued to cultivate learning, in which their brethren in Portugal also joined. In that kingdom, none of the sanguinary scenes that disgrace the annals of Spain had yet been acted. Among the many distinguished writers of this period, the major part of whom became exiles at the general expulsion from those kingdoms, may be enumerated:—

R. JOSEPH BEN SHEM TOB—born in 1420, a philosopher and jurist; was deeply versed in the Talmud and Arabic; he wrote a philosophical work under the title of "Superior Knowledge," "The glory of God," on the excellence of man, and the law of Moses. He also wrote an Arabic commentary on "Aristotle's Ethics."

R. DON DAVID BEN SOLOMON JACHIA—born at Lisbon, in 1430, where he died in 1465, a grammarian, poet, and Talmudist of repute; has left a grammatical work with the title of "The Tongue of the Erudite." His son Jacob finished his "Praise of David," a philosophical Talmudical work.

R. ABRAHAM SALOM—a native of Catalonia, born 1430, wrote a dogmatical work, connecting the divine with the human; under the title of "The Habitation of Peace."

R. ISAAC ABOAB—born in 1432, in Castile, succeeded R. Isaac Campanton, as chief of the Jews in Spain; he was a jurist, philosopher, and theologian; his profound learning procured him the esteem of John II. of Portugal, to which kingdom he retired at the expulsion, where he died six months after. He wrote a highly moral work, entitled "The Candlestick of Light;" "The River Pishon;" sermons; and a commentary on the Pentateuch.

[9] Acuerdos de Vit. vol. i., p. 187.

R. DON ISAAC ABARBANEL — the greatest and most illustrious man of the Hebrew people of this period and age, was born at Lisbon in 1437. He states, in his commentary on Zechariah, that his family settled in Spain, shortly after the destruction of the first Temple, and claims to be of the royal house of David. He was a great favourite and the confidant of Alphonso V., who was entirely guided by his advice. To avoid the fate the friends of that monarch experienced from his successor, John II., by the timely notice of a friend, when he was sent for to the palace he fled to Castile, abandoning his immense property, which the king confiscated. He there established a bank, and jointly with Abraham Senior farmed the royal revenues, by which he soon repaired his broken fortune. In 1484, he was summoned to the court of Ferdinand and Isabella, in whose service he was employed until the expulsion in 1492, which he endeavoured in vain to avert. On quitting Spain, he repaired to Naples, where he was kindly received by Ferdinand, to whom he rendered important services. Charles VIII. of France, on the death of that monarch, invaded Italy. Alphonso II., who had succeeded his father as king of Naples, fled to Sicily, whither Abarbanel accompanied him, and remained with the unfortunate monarch until his death. On the demise of that sovereign he retired to Corfu, and ultimately to Venice. The senate, knowing his abilities as a statesman, employed him to negotiate a treaty respecting the spice trade with Portugal. He died in that city in 1508, beloved and esteemed by all who knew him. Notwithstanding his political occupations in the service of so many sovereigns, and constant troubles, his inexhaustible mind enabled him to write many works. His language is pure and elegant, and so impressive, that popes forbade his commentaries on Isaiah being read by Jews. He was so quick a writer, that in fifteen days he completed his commentary on Joshua, and in seventy-two those on the books of Samuel and Kings. During his residence of ten years in Castile, his intimate friendship with R. Isaac Aboab, assisted him greatly in the study of the law. His works are, besides his valuable commentaries on the Pentateuch, and the Early and Later Prophets, from which are gathered the principal incidents of his eventful life; " The Paschal Sacrifice," an account of Passover ceremonies; " The Works of God," on the creation, and impugning the doctrine of the world's eternity; " The Proclaimer of Salvation," explanatory of the prophets; " The Inheritance of the Fathers," on their ethics; " The Crown of the Elders," on the promises to the fathers; " The Head of Faith," on the Jewish creed; answers to questions propounded by R. Saul Cohen, on some passages of Maimonides' Guide; " The Salvation of His Anointed," an exposition of the sayings of the ancient rabbis respecting the Messiah; " Assemblage of the Prophets," on the prophets; " The Vision of the Almighty," on the different degrees of prophecy; " The Days of the World," relating all the calamities the Jews had suffered until his time; " The Justice of the Worlds," on the creation, the new year, the day of atonement, Paradise, hell, the resurrection, and future rewards and punishments; " The New Heavens," on the creation, and elucidating chap. xix. b. 2, of Maimonides' Guide. Some minor tracts are also attributed to him.

R. JUDAH BEN JOSEPH - of Saragossa, where he was born in 1440, much esteemed for his talmudical knowledge. He wrote a commentary on the affirmative precepts, and two treatises, one on " Mourning," and another on " Unclean Animals."

R. GALAB—a native of Lerida, in Catalonia, born about 1445, was highly considered for his literary talents, medical abilities, and proficiency in the Latin language, in which he wrote a work entitled *Antedotarium*.

R. ABRAHAM BIBAS—born in Aragon, in 1447, was a theologian, philosopher, physician, and jurist. He wrote a philosophical work, entitled " The Book of Demonstration;" " The Tree of Life," also philosophical; a medical one, with the title of " Medical Collections;" " The High Road of Faith," on faith; and some sermons.

R. Jacob — His son wrote a commentary on the Talmudical Tales.

R. Samuel ben Habib — also of Aragon, was a philosopher, physician, and poet of repute. He studied under R. Abraham Bibas, and has immortalised his name by his Hebrew poems.

R. Jacob ben Habib — born in 1450, a celebrated jurist, theologian, and cabalist of Aragon, was one of the exiles at the expulsion from Spain. He wrote some talmudical works under the titles of " The Fountain of Jacob," or " The Fountain of Israel;" " The House of Israel," which at his death not being completed, was finished by his son R. Levi, who also wrote some solutions to questions.

R. Solomon ben Virga — an historian, talmudist, physician, and astronomer of great repute, born about 1450. He composed some astronomical tables. His historical work, " The Sceptre of Judah," is highly esteemed, and has been translated into Latin, Spanish, Portuguese, and German. His Practice of Medicine was greatly approved.

R. Abraham Sabah — born at Lisbon in 1450, which he quitted at the expulsion in 1497, having returned, at the risk of his life, to Portugal, to endeavour to obtain permission for his brethren to return to that kingdom; he died there in 1509. He was a celebrated cabalistical commentator. His " Bundle of Myrrh" is on the Pentateuch, and his " Bundle of Silver" on the five rolls.

R. Isaac Caro — born at Toledo, but in what year is not known, was a cotemporary of the foregoing. In 1492 he quitted his native city and went to Portugal, but was obliged in 1498 to depart that kingdom. In his voyage from Lisbon to the Holy Land he lost his wife, children, and books by shipwreck. He was an able expositor, jurist, and cabalist. He wrote a commentary on the Pentateuch, under the title of " The Generations of Isaac."

R. Isaac Arama — a native of Zamora, was also a cotemporaneous philosopher, theologian, expositor, and one of the most able Talmudists of his time; he was among the exiles in 1492. His " Ligation of Isaac" is a philosophical commentary on the ancient Rabbinical writers, in opposition to the Grecian philosophy; a " Commentary on the Five Rolls;" he wrote also " The Heavy Vision," impugning the dogmas of catholicism.

R. ISAAC BEN JOSEPH — was likewise a cotemporary professor of philosophy and medicine in Castile; he wrote a commentary on Maimonides' Guide.

R. VIDAL CASLARI — was at this period an eminent physician in Catalonia.

R. DON DAVID BEN JOSEPH JACHIA — born at Lisbon in 1465, where he was highly esteemed for his learning by Alphonso V. On the expulsion from Portugal, he retired to Italy and settled at Imola; the fame of his abilities as a philosopher, grammarian, and poet, induced the Jews of Naples to invite him to become their chief, which post he occupied for twenty-two years, when he returned to Imola, where he died in 1541.

R. DAVID VIDAL — a celebrated talmudist, physician, musician, and poet, born at Toledo in 1467, where he successfully practised medicine. He wrote an exposition of the precepts under the title of " The Crown of the Law," and another on " The Thirteen Articles of the Creed."

R. ABRAHAM ZACUT — born at Salamanca, and professor of astronomy at Saragossa, and which he had also taught in his native city and at Carthagena; on quitting Spain in 1492 he went to Lisbon, where he was appointed astronomer and historiographer to the king, Don Emanuel. On the banishment of the Jews from Portugal he retired to Tunis. His historical work, " The Book of Genealogies," is the best Hebrew work of the kind. He also wrote an astronomical and an astrological work, a perpetual almanac, and " Sweet to the Soul," on the future state and separation of the soul from the body.

R. JOSHUA BEN JOSEPH A LEVI — born at Toledo in 1467,

where after a persecution he lived under the protection of Don Vidal; being profoundly versed in the Guemara, he wrote rules for understanding it.

R. ISAAC ALHADAHEF — of Aragon; a mathematician and Talmudist, highly esteemed for his learning and works; which are—" The Plain Road," a mathematical work; " The Work of the Artificer," on arithmetic; and, " The Golden Tongue," an explanation of scriptural measures.

R. HASDAI KRESKAS — a native of Saragossa; a profound moral philosopher and Arabic scholar, from which language he translated into Hebrew a moral work of Abumat Algazel, and a philosophical one of an unknown author; he also wrote a treatise on " The Transmigration of Souls."

R. MOSES BEN HABIB — a native of Lisbon, and member of its academy; a talented grammarian, philosopher, and theologian. He wrote three grammatical works, entitled, " Pleasant Paths;" " Medicine of the Tongue;" and, " The Flower of the Lily;" " The Camp of God," a philosophical and theological work; a biblical commentary, and another on Hapenini's " Examination of the World."

R. JOSEPH GUIKATILLA — born in Castile, which he quitted at the expulsion. He was much esteemed for his literary acquirements, good qualities, and profound Cabalistical learning, on which subject he wrote six works, and a theological commentary on the passover service.

R. JOSEPH HIVAN — a native of Lisbon. His commentaries on Proverbs, Psalms, the Prophets, and the Ethics of the Fathers, are much esteemed.

R. DON JUDAH ABARBANEL — son of Don Isaac, was born at Lisbon. He accompanied his father in all his peregrinations, and ultimately settled at Genoa, where he practised medicine with great repute. He was a profound philosopher, and an excellent poet. His " Philography, or Dialogues of Love," is translated into most European languages; he also wrote some poems in honour of his father; an elegy on his death; and a poem of 130 stanzas, descriptive of the vicissitudes of his life, and containing exhortations to his son. He is commonly styled "The Hebrew Lion."

R. DON JOSEPH ABARBANEL,—second son of Don Isaac, after the expulsion, accompanied his father, and settled at Ferrara, where he practised as a physician.

DON SAMUEL ABARBANEL,—third son of the minister, whom R. Abraham Usque styles Trismegistus (thrice great), for he was great in learning, great in liberality, and had great means for being charitable. He established a house of commerce at Naples, and is said to have possessed 200,000 sequins of gold. His wealth was employed in assisting the indigent, redeeming captives, and giving dowers to poor orphan girls. His house is represented as having been a school for the virtuous—a hospital for the poor—and a refuge for the unfortunate. His wife, Donna Benvenida, was a pattern of piety, virtue, and prudence. The viceroy, Don Pedro de Toledo, placed his daughter, Donna Leonora (who was afterwards married to the grand duke of Tuscany, Cosmo de Medicis) under her care and tuition: the princess always styled and treated her as a mother. Donna Benvenida procured the most distinguished ladies of Naples to interest themselves with Charles V. to obtain the recall of her exiled people. The emperor was inclined to grant the request, but was dissuaded.

R. JACOB BERAB—at the expulsion went from Spain to Saphet, where he was appointed chief rabbi. He wrote solutions to questions and rules for understanding the style of the Prophets, under the title of " A Collection of Lilies."

R. JACOB CASTILE—born at Alcala la Real, was an eminent surgeon. He translated from Latin into Hebrew a surgical work of one Brunon.

R. JACOB MANTENU—born at Tortosa, in 1490, was taken by his parents, at the expulsion, to Venice. Under the instruction of his father, he became profoundly versed in jurisprudence, medicine, philosophy, and languages. He obtained a great reputation by his translations into Latin of Maimonides' Guide, and his Preface to the Mishna, Avicenna's general principles for the cure of pains in the head, and other versions of Maimonides, Plato, Aristotle, and Averroes, on physics, metaphysics, and jurisprudence. He practised medicine with great success at Venice; from whence he went to Rome, and was appointed first physician to Paul III.

R. MEIR ARAMA—son of R. Isaac Arama, wrote "Illustrations of Psalms," and "Illustrations of Job."

R. JOSEPH JACHIA,—son of R. Don David, born in 1494, at Lisbon, which he quitted with his parents for Italy, and was head of the congregation of Imola for many years. He commented on the Pentateuch, and wrote three Talmudical works. He died in 1539, leaving three sons, R. David, R. Guedaliah, author of "The Chain of Tradition," a historical work; and R. Judah, doctor of medicine and arts, at Padua.

BONPOS BONFIL—a native of Barcelona, was a celebrated physician, philosopher, and linguist. He translated into Hebrew Boetius' "*Consolationæ Philosophiæ;*" from the Arabic, "Esop's Fables;" and from the Greek, "*Pathologia et Hygienes ex Galeno,*" and "The Books of Hippocrates."

## CHAPTER XXIV.

*War of Granada.—Assistance rendered by the Jews.— Four Hundred and Fifty Captives redeemed by Abraham Senior.— Improbable Accusations.—Overcharge of Taxes refunded. — Fall of Granada.—The Edict of Banishment.*

ON peace being concluded with Portugal, Ferdinand resolved to avenge the insolent answer to his demand for the arrears of tribute due by Granada to the crown of Castile and Leon. The capture of Zahara by Muley Hassan, afforded him the excuse for commencing a war against the last Moorish kingdom of Spain, and driving the crescent from the Iberian soil. Yet notwithstanding the heroism and bravery displayed, the undertaking might have failed without the assistance of the Jews. During the warlike preparations they were left quiet and unmolested in their Jewries, peaceably occupied in their customary occupations and trade. While this war absorbed the general attention, and every one was earnestly engaged in preparations for it, the Jews, although they did not arm, were eminently useful. The immense permanent armies required providers, whose capitals should be employed in advancing money to procure provisions and supplies. This kind of commerce was a species of speculation the Jews had constantly entered into. Their wealth was every where expended in purchasing provisions, not without the hope of profiting by their enormous sacrifices. Thus the co-operation of the Jews was necessary and expedient for the success and hopes of the Catholic sovereigns, and the whole nation; and although Christians did not regard the Hebrew people kindly, their rancour towards them was suspended for a time. The Jews constantly followed the Christian armies, supplying their wants, and thus rendering most important services to the cause of Christendom. Ferdinand had declared that he would pick one by one the seeds from " The Pomegranate" *(Granada)*. After experiencing some reverses and checks, in 1485 he began to accomplish his promise. Zahara was retaken by assault; Cartama,

Coin, Ronda, Cambil, Alhabar, and Zalea, all fortresses of the greatest importance, fell under the empire of the Cross. In the following years, the same fate befell Loja, Higora, Morbrin, Velez Malaga, and Malaca, with many other castles and fortresses, on which the banners of Castile triumphantly floated over the crescent.

On the taking of Malaga, some Christians were found who had embraced Mahomedanism. Ferdinand had them burnt; and some baptised Jews, who had returned to the religion of their forefathers, with a refinement of cruelty he had impaled alive. Four hundred and fifty Moorish Jews, mostly women, found in the city, were ransomed for 20,000 doblas of gold, by the generosity of Abraham Senior, the wealthy contractor of Castile. They were taken away in two armed galleys.[1]

During the long and obstinate siege of Baza, nothing was wanting to the Castilian army. Not only were the necessaries of life abundant, but even those of luxury and convenience. Owing to the zeal and foresight of the Catholic queen, under the protection of convoys, and attracted by interest, traders and artificers from all parts repaired to this military mart, where, in a short time, they established warehouses for every description of goods, and workshops for various manufactures. Armourers manufactured those sumptuous helmets and splendid cuirasses, that were the ornament and pride of the Christian knights; saddlers and embroiderers made saddles glittering with gold and silver; traders' shops abounded with valuable cloths, brocades, fine linen, and tapestry; in

---

[1] Bernaldez MS.

short, every thing that could gratify the taste of youth, inclined to magnificence and grandeur.[2]

Thus had the Jews served the cause of the Catholic sovereigns. The camp experienced no scarcity; convoys arrived and departed at their stated times; the price of provisions, and even of articles of luxury, remained unchanged, laying the foundation for a new city in the midst of the Vega, to establish more commodious dwellings and shops.

In 1491, the following incredible tale was propagated by the monks:—At La Guardia, a village about nine leagues from Toledo, some Jews of that place, Quintanar and Tembleque, agreed to make a spell with a Host and the heart of a young boy, for the purpose of poisoning Christians, particularly the inquisitors, and to cause them to die raving mad. They stole a boy three or four years old and carried him to a neighbouring cavern, where after severely flogging they crucified him, then they took out the heart and buried the body in a vineyard at a short distance. They purchased a Host from the sacristan of La Guardia, which together with the heart was reduced to a powder, and sent to the celebrated synagogue of Zamora. One Benedict de las Mesuras had put some of the powder between the leaves of a prayer-book he used; going to church with it one day, a person noticed a radiance proceed from the leaves of the book, and informed the inquisitors; their officials discovered the plot, all the accused were put to the torture, condemned, and burnt at Avila. Neither the heart nor the body of the child was found, but the Host being discovered was

[2] Rios.

carried in solemn procession to the monastery of St. Thomas. An old Christian of Tembleque, named Fernando de Ribera, was taken up in 1521, for being concerned in this affair; he denied the accusation, but acknowledged that he had embraced Judaism and followed the law of Moses. Such were the tales fabricated by monks to inflame the minds of the people against the descendants of Israel! The credulity of the deluded populace appears astonishing in the present age. In July of this year (1491), the Jews of Vittoria complained that they had been overcharged in the assessment of 1489. It was ordered that the surcharge should be deducted from the amount to be paid on the present year.[3] And on the 20th it was resolved that the gates of the Jewry should be repaired, the expense to be paid from the city funds; and that the said Jews should close the back part of the Jewry from the Calle de la Pintoreria, at the expense of the owners of the houses and lands, by Michaelmas next, under the penalty of five thousand maravedis.[4]

The municipality condemned Moses Balid, chief of the Jews at Vittoria, to pay a fine of a dobla of gold for disrespect, in using insulting expressions to some persons of the tower, at a meeting on the preceding Friday.[5]

After a protracted siege and brave defence, the city of Granada capitulated, and the Catholic sovereigns added to their dominions the last Moorish Kingdom of Spain. The sun of the 2nd January, 1492, was the last that saw the crescent float over the Iberian soil, where it had shone with such splendour for nearly eight centuries. The internal dissensions that reigned among the Moorish princes had greatly contributed

[3] Acuerdos de Vit. vol. i., 421*b*.   [4] Ibid. p. 422*b*.   [5] Ibid. p. 423*b*.

to the success of the arms of Ferdinand and Isabella. Elated with the conquest, and instigated by the Inquisition, they resolved that Spain should no longer afford an asylum, nor its soil be polluted by the tread of any one not professing the Catholic religion. Those whose ancestors had resided in it, from time immemorial, were doomed by a fanatic zeal and insatiable avarice to be banished for ever from the happy scenes of their youth, the graves of their dearest ties, the land they had cultivated, and the country they had enlightened by their learning and talents in ages of darkness and ignorance. Regardless of every consideration, their blind policy induced the sovereigns to sign, in the halls of the Alhambra, the decree that expatriated a hundred and sixty thousand families from their peaceful homes, to wander they knew not whither. Under the specious hypocritical mask of zeal for religion, the crafty Ferdinand sought to gratify his avarice. Large sums had come into his coffers, from the confiscations of the property of the converts by his diabolical tribunal, the Inquisition, which increased his insatiable thirst for wealth.

The Jews were the only body of his subjects possessing large fortunes whom he could plunder with impunity; among them were many opulent men who had immense wealth, and property worth one and two millions. Three were reported to possess ten millions, one of whom was Abraham Senior, who farmed the revenues of Castile, the same generous philanthropic individual who had from his private purse redeemed the four hundred and fifty captives of Malaga; others also who were merchants had large fortunes.

Notwithstanding the tribute they paid to the lord of the soil, they were very charitable towards each other; none ever came to great want, for the councils of the Jewries liberally supplied the wants of the needy. They were landholders, and established in the finest cities, and settled on the most fertile and richest soils, and also merchants, traders, farmers of the excise, taxes and customs, stewards and bailiffs of grandees, founders, tailors, shoemakers, hide-dressers, tanners, silk-mercers, spice-dealers, silversmiths, weavers, pedlars, and similar trades.[6]

The mass of the common people industriously gained a livelihood by their dexterity in various handicrafts, which rendered them far superior to similar classes of the Christian population. The opulence to which many had risen from their industrious pursuits, gave them an interest in the land of their birth and adoption; and although personal interest might have had a share, they had shewn their loyalty in the assistance rendered to the catholic sovereigns in the late war with Granada. It gave to the descendants of Israel a claim on the gratitude of the victorious monarchs, to which might be added the obligation Ferdinand was under to a Jew for restoring sight to his aged father. But gratitude was a virtue the royal breasts did not possess, as further proved by their conduct to Columbus, who gave a new world to the crown of Castile.

The bloody records of the sanguinary Inquisition state not a single instance of the Hebrew people acting irreverently to the catholic worship. The faithful discharge of their social duties, and the protection of the laws, which guaranteed to them their landed possessions to a certain amount, had led them to hope for further immunities.

But all their hopes were frustrated. Neither humanity, gratitude, justice, nor the injury done to the state, by banishing so many useful subjects from his dominions, were powerful enough to operate against the personal avaricious disposition of Ferdinand.

[6] MS. Bernaldez's Reyes Cath. chap. cxii.

The following decree fell like a thunderbolt on the devoted heads of the Israelites:—

*Edict of Ferdinand and Isabella for the Expulsion of the Jews, dated Granada, 30th March, 1492.*

Whereas, having been informed that in these our kingdoms, there were some bad Christians who judaized and apostatized from our holy catholic faith, the chief cause of which was the communication of Jews with Christians; at the Cortes we held in the city of Toledo in the year 1480, we ordered the said Jews in all the cities, towns, and places in our kingdoms and dominions, to separate into Jewries and places apart, where they should live and reside, hoping by their separation alone to remedy the evil. Furthermore, we have sought and given orders, that inquisition should be made in our said kingdoms, which, as is known, for upwards of twelve years has been, and is done, whereby many guilty persons have been discovered, as is notorious. And as we are informed by the inquisitors, and many other religious, ecclesiastical, and secular persons, that great injury has resulted, and does result, and it is stated, and appears to be, from the participation, society, and communication they held and do hold with Jews, who it appears always endeavour in every way they can to subvert our holy catholic faith, and to make faithful Christians withdraw and separate themselves therefrom, and attract and pervert them to their injurious opinions and belief, instructing them in the ceremonies and observances of their religion, holding meetings where they read and teach them what they are to believe and observe according to their religion; seeking to circumcise them and their children; giving them books from which they may read their prayers; and explaining to them the fasts they are to observe; assembling with them to read and to teach them the histories of their law; notifying to them the festivals previous to their occurring, and instructing them what they are to do and observe thereon; giving and carrying to them from their houses unleavened bread, and meat slaughtered with ceremonies; instructing them what they are to refrain from, as well in food as in other matters, for the due observance of their religion, and persuading them all they can to profess and keep the law of Moses; giving them to understand, that except that, there is no other law or truth, which is proved by many declarations and confessions, as well of Jews themselves as of those who have been perverted and deceived by them, which has greatly redounded to the injury, detriment, and opprobrium of our holy catholic faith.

Notwithstanding we were informed of the major part of this before, and we knew the certain remedy for all these injuries and inconveniences was to separate the said Jews from all communication with Christians, and banish them from all our kingdoms, yet we were desirous to content ourselves by ordering them to quit all the cities, towns, and places of Andalusia, where, it appears, they had done the greatest mischief, considering that would suffice, and that those of other cities, towns and places would cease to do and commit the same.

But as we are informed that neither that, nor the execution of some of the said Jews, who have been guilty of the said crimes and offences against our holy Catholic faith, has been sufficient for a complete remedy to obviate and arrest so great an opprobrium and offence to the Catholic faith and religion.

And as it is found and appears, that the said Jews, wherever they live and congregate, daily increase in continuing their wicked and injurious purposes; to afford them no further opportunity for insulting our holy Catholic faith, and those whom until now God has been pleased to preserve, as well as those who had fallen, but have amended and are brought back to our holy mother church, which, according to the weakness of our human nature and the diabolical suggestion that continually wages war with us, may easily occur, unless the principal cause of it be removed, which is to banish the said Jews from our kingdoms.

And when any serious and detestable crime is committed by some persons of a college or university, it is right that such college or university should be dissolved and annihilated, and the lesser suffer for the greater, and one be punished for the other; and those that disturb the welfare and proper living of cities and towns, that by contagion may injure others, should be expelled therefrom, and even for lighter causes that might be injurious to the state, how much more then for the greatest, most dangerous, and contagious of crimes like this.

Therefore we, by and with the counsel and advice of some prelates and high noblemen of our kingdoms, and other learned persons of our council, having maturely deliberated thereon, resolve to order all the said Jews and Jewesses to quit our kingdoms, and never to return or come back tó them, or any of them. Therefore we command this our edict to be issued, whereby we command all Jews and Jewesses, of whatever age they may be, that live, reside, and dwell in our said kingdoms and dominions, as well natives as those who are not, who in any manner or for any cause may have come to dwell therein, that by the end of the month of July next, of the present year 1492, they depart from all our said kingdoms and dominions, with their sons, daughters, man-servants, maid-servants, and Jewish attendants, both great and small, of whatever age they may be; and they shall not presume to return to, nor reside therein, or in any part of them, either as residents, travellers, or in any other manner whatever, under pain that if they do not perform and execute the same, and are found to reside in our said kingdoms and dominions, or should in any manner live therein, they incur the penalty of death, and confiscation of all their property to our treasury, which penalty they incur by the act itself, without further process, declaration, or sentence.

And we command and forbid any person or persons of our said kingdoms, of whatsoever rank, station, or condition they may be, that they do not presume publicly or secretly to receive, shelter, protect, or defend any Jew or Jewess, after the said term of the end of July, in their lands or houses, or in any other part of our said kingdoms and dominions, henceforward for ever and ever, under pain of losing all their property, vassals, castles, and other possessions; and furthermore forfeit to our treasury any sums they have, or receive from us.

And that the said Jews and Jewesses during the said time, until the end of the said month of July, may be the better able to dispose of themselves, their property, and estates, we hereby take and receive them under our security, protection, and royal safeguard; and insure to them and their properties, that during the said period, until the said day, the end of the said month of July, they may travel in safety, and may enter, sell, barter, and alienate all their moveable and immoveable property, and freely dispose thereof at their pleasure.

And that during the said time, no harm, injury, or wrong whatever shall be done to their persons or properties contrary to justice, under the pains those persons incur and are liable to, that violate our royal safeguard.

We likewise grant permission and authority to the said Jews and Jewesses, to export their wealth and property, by sea or land, from our said kingdoms and dominions, provided they do not take away gold, silver, money, or other articles prohibited by the laws of our kingdoms, but in merchandise and goods that are not prohibited.

And we command all the justices of our kingdoms, that they cause the whole of the above herein contained to be observed and fulfilled, and that they do not act contrary hereto; and that they afford all necessary favour, under pain of being deprived of office, and the confiscation of all their property to our exchequer.

## CHAPTER XXV.

*The offer of Abarbanel.— Conduct of Torquemada.— Jews of Vittoria save their Cemetery from Desecration.—Abarbanel's Account of their Departure.—Bernaldez's.—Jews of Segovia.— Sufferings. — Some are baptised. —Number that go to Portugal—to Navarre.—Orders of the King to assist the Refugees.— Embark.— Cruelties and Misery experienced in their Voyages.—The Synagogues converted into Churches.*

The tempting offer of 600,000 crowns made by Abarbanel, caused the cold-hearted calculating Ferdinand to hesitate about revoking the cruel decree, when Torquemada rushed into the royal presence, with a crucifix in his hand. Casting it on the table, the proud Dominican said, "Behold him whom Judas sold for thirty pieces of silver; do you sell him for more?"— The churchman succeeded;—the decree was not repealed. This unmerciful persecutor of the Hebrew people rendered their fate worse, by forbidding Christians to supply them with food, or the necessaries of life; or to receive, or even to hold communication with them after the month of April; thus usurping and superseding the royal authority, which had guaranteed them security from the date of the edict until the end of July. Yet the Catholic sovereigns winked at the daring insolence of the monk in assuming an authority over the regal power; but

Torquemada was the creature of Ferdinand. In Aragon, Valencia, and Catalonia (where they were exceedingly wealthy), the inquisitor ordered that the property of the Jewries and individuals should be sequestrated, to pay any mortgages the king, the church, and monasteries might hold, and that twice the amount of the principal should be retained to defray expenses; and that a further sum should be taken to indemnify the land-proprietors and monasteries, for the loss they would sustain by their involuntary departure. Many Jews had emigrated after the establishment of the Inquisition, foreseeing that its cruel power would one day turn from the converts, on those who adhered to the religion of their ancestors. Ten years had scarcely elapsed, when their predictions were too fully and fatally accomplished.

When the Jews of Vittoria found that the edict of Granada was irrevocable, they sought to protect the graves of their relatives and friends from desecration, and entered into the following agreement with the municipality:—

Wednesday, 27th June, 1492.—In the street of the Jewry of this city, present, the members of the council, together with Moses Balid as judge of the Jews; their magistrate and representative, Ismael Moratan, Samuel Benjamin, the Gaon, and his cousin Abiatar Tello, Judah and Joseph Farral, and Samuel de Mijancas, Jews, inhabitants of the said city, who said, that whereas, as was notorious, the Jews were to quit for ever all these kingdoms, by the month of July next ensuing, by order of the king and our lords, in consideration of the good and neighbourly treatment they had received from this city, for themselves, and in the name of the whole Jewry of the said city, they did present, and make, *inter vivo*, an irrevocable gift of the field and cemetery of the said Jewry, called the Judemendi, with all its appurtenances, entrances, and outgoings; that from now, and for ever hereafter, it may remain for a pasture and public common of the corporation of the said city. Whereupon the representative of the city engaged and made oath in its name, as Juan Martinez de Olabe, the representative of the said city, does engage and make oath to them, that it never shall be broken up or ploughed, but remain for the public benefit of the corporation of the said city, as aforesaid. They granted a full and ample deed of gift, under legal advice, renouncing all laws that might appear opposed thereto. Signed by my hand.

Witnesses, Andres Martinez de Heredio, Pedro Gonsalez de Tungiter, Juan de San Juan, provision-dealer, and Pedro Galaretta, tailor, inhabitants of Vittoria.[1]

The field where the Jews had their cemetery is yet preserved. It is at a short distance from the Calle Nueva, which was the former Jewry, and is bounded by the adjoining land. It is called in the Basque dialect Judemendi, which means the Jews' hill.

What probably gave them the idea of this deed, was its having been reported, that Juan Lopes de Escoriaga had bought, or intended to buy it, from the Jews. The town council summoned him to a meeting held a week before, to inform him that it was, and ought to be, a public common for the benefit of the city.[2]

Their precaution to secure the sepulchres of their ancestors from desecration proved to be a wise step, for in 1580, Spanish fanaticism led the people of Seville, without respect for the ashes of the dead, to open and demolish the graves and monuments in the cemetery of the Jews, near the gate of Minjoar (so named from a wealthy Israelite who resided there), and robbed the corpses of everything of value. In some graves they

---

[1] Acuerdos de Vit., vol. i., p. 456.  [2] Idem 455.

found manuscripts, which they took to the celebrated Arias Montanus.[3]

As before said, on the publication of the edict, Abarbanel used his utmost exertions to obtain its revocation, but in vain; his own words are the best statement of what passed.

I was at court when the royal decree was announced. I wearied myself to distraction in imploring compassion. Thrice on my knees I besought the king. "Regard us, O king, use not thy subjects so cruelly. Why do thus to thy servants? Rather exact from us our gold and silver, even all the house of Israel possesses, if he may remain in his country." I likewise entreated my friends, the king's officers, to allay his anger against my people. I implored the councillors to advise the king to repeal the decree. But as the adder closes its ear with dust against the voice of the charmer, so the king hardened his heart against the entreaties of his suppliants, and declared he would not revoke the edict for all the wealth of the Jews. The queen at his right hand opposed it, and urged him to continue what he had begun. We exhausted all our power for the repeal of the king's sentence; but there was neither wisdom nor help remaining. Wherever the evil decree was proclaimed, or the report of it had spread, our nation bewailed their condition with great lamentations; for there had not been such a banishment since Judah had been driven from his land. They exhorted and encouraged each other to keep firm to the law: Let us surmount every trouble for the honour of our nation and our religion; let us defend these against the hateful persecutors. If they leave us with life, we will live; if they deprive us of it, we will die; but never let us violate our holy law. If his heart turn not, let us go, in the name of "the Lord our portion." Let us abandon our settlements, and seek for homes elsewhere. In one day, on foot and unarmed, 300,000 collected from every province, young and old, aged and infirm, women and children, all ready to go anywhere. Among the number was I, and, with God for our leader, we set out.[4]

[3] Caro, Ant. of Seville.     [4] Pref. to Abar. Com. on Kings.

Such is the recital of Abarbanel.

Another contemporary and eye-witness gives the following harrowing account.

Within the term fixed by the edict the Jews sold and disposed of their property for a mere nothing; they went about begging Christians to buy, but found no purchasers; fine houses and estates were sold for trifles; a house was exchanged for an ass; and a vineyard given for a little cloth or linen. Although prohibited carrying away gold and silver, they secretly took large quantities in their saddles, and in the halters and harness of their loaded beasts. Some swallowed as many as thirty ducats to avoid the rigorous search made at the frontier towns and sea-ports, by the officers appointed for the purpose. The rich Jews defrayed the expenses of the departure of the poor, practising towards each other the greatest charity, so that except very few of the most necessitous, they would not become converts. In the first week of July they took the route for quitting their native land, great and small, old and young; on foot, on horses, asses, and in carts; each continuing his journey to his destined port. They experienced great trouble and suffered indescribable misfortunes on the roads and country they travelled; some falling, others rising; some dying, others coming into the world; some fainting, others being attacked with illness; that there was not a Christian but what felt for them, and persuaded them to be baptised. Some from misery were converted; but they were very few. The rabbins encouraged them, and made the young people and women sing, and play on pipes and tabors to enliven them, and keep up their spirits.[5]

The unfortunate Hebrews who had peaceably resided at Segovia, until the promulgation of the decree, previous to abandoning their homes, were three days in the cemetery, watering with their tears the ashes of their fathers; their lamentations excited the pity of all who heard them.[6]

[5] Bernaldez, MS. Chron. de los Reyes Cathol.
[6] Colmenares, Hist. de Segovia.

The perils and privations of their dreary pilgrimage were most severely felt by many whose families had been reared in all the refinements wealth and education could procure, by which they had ennobled their characters, and were ornaments to the country that had given them birth. From the manner in which the departure of so many thousands of families was hurried, the property of the unfortunate Hebrews was disposed of for trifles; the sale of their effects had more the appearance of a spoliation than a fair alienation. It was every where a general desolation; Christians witnessed the most heart-rending scenes: the inexorable Ferdinand and the odious Torquemada alone remained unmoved. With the sincerest sorrow, the profoundest grief, they quitted a country where their nation had flourished for many ages; it had become their country. Some of the proscribed, yielding to imperious necessity, preferred abjuring the faith of their fore-fathers to quitting the soil to which all their fondest affections attached them; others to retain their possessions. But many of these dissemblers, who were so fortunate as to escape the lynx-eyed inquisitors, when opportunity offered, rejoined their brethren and openly avowed their Judaism. Those whom fear or attachment to their native soil had made converts, remained objects of suspicion to the clergy. They compelled them to prove their baptism and to live among Christians, instead of together as formerly; those who had been Rabbins were obliged to leave the towns where they had resided, so much was their influence with their former co-religionists feared.

Fifteen hundred powerful and wealthy families that had resided in the kingdom of Granada, were the first that quitted the inhospitable shores of Spain.

Mariana estimates the number that emigrated at 800,000 souls. The major part of those from Castile, yet clinging to the Iberian soil, retired to Portugal.

Bernaldez states that upwards of 3,000 souls went from Benevente to Braganza; 30,000 from Zamora to Miranda; 35,000 from Ciudad Rodrigo to Villar; 15,000 from Miranda de Alcantara to Marbao; 10,000 from Badajoz to Yelves. Those from Merida also went to Portugal, so that upwards of 100,000 entered that kingdom, where they received the most disinterested hospitality from their co-religionists. Many learned men settled in various Portuguese cities, where rabbinism already flourished, some of whom were highly esteemed by the sovereign.

From the frontiers of Navarre, 12,000 entered that kingdom, where they were kindly received in consequence of a letter dated 8th June, addressed by the king, John Labrit, and Donna Leonora, his queen, to the magistrate, judge, and commander of Estella, ordering, "that if any Jews of those expelled from Castile and Aragon, by order of Ferdinand and Isabella, should come to that city, they should afford them a safe transit, and every possible accommodation, because they are a docile people, that can easily be brought to reason." The sovereigns fearing that the Jews who resided at Estella might be maltreated, as their ancestors had been exactly a century before, announced that their officers would incur their high displeasure if they did not prevent such an occurrence.[7] The municipality of Tudela, actuated by feelings unlike those of their humane sovereigns, wrote to that of Tafalla, that the Jews exiled from Castile intended entering Navarre, but that neither city ought

---
[7] MS. Hist. de Estella.

to receive them, as it was contrary and opposed to the service of God and the king. From Andalusia and the commandery of St. Jago eight thousand souls, and from Medina de Pumar three hundred families, repaired to Cadiz.

An immense concourse assembled at Carthagena, Valencia, Barcelona, and other ports of Aragon and Catalonia, to embark for Italy, Morocco, Barbary, and the Levant. Ferdinand had provided vessels at those ports to transport them wherever they might choose to go. A fleet of twenty-five sail, under the command of Pedro Cabron, conveyed a large number from Port Maria and Gibraltar to Oran. Bernaldez states that seventeen of the vessels of Cabron's fleet entered into the port of Carthagena, where a hundred and fifty persons demanded the rite of baptism, which was given to them; and when the fleet was at Malaga, four hundred asked to be baptised, and they returned Christians to Castile; the rest were landed at Archilla, from whence they went to Fez. But owing to a long drought, great scarcity prevailed there; consequently, the Moors refused to admit them into the city. The sufferings they experienced on the voyage must have been dreadful—as is evident from the circumstance of the baptisms mentioned by Bernaldez; for it can be attributed to no other reason, that five hundred and fifty persons, who had so recently sacrificed their property and abandoned their happy homes, should so suddenly become converts to a religion, to avoid which they had made such sacrifices and submitted so resignedly to the perils and dangers that surrounded them. On their arrival at Fez, they were forced to encamp in an open plain; and, to satisfy their hunger, these wretched beings had to subsist on the dried roots and withered grass the barren parched-up African soil then produced. Some sold their children to procure bread, others expired in the midst of theirs, who were also dying from hunger; some few, in despair, returned to Spain, and were baptised. Those who had been sold, the king subsequently ordered to be liberated. What a contrast between the conduct of a prince considered as a barbarian and that of the Catholic sovereigns, misnamed Christians!

The misery suffered by the unfortunate exiles is almost indescribable. Some of the vessels took fire, and they either perished in the flames or were drowned, others were so overloaded that they sunk. Many were wrecked on barren coasts, and perished with hunger and cold; those who survived were exposed to further troubles and misfortunes. Some captains purposely prolonged their voyage, to force them to buy water and provisions, at any price they chose to exact from their unfortunate victims.

No one can describe nor even imagine all the calamities that befell the Hebrews in quitting Spain,— such as the dreadful want of food that some experienced at sea,— the ferocity of brigands, who on land plundered them of every thing they possessed,— the barbarity of captains, who conveyed others to distant islands, there selling them for slaves, pretending they were prisoners of war, or those who threw the sick overboard to take their property. On board one vessel full of emigrants a pestilential disease broke out; the captain landed all on a desert island, where they wandered about in quest of assistance. A mother carrying two infants, walking with her husband, expired on the road; the father, overcome with fatigue, fell fainting near his two children; on awakening he found them dead from hunger. He covered them with sand: "My God," exclaimed he, "my misfortunes seem to induce me to abandon thy law; but I am a Jew, and will ever remain so."

Another captain deprived them of their clothes, and landed them naked on a barren coast, where they found a spring of water. At night, climbing some rocks in search of human habitations, a number were devoured by wild beasts. After being there for five days, the captain of a passing ship perceived naked people on the shore; he took them on board, clothed them with old sails, gave them food, and conveyed them to Genoa. Seeing their miserable condition, the inhabitants inquired if he had slaves for sale? He nobly answered, "No!" and delivered them to their brethren in the city, on payment of reasonable expenses. They gladly made him an additional present, and loaded him with their blessings.[a] One wretch is said to have violated a Jewish maiden in her parents' presence: after quitting her, he returned and cut her throat, for fear, as he said, she should have conceived, and should bring forth a Jew.

The miseries suffered by those who went to Morocco are equally appalling. The Moors plundered them of almost everything they had. Hearing that many men and women had swallowed gold to bring away, they murdered a number, and then ripped them open to search for it.

At Sallee, the crew of a large vessel enticed a number of children on board, with promises of giving them bread, and then set sail, while their frantic

[a] Shebet Jeudah.

mothers implored them from the beach to restore them their only treasure.

Nine crowded vessels, infected with disease, arising from the hardships and privations of the voyage, arrived at Naples. The pestilence was communicated to the city, and 20,000 of its inhabitants fell victims to it.

Others repaired to Genoa, where a famine prevailed. They were permitted to land, but were met by priests carrying a crucifix in one hand and a loaf of bread in the other; thus intimating, that by receiving baptism they should have food.

This is but a brief account of the horrors and atrocities suffered by the unfortunate descendants of Judah on quitting, by the cruel mandate of Ferdinand and Isabella, a country to which, notwithstanding the persecutions they had occasionally experienced from the populace instigated by fanatic monks, they were sincerely and devotedly attached.

Many of the expatriated Hebrews went to the Levant. Those that repaired to the various Italian states were hospitably received, notwithstanding the existence of inquisitions; but no Torquemada governed them. Even Pope Alexander VI. kindly afforded them an asylum in the papal dominions, and subsequently wrote to all the Italian States to grant the exiles from Spain and Portugal the same privileges as resident Jews enjoyed.

Besides the gold and silver they had secreted, and the valuable effects they were permitted to carry away, which an author has estimated at thirty millions of ducats, they took with them a great many Hebrew manuscripts, that had been the ornaments of the synagogues, or which opulent families had had written for their private use by able scribes, which are to the present day admired specimens of Hebrew calligraphy.

They were not permitted to dispose of property that belonged to the congregations. The synagogues were for the most part converted into churches.

The following appears on the records of the city of Vittoria, 9th July, 1492 :[9]—

The town council notified to Juan Martinez de Ulbarri, that it was reported he had bought the synagogue the Jews had in that city, which the civic authorities had ordered no inhabitant should purchase, because they were not permitted to be sold in the whole kingdom; and that if he had not bought it, he was not to buy it; and if he had, he should not pay the sum agreed for; and if he had already paid, he must have recourse to the persons who sold it, particularly to the chief of the Jews of the city, to recover what he had paid, as afterwards he could make no claim on the city, as the said synagogue must remain as other synagogues in the kingdom. Not acting accordingly, he would lose whatever he may have given for it. The said Juan Martinez demanded a copy.

Diego Martinez de Alava, notary, and Alvaro de Urquibel, inhabitants of the said city, witnesses.

[9] Acuerdos de Vit., vol. i., p. 857.

## CHAPTER XXVI.

*Review of the consequences of Ferdinand's conduct.— Condemned by Mariana. — Surprise of Bajazet. — Declarations of the Grandees.— Forgeries to impose on the People. — Images of Rabbinism. — Opinions thereon of Spaniards of the present day. —The consequences of the Expulsion.— Extracts from Morejon on the Act.—Assistance.— The Second Inquisitor-general Deza.— Additional Decree obtained by him.— A private Synagogue discovered at Valencia.*

The conduct of Ferdinand in issuing and putting into execution this decree, was severely reprobated and disapproved by every one. But for the submission always shewn by the Hebrew people to the will of the sovereign, and their resignation to the decrees of the Omnipotent, a civil war might have been the result of this intemperate and cruel act. But the crafty monarch calculated on the peaceable demeanour of his Jewish subjects, whose conduct on this occasion Abarbanel justly praised. A prudent sovereign would have taken into consideration the fearful consequences that might have ensued from this cruel and insensate mandate. Instigated by that monster in human shape, the Dominican inquisitor, Torquemada, under the hypocritical mask of religion, he risked crown and throne to gratify his avarice.

Spain, although apparently then at peace, possessed

within itself the germs that might have proved the overthrow of the catholic sovereigns, its ramifications might easily have undermined the royal authority.

Had these 800,000 souls in their despair have raised the standard of revolt, they would soon have found numerous auxiliaries. Granada had surrendered; but the martial spirit of the hardy race of Moors in the Alpuxara mountains was not subdued. The new Christians, who the year before had sought to render themselves independent by the purchase of Gibraltar from the duke of Medina Sidonia, on whom by deed of gift dated 3rd June, 1469, Henry IV. had conferred it,[1] would gladly have thrown off the disguise they had been forced to assume. Portugal, forced to conclude a peace after her defeat on the plains of Toro, would gladly have seized so favourable an opportunity to avenge her discomfiture. Surrounded by such perils, what might not have been the fate of the Castilian monarchs?

The fanatical jesuit, Mariana, who could write in defence of Jacques Clement, the assassin of Henry III. of France, condemned it; he says :—

The number of Jews that quitted Castile is not known; most authors say they amounted to 160,000 families; and some, that they amounted to 800,000 souls; undoubtedly an immense multitude, which induced many persons to reprobate the resolution adopted by the king, Don Ferdinand, in expelling from his dominions so profitable and opulent a people, acquainted with every mode of collecting wealth. Carrying with them a large portion of the riches of Spain in gold, precious stones, and jewels of inestimable value, the states they went to derived incalculable benefit.

When the exiles from Spain came to Turkey, the sultan, Bajazet, who had been led to form a high

[1] Ayala, Hist. Gib.

opinion of Ferdinand, exclaimed, " Do you term this a political king, who impoverishes his country and enriches ours?"

Had the Catholic sovereigns a right to drive so many thousand families from their native soil? Or should they have confined themselves to the laws that existed in Spain? These are questions that may be asked; for, from the earliest period of Christianity, the dispersed and wandering Hebrew people had been everywhere tolerated; such conduct was considered one of the greatest triumphs of Christianity. In Spain they had been established long anterior.

The sovereigns of the second Gothic monarchy not only afforded their protection to the Jews, but secured to them their individual freedom, granting them in the civil order remarkable concessions. In the Fuero Viejo of Castile, Alphonso VIII. placed their property in security from unjust aggressions.

Ferdinand III. granted them the privilege of being tried by their own judges, and that Christians should not serve as witnesses against them.

Alphonso the Wise, in the Seven Codes, ordained that the existence of Jews among Spaniards should be respected, that the holy scriptures might be fulfilled. Alphonso XI. desired that the Jews should never quit Spain, and they would be converted to Christianity. While he forbade their usury, he authorized them to acquire landed property in all his dominions.

In nearly all the laws made by the Cortes regarding the Jews, in all the privileges and charters granted them by sovereigns, the desire that they should reside in Spain is perceptible, flattering themselves with the hope that they would abjure their religion, and be of great advantage to the state. How then could the Catholic sovereigns infringe the laws of the kingdom, and by a single stroke of the pen drive from their hearths the descendants of Judah, who for so many centuries had reposed under the shadow of the throne in the Iberian peninsula? The only answer that can be given is, that they had no right; they were bound to act in conformity to the existing laws enacted constitutionally.

Examining the edict politically, did it affect the interest of the state? Undoubtedly it did; for notwithstanding the prohibition, the Jews carried away immense wealth, to aggrandise and enrich foreign states. By the expulsion of the Hebrews, the true sources of public welfare, commerce and industry, suffered a mortal blow. The latter, owing to the recent conquest of Granada, was at first less felt, as thereby Castile obtained new cultivators. Commerce, on the contrary, closed its gates, by the banishment of the proscribed people, and for a time lost all its activity.

The act of Ferdinand and Isabella is condemnable, as injurious to literature and the arts and sciences. For many ages, the efforts of the Jews had been directed to acquire knowledge. The triumphs gained by them in the sciences and literature, the constant example of their studies, exercised no little influence on Spanish civilisation. The earliest writers of antiquity, down to the most modern authors, had been consulted and studied by the rabbins. Innumerable works on every science, whether in Hebrew or in Arabic, had been translated into Spanish, or more frequently into Latin, the language of the learned.

The academies, schools, synagogues, meetings of learned men, commercial establishments, all were destroyed at a single blow. What a return for the assistance rendered by them in the war with Granada!

The grandees, when they found their towns and villages depopulated, their lands uncultivated, declared, that, could they have imagined the desolation would have been so great, they would have resisted its execution.

The people generally seem to have disapproved of the measure; for although the rabble, when incited by fanatic monks, committed the most horrid outrages, the Jews would not otherwise so earnestly have sought to remain in the midst of a hostile population. The following forgeries became necessary, and were widely spread, to induce a belief in the necessity of banishing them for ever. They are yet on record.[2]

*Letter of the Jews of Spain to those of Constantinople.*

RESPECTED JEWS,—Health and grace. Know ye, that the king of Spain, by public proclamation, makes us become Christians, takes away our property, deprives us of existence, destroys our synagogues, and commits other vexations towards us, which confuses us, and we know not what to do, conformably to the law of Moses. We beg and entreat you to be kind enough to convene a meeting, and forward us with all despatch, the resolutions you may therein adopt.    CHAMORO,
Chief of the Jews of Spain.

*Answer of the Jews of Constantinople to those of Spain.*

BELOVED BRETHREN IN MOSES,—We received a letter, wherein you inform us of the troubles and misfortunes you suffer; for which we feel as much as yourselves. The opinion of the authorities and rabbins is the following:—In regard to what you say, that the king of Spain makes you become

[2] Arch. Nav. § Ecc. Aff. leg. i., ch. 21.

Christians, submit to it since you cannot do otherwise. As to what you say, that they take away your property, make your sons merchants that they may take away theirs. In regard to taking away your lives, make your sons physicians and apothecaries, that they may deprive them of theirs. In respect to your saying that they destroy your synagogues, make your sons ecclesiastics, that they may destroy their temples. As to saying they otherwise vex you, endeavour that your sons enter into the offices of the state, that you may avenge yourselves by having them under you. Depart not from this order which we give you, and you will find from being low, you will become very high. USUFU,
Chief of the Jews of Constantinople.

This infamous imposture and calumny was the fabrication of some ignorant ecclesiastic; for the Spanish Jews never acknowledged those of Constantinople, or any others, after the closing of the Persian schools, and the death of Rabenu Hayé, in Persia, whom all Israel recognised as supreme head and judge. The Jews of Spain acknowledged only their own rabbanim, of whom they reckon ten generations.

1. R. Samuel a Levi, the prince.
2. R. Joseph a Levi, his unfortunate son.
3. R. Isaac Al Fez.
4. R. Joseph a Levi ben Megas.
5. R. Moses ben Maimon (Maimonides).
6. R. Moses Micozi, and R. Moses ben Nachman (Nachmanides).
7. R. Solomon ben Adereth.
8. The famed Rabenu Asher, a German.
9. R. Isaac Campanton.
10. R. Isaac Aboab.

The author has the honour of being personally acquainted (here and in Spain), with many of the illustrious Spaniards of the present day; and all, without exception, attribute the fall of their country from the highest pinnacle of glory and power, to its present state, to the banishment of its most industrious population. For, a few years after the expulsion of the Jews, the Catholic sovereigns, in violation of a sacred treaty, forced the Moors to quit the Iberian soil.

The consequences are visible: Spain, which formerly contained forty millions of inhabitants, to which its productive soil afforded subsistence, now can barely number fifteen, and although at one time it was complained that the immense Jewish population enhanced the price of provisions, political economy, properly understood, teaches that the chief source of the wealth of nations is their population; and whilst in every other country it has considerably increased, in Spain it has fearfully diminished.

From being the first among the nations, she has fallen into a secondary rank in the European family. Such has been the effect of impolicy, fanaticism, and persecution!

I shall close this digression with extracts from a modern Spanish author of note.

I will not speak of that cruel persecution, of that horrid banishment of four hundred thousand Jews by order of the Catholic sovereigns in 1492, without permitting them to take away the gold and silver that belonged to them.

Would that a thick veil could hide this act from us which casts such a stain on the happy epoch of that reign, and obscures the glory acquired by other noble deeds of those who counselled such a political assassination.

Would that this black page could be blotted from history, which exhibits to us the blindness of fanaticism, and the obduracy of heart, when once religious prejudices are instilled into it.[1] The dislike with which some persons regard this unfortunate people, is an injustice towards them, an insult they do not deserve, and their banishment from Spain must be considered a political crime.[3]

Considered humanely, this painful and ever to be regretted act against a race that had for many centuries peaceably resided in our Peninsula, among whom so many men of worth, talents, and learning had shone, cannot contribute to dispel the opinion all Europe has formed of our ancestors, " that they were pre-eminently intolerant."[4]

If to this be added, that the Jews neither could, nor ever attempted to invade our territories, to subvert our laws, to act hostilely to our religious belief, or to disturb our social order, it will be seen how wrong our legislators were in proscribing and placing under a perpetual ostracism thousands of families, who, by their departure from the kingdom, only diminished our public wealth and reduced our population, the value of which is well known in political economy.[5]

The Christian population were by the expulsion deprived of sufficient medical assistance; for, although the laws prohibited them employing Jew physicians, surgeons, and apothecaries, their known abilities and professional skill in the practice of medicine, rendered their services indispensable and sought after by their Christian fellow citizens, as is proved by the following record of the municipality of Vittoria, dated 29th October, 1492.

Knowing the want of physicians, the city, its territory, and vicinity experience, from the departure and absence of the Jews and the physicians of the said city and its neighbourhood, they agree to request, and do hereby request, the licentiate Doctor Antonio de Tournay, physician, to remain and reside in the said city, there to practise his profession and art for the following year; that is, from the day of All Saints for one complete year; for which, in the name of the city, they would give

[3] Morejon, Hist. Med. Espag., vol. i., p. 74.   [4] Ibid. p. 75.   [5] Ibid. p. 344.

and pay him ten thousand maravedis for his services during the said year.[6]

This want of medical assistance continued to be felt the following year; for in the record of a meeting of the town council, held 10th June, 1493, mention is made "that there was a great scarcity of physicians, owing to the departure and absence of the Jews."[7]

At a meeting held 20th August, they resolved and ordered —

Whereas many of the new Christians resident in this city, who were formerly Jews, have come to live in the new street, formerly called the Jewry; from which arises a disservice to God, and a great inconvenience; although some inhabitants have complained thereof, none of them are to reside in the said street; but, on the contrary, all such as now reside in it are to seek other dwellings, and are to remove thereto within fifteen days after it shall be notified to them. The magistrates are charged to notify and remedy the same.[8]

It would appear from this, fears were entertained that the forced converts might relapse to Judaism, if their early habits and associations were permitted. The last notice of the Jews on the records of Vittoria is, that by an order from Madrid, dated 10th January, 1495, any public property there might be that belonged to the Jews, was to be delivered over to the city for 1,000 maravedis the Jewry owed for taxes.

On the death of Torquemada, in 1498, another Dominican, Don Diego Deza, archbishop of Seville, was appointed inquisitor-general: his hatred of the Jews equalled that of his cruel predecessor. The Jews were so attached to the country where the learning of the Hebrews had immortalized their names, that some sought to settle in Spain a few years after the expul-

[6] Acuerdos de Vit., vol. i. p. 487, b.   [7] Ibid., p. 506.   [8] Ibid., p. 548.

sion. Deza applied to the Catholic sovereigns to prevent it; in consequence, on the 5th September, 1499, after repeating the former edict of 1492, they added the following:—

As we have been informed that some Jews have presumed to come to these our kingdoms, saying, they are not the persons that were banished, and that the foregoing law does not extend to them, being from foreign states, and on being arrested, declare that they wish to become Christians, as the punishment is doubtful. We therefore order all and each of the justices of our kingdoms, that if now, or at any time hereafter, any Jews or Jewesses should enter our kingdoms, whether those that were banished, or whatsoever others from foreign kingdoms or states, you are immediately to inflict on them the punishment of death, confiscation of their property, and every other penalty contained in the aforesaid law. Fail not to execute it, although such Jews declare they desire to become Christians, except previous to entering our kingdoms they send to manifest and make known to you that they come to turn Christians and be converted to our holy Catholic faith, and execute a deed in presence of a notary and witnesses, to that effect, at the first town they enter. Such persons, on publicly becoming Christians at the place where they arrive, in conformity to the above, we permit to reside in our kingdoms as Christians; but if any of them should have Jew servants, they must send them out of the kingdom within two months, or at the expiration of that time they must become Christians: failing so to do, they incur the aforesaid penalties and punishments.

But they could not eradicate Judaism from the Hebrew breast; and the converts, although apparently the devoutest Catholics, secretly observed the religious rites enjoined by the Mosaical law, and even assembled to join in worship to the God of Israel. A private synagogue, in 1501, was discovered at Valencia. The owner of the premises suffered at an Auto da Fe; the house was rased; and the Inquisition built a chapel on the site, which is yet known by the name of *La Cruz Nueva* (the new cross).

## CHAPTER XXVII.

*Jews of Portugal. — Don Solomon Jachia holds the highest Offices of State.—Order of Gregory IX. — Favoured by all the Sovereigns. — Their Civil and Religious Government.— Privileges.— Laws respecting Converts.—Bull of Clement VI. — Cortes of Lisbon — of Evora.—Paid a Property Tax of Two per Cent. —Ordinance of Duarte — of Alphonso V. — Cortes of Santarem—of Lisbon.*

THE settlement of the Jews in the ancient Lusitania was as early as in the other parts of the Iberian peninsula. From the earliest period of the Portuguese monarchy, they enjoyed the confidence of its sovereigns. We find, in the reign of Sancho I., in 1190, Don Solomon Jachia, by his merit and fidelity, obtained the command of the army, and was appointed field-marshal-general. His bravery and success raised many powerful enemies against him; but by his humility he disarmed their angry feelings, and eluded the cabals and intrigues of the ministry. He prevailed on his co-religionists not to ride on horses or wear silk, as he observed it caused the envy and jealousy of the Christians. His family must have been ennobled, as all his descendants had the title of *Don*, a title then only conferred on noblemen, and not used in common as at the present day.

Sancho II. appointed Jews, in preference to Christians, to various public offices, undoubtedly because he found them to be better financiers, and more adapted for the public service than the latter. Complaints being made to Pope Gregory IX. that he favoured the Jewish religion, he ordered the bishop of Astorga and Lugo to admonish him on the subject. He also desired the king, when the posts of receivers, collectors, or farmers-general were held by Jews or Moors, to appoint a Christian superintendant, who might look into the vexations and impositions they practised on ecclesiastics and Christians generally, by their rigorous exactions and mode of recovery. In return for the protection afforded them, the Jews furnished an anchor and a cable of sixty fathoms to every king's vessel on her first leaving port. The origin of this custom is not stated; but that it existed is proved by a commission appointed in 1320 by King Dennis, to inquire respecting it; therefore it must have fallen into desuetude during the reign of his father.[1]

The crown of Portugal had rendered itself tributary to the Holy See, a power which, once obtained, was never willingly relinquished by the representatives of St. Peter. In virtue of this authority, Innocent IV. nominated Alfonzo III. regent of the kingdom, thus virtually deposing his brother, the king, who, through the influence of the discontented clergy and nobles, became the victim of the court of Rome.[2]

The undisturbed residence of the Jews in Portugal, proves that the Papal See was not opposed to the

[1] Britto's Hist. de Portugal.   [2] Brandaōs Monar. Lusitania.

Hebrew people residing in Catholic countries; for until the reign of Emanuel, we find none of the pages of the history of Portugal stained with the sanguinary records that so frequently disgrace the annals of Spain. That it should be opposed to Jews holding the highest offices of state is not surprising, as thereby they might exercise a powerful influence over the Christian population.

But the Portuguese sovereigns found their financial and commercial talents necessary, and continued to employ them in various departments of government; for when the clergy, in 1289, made forty charges against King Dennis to the Papal See, the 27th was, that he appointed Jews to the highest offices of state, —the chief rabbi Judah being his high treasurer and minister of finance,—and that, in consequence, he permitted Jews to be without the distinguishing mark, and did not compel them to pay tithes, according to canonical law; which he promised to remedy, and that year ordered them to wear the sign; but what it was is not stated. In 1317, the king agreed that the Jews of Braganza, in lieu of extraordinary taxes, should pay annually 600 maravedis of eight, in white Leonese sous. At a cortes held in 1325 at Evora, sumptuary laws respecting dress were enacted; and no exceptions were made in regard to the Jews. During his reign, except the favour granted to the Jews of Braganza, they paid the ordinary and extraordinary taxes the same as in the time of his predecessors.

The sovereign of Portugal continued to favour them. His son, Alfonzo IV., in 1340, fixed a sum for the ordinary tribute; and, to put a stop to the exactions they were subject to, commuted for 50,000 livres the extraordinary impositions. This was a great boon, for the Jews of Portugal were much wealthier than those of Castile; the major part lived on their incomes, or by contracts with government and the cities, most of the revenues being farmed by them; they were also large landed proprietors. The commutation was regularly collected; for although in every town of Portugal there were Jewish communities, the whole formed a body under their own particular government, more resembling a foreign tributary nation than subjects of the Portuguese crown. Besides, being under the protection of the laws, which were better administered and observed than in Castile, they enjoyed from the sovereigns extraordinary privileges and immunities. Although generally regarded with mistrust and contumely by the Christian population, many were highly respected for their moral conduct, civil virtues, and immense wealth. They had various magistrates to watch over the economy, policy, and interest of the different communities, as well as for the administration of justice.

The head of their civil and religious government was the Chief Rabbi, who was elected by the king, and consequently either a person who had rendered some service to the state, or a personal friend of the sovereign; it was a post of high distinction and importance. His seal of office was the arms of Portugal, with the words, "Chief Rabbi of Portugal" round it, all documents and letters signed by him, or his ouvidor (the title of a magistrate who hears causes), who always accompanied him, were sealed with it.

All acts of appeal and other documents, that in the last instance were appealed to the ministers of state, began, "Judah (or A. B.), chief rabbi of my lord the king, of the communes of the Jews of Portugal and Algarve, to whomsoever these presents cometh," &c.

Besides having the same authority as noblemen who possessed seigneurial rights, he had the power of inflicting punishment, a power the sovereigns of Portugal did not often grant to other grandees.

He took cognizance of all wrongs and injuries committed by the magistrates he had appointed in the provinces, those committed by him or his ouvidor were only subject to the revision of the corregidor (the supreme magistrate) of the court. All causes and suits of which he was bound to take cognizance, were heard and determined by him. It was his duty from time to time to visit the different communes. He took, or commissioned other persons to take, an account from the administrators and treasurers of the property of communes, to see that they were placed to advantage, and by his usher could compel defaulters to pay to the utmost of their means. He was bound to examine and see that the property of orphans was properly secured, and to demand accounts from their curators and guardians; and to order the rabbis of provinces, under a penalty, to appoint within a certain time, curators or guardians for those who had not.[3] In places where the court was present, he could order immediate punishment to be inflicted, and could take cognizance of all causes of persons who from their rank, office, wealth, or protection, were exempted from the jurisdiction of the rabbis of provinces. It belonged to him to order the making of footpaths, and keeping them and the buildings of the Jewries in proper repair.

He had the same authority as magistrates of provinces to grant passports and safeguards: those made in his name ran thus:—

" I (A. B.), chief rabbi of my lord the king of the communes of the Jews of Portugal and Algarve, to you (C. D.) rabbi of the commune of Jews of * * * *. Know ye, that I hereby give safeguard and security to (E. F.), who is authorized to live and reside in your place," &c.

He could not grant any privilege, favour or grace, to exempt, or excuse any person from serving the offices, duties, and

[3] Mem. da Aca. real das scien do Lisboa, and Monteiro His. da Inquisicam.

charges in the community where he resides. Nor could he either in the first instance, or by appeal, take cognizance of complaints against the persons authorized to fix the market prices of articles, as each commune had its particular officer appointed for that purpose. Nor could he decide on verbal quarrels, as they belonged to the appointed officers of the respective districts. He could neither arrest nor have any person arrested, except on sworn evidence or declared witnesses. In consequence of the many inconveniences suffered by those who were imprisoned by him, they were forced to follow him to the place where the punishment was to be inflicted.

All sentences delivered by the chief rabbi or his ouvidor, were issued in the name of the reigning sovereign, and sealed with the royal arms. From the foregoing, it will be perceived that the chief rabbi exercised the same authority over the Jews as the chief civil magistrate of the court had over the other population. He had various officers attached to him. The principal was an ouvidor, who always accompanied him; his duties were the same as the chief civil magistrate; he joined the chief rabbi in taking cognizance of all causes that he could not determine by himself.

1. The ouvidor was to be a well-informed Jew, possessing all the necessary qualifications for an upright and just judge. He affixed the official seal to all letters, sentences, and releases or acquittals, given by the chief rabbi or himself.

2. A chancellor, in whose custody all the official papers were kept, which he carried with him to the respective provinces. He might either be a Jew or Christian, provided he was duly qualified for the office.

3. A notary, to note, and give notarial acts and documents of every thing that passed before him, for which he was entitled to make the same charges as the royal notaries. Before entering on his office, he was sworn before the chief rabbi, faithfully and truly to perform its duties. He might either be a Christian or a Jew, but must know to read and write well.

4. He had also an usher to make the seizures, and execute the sentences given by him, or his ouvidor.

## CONSTITUTION OF THE JEWS IN PORTUGAL.

No appeal or complaint could be made against any sentence or acquittal given by the ouvidor who accompanied the chief rabbi, as that person is considered the same as a minister appointed by the king.

The kingdom was divided into seven provinces. Each had its particular ouvidor. They were appointed by the chief rabbi, and their residence fixed by law. The ouvidor of Estremadura resided at Santarem; of Lower Beira, at Vizeu; of Upper Beira, at Covilha; of Entre Douro e Minho, at Porto; of Tras os Montes, at Torre de Moncorvo; of Alemtejo, at Evora; and of the kingdom of Algarve, at Faro.

Each used for his seal the arms of Portugal, around which was "Ouvidor of the Province of ****." They had their chancellor, who was bound to reside in the same city or town, and might be either a Jew or Christian. He affixed the official seals to all documents. They also had their respective notaries to record all matters that were brought before the ouvidor. He might be a Christian or Jew. The duty of the ouvidor was to hear and determine all complaints and appeals from the rabbis of the communes in their respective province. Their sentences were issued in the name of the chief rabbi.

Besides the magistrates in each province, every town had its rabbi, whose authority was only annual. These rabbis were elected by the votes of the Jews of the place, but could not act until their election was approved by the chief rabbi; and they had a commission signed by him or his ouvidor, sealed with his official seal, and issued in the name of the reigning sovereign.

They had civil and criminal jurisdiction over the Jews of their respective towns; but they could not take cognizance of causes that concerned royal rights, as there were particular judges specially appointed for that purpose. They attended to the economy, policy, and property of their respective communities, in each of which there was an assessor of markets, an intendant, a treasurer, and a representative. They also had their respective notaries, who in presence of the rabbis noted all proceedings that took place, and drew up all contracts made between Jews, which were in Hebrew.

In criminal cases, the rabbi of the place took cognizance of them in the first instance. From his interrogatories, or definite sentence, the parties might appeal or complain to the chief rabbi, in case it was in the town or province; or in his absence to the ouvidor of the province. But if the crime committed should be of the description that belonged to the superior tribunal of justice, they could not pass a final sentence thereon, as the royal ministers took cognizance of them in the last instance.

Civil actions were in the first instance decided by the rabbis of the towns. From their decisions, appeals or complaints might be made to the chief rabbi, if he were in the town or province; but if he were not, to the ouvidor of the respective province; but the parties condemned might appeal or complain to the royal ministers. Actions between themselves were to be proved in the same manner as suits between Christians were, that is by documentary evidence, witnesses, or by oath. But the word and testimony of a Jew might be impugned in a dispute between a Christian and a Jew, as in that case the testimony of a Jew against a Christian was not valid, unless corroborated by another Christian. But the testimony of Christians against Jews was always valid, even in causes among themselves.

Jews, whether in their own causes, or with Christians, were to be sworn by the rabbi on the five books of Moses in the synagogue, in presence of the party, and an usher of the court, who acquaints the judge that the Jew had been sworn; then the judge examines him, and learns the truth of the case.

In civil cases between a Christian and a Jew, or Jew and Moor, the Jew defendant can only be summoned before his rabbi; the plaintiff can only go to the court of the defendant. This rule has only two exceptions.

1. In places where judges are specially appointed to take cognizance of all civil causes that may occur between Christians and Jews.

2. When the action is for tithes, tolls, taxes or other royal dues, as there are particular judges appointed to try those causes.

In criminal actions, although a Jew is the defendant, they could only be tried by the criminal judge appointed by the king.

They could sue Christians for bond debts, even after the limitation of twenty years.

On Saturdays, passover, and other holidays enjoined by their religion, as they are prohibited to distract themselves with profane concerns, on those days the royal ministers could not proceed against them, nor could they be summoned to appear in any court.

In all cities and towns where ten Jews resided, they had their Jewry to live separate from Christians; they were closed at night, and guarded by two sentinels; they were better situated than the Moors, for the Jewries were always within the walls of the city. The street where the Jewry of Lisbon was, yet retains the name; the Moories were without the city walls.

It may now be necessary to state the laws regarding converts, for the kings of Portugal granted many advantages and favours to Jews and Moors who would enter the pale of the church. By a very ancient law—

Any person who called another "Turncoat," who from any other religion became a Christian, was to be fined sixty soldos by the alcalde.

No Jew could disinherit a child solely on account of embracing Christianity: on the contrary, it secured to the convert a large portion of the parents' property, even before their death.

The following was the law on the subject:—

If the convert was an only son or grandson, he received two-thirds of all the family property, and a third only was left for the parents: to which, or any other property he might acquire after the division had been made, the convert could never make any further claim, unless left to him by will.

If there were many sons, and the whole became Christians, the two thirds of the property were equally divided among them, under the same conditions as if there had been only a single convert.

If the convert had another brother who was a Jew, he was only to have half the property the parent possessed at the time of his conversion; and if he had more than one Jew brother, then he was only to have a third.

A convert might inherit from any Jew relation in the same way as he would were they Christians.

It has been stated that they were large landholders. No limits seem to have been made to their acquisitions; for the first mention of the subject is in the reign of Dom Pedro, who enacted,—

That when Jews bought, hired, assigned, farmed, or exchanged landed property with or from Christians, they should be sworn before the judge of the place, or the two notaries that draw up the deed, that the transaction is neither fraudulent nor usurious.

At this time they appear to have received titles or surnames from their landed possessions, for this sovereign granted to the chief rabbi, Don Moses, and his wife Donna Salva, and their heirs, the right and privilege of assuming the name of Navarro, on entailing a large property and many villas they possessed within the boundaries of Lisbon.

Dom Ferdinand, his successor, was also much attached to his Jewish subjects. Don Judah was the high treasurer of the royal treasury, and Don David Negro was a particular favorite with him. On his death Don David evinced his gratitude by his conduct towards John I., of Castile, the husband of Donna Beatrice, the daughter of the deceased monarch, as before related.

At the Cortes held in 1371, at Lisbon, he ordered

that the privileges which had been granted to the Jews and Moors should be observed.

On Dom John I. ascending the throne of Portugal, he continued favourable to the Hebrew people. His physician, Don Moses Salom, who had held the same post to his predecessors, fearing that the flame against the Israelitish people, which had caused such devastation in Castile and Aragon, might spread to Portugal, in 1391 presented to the king a bull of Boniface IX., confirming that of Clement VI., issued in 1348, wherein the Pope prohibited Christians molesting the Jews in the exercise of their religion, desecrating their cemeteries, or imposing on them any other taxes than what Christians were subject to. In consequence of this representation, the king, in the following year, ordered, "that the rights and privileges of the Israelites should be respected." Thus preventing bigoted ecclesiastics instigating the ignorant populace to perpetrate on the descendants of Judah those scenes of horror, that cast so indelible and bloody a stain on the pages of Spanish history.

The wearing a distinguishing sign having fallen into disuetude, complaint was made to the cortes held at Evora in 1391, that either they did not wear them, or had them so small, or wore them in such part of their dress, as not to be perceptible. Whereupon he ordained,—

That all Jews of his dominions should wear a red star, having six points, the size of his round seal, on the breast of the outer garment, at the pit of the stomach, in such manner as to be visible.

Hitherto all papers and documents among Jews were drawn up in Hebrew; but Dom John ordered that in future they should be made in the language of the country.

In the early périod of the monarchy, all the vassals were military, and every rich and powerful subject was bound to have his horse, to be prepared in case of war; as it was a measure for the defence and security of the kingdoms, the Jews were equally bound to the same until this reign, when the king ordered his master of horse not to compel Jews to have a horse, although they possessed property which, according to the regulations, would oblige them to it.

In 1404 it was ordered,—

That all Jews should inscribe the value of the produce, and the lands they possessed, or they should become the property of the occupiers.

It appears they paid a property-tax of 2 per cent.; for it is recorded that property worth 6,000 reis paid 120 to the king.

At the instance of the Jews, and by the advice of Dom Gil Alma, bishop of Lisbon, and other persons of his council, he ordered that a convert from Judaism should be compelled to give his wife *guet* (a divorce according to Jewish form), as without that document she would yet be considered bound to him as his wife.

For the protection of converts, he ordered,—

That any person that offended them should be summoned and tried before secular judges, as delinquents frequently were not punished when carried before ecclesiastical commissioners.

John was succeeded by his son Duarte (Edward). During his short reign of less than five years, he made many laws respecting the Jews and Moors. He appears to have taken example from his Castilian neighbour, John II. He ordained—

That no Jew or Moor should hold any office in the household of the king, queen, infantes, noblemen, or prelates.[4]

Fearing too much communication with Jews and Moors might be injurious to his Christian subjects, particularly to women, he enacted,—

That neither Jews nor Moors should have Christian boys or girls in their service, for hire or gratis.

They were prohibited entering the houses of single women, widows, or even of married women, in the absence of their husbands, unless in the company of two Christian men or women; except physicians, surgeons, apothecaries, and mechanics, who in virtue of their office, were permitted.

No Christian woman might enter the warehouses or shops of Jews or Moors, unless accompanied by a Christian man.

No Christian woman could enter the Jewry by herself under pain of death.

The same occurred here as in Spain: the extreme severity of the laws to prevent the intercourse of Jews and Moors with Christians, rendered them ineffective. The early death of this monarch probably saved the Hebrews of Portugal similar persecutions to what their co-religionists suffered at this period in Spain.

Alfonzo V., who succeeded to the throne in 1438, although constantly engaged in glorious but unprofitable wars with the Moors in Africa, or his Castilian neighbour, was a great benefactor to his country, for he revised and compiled the laws of the kingdom, forming a code which bears the title of the Alfonzine Code. The foregoing laws and privileges respecting the Hebrew people are embodied in it, with the following alterations and additions:—

A convert might continue to live with his unconverted wife for one year. If within that time she would not embrace Christianity, he should then be compelled to give her *guet*.

[4] Vit. de Santarem das Cortes.

That the privileges granted to converted Jews should be extended to Christians, who married Jewesses that had become Christians.

At the Cortes held in 1451, at Santarem, it was enacted,—

That Jews and Moors should not be permitted to wear silk dresses.

At another held at Lisbon in 1460, in consequence of a ruinous war he had entered into against Castile, a general contribution was ordered to be levied on the Jews and Moors; but their officers were exempted from it.

In 1468 a cortes was held at Santarem, which resolved,—

That Jews and Moors should not be permitted to reside without their Moories and Jewries, and that they should be compelled to wear the signs enacted by law.

Although ordered by John I., and now confirmed, it will be seen that it was not observed.

The Jews of Portugal, like those of Spain, were found to be more liberal in farming the public revenues than Christians; and the clergy, whatever might be their dislike to them for adherence to their faith, had none against them as farmers and collectors of the revenues of the church, as they paid better prices than could be obtained from any of their Catholic flock. To remedy this, in the last Cortes held by this sovereign at Lisbon, in 1473, it was enacted,—

That Jews should not be permitted to recover the revenues belonging to the church; and severe penalties were enacted against Christians who farmed or let them to either Jews or Moors.

At the same Cortes it was ordained—

That the Jewish rabbis and the muftis of the Moors might only take cognizance of affairs that occurred among themselves in their respective communities.

## CHAPTER XXVIII.

*John II.—Cortes of Evora.—The Exiles from Spain admitted—Forced to quit—Cruelties they suffered.—Emanuel succeeds to the Throne—Banishes them—Deliberations of the Council—Their Children taken from them—Bishop Osorio's Account—Usque's Relation of their Sufferings.*

On the accession of John II. in 1481, he held a Cortes at Evora; the following petitions against the Jews and Moors were presented to it.

Sire, it appears to our people that in regard to the dresses of Jews, Moors, and their wives, your highness might order that they should wear their signs and dress as formerly, in such manner that they may be known as Jews or Moors wherever they are, and thereby confer a great favour on your vassals.[1]

Whereas, at present we generally perceive, much injurious dissoluteness among Jews, Moors, and Christians, as well in living, in dress, and in association, which is disgraceful, improper, and abominable. And we notice Jew cavaliers, mounted on richly caparisoned horses and mules, in fine cloaks, cassocks, silk doublets, closed hoods, and with gilt swords, that it is impossible to recognise them. Further, they enter churches, mock the holy sacraments and mix with Christians, to the great injury of the Catholic faith. And besides this great

[1] Chap. ciii.

dissoluteness, there spring other errors and acts highly prejudicial and injurious to bodies and souls. What is worse, from being farmers-general they do not wear the distinguishing sign, but molest and annoy Christians by their strict exaction of payment.[2]

The king answered,—

As to the clothes of Jews, it is right that they should be of the same description of cloth as I have ordered other men to wear, but they may not wear silk, and are only to wear woollen. And they are to wear the customary sign of a star, according to the form of the ordinance, on the pit of the stomach.

A singular complaint was made against them at the Cortes held the following year:—

The representatives of the kingdom laid before the king that Jew workmen, as cobblers, renovators, etc., travel the country in search of work, and while the labourers are employed in the fields, they are connected with their wives and daughters, which (added the Cortes), is highly injurious to good morals and the Catholic faith; and, in consequence, they demanded that Jew workmen should not be permitted to travel the country, but be confined to their Jewries, where those who require their work will be sure to find them.

The king sensibly answered—

That it was for the convenience of the country people that he had permitted Jew workmen to offer their services to the labourers, and that if those workmen committed any crime they could be brought to justice.

This proves that the poor Jews were artisans, and sought industriously to gain their livelihood. The higher classes were men of learning, and great repute in the sciences generally; their physicians were held in the highest esteem, and rivalled in skill their medical brethren in Spain.

[2] Chap. cxviii.

In the early part of his reign, from an expedition made by Abraham de Beija and Joseph Zapatera to the Persian Gulf, by the coast of the Red Sea, the king gained such information as to induce him to expect that a passage to India by the western coast of Africa might be effected; but his premature death prevented the accomplishment of his wish to discover it, in which his successor succeeded in 1497 by the aid of the intrepid Vasco de Gama. John charged the Hebrew physicians, R. Rodrigues and R. Joseph, together with the geographer, Martin Belem, to form rules for taking the altitude of the sun, and tables of its declination, for his vassals who were making voyages on the coast of Africa. It was probably to these two eminent physicians and cosmographers, together with the bishop of Vizeu, that he referred the consideration of Columbus's project for the discovery of America, as he used to consult them on all matters of this description.

As early as in 1485, R. Eliezer and R. Tzorba introduced Hebrew printing into Portugal. From their press many valuable books were produced in 1491. Among other works a beautiful edition of the Pentateuch, with the Targum paraphrase of Onkelos, and the commentary of Rashi in two volumes, quarto; it is considered by bibliographers to be the finest specimen of Hebrew typography of the fifteenth century. It is extremely rare, as are most of the early editions of Hebrew books, probably the smallness of the editions in the beginning of that invaluable art, and the losses experienced in the frequent emigrations, have been the causes of their scarcity.

The Jews had seized with avidity an art that afforded the means of disseminating knowledge. The printing presses of the Jews were not confined to theological and religious books. Works of every description on jurisprudence, history, and medicine were printed from the manuscripts that circulated among the Hebrew people in the bright age of their literature. Soon after the discovery of the art, Hebrew presses were established in many cities of Italy, among the earliest may be reckoned those of Plebisario, Mantua, Padua, Sonsino, Venice, Naples, Pesaro, Faro and Rimini; and from those cities they introduced printing at Thessalonica and Constantinople. Ten years earlier the Jews of Italy had been actively employed in disseminating their sacred books, but they are so rare as to be accounted among the greatest curiosities of bibliographers. Learned Jews attended to the correction of the press, therefore the earliest editions of the sacred books of the Hebrews, are for the most part correct, and offer important instruction to establish the purity of the text of those books, having mostly been printed from ancient and esteemed manuscripts; so that not only bibliographers, but theologians also, seek those old editions which are regarded equal to manuscripts, their types are beautifully moulded, and are printed with fine black ink, having exceedingly wide margins.

Black slaves being imported into Portugal from the coast of Africa, in 1490 Jews and Moors were prohibited buying them.

When no alleviation to the cruel edict of Ferdinand and Isabella could be found, and the descendants of Israel prepared to quit the Spanish territory, numbers, as before stated, sought an asylum in Portugal, which had frequently offered a peaceable residence to the

Castilian Hebrew emigrants in the many persecutions they had suffered in that kingdom. Two causes may have led so many of the Spanish exiles to seek an asylum in Portugal, and submit to the harsh terms imposed by John II., which according to Portuguese historians were; that—

All persons, children at the breast excepted, were to pay eight crusados, for which they were to receive certificates from the officers appointed for the purpose. Those who should be found not to have paid, and who were unprovided with certificates, were to be slaves to the king. Under these conditions, they were permitted to remain eight months in the kingdom, within which period the king engaged to furnish them vessels on moderate terms, to carry them wherever they wished to go. Those who did not depart within the specified time were to become slaves.

Armourers, smiths, and braziers, who would remain in the kingdom, were only to pay four crusados each.[3]

Under these conditions, 20,000 families, some of ten and twelve persons, are said to have entered the kingdom.

Historians, to palliate the conduct of their sovereign, say that he then meditated an expedition against the Moors of Africa, and not being able to raise sufficient money from his subjects, he extorted this imposition from the unfortunate Israelites, which at his death was found intact, as he could not execute his intended project.[4]

The vicinity of the countries, and the similarity of language and customs, were inducements that naturally would lead them to seek refuge there, in preference to undertaking perilous voyages, and to find

[3] Damião de Goes.     [4] Garcia de Resende's Chro.

on their arrival, inhospitable shores; to which may be added that innate principle in every civilised breast, love of one's native land; fondly hoping the stern decree might be repealed, and themselves restored to the land of their birth, their homes, their fondest ties, and the graves of ancestors of whom they might so justly be proud. This made them linger on the Iberian soil of Lusitania; but, alas! their hopes were vain. The cruel mandate was irrevocable, the tyrants were inflexible, and even carried their hatred, vengeance, and persecution, against the unoffending descendants of Israel beyond their own dominions, as will be seen.

The consideration in which the Hebrew people was held in that country, the privileges and tranquillity they had long enjoyed, offered some security and peace to the expatriated Spanish descendants of Judah.

Although the schools of Portugal had not produced an Aben Ezra, or a Maimonides, they could boast of their Jachias, their Abarbanels, and many other learned men, whose names will be found in the preceding pages, and who cast a lustre on the Hebrew name, and the literature of their age.

But John, though favourable to the Jews of Portugal, was not so to the unfortunate Spanish exiles. Probably the great influx was the cause of his exacting the performance of the agreement under which they had been permitted to enter Portugal. Although the king had ordered that they should be charged moderately for their passages and freights, the captains and masters of vessels made them pay higher prices than they had agreed for. Besides ill-treating them, and taking advantage of their forlorn condition, as they had no means for obtaining redress, they prolonged the voyages for the purpose of selling provisions and water to them at any price they chose to exact. They insulted them in the most brutal manner, and even ravished their wives and daughters, so that in quitting Spain, the miseries of the unfortunate exiles had not yet terminated.

The Castilian Jews, who from poverty or any other cause had not departed at the limited time, the king ordered should be taken for slaves, according to the terms of their entrance, and distributed them to whoever asked for them. His inhumanity did not cease here. He tore their young children from them, and had them baptised. Being at the time desirous of peopling his newly discovered acquisition on the coast of Africa, the island of St. Thomas, he sent them to it, with the new governor, Alvaro de Cominha, so that by being separated from their parents, and marrying people in the island, they might become good Christians.

Fathers threw themselves at the feet of the king, entreating they might be sent with their children, which was cruelly denied them. A mother embracing her only child, and determined not to be separated from her infant, threw herself into the sea, and perished with it in her arms.

On the accession of Emanuel in 1495, the prospects of the unfortunate Spanish Hebrews brightened, and seemed to promise a happier future. This prince being sensible they had not wilfully, but only from necessity, remained in Portugal after the limited time, generously restored to their liberty those whom his predecessor had condemned to slavery. With a grateful sense for such extraordinary goodness, a treatment they had long been unaccustomed to, they offered the king a large sum of money, which he magnanimously refused, being resolved to gain their affection by kind treatment, and thereby gradually to allure them to the Christian faith.

But their hopes were soon blighted, for in a few months they were treated even worse, and suffered more, than when they quitted the Spanish dominions. The Portuguese Jews who had been among the first settlers of that kingdom, were doomed to suffer the same troubles that awaited their Castilian brethren, without even a cause being assigned for it. The Catholic sovereigns had given a reason, although false; but Emanuel drove from their homes the unfortunate descendants of Israel, who had enlightened and been the ornaments of his kingdom, only because they would not abjure the religion of their forefathers, nor abandon that law their ancestors had received from the Eternal at Mount Sinai.

The Academician Ribiero dos Santos, author of " Memoirs of the Sacred Literature of the Portuguese Jews," acknowledges that the Christians of Portugal, in regard to learning, owe innumerable obligations to the Hebrews established in Portugal.

Indeed (says he), we are chiefly indebted to them for the first knowledge of philosophy, botany, medicine, astronomy, and cosmography, as well as for the rudiments of the grammar of the holy language, and nearly all the studies of biblical literature. What contributed greatly to disseminate the knowledge of these subjects, was the introducing, and the perfecting of Portuguese typography, particularly the Hebrew, which put us in a state to enter into competition with the more advanced nations of Italy and Germany.

The following account of the cruel and inhuman conduct of Emanuel is extracted from the works of the Historian of the time,[5] and the learned bishop Osorio.[6]

As the Portuguese were anxious to see their sovereign married, they recommended an alliance with one of the daughters of Ferdinand, king of Castile; Emanuel consented, provided he could obtain the hand of the young and beautiful widow of Alphonso, the son of Don John. The princess Isabella was weak, and animated with a false zeal; and although opposed to a second marriage, gave her consent, on condition that Emanuel should previously banish the Jews and Moors from his states. Ferdinand also wrote to the king and earnestly entreated him not to permit so perverse a people, who were under the displeasure of God and the odium of mankind, to remain in his dominions. Emanuel considering it a subject of the utmost delicacy and worthy the greatest consideration, thereupon consulted his council.

Some of the councillors were of opinion, that they ought not to be driven away, since the pope himself permitted them to reside in the papal dominions. Induced by his example, several Italian states, and many Christian princes, not only in Italy, but in Germany, Hungary, and other parts of Europe, had also granted them the same liberty, and permitted them to trade and carry on all kinds of business. Besides (said they), their banishment will never reclaim them, for wherever they go, they will carry their perverse dispositions; a change of country will not make any alteration in the depravity of their minds. If they should go over to Africa, as it is probable they would if driven from Portugal, all hopes of their conversion would be lost. While they have lived among Christians, many of them, influenced by friendship and example, have embraced the Christian faith, which will never be the case when they come to mingle with blind and superstitious Mahomedans. Moreover, it will be highly detrimental to the public benefit, if this people, who are extremely rich, should carry

---

[5] Damiaõ de Goes.    [6] De rebus Emanuelis.

their wealth to the Moors, and enrich our enemies. They would be able to teach the Moors what is necessary to oppose us, and instruct them in the mechanical arts, in which they are very expert, particularly in the manufacture of arms, from which great injury, trouble, and loss might accrue both to the people and property of all Christendom.

Those of a different opinion acknowledged that what had been said was true, but that it was not without reason that the Jews had been banished from Spain, France, England, Scotland, Denmark, Norway, Sweden, and many adjoining states, from the whole of Flanders, Burgundy, and many places in Germany. Those princes did not set a higher value on the increase of their revenues than the interests of religion. They had perceived the dangerous consequences of allowing such a people to remain in their dominions, for they were apt to impose their pernicious errors on the simple and vulgar. That, in fact, it would be highly imprudent to place confidence in men who were so inveterate against our religion, who were bound by no ties nor obligations, but would be ready to sacrifice every thing to their interests, by prying into the secrets of state, and giving intelligence to our enemies. It would be much more to the public benefit that they should be banished immediately, when they could only carry away the wealth they had scraped together in other countries; this (they said) would be more advisable than allowing them to remain longer, and then send them away after they had amassed considerable wealth, which they scrupled not to obtain by the most fraudulent means. As the latter opinion was more agreeable to the passion of Emanuel, influenced by it, in December 1496, he issued a decree from Muja, ordering all Jews and Moors who would not embrace the Christian faith to quit his dominions. A day was fixed, after which all who remained in Portugal were to lose their liberty. Three months was the time allowed them.

The time approached, when the Jews who would not become Christians were to quit Portugal. All prepared with alacrity and firm resolution for their departure. It caused Emanuel great uneasiness, to think of so many thousand men leaving his kingdom, and being driven into banishment; and he was desirous at least of converting their sons. For this purpose he devised a plan that in fact was contrary to justice and equity, although the act was attended with the good consequences he wished. He ordered all the sons of Jews under fourteen years of age to be forcibly taken from their parents, that they might be instructed and initiated in the Christian faith. This could not be executed without causing the most affecting and heart-rending scenes. It was a horrid and wretched spectacle to see tender children torn from the arms and breasts of their distressed mothers; fathers who fondly held them in their embrace, dragged about to force them from their arms. To hear the cries, sighs, groans, lamentations, and female shrieks that filled the air, was dreadful. Some were so distracted, that they destroyed their children by casting them into wells; others, in fits of despair, made away with themselves. These wretched mortals were yet doomed to suffer further calamity and misery. Those who were desirous of quitting a country where they had met such barbarous treatment were not permitted. The king was so determined on making converts of this people, that he resolved to induce them by rewards, or compel them by necessity to embrace Christianity.

By the arrangement the king was to have provided vessels for the Jews, and to permit them freely to depart; but this he purposely delayed from time to time. Three ports (Lisbon, Oporto, and Setubal), were at first assigned for their embarkation; but it was subsequently ordered they should only embark at Lisbon. This obliged them from all parts of the country to repair to that capital, which became so crowded with them, that they were like sheep in a pen. The motive for reducing the number of ports of embarkation by the inhuman and wily Emanuel was, that by compelling all to come to Lisbon, the limited time would expire, numbers would be unable to leave, and thus forfeit their freedom. Many, wearied by these hardships, became Christians. Some perhaps were sincere in their conversion, but far more were only so in outward appearance, to render their existence less painful and irksome. They were, however, baptised, and initiated into the mysteries of our holy religion. By this means they recovered their children, and were restored to their freedom. The king was extremely kind to these, and gave them great encouragement, so that many Jews continued to live comfortably in the Portuguese dominions.

Such was the mode used to bring about the conversion of this people; but it must be owned it was unwarrantable. Will any one pretend to maintain that it was consistent with the principles of justice or religion, to force perverse and obstinate minds into the belief of things which in reality they despised and rejected? Will any one pretend to take on himself to prevent the freedom of will, or put fetters on the understanding? This is impossible to be done, and is directly opposed to the doctrine of Christ. He does not take pleasure in any thing that proceeds from force or restraint, and is pleased only with a voluntary sacrifice that flows from the heart. He does not command violence to be offered to the minds of men, but that, by persuasion and mild treatment, they should be invited to the study of the true religion. Besides, what is more presumptuous, than for a mortal to do what the Divine Spirit only can effect? It alone is able to enlighten and purify the minds of men. Those it finds not altogether perverse and repugnant to its influence, it removes from darkness, and makes them see the truths of Christianity. Is it not scandalous and disgraceful, that religion should be so far prostituted, as to admit men of so much infidelity and dissimulation into her holy mysteries? That those who contemn the doctrine of Christ, should have such opportunities afforded them to exercise their impiety and ridicule? That religion should be violated and debased under a religious pretence?

Yet there were some persons who highly applauded the conduct of Emanuel towards the Jews, especially as some religious and learned men were of opinion that it was lawful, and had been done before by Christian princes. But there never was, nor will there ever be wanting persons, who, to insinuate themselves into the favour of their prince, will accommodate their sentiments with his humours. This step of the king, although unjust in itself, produced, as we see daily, most excellent effects, for, notwithstanding many only put on a religious mask, their sons, having forgotten the impiety of their fathers, influenced by custom and example, now worship Christ most devoutly, and live according to his rules. Thus it was that part of the Jews were removed by banishment, and part lost the name of Jews.

But the Moors, who would not renounce the pernicious errors of Mahomedanism, were allowed, unmolested, to depart for Africa, lest if they had been injured, the Christians that lived in Asia and Africa should suffer for it.

The foregoing leaves but little room for comment. The worthy and learned prelate acknowledges the injustice and iniquity of the conduct of Emanuel, although he attempts to palliate it by the effects produced. But his ideas of forcing man to change his religious belief, cannot fail to meet the approbation of every reflecting mind. Fear of retaliation induced the Portuguese monarch to show greater mercy towards the Moors than to the descendants of Israel.

As to the assertion of some of the councillors, fearing the treachery of the Jews, universal history shews it was unfounded and untrue: for no country in the world can produce a single instance of a Jew being a traitor,—their fidelity to their native country has ever been a most remarkable characteristic in their conduct, as faithful and devoted subjects. As to getting wealth by fraudulent means, in the history of Portugal they are not accused, as in other countries, of usury, in any one instance.

Usqué adds to the relation of Osorio,—

That on the children being taken from their parents, many fine promises were made to induce them voluntarily to become Christians, but they were firm and refused; whereupon they were dragged by the legs and arms to the churches, where water was thrown on them. After this they were sent back to their afflicted parents, who sustained a miserable existence, who were told they were now Christians, and would hate them unless they did the same; but they would not submit. The king ordered them to be deprived of food and drink. At the end of three days, finding they would rather die than abandon their faith, they were dragged by the hair and beards, with blows and wounds, to the churches, where water was sprinkled on them. Those who were thus baptized had Christian names given to them, and were given in charge to old Christians, to watch that they observed Catholicism and kept to the faith. A father who had thus been taken with his six children, by learned reasoning recommended them to die, rather than renounce their religion; they were all murdered. Some, sooner than abandon the religion of their fathers, threw themselves into wells, or from their windows. Their corpses were taken up and burnt, to inspire their surviving friends and relatives with fear and dread.[7]

A wretched mother, from whom six children had been taken, cast herself before the king's carriage, and entreated that the youngest might be restored to her, to console her for the loss of the others. The king, inhumanly smiling at her distress, ordered her to be taken away, while his attendant courtiers ridiculed her maternal affliction. The people were not as unfeeling or inhuman as their sovereign: many of them secreted the children of the unfortunate Israelites for their wretched parents.

Many yielding to necessity received baptism, solely to preserve their lives, for it will be seen numbers of those dissembling Catholics only waited the oppor-

[7] Consolaçao.

tunity of escaping from the fangs of these ferocious monsters. Learning the deplorable state in which the holy office held the converts in Spain, they stipulated that for twenty years the Inquisition should not be introduced into Portugal, and after its establishment, that the accused should be informed who were the witnesses against them, and in case of condemnation their property should not be taken from their families.[8]

These were but feeble guarantees which the Jews asked against the tyranny of inquisitors; but it shews the odious reputation they had acquired in a few years. Emanuel acceded to the demand.

The expulsion of so many useful subjects, which took place at a time when the expeditions and maritime conquests took away so many thousands of Portuguese from the peninsula, and the establishment of innumerable convents, hastened the decline of the population of the kingdoms.[9]

The blind policy of Spain and Portugal in expelling this industrious and commercial people prevented their reaping the rich harvests their discoveries in the east and west would otherwise have afforded them, by which they might have preserved that ascendancy they held at the commencement of the sixteenth century.

[8] Monteiro Inq. do Portugal.
[9] Mem. para a Hist. de Agricul. em Portugal.

## CHAPTER XXIX.

*The Exiles protected by the Papal See—The Senate of Venice welcomes them.—Privileges granted them at Leghorn, and other Italian States.—Heroism of Esther Cohen.—Solomon Rophé—In the Barbary States, raised to the Highest Offices.—Egypt.— Morocco.—Heroism of Alvarensi.—Noble conduct of the Jews to the Portuguese Prisoners.—Parliament of Paris—Settle at Bourdeaux and Bayonne.—Deputation to Charles V.—Independence of Holland— The Jews protected there—at Hamburg—in South America and the West Indies—the North of Europe —England—Sir Moses Montefiore, Baronet of the United Kingdom—employed and ennobled by Spain and Portugal.—An Article of the Treaty of Utrecht.*

The cruelties suffered by the unfortunate Hebrews in these two banishments, induced those who were not nominally, but in reality Christian states, to afford an asylum to the expatriated Spanish and Portuguese refugees.

Besides the Jews who had resided in Italy from time immemorial, the many emigrations from Spain had vastly increased the Jewish population in the south of Europe, and they had held the highest situations, not only in the palaces of the lay princes, but also in the households of popes. In proof of this assertion, in 1414, the republic of Florence sent a Jew banker, named Valori, to Milan, with a complaint to the Duke Visconti, against the act of the lord of Forli, who, at his death, had appointed the duke administrator of his estates. The duke refused to receive a Jew as ambassador, and referred him to his secretary. Florence considered itself insulted by the affront offered to its envoy, and declared war against Visconti.[1] As a proof of the ignorance of Christianity of the bigoted Spanish and Portuguese sovereigns, Rome opened its gates to the banished Israelites, and Alexander VI., who probably laughed at their intemperate zeal, kindly received the exiled Hebrews, and afforded them his protection. Zurita relates, " that the Jews of Rome, fearing the competition of the exiles, exerted themselves to prevent their establishment in that capital, and even offered a thousand pieces of gold to the pope to prohibit it." But the more humane and politic pontiff threatened to banish them, unless they received and assisted their co-religionists. When the well-known liberality and compassion ever shewn by the Jews to their indigent and distressed brethren are considered, the veracity of this historian on this point may be justly doubted, and a Spaniard of that bigoted age, may be excused for vilifying the Hebrew people. After the persecution the new Christians suffered in Portugal, Clement VII. invited them to settle in the papal states, and offered the Jews that had forcibly been baptized, to come and live in his dominions as they pleased, without enquiry being made how they had lived in Portugal. His successors, finding the benefit of this policy, continued to follow it. Nearly 20,000 repaired to the States of the Church, and by their commerce and industry Ancona became a flourishing commercial port. The family of

[1] Daru Hist. de Venise.

Corcos was highly esteemed by the noble families of Rome, and had great influence at court. But when the king and cardinal of Portugal found that many of the new Christians prepared to go there, in 1524 they made it death and confiscation of property for any to attempt to depart the kingdom.

The senate of Venice, which, in its deliberations, was ever most prudent and cautious, reprobated the conduct of these sovereigns, in thus banishing from their dominions without any cause, people who were publicly and privately so beneficial to the state. The emigrants were welcomed in all the Venetian states, and were so powerfully protected at Florence, that it was commonly said, a person might as soon insult the grand duke as a Jew. Two Jews had permission granted them in the latter part of the 14th century, to establish a bank to lend money at interest. The emigrants were employed by the senate in various affairs of state. Don Isaac Abarbanel negociated for it the spice treaty with Portugal; and Daniel Rodrigues was sent in 1589 to appease the troubles in Dalmatia, which he successfully effected.

Leghorn had just been founded by the Medici; its situation promised to render it an important commercial place. A quarter was assigned to the Spanish and Portuguese emigrants; they were received more as colonists, than as tolerated foreigners. It was in reality a Jewish colony, which has prospered and lasted longer than any of their establishments in the south of Europe; for it is yet in the most flourishing and solid condition. Whether misfortunes had rendered the exiles prudent, or that the colonists, admitted by the Medici, were naturally the friends of order and justice, and provided with means for maintaining a rising establishment, it is certain they proceeded with great wisdom in the foundation of their colony, which secured them the favor of the grand duke. They formed a constitution where theocracy does not govern; a proof that it was merchants, and not rabbis, that founded the Jewish community at Leghorn. The exiles modelled their government on the Italian republics; they placed it in an aristocratical body, a senate of sixty persons, who elected from themselves an administration of five members, part of which were chosen every six months; but they were only elected on the approval of the grand duke, to whom a list of candidates was submitted. This senate judged the suits of the community, and could even inflict corporal punishment, and banish culprits from Leghorn. The Spanish language is yet preserved in congregational matters, and even in their daily transactions; the Mosaic worship is performed with great splendour. The community possesses a considerable income, which, together with some imposts, serves to support the synagogue, schools, and hospital. Medicine and surgery are studied and practised as formerly by many Israelites, both merchants and rabbis. The former, by their commercial speculations, especially with Africa, have made immense fortunes; the wealth of the Ghetto (the Jewry) of Leghorn has so increased, that the 10,000 inhabitants of that obscure and dirty quarter, are owners of a large part of the city, and the surrounding country. They are likewise bankers and brokers. The invasion of the French during the revolution, placed them on an equality with other citizens, since which, the senate no longer exercises judicial power except in religious matters, and has been reduced to forty.

It has been before stated, that a number of the emigrants had repaired to Naples, where they soon amalgamated with the Neapolitan Jews. Owing to their security and ease of life under the fine Parthenopian sky, they began to signalise themselves in literature. The invasion of Charles VIII. of France destroyed their happiness, and exposed them to new persecutions. The major part fled; those that remained, panic struck, seemed inclined to embrace Christianity to save their property and liberty. But as soon as the danger was over, they forgot their baptism and profession of faith, and returned to Judaism; or at least ceased to practise the Catholic worship. When, in 1504, Gonzalve de Cordova, took Naples for the king of Spain, to appear consistent, as the Jews had been banished from the Spanish dominions, the question of expelling the Jews was mooted. But the Great Captain, as Gonzalve is styled, considered it would be a great detriment to the state, if they retired to Venice; he preferred prosecuting them as bad Christians, to expelling them as Jews. In consequence, instead of promulgating an edict of banishment, he wished to introduce the Inquisition. But other affairs occupied the government in this recent conquest, so difficult to maintain. At length, in 1510, the attempt was made to introduce the tribunal of the Inquisition. When the people saw that it was intended to impose on the conquered nation an ecclesiastical authority, which had shed torrents of blood and diffused mourning throughout Spain, a general insurrection took place. The Spanish government found it most prudent to yield; but, in promising the Neapolitans not to introduce the Inquisition, it avenged itself for this concession, on the Jews, who were all banished the kingdom, and obliged to retire to other Italian states.

The duke of Ferrara admitted the Portuguese exiles to reside in his capital and states, and granted them the same privileges as the other Italian princes; but the great influx of Jews and new Christians, induced him to renew an old law, that they should wear a small yellow circle on the breast. In 1551, he was obliged to enact a law again exiling the unfortunate Israelites, in consequence of the plague which had been brought by some Swiss and Germans; but as some of the expatriated Hebrews had arrived from the Grisons, the people exclaimed they had spread the contagion, although they were equally suffering, so that many found the utmost difficulty to drag themselves to the vessels that were to take them away. Some fell into the hands of pirates; others, repulsed, from the fear of infection, from the ports of the Adriatic, were charitably received by their brethren in Pesaro. At the intercession of Emanuel Bichacho, a noble emigrant, from Portugal, the duke of Urbino granted them his protection. One night, in 1553, a mob secretly entered their synagogue, and destroyed everything they found in it, as well as in another synagogue belonging to the Italian Jews. The duke had only signed this decree of banishment to quiet his riotous subjects. They soon returned to Ferrara; for the famed edition of the Ferrara Bible bears the date of 1553; and, in the same year, R. Samuel Usque printed in that city, *As Consalaçams os tribulaçoens de Ysrael*, which gives the most impartial account of the various persecutions the Jews suffered from the earliest period until his time. It is a most curious work, written in the Portuguese language of that age. He often borders on the poetic, as may be seen by his description of the Inquisition. The work is extremely scarce.

A number repaired to Bologna, where they were so much esteemed, that, when in 1529, the Emperor Charles V. wished to banish them from it, the nobles interfered, and dissuaded him; but, in 1534, he banished them from Sicily.

Many went to Cremona, where renowned Jewish academies flourished. They possessed a most valuable library of Hebrew works. In 1559, the Inquisition of Rome resolved on its destruction, and despatched Sextus of Sienna for the purpose. The fanatical Dominican proved himself a fit envoy for such a mission; he condemned 12,000 volumes to the flames, and, had he not been restrained by the more enlightened Italian princes, would not have left a single Hebrew book; for, he regrets, "that the avarice and weakness of princes permitted them to retain Talmudical works."

The duke of Modena also granted them the privilege of having judges of their own people. At Mantua, Padua, Verona, Ragusa, and every other city and independent state, they were kindly received.

Before quitting Italy, the following historical fact deserves to be recorded. When Andrew Doria ravaged Sicily and the Morea, he made many Jews prisoners, who were redeemed by their brethren in Italy. In every congregation, funds were appropriated for the redemption of captives. Among the prisoners made at Coron, was Jacob Cohen and his wife, Esther. The captain of the galley on which she was on board, became enamoured of her. Finding that her tears and entreaties did not divert him from his wicked purpose, she begged him to grant her a little delay, and she would submit to his wishes. The tyrant, quieted thereby, desisted; in the meanwhile the virtuous and afflicted wife mounted to a part of the galley suited to her purpose, tied her clothes to her feet, and threw herself into the sea; sacrificing her life to preserve her honour and chastity.[1]

Many joined their brethren in Turkey, where the Spanish exiles had been kindly received. The free and undisturbed practice of their religion was permitted, and many privileges granted to them. R. Joseph Peso, a disciple of R. Isaac Aboab, opened a college at Constantinople, which produced many learned men. Selim I. appointed Joseph Amon, a native of Andalusia, to be his chief physician. His son, Moses Amon, who, by order of the sultan, had translated the Hebrew ritual into the Turkish language, occupied the same post under Solyman, his successor. From his influence, he saved the Jews from being massacred in that capital under the following circumstance:—

A virtuous married Turkish woman having been much importuned and persecuted by a Turk, she informed her husband, who advised her to give him a rendezvous. Lying in wait for the intended adulterer, he assassinated him, and to avoid discovery threw the corpse into the Jews' quarter. The populace rose against them, and false testimony being adduced to the bashaws, they had a number imprisoned; when the physician requested the sultan to have a rigid

[1] Nomologia.

enquiry made into the affair, by which the whole was discovered.[2]

Shortly after, Solyman granted them permission to establish a printing-press at Constantinople, which was of great advantage to the nation; for copies of the law which had become scarce were now universally circulated, and people applied more earnestly to its study. The Muftis were opposed to this grant, fearing the Alcoran might be printed; but their opposition could have had little or no effect, for Zacut, in 1566, there published the first edition (the only correct one), which is now very scarce, of his " Juchasin," the Book of Genealogies. Successive sultans continued their protection, and employed them and their descendants in various honorable posts. After the battle of Lepanto, Selim II. sent Solomon Rophé to conclude and negotiate a treaty of peace with the republic of Venice.

Numbers repaired to the Barbary states of Algiers, Tunis, and Tripoli, where many of their brethren had long resided. The Deys employed and still continue their descendants in the highest offices of state, as secretaries, treasurers, and envoys to foreign powers; although in general disliked by the people, the protection they received from the government secured them from the persecutions the Israelites suffered in Europe; they were only molested in the various revolutions that so frequently happened in those piratical states. On those occasions they were unmercifully plundered. When Tunis, in 1535, was taken by Charles V., the Jews were made prisoners, and one hundred and fifty captives were redeemed by the congregations of Naples and Venice.

[2] Consol. de Israel.

At Salonica, where many of the exiled European Jews repaired, they established a famous college, which had as many as five thousand students. The poor were maintained, clothed, had salaries allowed them, and qualified instructors provided. They also had other academies, and thirty-six synagogues, all of which, with a valuable library, were destroyed in 1545, by an accidental fire.

Numbers went to Saphet, where they enjoyed many privileges. A college of high repute had long existed there; and the famed R. Moses, of Cordova, is considered to have been among its first founders.

Egypt also offered an asylum from persecution, to the descendants of Israel. They were numerous in that country, and possessed great privileges; and most were merchants who carried on an immense trade; for the frequent emigrations from Spain had greatly increased the Jewish population of Egypt. R. Samuel Serralvo removed his college to Cairo. In 1524, Achmed, the governor, revolted against the sultan, and the lawless soldiery began to plunder the houses of the Jews. Achmed, determined to enrich himself, at once taxed them two hundred talents. They represented their inability to pay so large an amount, but carried fifteen talents to his treasury. Achmed, enraged, ordered all who had not paid to be imprisoned. While one of his officers was executing his order, a conspiracy broke out, and Achmed was obliged to flee; but being overtaken by Ibrahim and put to death, peace was restored to Cairo, and the Jews escaped this danger.

Many retired to Morocco. R. Joseph Uziel and R. Shemtob re-opened their colleges at Fez, where the

Portuguese refugees were kindly received by their brethren and the emperor. They were allowed to have their own judges; twelve of the most eminent sages were chosen, three officiated weekly; and on important cases all assembled, and the governor was bound to have their sentences executed. They were so much respected, that for many years the family of Rutès were *Xeques* or governors of Fez and Tarudante.

At this period the throne of Fez was occupied by the Merinès, the Xeriffès rose against them, and plundered the kingdom. Samuel Alvarensi, a Spanish emigrant, was a great favourite with the reigning sovereign. The Xeriffès laid siege to Ceuta, then occupied by the Portuguese troops of Emanuel. Alvarensi, in gratitude to the monarch from whom he had received so much kindness, risked his life, property, and all he possessed, to serve against the enemies of his sovereign. Providing some vessels, he joined some officers of the Merinès, who appointed him their commander, and embarked with about four hundred men. They landed at Ceuta, and at night, with that small force, attacked the besieging army of the Xeriffès, amounting to thirty thousand men, and completely defeated them, so that the next day they raised the siege.[3] R. Judah Aboab transferred his college to Alcaçarquiver, a place renowned in history for the defeat and death of Dom Sebastian, in 1578, when the flower of the Portuguese nobility were slain or made prisoners. From thence they were taken to Fez, where, in the market-places, they were sold by public auction for slaves, and considered themselves fortunate when purchased by the descendants of those whom their

[3] Nomologia.

ancestors had so cruelly persecuted. They permitted many to return to Portugal, depending on their promise to repay the sums they had advanced to redeem them, which they fulfilled, and sent many valuable presents in return for the kindness they had received.[4] Such was the revenge the Portuguese Jews took for the wrongs they had suffered. They enjoyed great favour at court, and the emperor intrusted the most important offices to them, and frequently sent them as ambassadors and envoys to foreign states. Great numbers were employed in the iron works on the mountains of Morocco, in building, and many laborious works, which the indolent habits of the Moors rendered them averse to; and many were industrious agriculturists. They were governed by their own judges, who exercised an arbitrary power, and kept the lower classes, who were extremely ignorant except of the outward forms of Judaism, in the most abject state; and although there were many Jews in Morocco of high attainments, they required the polish of European civilization to procure for them that consideration their learning might otherwise have entitled them to. The want of printing in Morocco probably hides from us many valuable treasures; therefore the Jews of that country should not be judged by the few we see from it.

The parliament of Paris reprobated in severe terms the inhuman conduct of the Castilian and Portuguese monarchs, which probably induced Henry II. (as the Jews were not then tolerated in France), to invite some Jews from Mantua to settle in that kingdom; and in 1550, by letters patent, he granted them protection, and various privileges, which led a number

[4] Cardozo Excel de los Hebrees.

of Portuguese emigrants to establish themselves at Bourdeaux and Bayonne, where to the present day their descendants carry on the trade and commerce of their ancestors, and enjoy every right as French subjects.

On the accession of Charles V. to the throne of Spain, in 1519, some of the sincere Jews and pretended converts made a last effort to return to the Iberian Peninsula. They deputed some of the most considerable of their people to him in Flanders, to represent that they groaned under the yoke of a religion which they had been forced to embrace, and were daily exposed to the merciless tribunal of the Inquisition,— that they carried on with honour nearly the whole commerce of the nation, and were the most useful, and perhaps the most faithful subjects of the kingdom,— on which account they trusted in his justice and goodness that he would grant them the free exercise of their religion, and engaged on that condition, to give him all the assistance they could, and in return for his kindness, would make him a present of 800,000 crowns in gold. The deputation met with a very gracious reception from that monarch, and the council of Flanders was likewise of opinion that he ought to accept their offer, and grant their request; but Cardinal Ximenes, who by the death of Deza had become inquisitor-general, no sooner heard of this resolution, than he despatched a courier express, to inform Charles that it was not lawful to make a traffic of religion, and to barter the blood of Christ for gold; that the Inquisition had been instituted for very good and wise purposes; that he ought therefore to follow the example of King Ferdinand the

Catholic, who in his greatest need, had refused 600,000 crowns which those very Jews had offered him for the liberty of continuing peaceably in his dominions. What other advice could be expected from an inquisitor-general, who was enriching himself with the spoil of his victims? Charles yielded to it, and their request was refused. Many from Portugal had sought refuge in the Low Countries; but in 1532, Charles forbade them remaining, unless they had been residents there for six years. No favour was shewn to the Portuguese converts. They were also included in the proscription, being undoubtedly considered better Jews than Christians.

Spanish tyranny and intolerance, at length forced Holland to declare its independence, and the Spanish and Portuguese Jews were gladly welcomed in the Seven United Provinces. They brought large properties with them; the States-General took them under their protection; and Amsterdam became in a manner their head-quarters, as the Reformation offered them security from the persecutions of ignorant friars and fiendish Dominican monks. Most of the new Christians that escaped the fangs of the merciless Inquisition repaired to that city, where they could throw off their Catholic mask, openly profess their Judaism, and freely exercise the religion of their forefathers. At the Hague also they have a handsome synagogue, and enjoy the greatest prosperity. They live in the most sumptuous edifices, in the utmost luxury, and enjoy their wealth and grandeur, without exciting the jealousy, zeal, or envy of the populace. Their extensive commerce tended greatly to the prosperity of Amsterdam, Rotterdam, and Antwerp; and so careful was the government of protecting them, that in a treaty in 1627 with Algiers, the vessels and trade of Israelites residing in the Netherlands, by articles 2, 12, 14, 15, and 19, are specially provided for, and protected with the same privileges as other subjects of the Dutch nation, as probably, without these stipulations, the Algerine pirates might have yet considered them as belonging to Spain and Portugal.

A few years after they were settled in Holland, some went to Hamburgh, where they were permitted to build a synagogue, although the Catholics were not allowed to erect a church.

The discovery of the New World opened a wide field for their commercial enterprise. Many of the New Christians from Portugal had emigrated to the Brazils, to live unmolested by the Inquisition. As soon as the Dutch became masters of that rich and fertile country, a large number of Jews from Amsterdam repaired to the new conquest of Holland, and to their agricultural industry the Abbé Raynal attributes in a great measure its fertility. On their arrival, many of the Portuguese Brazilians threw off the Catholic disguise they had been forced to assume, and returned to the religion of their forefathers. When the Portuguese regained possession of the country, the emigrants from Amsterdam returned to Holland, accompanied by those who had abandoned a religion they had feigned to profess; and every facility for their departure was afforded them by the Portuguese authorities. The Jews, perceiving the commercial advantages the discoveries in America offered, were anxious to return to the Western hemisphere. David Nassy, and other Portuguese Jews, who had returned to Holland from the Brazils, obtained a charter from the Dutch West India Company, to establish a colony in the island of Cayenne, to which a number of Jews from Amsterdam, Leghorn, and other places, repaired and flourished, until driven from it by the French under M. de la Barre. Many then retired to Surinam, where they were soon joined by a number from England, and obtained extraordinary privileges from the British government,[5] which gave great encouragement to settlers in its colonies. After the cession of Surinam to the Dutch, all the privileges that had been granted to the Jews were confirmed; but the major part of those who had come from England quitted with the fleet under Captain Willoughby, and settled at Barbadoes and Jamaica. In the North American possessions of England, the Spanish and Portuguese Jews also settled. The earliest synagogues in the United States were founded by them; and Jews enjoy equal rights with other American citizens; and at the present day, an Israelite (David Levy Yulé), is a member of the Senate of the United States.

Their abilities, commercial enterprise, and peaceable conduct soon attracted attention in the north of Europe. Christina, queen of Sweden, appointed the Teixeiras her agents in Holland and Hamburgh; and the king of Denmark invited them to settle at Gluckstadt.

During the Protectorate, they were invited to England by Mr. Secretary Thurlow. Manasseh ben Israel came over from Amsterdam, and proposed some conditions,[6] which, although it does not appear by any official document, were probably consented to by Cromwell, as the third is—

[5] Appendix, No. VII.  [6] Jewish Calendar.

That we may have a place or cemetery out of the town to inter our dead without being troubled by any.

Two months after, they leased the burial ground at Mile End for 999 years, which it cannot be supposed they would have done, unless they were assured of remaining unmolested. On the restoration, Charles II. continued to afford them his protection; and overtures for his marriage with Catharine of Braganza were made to General Monk by a Portuguese Jew. In this, and the following reign, upwards of one hundred Jews were naturalized. Under the protection of the laws of the country, the Jewish population of the United Kingdom and her numerous colonies has greatly increased. Successive British sovereigns have continued their favour. Our present gracious sovereign created Sir Moses Montefiore, a baronet of the United Kingdom, on his return from his philanthropic journey in the winter of 1847, to Russia, to intercede with the Emperor in behalf of his co-religionists, and avert the misfortune that threatened them. Her Majesty had previously conferred on him the distinguished honour of supporters to his arms, as she is pleased to say in the grant, "as an especial mark of our royal favor, to the said Sir Moses Montefiore, in commemoration of his unceasing exertions in behalf of his injured and persecuted brethren in the East, and the Jewish nation at large."

Undaunted by the cold of a Russian winter, and the heat of an Egyptian summer, or the dreaded sirocco, his lady accompanied him in his philanthropic expeditions to serve and rescue their fellow Israelites from danger.

Sir I. L. Goldsmid, and Baron A. de Rothschild,

have also been created baronets of the United Kingdom. To the unremitting exertions of David Salomons, Esq., are the Jews of England indebted for their admission to the highest municipal offices in the kingdom; and he has deservedly been chosen an alderman of the city of London. The only disability the Jews are now under in Great Britain is, that they are not yet admitted by law to sit in parliament, although Baronel Lionel de Rothschild, at the last election, was chosen a member for the city of London, which was recognised by a majority of the House of Commons.

Spain and Portugal made it death for a Jew to be found in their dominions, yet they employed the pretended Catholics in high offices; for Charles V. sent Jacob Casino on various embassies to the Barbary States, and appointed him as ambassador to the emperor of Morocco; and the two intolerant Philips continued the family in that post for many years. Charles II. of Spain appointed Emanuel Belmonte accredited agent for Spain to the United Provinces, and created him Baron de Belmonte, and Fr. Lopes Suasso, baron d'Averna, for the assistance these two Jews residing at Amsterdam had rendered the allies, by all of whom they were much esteemed. John IV. of Portugal appointed Gabriel Nunes da Costa, Portuguese consul, agent, and resident at the Hague, and honored him with letters patent of nobility, to all of which his son, Alexander, succeeded. This sovereign shewed his confidence in persons who were known to be Jews; for the cargo of produce destined to pay the dower of Catherine of Braganza, was entrusted to Diego da Silva. The descendants of the forced Portuguese converts were all employed in the most honourable posts. Antonio Mendes was the king's physician, and head professor of medicine at Coimbra. His talents were so highly considered, that an express was sent for him to attend Catherine of Braganza, the queen of Charles II., in an attack of erysipelas she suffered in Castile, on her journey to Portugal; and his brother, Andrea, was appointed her chamberlain. They, with their brother, came to England, openly professed their Judaism, and assumed their real name of Mendes da Costa.

Yet, although the sovereigns of Spain employed and conferred honours on Jews when their services were wanted, a latent hatred continued in the breasts of Spanish monarchs, as if intolerance was an appendage and peculiarity of the Castilian crown; not only demonstrated by their attendance at those religious butcheries, termed Autos da Fé, but by their treaties with foreign powers. By Art. 10 of the treaty of Utrecht, in 1713, Gibraltar was ceded to Great Britain: one of the conditions is—

And her Britannic Majesty, at the request of the Catholic king, consents and agrees, that on no account whatever shall Jews or Moors be permitted to reside, or have domiciles, in the said city of Gibraltar; and that no refuge nor shelter shall be allowed to any Moorish vessel of war in the harbour of the said town, whereby the communication between Spain and Ceuta may be obstructed, or the coasts of Spain be infested by the excursions of the Moors. But whereas, there are treaties of friendship and freedom of commerce existing between British subjects, and certain parts of the coast of Africa, it is always to be understood, that entrance cannot be refused to Moors, and their vessels, that come solely to trade.

Notwithstanding Moorish vessels were admitted, and the Jews were allowed to establish themselves there, who, by their commerce and industry soon rendered it a trading port of the utmost importance to British interests in the Mediterranean, representations were made by the court of Madrid in 1723, respecting the admission of Moorish vessels; but nothing was said about the Jews, probably from the British government permitting Catholics the free exercise of their religion.

## CHAPTER XXX.

*New Christians.—Massacres at Lisbon.—John III.—Inquisition established in Portugal.—Jew Physicians.—Anecdote of Francis I.—Learned Men—Amatus Lusitanus—Solomon Malcho, etc.*

HAVING given in the preceding chapter an account of the dispersion of the banished Spanish and Portuguese Hebrews from their native land, I shall return to those who remained in those countries, under the denomination of New Christians.

Those of Spain were not murdered by the populace, but thousands were immolated by the infernal tribunal of the Inquisition, which, not to stain its hands with blood, condemned its victims to the flames. It was next to impossible to escape from those human, or rather inhuman blood-hounds, yet some who continued their medical studies in the famed Spanish universities, were so fortunate, as will be seen in the following pages. Llorente, who had been secretary to it in its latter days, in his " Critical History of the

Inquisition," in four volumes, octavo, relates horrors that are inconceivable.

In Portugal that merciless tribunal had not yet been established, when upwards of 2,000 of the forced converts were murdered and plundered by the mob of Lisbon, on Easter Sunday, the 19th April, 1506.

In the monastery of St. Domingo there was a celebrated chapel called Jesus' chapel: on the altar was a crucifix having a bit of red glass to represent the wound in the side, the monks to delude the ignorant populace, caused a candle to cast its light through the glass, which they proclaimed to be a miracle. A New Christian, who perceived the imposture, and saw that the reflection of the light proceeded from the situation of the candle, incautiously made the remark, whereupon they dragged him by the hair from the church, killed him, and burnt his corpse. While one monk was inveighing from the pulpit, two other Dominicans sallied forth with crucifixes in their hands, exclaiming, Heresy! Heresy! and offering a hundred days' indulgence to every Christian who should kill a Jew or any one who conformed to Judaism. They soon collected a mob, which was increased by a number of Dutch and Danish sailors who landed from their vessels then lying in the Tagus. They slew and mangled their victims, casting many while yet living into the fires the negroes and vilest rabble had kindled at the church doors, to which they kept constantly adding fuel. On the Monday, the numbers of the mob were considerably augmented from the neighbouring villages, the massacre and butchery of the New Christians were continued, their houses were broken open, whole families were murdered, the merciless wretches dashed out the brains of infants against the walls, pregnant women were thrown from the windows on the pikes of those below, women were violated and virgins ravished; such were the horrors committed in the capital of Portugal on that day. One woman courageously drew from the belt of a monk a knife he carried, and when attempting to violate her, stabbed him to the heart. On the Tuesday the scene of carnage was renewed; the mob were equally eager for blood and plunder, but were nearly exhausted; many of their intended victims had escaped from the city, and were secreted and protected at the risk of their own lives by Christian friends. All who were discovered were murdered, many Christians only from resembling Jews were sacrificed, private animosities eagerly seized the opportunity of wreaking vengeance. Sanctuaries were desecrated, and the poor suppliants were dragged from the crucifixes they embraced to be immolated with the others. Plunder was not lost sight of; the sailors took the booty they had got on board their vessels, weighed anchor, and sailed away from the port. Thus for three days Lisbon was completely in the hands of a lawless infuriated populacé. Owing to the plague then raging, the court had removed to Abrantes; and the magistrates, when they found they could not suppress the riot, abandoned the city: they then returned with soldiers, and quelled the tumult. Emanuel sent commissioners with orders to use the utmost severity; the monks who had instigated the riot were divested of their religious habits, strangled, and burnt. The magistrates who had not performed their duty, were heavily fined and deprived of office. The title of "Most Faithful City," was taken from the metropolis, and it was divested of its decorations. Had he not been dissuaded by his council, the king would have demolished the church, and had all persons convicted of having been concerned in the outrage executed. But by an ancient law of Portugal, when fifty or more persons were concerned in any riot where loss of life occurred, the ringleaders only were responsible. He confirmed the agreement made with the New Christians in 1497, and ordered that in future no distinction should be made between Old and New Christians.[1]

John III. succeeded his father Emanuel in 1521. Shortly after his accession he wished to introduce the Inquisition in Portugal. The anonymous author of "Authentic Memoirs of the Portuguese Inquisition,"

[1] Chron. do Rey Manuel.

gives the following improbable account of its introduction.

A Spaniard named Saavedra, who had amassed great wealth by forging apostolical briefs, pretended to have been sent as a Legate from Rome, and having set up a splendid equipage he was received in that quality by the archbishop of Seville, and lodged in his palace. Arriving on the frontiers of Portugal, he despatched his secretary to the king to advise his coming, and transmitted several fictitious letters, as from the pope, the emperor, and other princes, requesting the king to favour so pious a design. John, giving implicit faith to such a messenger, sent a nobleman of the highest rank to pay his compliments, with orders to accompany the pretended legate to the royal palace, where he resided for three months in great pomp; during which time he took his measures so well, as to fix the holy office in 1526 on a solid basis. Saavedra having effected this business took leave of the king, and arriving on the frontiers of Castile, was discovered by a domestic of the Marquis of Villa Nova, who recognised him; upon which he was seized and condemned to the galleys, from which Paul IV. afterwards procured his release.

The writer in support of this extraordinary relation declares to have seen it in manuscript in the libraries of the marquis of Abrantes, of the count of Vimioso, and of cardinal de Souza, and that the story has been dramatised under the title of " *O falso Nuncio de Portugal.*"

But a far more probable account is given by a renowned jurisconsult at Rome, as stated by Aboab in his " Nomologia."

On the death of Emanuel, his son, John III., succeeded to the throne. Instigated by others that his father's promises to the New Christians were of no value, as they did not live as they ought, and that his father could not grant them without the

1535.]  ORIGIN OF THE PORTUGUESE INQUISITION.   355

authority of the pope, he (the king) wished to proceed against them, in the same manner as the Spaniards were then acting towards the Moors. He sent to Rome to obtain permission to cancel those engagements, which was not only refused, but his idea was reprobated; the promises of his father were confirmed, and a general pardon proclaimed for all who had been imprisoned, and one thousand five hundred were restored to liberty. This was done by Clement VII., and the whole conclave of cardinals. John repeated his request with so many replications and triplications, that ultimately the pontiff granted it, although he revoked it a few days after, declaring no such licence should ever be granted, as being contrary to reason and justice, and, to the great dissatisfaction of the king and his brother the cardinal, proclaimed a general amnesty for all who had been imprisoned, which were one thousand two hundred persons. Paul III. succeeded Clement, and they endeavoured to obtain from the new pontiff permission to establish the Inquisition, but holding the same opinion as his predecessor, that it was opposed to justice and reason, he would not grant it; he confirmed the promises made by Emanuel, and pardoned all delinquents from the time compulsion had been used.

John, hereupon, sent an ambassador to Rome expressly on that business; but the pope would not grant permission. John then resolved to apply to the Emperor Charles V., who in passing through Rome on his victorious return from Tunis, would be entitled to a triumph, when, as was customary, he might ask the pope for any favour he wished. John requested him to ask permission for the king of Portugal to establish the Inquisition in his kingdom. The emperor asked it; but the pope replied that he could not grant it, in consequence of the promises made by Emanuel in 1497, at which time he was apostolic nuncio, when the Jews were forced to become Christians, and those promises were made. The emperor answered, Let the sin fall on him and his son, and the apostolic see be free from it; whereupon the pope granted it. Charles had interested himself in this affair from being brother-in-law to John, and they were, at the time, also in treaty for an alliance between their children, which was afterwards concluded. At the time Paul III. granted it, he decreed a general pardon for all who had been imprisoned up to that period, and that they should be released. The king would neither obey this pardon nor release the prisoners, which the pontiff considered so ill-done, that he sent Monsignor Monte Puliciano, as nuncio, expressly on this subject. Nevertheless the king would not obey, whereupon the nuncio had the pardon put on the doors of the churches, personally opened the prisons, and released one thousand eight hundred persons. The New Christians had engaged Duarte de Paz, a knight of St. John's, to watch over and frustrate the machinations of their enemies at Rome; he was highly esteemed by the pope, the cardinals, and the whole court. While the emperor, with his troops, was in that capital, ten masked men attacked De Paz one night, gave him a number of wounds, and left him for dead. The persons who discovered him in this state, carried him to the house of Philip Estozzi. As soon as Paul III. heard of it, he had him for safety conveyed to the castle of St. Angelo, where he was magnificently entertained and attended by the pope's physicians.

The great reputation the Jew physicians of Spain enjoyed, will have been seen by R. Jacob Mantenu becoming first physician to Pope Alexander VI., and Joseph Amon to Sultan Selim I. Their acquaintance with all the medical writers of antiquity, whose works had been translated into Hebrew or Arabic, procured for them this pre-eminence, enabling them to prosecute their studies in languages they understood perfectly, and which many of the New Christians continued to cultivate.

Printing, yet in its infancy, had not then disseminated knowledge sufficiently to enable other students of the Esculapian art to acquire that celebrity so many have since so deservedly attained. That Jews were at this period considered amongst the best physicians, is further exemplified by the following anecdote of Francis I., recorded by Huarte.[2]

Francis de Valois, king of France, suffering a long illness, and finding that all the physicians of his household and court could not cure him, whenever the fever increased, he said Christians did not understand how to cure, and that he never expected to be cured by them. Once, in despair at the continuance of the malady, he sent a courier to the Emperor Charles V., requesting him to send the best Jew physician he had in his capital, who, he understood, could cure his disease. The request was heartily laughed at in Madrid, and every one considered it to be the wanderings of a person under a fever; yet the emperor ordered one to be sought, even out of the kingdom, but not finding one, he sent a physician who was a New Christian, thinking that would fulfil the king's wish. On the arrival of the physician in France, and being introduced to the king, a curious conversation took place between them, by which, discovering that he was a Christian, the king would not be cured by him.

The king, under the idea that the physician was a Jew, in conversation asked him if he was not tired of waiting for the Messiah promised in the law?

Physician.— Sire, I do not expect the Messiah promised by the Jewish law.

King.— You are very discreet thereon, for the signs given in Holy Scripture to know his coming, have long since been fulfilled.

Physician.— We Christians have reckoned the time correctly: it is now 1542 years; he was 33 years in the world, and then died on the cross; on the third day he rose and ascended to heaven, where he now is.

King.— Then you are a Christian?

Physician.— Yes, Sire, by the grace of God.

King.— Then in a good hour return to your country; for I have Christian physicians enough in my household and court; I want a Jew, for in my opinion they possess the natural ability of curing.

[2] Examen de ingenios.

The king despatched him without speaking to him about his disorder, or permitting him to feel his pulse. He then sent to Constantinople for a Jew, who cured him with ass's milk.

But the New Christians did not confine themselves to the study of medicine; every other branch of science and literature was cultivated by them. The following list will shew that Spain and Portugal continued to produce among the descendants of Israel, men of first-rate talents; and that, notwithstanding the Inquisition, Judaism continued secretly to be practised, and Hebrew learning taught and inculcated in succeeding generations.

ALPHONSO DE ALCALA — born in 1465, at Alcala la Real, was a profound Hebrew, Greek, and Latin scholar; graduated as doctor of medicine at the University of Salamanca, where he practised. He abjured Judaism in 1492, when he applied himself to the study of theology.

PABLO CORONEL — a native of Segovia, born in 1480, was a celebrated talmudist, and deeply versed in Hebrew, Latin, Greek, and the Oriental languages. After his baptism, in 1492, he studied theology, and was appointed professor of it at the University of Salamanca.

ALPHONSO DE ZAMORA — where he was born in 1480, also became a convert from Judaism in 1492. From his profound knowledge of Hebrew, Chaldee, and Greek, Cardinal Ximenes employed him with the two preceding, to translate the Hebrew Bible into Latin, for the famed *Polyglotta Biblia Complutense;* and by desire of Don Alphonso de Fonseca, archbishop of Toledo, he wrote a Hebrew grammar for the instruction of Spaniards.

R. JOSEPH CARO — was born in Castile previous to 1492. At the expulsion he was carried by his parents to Saphet, where he became chief of its famed college. He wrote under the title of "The House of Joseph," a commentary on the

"Four Orders" of R. Jacob ben Asher, which he afterwards abridged under the title of "Shulchan Aruch, the prepared Table," which is followed by the Jews to this day as the best digest of Jewish laws and customs. He also commented on "The Powerful Hand" of Maimonides; he wrote rules for the study of the Talmud and Guemara, and an exposition of the Pentateuch.

R. SAMUEL DE MEDINA—was a contemporary of the preceding, born at Medina del Campo. He was a philosopher, jurist, and teacher of repute: he became head of the college of Salonica. He has left a volume of sermons, and another of answers to legal questions.

R. JACOB JUDAH ARIÉ—a native of Leon, retired to Middleburgh in Holland. To gain a more perfect idea of the temple of Solomon, he made a wooden model of it, from the plans described by Jewish authors, and then published a description of it in French, which he afterwards augmented, and translated into Hebrew, under the title of "The Figure of the Temple;" to which he added a description of the Tabernacle, and a treatise on the Ark and Cherubim; he also wrote a commentary on Psalms.

R. MOSES DE CORDOVA — born at that place in 1508, and afterwards went to Saphet. He was a philosopher, jurist, and profound cabalist, on which science he wrote a number of works, and various expositions on the prayers.

R. AARON ABIAH—a moral philosopher and metaphysician of high repute. He wrote in Spanish a work entitled "Opinions on the Soul," taken from the most eminent philosophical writers, and quotes those of upwards of twenty of the most renowned philosophers of antiquity.

R. JUDAH BEN BILHAM—a native of Toledo, was a grammarian and talmudist. He wrote a work on the accents of the Holy Scriptures.

AMATUS LUSITANUS—born at Castelbranco, in Portugal. He professed Christianity under the name of Juan Rodrigo;

was a physician and surgeon of great repute. He practised surgery at eighteen years of age at Salamanca, at the university of which city he graduated. He then went to Lisbon, from thence to Rome, Ferrara, and Venice, where he declared himself a Jew, and ultimately retired to Salonica, where he died. He was professor of medicine at Ferrara. He travelled through nearly all Europe, and refused advantageous offers from the king of Poland, and the Republic of Ragusa. His works are well known and appreciated by medical practitioners. Under the name of Juan Rodriguez he commented on the first two books of Dioscorides, as well as the five books of Materia Medica of the same author, in which he explains simples in Greek, Latin, Italian, Spanish, German, and French. Under the name of Amatus Lusitanus, he wrote a work entitled "Centurias of Medicinal Cures," which was highly recommended to young practitioners. He also commented in Latin on the fourth fen of the first book of Avicenna, and translated into Spanish the "History of Utopia."

R. JUDAH LERMA—was a philosopher, jurist, and talmudist of high repute. After quitting Spain, he became rabbi at Belgrade. Under the title of "The Bread of Judah," he wrote a commentary on "The Ethics of the Fathers," and a talmudical work entitled "The Remnant of the House of Judah."

R. ISRAEL BEN MOSES NAGERA—of which city he was a native, was a celebrated mathematician and poet, went to Damascus. He wrote many much admired hymns, which he set to Turkish airs. His work, "The Waters of Israel," contains some hymns, prayers, and elegantly written letters.

R. JOEL BEN SOHEB—an Aragonese, wrote a commentary on the Psalms, with the title of "Fearful in Praise;" and "The Sabbath Offering," containing doctrinal sermons for the Sabbath-day.

R. ABRAHAM ZAHALON—an astronomer, poet, moral philosopher, and jurist of high repute, wrote "The Salvation of God," a moral and literal commentary on the Book of Esther;

" Medicine for the Soul," on conversion and repentance; and "The Hand of the Diligent," on the Jewish, Christian, and Mahomedan calendars.

R. ISAAC LEON—so named from the city where he was born, wrote a commentary on the Book of Esther; and under the title of " The New Book," novel observations on the books of the Talmud.

R. JOSEPH BEN JOSHUA A COHEN—born in 1496, at Avignon, whither his father had retired on leaving Spain, wrote a historical work, entitled " Chronicles of the Kings of France and the Ottoman Sovereigns." It contains a very detailed account of the wars between Francis I. and Charles V., particularly in Italy, and the inroads of the Turks in Europe. Disinterested and cotemporary with those events, he must be regarded as an impartial historian.

DUARTE PINEL—born at Lisbon, in the latter part of the fifteenth century, wrote in his native city, in 1543, a Latin Grammar. On retiring to Ferrara, he there published, in 1553, a Spanish translation of the Bible. He was also an excellent mathematician.

R. ABRAHAM USQUE—born also about the same period at Lisbon, went to Ferrara, where, together with R. Yom tob Athias, he published a Spanish translation of the Bible in 1553, and wrote a treatise on the rites of the New Year and the Day of Atonement.

R. SOLOMON MALCHO—became a convert to Christianity in the time of Dom Manuel, and was employed in the office of the king's secretary. A few years after, he returned to Judaism, by the persuasion of R. David Ruben, who had come from the East, and was much esteemed for his learning by Clement VII. Ruben went to Portugal. On his return to Italy, Malcho accompanied him, and made such progress in the study of the Talmud, that he became head of the college at Mantua. He was so zealous for Judaism, that he entertained the idea of converting the pope, King Francis I., and the Emperor

Charles V. to it. The latter, offended at his temerity, ordered him to be burnt at Mantua, in 1532. A more humane sovereign would have confined him in a mad-house; for he was an object rather for a lunatic asylum than the stake.

R. ABRAHAM ZACUT—born at Lisbon in 1575, was one of the most erudite of the Hebrew physicians; he studied at Salamanca and Coimbra; at the age of eighteen he received the degree of doctor of medicine, at the university of Siguenza. His works are much esteemed; he wrote "*Historia Medicorum Principium;*" "*De Praxi Medica Admiranda;*" "*Introitus ad Praxim et Pharmacopeam;*" "*De Calcolorum Morbis;*" "A History of the most renowned Surgeons;" "On the Government of Princes;" a treatise on the errors of modern physicians, and an epitome of the select doctrine of Hippocrates and Galen. He practised medicine for thirty years. At the age of fifty, he returned to the religion of his forefathers, in which faith he died in 1642.

RODRIGUES DE CASTRO—a native of Lisbon, was a doctor of philosophy and medicine, and student of the university of Salamanca, from whence he went to Hamburgh, where he practised medicine with general satisfaction; he died in 1627. He wrote in Latin on "Female Diseases;" "Advice to Physicians;" and on "The Plague."

R. ABRAHAM NEHEMIAS — born at Lisbon about the middle of the sixteenth century; wrote in Latin various medical works. On leaving Portugal he settled at Amsterdam, where he practised medicine.

R. JOSEPH SEMACH ARIAS — a native of Portugal; he held the commission of captain in the army; was a historian, grammarian and Talmudist of repute at Amsterdam, where he translated Josephus' answer to Apion from the Greek into Spanish.

ELIAS MONTALTO—born in Portugal; while professing Christianity he went under the names of Philip and Eliano. He wrote some esteemed medical works in Latin; the fame of his abilities procured his being appointed principal physician to Mary de Medici, queen of Henry IV. of France, who obtained for him the free exercise of his religion. He was subsequently physician and counsellor to Louis XIII., and died at Paris in 1616.

R. SOLOMON ELESMI — a native of Lisbon, born in the latter part of the sixteenth century, was much esteemed for his abilities as a moral philosopher; he wrote a moral philosophical treatise, entitled, " An Exhortatory Letter," for the instruction of his scholars.

R. ABRAHAM FERRAR — practised as a physician at Lisbon, where he was born; on retiring to Amsterdam, he wrote, in 1627, " An Exposition of the Precepts," in Portuguese.

R. JOSEPH ABEN EZRA — born at the latter part of the sixteenth century, was one of the most renowned Talmudists of his time. He wrote two talmudical works.

R. ABRAHAM COHEN HERRERA — born at Lisbon about the same period, went to Morocco, and from thence to Vienna; was a famed cabalist, and wrote a work on it in Latin, which was translated into Hebrew under the title of, " The House of the Lord;" another entitled, " The Gate of Heaven," and a treatise on logic in Spanish.

R. SHEM TOB BEN PALKIRA — born in Spain about the middle of the sixteenth century; was a philosopher, poet, and jurist, of repute. He wrote in verse two moral philosophical works, entitled, " Rules for Body and Soul," and " The Book of the Enquirer." In prose, " The Science of Philosophers," following the doctrine of Aristotle; " The Book of Degrees," to demonstrate the utility of the Aristotelian philosophy for advancement in Jewish studies; " A Letter of Disputation," a dialogue between a moral philosopher and a jurist, and " The Beginning of Wisdom," shewing the necessity of philosophy for real happiness.

R. EMANUEL ROSALES — born at Lisbon in the middle of the sixteenth century; wrote in Portuguese, " Three true Propositions of Astrology, Astronomy, and Philosophy," and various heroic poems; he was an excellent poet, philosopher, and astronomer.

R. EMANUEL ABOAB—of Spanish origin; resided at Venice, and subsequently at Amsterdam; was a jurist and historian of repute. His " Nomology, or legal arguments in defence of the oral law," is highly esteemed; it contains an excellent account of the banishments from Spain and Portugal; he died in 1629.

## CHAPTER XXXI.

*New Christians that escape from Spain and Portugal—R. Manasseh ben Israel—Learned Men—R. Isaac Cardozo, Specimen of his Writings—Isaac Orobio, his sufferings in the Inquisition—R. David Nieto—Prevented from quitting Portugal.—Sugar introduced by them into South America and the West Indies—Jews permitted to trade in Portugal.—Anecdote of the Marquis of Pombal.—Re-admitted into Portugal.—Sir I. L. Goldsmid created a Portuguese Baron.—Laws of Spain unrepealed.—Some established and trade with it unmolested.—Opinions of the enlightened Spaniards of the present Day.—The End.*

NOTWITHSTANDING the numerous New Christians, or rather dissembling Catholics (from that faith having been forced on them) who found means to escape from the Inquisitions of Spain and Portugal, to places where they could freely exercise the religion of their forefathers, Judaism yet continued to be practised secretly in the Iberian Peninsula.

The numbers reflecting honor on the Hebrew name, who rejoined their brethren, particularly in Holland, in the 17th century, shew, that, while residing under the bigoted Most Catholic, and Most Faithful Sovereigns, and in the constant dread of the horrors of that merciless tribunal, the Inquisition, their parents strictly attended to the education and instruction of their children in the Mosaical rites. Many in this country possess and preserve mementos of their ancestors, who perished in the flames of those disgraceful and horrid misnamed religious acts, termed Autos da Fé.

The following are some of the learned Hebrews, whose works are highly esteemed, and whose talents procured for them the esteem of the *literati* of the 17th century, the age in which they were born in the Peninsula; to which are added, a few descendants of Spanish and Portuguese Jews, who, at the same period, rendered themselves illustrious in the annals of literature.

R. MANASSEH BEN ISRAEL — born in Lisbon in 1605; his father had thrice been incarcerated in the prisons of the Inquisition, from which he effected his escape, and settled with his family at Amsterdam. Manasseh was an able philosopher, poet, physician, and theologian; he wrote Hebrew, Greek, Latin, Spanish, and Portuguese, with elegance and fluency. His literary fame procured him the esteem of the learned throughout Europe, with many of whom he corresponded. At the age of seventeen, he commenced his Hebrew Grammar, "The Pure Lip;" and at twenty-seven, his grand work, "The Conciliator," reconciling the apparent contradictions in the Bible. This valuable work has lately been translated into English, and is highly appreciated as a valuable appendage to the Holy Scriptures. "A Spanish Version of the Pentateuch;"

"The Customs, Rites, and Ceremonies of the Jews." In Hebrew, "The Precious Stone," a comment on the statue of Nebuchadnezzar; "The Soul of Life," on the resurrection and immortality of the soul; "Many Faces," an index of the passages of Scripture explained by the rabbins; "The Hope of Israel." "A Spanish and Arabic nomênclature;" "A Rabbinical Catalogue," "Phocylides," with notes in Spanish; "On Human Frailty." In Latin, "Thirty Problems on the Creation;" "On the Duration of Human Life;" "Defence of the Jews," in English. His exertions procured the present establishment of the Jews in England; after which he retired to Middleburgh, where he died in 1657.

R. DAVID COHEN DE LARA—born at Lisbon in the beginning of the 17th century; was a grammarian, moral philosopher, and jurist of repute. He translated into Latin, and wrote notes to, Aben Ezra's enigma of the letters אהוי; "The Ethics of Maimonides;" "His treatises on the Law, and on Penitence," into Spanish. He commenced a Rabbinical Talmudical dictionary, with the meaning of each word in Chaldee, Syriac, Arabic, Persian, Turkish, Greek, Latin, Italian, Spanish, Portuguese, French, German, Saxon, and English. After labouring forty years on this work, he had only completed the tenth letter; to which he gave the title of "The Crown of the Priesthood." He retired from Portugal to Amsterdam.

R. MOSES ABUDIENTE—a native of Lisbon, where he was born in the early part of the 17th century; went to Hamburgh, and is celebrated by De Barrios as an able poet. He wrote a Hebrew and Portuguese grammar.

R. JOSIAS BEN JOSEPH PINTO—born at the beginning of the 17th century at Lisbon, settled at Damascus, where he wrote "Light of the Eyes," annotations on the Fountain of Jacob; "Purified Silver," a diffuse exposition of the Pentateuch, and a more succinct one, with the title of, "Choice Silver."

R. MOSES TOLEDO—born in that city about the same time, was a philosopher and Talmudist of repute; from Spain he went to France, and from thence to Amsterdam, and became a member of the Hebrew college of that city, but retired to Venice, where he wrote a moral philosophical work, under the title of, "The Trumpet of Moses of Toledo."

R. JACOB LUMBROSO—doctor of medicine, flourished in the early part of the 17th century, in Tuscany, where he was president of the council of the grand duke, but retired to Venice to live openly as a Jew, where he practised medicine. He wrote a "Grammatical Commentary;" that is, a treatise on the points and accents, and the most necessary rules for reading Hebrew. The most difficult words are explained in Spanish, written in Hebrew characters. He also wrote a work against Grotius, in defence of the Jewish religion.

R. ISAAC CARDOZO—a native of Lisbon, born the beginning of the 17th century, practised as a physician at Valladolid and Madrid. While professing Christianity he bore the name of Ferdinand; he quitted Spain and went to Venice openly to profess himself a Jew, and retired to Verona where he died; he was an eminent practitioner, he wrote various medical works; his style borders on the sublime, as the following extract from his work "On the benefit of Water and Snow" shews. "Nature appears to have surpassed itself in the superiority of this element, adorning its waters with different properties, and enclosing mysterious wonders in its waves. There is no part of the liquid crystal, from the minuteness of the spring to the immensity of the ocean, that does not proclaim wonders. In the beginning they overflowed the earth, seeking new concavities; they retired within the limits fixed by the divine command, making so light an object as sand, which a breath of air can disperse, to break the vivacity of its arrogance, that it may be seen how the greatest pride can be overcome by the most humble instrument." This work, as well as "The Excellencies of the Hebrews," divided into ten classes, and refuting ten calumnies against them; and "The Origin and Restoration of the World," are written in Spanish. His medical work "*De Fiebri Syncopale*" and "Liberal Philosophy," he wrote in Latin.

R. ABRAHAM CARDOZO—brother of the preceding, was physician to the Dey of Tripoli, he wrote a philosophical work entitled "Jacob's Ladder."

R. BENJAMIN MUSAPHIA—born at the early part of the 17th century, was a celebrated physician and scholar; he practised medicine with great repute at Hamburg and Gluckstadt. He wrote a treatise on "Potable Gold," and made additions to the "Hebrew Lexicon," under the title of "The Remembrance of Many;" "The Hebrew Roots;" the disputes between R. Jacob Sasportas and himself; entitled, "The Testimony in Jacob." He commented on the Jerusalem Talmud, and applied himself to search into the causes of the tides of the ocean.

EMANUEL GOMEZ—a native of Portugal; after serving in the army, he graduated at the university of Evora, for Doctor of Medicine, which science he practised at Antwerp. Like many other Spanish physicians, to great practical knowledge he united the talent of versification; he commented in Spanish verse on the first aphorism of Hippocrates, applying with great ingenuity his doctrine to the art of war. He highly eulogised surgery, wrote on the plague, and was among the first who called attention to the inutility of an implicit reliance on the use of milk in the treatment of confirmed phthisis. His works are highly praised by Morejon.

R. SAUL LEVI MORTEIRA—studied at Venice, but settled at Amsterdam, and was sent for to Paris to convey the corpse of Montalto for interment in that city; he wrote a work entitled "The Divine Providence of God towards Israel," impugning Catholicism so severely that it has never been printed.

R. SOLOMON DE OLIVIERA—born at Lisbon in the middle of the 17th century, was a moral philosopher, astronomer, and grammarian of repute. On settling at Amsterdam he published a complete Hebrew and Portuguese dictionary; an abridgment of it; a grammar; a dictionary of Hebrew words, having the same terminations, a useful work for poets; a calendar; an astronomical work; a moral philosophical one, entitled "The Loving Hind" and "The Ways of the Lord;" an alphabetical index of the precepts.

R. SAMUEL COHEN DE PIZA—a native of Lisbon, was one of the most profound Talmudists of his age; he wrote "The Revealer of Secrets," a commentary on part of Ecclesiastes.

R. EZEKIEL DE CASTRO—a celebrated physician, flourished at Verona in the middle of the 17th century, where he wrote the following medical works: "*Amphitheatrum Medicum;*" "*Ignis Lambens;*" "*Historia Medica;*" and "*Prolusiones Medicæ.*"

R. ISAAC JESSURUN—flourished at Hamburgh about the same time; he was a celebrated jurist and moral philosopher, and wrote in Hebrew, "New Faces," a compilation of Jewish customs since the "House of Joseph," of R. Joseph Caro; a compendium of "The Path of Life," under the title of "The Collection of Meal;" and a moral philosophical work, "On Divine Providence," in Portuguese.

R. ABRAHAM ISRAEL PEREIRA—of Portuguese origin, born at Amsterdam, where he flourished in the middle of the 17th century, was one of the students of the college of that city; highly considered for his literary talents. He wrote in Spanish, "The Mirror of Worldly Vanity," and "The Sure Path."

R. MOSES RAPHAEL AGUILAR—also of Amsterdam, and member of its college; he went in 1641 with the Jews that emigrated to the Brazils. On his return to his native city, he wrote in Hebrew, "An Alphabetical Index to the Guemara and Talmud;" "The Book of Narratives," all those contained in the Talmud, and a Portuguese and Hebrew Grammar.

R. ABRAHAM ISRAEL PILZARRO—flourished likewise at Amsterdam; he wrote an exposition of Jacob's prophecy, entitled, "The Sceptre of Judah;" in which he complains of the unfair manner in which Christians expound the Scriptures, of their unfitness for such a task, and the danger of confuting their interpretations. The governors of the congregation very properly suppressed the work.

R. DAVID PARDO — of Spanish origin, was head of the congregation in London; he was born at Amsterdam. He wrote in Hebrew, "The Pure Table," an abridgment of the Jewish rites; and translated into Spanish, "The Duties of the Heart" of Rabenu Behayé; it is printed in Hebrew characters.

R. JACOB ABENDANA — a native of Amsterdam, in 1682 was appointed head of the congregation of London, where he died in 1685. He made an elegant translation of "The Cuzari" of R. Judah a Levi; it is preferred to any other translation.

R. ISAAC ABENDANA — brother of the preceding; they were of Spanish origin. He came from Amsterdam where he practised as a physician, and settled at Oxford; and he became professor of Hebrew in that city; he translated the Mishna, with the commentaries of Bartenora and Maimonides into Spanish. Surenhusius profited by it for his celebrated Latin translation.

DANIEL LEVI DE BARRIOS — born at Montilla. While outwardly professing Catholicism, he bore the name of Michael, and was a captain in the Portuguese army. He retired to Amsterdam to follow the religion of his fathers openly; was a historian, philosopher, and poet of great celebrity; his numerous poetical works and comedies have become scarce. He wrote "The triumph of Popular Government;" "An Essay on Jewish History;" and an account of a long list of Spanish and Portuguese Jews, who were poets in those languages.

DON ISAAC OROBIO DE CASTRO — a native of Portugal, was a philosopher and physician of eminence in the seventeenth century. His parents, who were Jews, although outwardly professing Catholicism, educated him in Judaism. Orobio studied the scholastic philosophy usual in Spain, and became so skilled in it, that he was made professor of metaphysics at the university of Salamanca. Afterwards applying himself to the study of physic, he practised that art with great reputation at

Seville, until, suspected of Judaism, he was thrown into the Inquisition, and suffered the most dreadful cruelties to extort a confession. His own account is the best we have of the sufferings of those persons who incurred the displeasure or suspicion of that merciless tribunal. He tells us that he was put into a dark dungeon, so narrow, that he could scarcely turn in it, and suffered so many hardships, that his brain became disturbed. He would ask himself, "Am I that Don Balthasar (his baptismal name) Orobio, who walked about freely in Seville, who lived at ease, and had the blessing of a wife and children?" Sometimes he would suppose his past life to have been a dream, and that the dungeon where he then lay was his birth-place, and which to all appearance would be that of his death. At other times, as he had a very metaphysical mind, he formed arguments and then resolved them, thus performing the parts of opponent, respondent, and moderator at the same time. In this way he amused himself, and constantly denied that he was a Jew. After appearing twice or thrice before the inquisitors, he was used as follows:—At the bottom of a subterraneous vault, lighted by two or three small lamps, he appeared before two persons. One was the judge, and the other the secretary of the Inquisition, who asking him to confess the truth, declared, that in case of a criminal's denial, the holy office would not be deemed the cause of his death if he should expire under the torture,.but it must be attributed to his own obstinacy. Then the executioner stripped off his clothes, tied his hands and feet with a strong cord, and set him on a low stool, while he passed the cord through some iron rings fixed in the walls; then drawing away the stool, he remained suspended by the cord, which the executioner drew tighter and tighter to make him confess, until a surgeon assured the court he could not bear more without expiring. These cords put him to exquisite torture, by cutting into the flesh, and making the blood burst from under his nails. To prevent the cords tearing off the flesh, of which there was danger, bands were girded about the breast, which were drawn so tight, that he would not have been able to breathe, if he had not held his breath in while the executioners put the bands round him. By this device his lungs were enabled to perform their functions. During the severest of his sufferings, he was told that was but the beginning of his torments, and that he had better confess before they proceeded to extremities. Orobio adds, that the executioner being on a small ladder, to frighten him, frequently let it fall against his shin-bones. The staves being sharp, caused him dreadful pain. After three years' confinement, as he persevered in denying his Judaism, they ordered his wounds to be cured, and released him. Shortly after he quitted Spain, and retired to France, and was made professor of medicine at Toulouse. The theses he chose for obtaining that place were on putrefaction, and he maintained them with so much metaphysical subtlety that he embarrassed all his competitors. He continued there to appear a Christian; but weary of dissembling, he went to Amsterdam, where he was circumcised, and took the name of Isaac. He wrote " Israel Avenged," an exposition of the prophecies Christians apply to the Messiah; " A Philosophical Defence of the Revealed and Natural Law;" "A Letter in Defence of the Law of Moses;" " The Divine Prohibition of Heathen Idolatry;" " Reflections on the Seventy Weeks of Daniel;" and " Fifty-third Chapter of Isaiah;" " On the Perpetuity of the Mosaic Law;" and " Three Treatises in favour of Judaism." He died at Amsterdam in 1687.

R. DAVID NIETO — of Spanish origin, born at Venice in 1654, was a philosopher, physician, poet, mathematician, astronomer, historian, and theologian of high repute. He practised medicine at Leghorn, where he wrote in Italian a work entitled " Pascalogia," dedicated to Cardinal de Medici, demonstrating the errors which had crept into the calendar, from the Council of Nice to 1699, and rules for correcting it in perpetuity. The fame of his talents led the congregation of London to invite him to be their head. He arrived here in 1701. He wrote a Theological Treatise on " Divine Providence;" " A Jewish Calendar." In Hebrew, " The Fire of the Law," impugning the doctrine of R. Nehemiah Chiyon; " The Rod of Judgment," or second part of the Cuzari, to prove the divine authority of the oral law; and under the assumed name of Carlos Vera, " A Reply to the Sermon of the Archbishop of Cranganor," at the Auto da Fé, at Lisbon, in 1705. He died in 1728.

To the above, as well as to those of preceding centuries, many other names might be added; but sufficient has been said, to shew that the Jews of Spain have been the preservers not only of Holy Writ in its purity, but also of the arts and sciences. To them is due the preservation of the most valued works of the ancient philosophers, while Europe was involved in Gothic barbarism.

Apparently as Christians, it will be seen they continued long to linger in Portugal after the proscription. During the first ten years, so many had quitted their native land, that Emanuel, perceiving the injury his kingdom suffered by the emigration of the most wealthy and most industrious of its population, ordered in 1507 the seizure of the persons, and confiscation of the property of all who should be found preparing to quit the country. Yet so many ventured, at all hazards, to abandon the Portuguese soil, that in 1524, John III. found it requisite to renew the edict; and the emigration must have continued, for Dom Sebastian repeated it in 1567, and again in 1573. But in return for the assistance they rendered him, by advancing £250,000 towards fitting out his unfortunate expedition against Morocco in 1577, he revoked all prohibitions and penalties. They eagerly embraced the opportunity of emigrating to where they could openly profess the religion their parents had diligently taught them.

Before the establishment of the Inquisition, all

crimes against the faith (as the return of the New Christians to the religion of their ancestors was termed), were taken cognizance of by the bishops, who confiscated the property of the accused, and banished them to the Brazils, then considered by the Portuguese as a penal settlement. There they found kind relations and old friends; others, known as men of probity and intelligence, obtained advances from merchants of other countries with whom they had formerly been in correspondence. By the assistance of some enterprising men, they began to cultivate the sugar cane, which in 1531 they had procured from Madeira. Sugar until then had only been used in medicine; now it became a luxury. In Surinam, they were also the earliest cultivators of the cane; at Martinique its culture was introduced in 1650, by Benjamin da Costa, also a Portuguese Jew; so that to their industry is the world chiefly indebted for the enormous production, in the West, of an article that has now become almost a necessary of life.

The Inquisition of Portugal exercised the same cruelty as that of Spain towards the New Christians. Those who were discovered or suspected of practising Jewish rites, and under torture confessed their Judaism, suffered death, and expired in the flames of the Autos da Fé.

Yet Jews seem to have been permitted to trade with that country. Through them all the rich products of India that were brought to Lisbon, were carried to every other part of Europe, from which the crown of Portugal derived great profit. This is confirmed by an edict of John III., dated 7th February, 1537, ordering " that all Jews should wear a badge by which they might be distinguished from Christians." While Portugal was united to Spain during the reigns of the bigoted Philips, they were treated as cruelly as in all the other Spanish dominions; but on the revolution and the accession of the house of Braganza, as their wealth had assisted John IV. to defend his crown, he again tacitly tolerated them.

In Portugal, in proportion to its population, they had been as numerous as in Spain, and were there also allied with the chief nobility of that kingdom. Orobio states that in the synagogue at Amsterdam he met brothers, sisters, and near relations of the first Portuguese families, and that the greater part of the clergy, even archbishops and bishops, are descended from them; this is corroborated by the following anecdote of the famed Marquis de Pombal. Joseph I. ordered that all Portuguese, who were in any way allied or descended from the Hebrew race, should wear a yellow hat. The old marquis shortly after appeared at court with three of them under his arm. The king, smiling, asked him, "What he had to do with them?" He replied, "That he had them in obedience to his majesty's command, for he did not know a single Portuguese of note who had not Jewish blood in his veins." But said the king, "Why have you three?" He answered, "One for myself, one for the inquisitor-general, and one in case your majesty should wish to be covered."

Many who had been friars and nuns, of almost every monastic order, not excepting the Jesuits, sought at Amsterdam, Leghorn, and other places, to make atonement for their former apostasy, and to re-enter the flock of Israel. Among other instances is that of a New Christian, whose catholicity was so undoubted, that he was entrusted with the sale of indulgences in Spain; from Malaga he went to Barbary, where he disposed of the remainder of his stock to some resident Catholics. As soon as he received payment, he declared himself to be a Jew, upon which the purchasers appealed to the Cadi against the imposition; but he claimed the privilege of a free port to sell any description of goods.

In the congregations of the Spanish and Portuguese Jews, those languages are yet more or less preserved, and many in Europe keep their records in them; but the custom is falling into desuetude, and since their closer amalgamation with the inhabitants of the north of Europe, they have generally adopted the language of their respective countries. Notwithstanding, some remembrance of them is yet preserved; even here, in London (where the congregational records are kept in English), this is the case; and many of its members, who have never visited the Peninsula, speak the languages of their ancestors.

At Jerusalem, where the major part of its Jew inhabitants are of Spanish descent, that language is generally spoken, as well as throughout the East and in Italy.

From the general knowledge of these languages by their co-religionists, many of the Hebrew authors of the seventeenth century, at Amsterdam and in Italy, wrote and translated from the Hebrew into them, some of the most esteemed works of the ancient Spanish rabbins.

With the destruction of the Inquisition, persecution has ceased in those countries; and in return for the assistance rendered by the Jews during the scarcity in Portugal, John VI., in 1820, granted them permission to settle at Lisbon, where, by their conduct, they have gained the esteem of the other inhabitants. They have there a synagogue, and follow the religion of their forefathers unmolested. They are allowed to hold and possess landed property; for Sir Isaac Lyon Goldsmid has bought from government the estates of San Antonio e Palmeira, in the suburbs of Lisbon, adjoining the ancient Moory. In 1840, the present queen conferred on him a commandership of the Tower and Sword; and in 1845, created him a baron, with the title of Baron de Goldsmid and da Palmeira, as she expresses in the patent, "in manifestation of the important services rendered by him on various occasions to the Portuguese nation;" and our gracious sovereign has been pleased to grant her royal sanction to his bearing the title in Great Britain. Since the independence of the former Spanish and Portuguese possessions in the Americas, where formerly Autos da Fé blazed, Jews are now freely admitted; and the emperor of the Brazils, following the enlightened policy of the Braganza family in Europe, has created Sir I. L. Goldsmid an officer of the Order of the Rose.

In Spain, the laws against the Hebrews are yet unrepealed; which may be attributed more to the frequent ministerial changes than to the disinclination of the ruling powers. The Israelites of Bayonne have formed establishments at St. Sebastian, where they are respected, and carry on their commerce unmolested. The Hebrews of Gibraltar trade openly with Cadiz and the ports of the Mediterranean without obstruction; and a Jew can at the present day travel in Spain without fear of insult, as the author has experienced.

A late minister of justice in that country informed the author, that no judge in Spain would now dare to act on the antiquated laws against the Jews; and an ambassador to this court assured him of personal safety in travelling in a country from which his ancestors had been exiled.

To them, and a late prime minister of Spain, he is indebted for introductions to some of the most enlightened individuals of the Spanish capital. They, as well as all other illustrious Spaniards resident in this country, are of opinion that Spain must, and shortly will acknowledge the principle of universal toleration and freedom of conscience, as necessary to its welfare.

May the day soon arrive when a difference in serving the Creator of all shall cease to disturb the harmony and union the Eternal intended should ever exist among mankind!

# APPENDIX.

No. I.—*Extract from Power's History of the Empire of the Mussulmans.*

THE writers from whom these details are taken, relate also the sums which it cost to build this palace, and the town of Zahara, which amounted to 300,000 dinars of gold (about sixty millions of our money) per annum; and it occupied a space of time of nearly twenty-five years to complete the work. To these immense expenses, it is necessary to add, the maintenance of a seraglio, in which his wives, his concubines, and slaves, together with his black and white eunuchs, amounted to 6,300 persons. The officers of the palace of the caliph, and the horses, set apart for himself, were in equal proportion. 12,000 horsemen composed his guard alone; and if one reflects that Abderachman, in a state of continual war with the Spanish princes, was obliged to keep on foot a numerous army, to maintain a marine, to purchase frequent stipendiaries from Africa, and to fortify those places on the frontiers which were continually menaced, it is difficult to conceive how his revenues could have been sufficient. But his resources were immense; and the sovereign of Cordova was perhaps the richest and most powerful potentate in Europe. An idea of his opulence may be formed, from the presents Abderachman received from one of his subjects, Abdulmelec ben Chica, who was elevated to the dignity of grand vizier. They consisted of 400 lbs. of gold; the value of 420,000 sequins in bars of silver; 420 lbs. wood of aloes; 500 ounces of ambergris; 300 ounces of camphor; 30 pieces of drapery of gold and silk, so costly that none but the caliphs had the privilege of wearing them; 10 furs of the sable or martin of Khorasan; 100 other of common martins; 48 trailing housings of cloth of gold of Bagdad; 4000lbs. of silk; 30 Persian carpets of superior beauty; 800 suits of steel armour for horses of war; 1000 bucklers; 100,000 arrows; 15 Arabian led horses, adorned as richly as those of the caliph; 100 inferior Arabian horses for the suite of the prince; 20 mules with their saddles and trailing housings; 40 young boys and 20 girls of exquisite beauty, dressed most splendidly. The vizier accompanied this present with a copy of verses, in which the praises of him to whom it was offered, and the protestations of the zeal and devotion of him who offered it, were not forgotten. The present and poem pleased the caliph extremely, and contributed not a little to the favour the vizier enjoyed during his administration; and the prince, as a recompence, assigned him a revenue of 100,000 pieces of gold. Abderachman possessed Portugal, Andalusia, the kingdoms of Granada, Murcia, Valencia, and the greatest portion of New Castile; that is to say, all the most beautiful provinces of Spain. These provinces were at this time extremely populous; and the

Mussulmans had carried agriculture to the highest degree of perfection. Historians assure us, that on the borders of the Guadalquivir, there stood 12,000 villages; and that a traveller could not advance for a quarter of an hour, without meeting a hamlet. The states of the caliph contained 80 great towns, 300 of the second order, and an infinite number of country villages. Cordova, the capital, enclosed within its walls 200,000 houses, and 900 public baths. All these have suffered a great change since the expulsion of the Mussulmans; the reason of which is obvious, for the Mussulmans, conquerors of the Spaniards, who conquered them, not only persecuted, but deprived them of their possessions. It is calculated, that the revenue of the caliphs of Cordova amounted to 12,045,000 dinars of gold, which is more than 130 millions of our money.\* Independently of this gold, a number of the imposts were paid in the produce of the land; and amongst a people laborious and prone to agricultural pursuits, and possessing a country the most fertile in the world, these riches must have been incalculable. The mines of gold and silver at all times common in Spain, were another source of wealth. Commerce, too, that fruitful tree of treasure, which enriches at the same time the sovereign and people, had many branches. The silks, the oil, the sugar, the cochineal, the iron, and the wool of Spain, were peculiarly estimable at that period; to which may be added, ambergris, amber, the loadstone, antimony, the marcassite stone, rock crystal, sulphur, saffron, and ginger; the coral collected on the shores of Andalusia, and the pearl fisheries of Catalonia; the rubies, of which they had discovered two mines, one at Malaga, and one at Beja. All these productions of the earth were transported into Africa, Egypt, and the East. The emperor of Constantinople, always a necessary ally to the caliphs of Cordova, favoured these branches of commerce; and the immense extent of coast, and the vicinity of Africa, Italy, and France, contributed to render them more flourishing. Such was the state of Cordova during the reign of Abderachman, who occupied the throne more than fifty years. Must we not acknowledge that it was with glory?

No. II.—*Extract from Epitaph of R. Joseph Ben Shoshan.*

כי נגנז תחתיה הנשר בעל הכנפים
וכל שרי המלך משתחוים לו אפים
הנשיא הגדול
גבור התורה ואלוף המשרה

*Abné Zicaron*, No. 75.

\* The author here calculates the dinar at about half what he states it to be at the beginning of this extract.

No. III.—*Extract from Epitaph of R. Joseph Ben Daoud.*

עבד לעבריים וחלקו לו מלכי ערב כבוד וגם משרה
*Abné Zicaron*, No. 49.

No. IV.—*Extract from Epitaph of R. Joseph Levi Abulaphia.*

האיש אשר המלך חפץ ביקרו
וישם רביד הזהב על צוארו
*Abné Zicaron*, No. 22.

No. V.—*Extract from a Poetical Satire on Sancho the Brave for his Protection of the Jews.*

Despues desto llego Don Abram y Don Samuel,
Con sus dulces palabras que parecen la miel;
Y facen una puja sobre los de Ysraél,
Que monta en todo el Reyno cuento y medio de fiel.
*Discurso sobre los Judios de España.*

Which may be thus rendered in English :—

Then Don Abram and Don Samuel stood forth and pleaded well,
And words of honied sweetness and of wisdom from them fell;
And they magnified the sons of the faithful Israel,
Of whom a million and a half do in the kingdom dwell.

No. VI.—*Extract from Epitaph of R. Abraham ben Alnakova.*

דורש טוב לעמו וגודר בפרץ
עם מלכים ויועצי ארץ
ומדרש בנה לרגנות בו התורה היקרה
לאור היום והלילה בנר מצוה ותורה
ובית דירה לאברהם למקנה
והקדישו לאורחים הבאים מכל פנה
ונתן בו מטה שלחן וכסא ומנורה ומזון לסעודה
*Abné Zicaron*, No. 28.

No. VII.—*Privileges granted by the British Government to the Jews of Surinam.*

Whereas it is good and sound policy to encourage as much as possible whatever may tend to the increase of a new colony, and to invite persons of whatsoever country and religion, to come and reside here and traffic with us: and whereas we have found that the Hebrew nation, now already resident here, have, with their persons and property, proved themselves useful and beneficial to this colony; and being desirous further to encourage them to continue their residence and trade here: we have, with the authority of the governor, his council, and assembly, passed the following act: —

Every person belonging to the Hebrew nation now resident here, or who may hereafter come to reside and trade here, or in any place or district within the limits of this colony, shall possess and enjoy every privilege and liberty possessed by and granted to the citizens and inhabitants of this colony, and shall be considered as English-born; and they and their heirs shall in this manner possess their property, whether real or personal.

It is also hereby declared, that they shall not be compelled to serve any public office in this colony, and that we receive them under the protection and safeguard of our government, with all the property they now hold, or shall hereafter possess or import from any foreign place or kingdom abroad. We also grant them every privilege and liberty which we ourselves enjoy, whether derived from laws, acts, or customs, either regarding our lands, our persons, or other property, promising them that nothing of what they now possess, or shall hereafter acquire, shall be taken from them or be appropriated among ourselves, by any person of whatsoever rank: but that, on the contrary, they shall have full liberty to plant, trade, and do whatsoever they may consider conducive to their advantage and profit, on condition that they shall be true subjects of our Sovereign Lord the King of England, and shall obey all orders already issued by him, or which he may hereafter promulgate. It is, however, to be well understood, that none of these orders shall be contrary to what is herein contained.

It is also hereby granted and permitted, in the most ample manner possible, to the Hebrew nation, to practise and perform all ceremonies and customs of their religion, according to their usages; also those relating to their marriages and last wills or testaments; and that the acts of marriage made according to their rites and customs shall be held valid in every respect. It is also hereby declared that they shall not suffer any let or hindrance in the observance of their sabbaths or festivals, and those who shall trouble them on that account, shall be considered disturbers of the public peace, and shall be punished accordingly. Also that they shall not be bound to appear, on the said days, before any court or magistrate; and that all summonses and citations for the said days shall be null and void. Neither shall their refusal of payment of any claim made against them on these days prejudice them in any way, or diminish any right they may have. The possession of ten acres of land at Thoxarica, is also hereby granted to them, that they may build thereon places of worship and schools; also for the burial of their dead. They shall, moreover, not be compelled to do personal duty, but shall be permitted to send a substitute, except in case of war, when they also shall be bound to come forward with the other inhabitants. Permission is also hereby granted them to have a tribunal of their own; and that in cases so litigated, the deputies of their nation may pronounce sentence in all cases not exceeding the value of ten thousand pounds of sugar. Upon which sentence, pronounced by the said deputies, the judge of our court shall grant execution to issue; and they shall keep registers and records of the same according to custom. When an oath shall be required, it shall be administered in conformity with the customs of the Hebrew nation, and such oath shall be deemed valid, and have all the force and effect of a judicial oath, notwithstanding any law to the contrary.

That all this may be fully known, I have, by order of his excellency the governor, his council and assembly, signed the present on the seventh of August, 1665.

(Signed) JOHN PARRY, SECRETARY.

No. VIII.—*Fac-simile of the Inscription in the Synagogue of Toledo, taken in 1752.*

The following is a translation, as far as it could be made, of the Hebrew inscription of the synagogue at Toledo, as taken by Don Francisco Perez Bayer, in 1752, for the Royal Academy at Madrid, according to the annexed fac-simile; being formed of stucco, many letters have fallen off. To render it intelligible in English, it has been necessary to add some words, which are printed in italics; they are mostly passages from scripture.

### ON THE RIGHT HAND SIDE.

*I will mention* the loving kindnesses of the Lord, *and his praises*, in respect to all he hath bestowed upon us, and *according to the great things that he hath* done for us. He rescued us from the hands of enemies and persecutors. Although there is no king in Israel, he hath not left us without a protector . . . . . even he (*whom as a mark of respect we call*) the mighty tower. Since the captivity of Ariel, none like him has arisen in Israel. *He is distinguished by his* noble lineage; *his descent from those who in past times* were the fundamental pillars of the state, the princes and valiant leaders, known from the high position in which they stood. His name is known in Israel by praise, fame and glory. Throughout his life he stood before sovereigns as a hero in the breach, to preserve the welfare of his people. Chief of the captivity of Ariel, the chosen one of the nobles, the crown of grace and *honour*, and great among the Jews. To him came Gentiles from the farthest parts of the earth, to adopt him as the protector of their paths, that he might defend them in the breach of danger. He was commander over the land, the lofty tree, the mighty tower; he ascended to the height of princely rule. From the high praise *he enjoys*, and the magnanimity *he displays*, he may justly be termed a holy man. He is the main pillar that supports the house of Levi, and the house of Israel. Who can recount the praise he merits, and the good attributes that belong to him? Where is the man who can sufficiently celebrate his worthiness? He is the crown of the nobility, the wondrous glory, standing first in rank of the Levite princes, Samuel a Levi, the man who was raised on high. May his God be with him, and may he rise higher. He found grace and favour in the sight of the Great Eagle, with mighty wings, the renowned warrior and champion, whose fear fell upon all nations. Great is his name among the people, the mighty King, our *Lord* and ruler. The KING, DON PEDRO, may God be his help, and augment his strength and majesty, and preserve him . . . . The king aggrandised him (*Samuel Levi*), advanced him, and set his seat above all the princes that were with him. And committed to his charge all *his house contained*, and *commanded, that without his consent* no man should lift his hand or his foot, and that all other noblemen should bow to him respectfully . . . . being thus mighty . . . . . *over* all the land . . . . . his fame was bruited in every kingdom, and he became a helper to Israel.

ON THE LEFT (*much defaced*).

. . . . He rescued them from their enemies. Since the time of our captivity there has been none among the children of Israel of so high a rank. He may be compared to a stately tree: the great, pious, and righteous man; the prince of the princes of Levi. . . .
. . . . . . In former days and years past there was not . . . . . And he added above all this, the building of a house of prayer to the name of the Lord God of Israel. And he began to build the house . . and finished in the year (לתולדות) טוֹב (*good to the Jews, numerically* 117—1357) . . . . Praise and glory be greatly given to Him (GOD) who aided him to commence . . . . May the glory of this house be extolled. Eyes never beheld like it, nor ears heard *the existence of its equal*. For thy name's sake, with thy hand ever open and extended, may his God remember him for good, and prolong *his* ₊*days* . . . *In this* everlasting house to stand and minister in the name of the Lord: he and his children; and to do unto him *what is merciful and kind*. . . . . Let thy eyes be open on this house, and thy ears open *to hearken to the prayers therein addressed unto thee. Thy servants* found grace in thy sight to build the sanctuary of Ariel, to save Judah and Israel, and may the Redeemer come to Zion.

THE END.

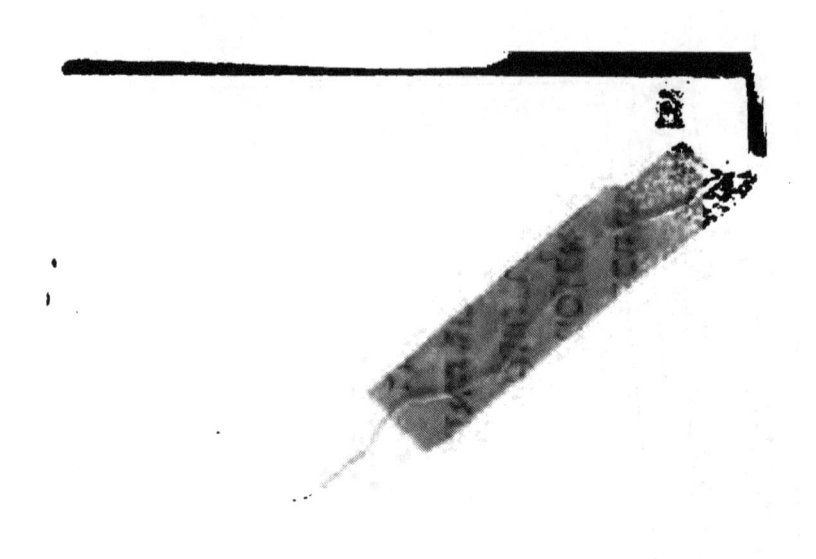

*In 2 vols. demy 8vo., bound in cloth, price 20s.*

# THE CONCILIATOR;

BY

## R. MANASSEH BEN ISRAEL:

A RECONCILEMENT OF THE APPARENT CONTRADICTIONS
IN HOLY SCRIPTURE.

TO WHICH ARE ADDED,

EXPLANATORY NOTES AND BIOGRAPHICAL NOTICES
OF THE QUOTED AUTHORITIES.

BY

### E. H. LINDO,
AUTHOR OF "THE JEWISH CALENDAR."

OPINIONS ON THE ORIGINAL WORK.

CELUI où il parait plus d'érudition Juive, est intitulé en Espagnol "*El Conciliador*," imprimé l'an 1632 à Francfort. Il tâche de concilier dans ce livre les passages de l'Ecriture, qui semble se contredire; et s'y sert des témoignages des Rabbins, tant anciens que nouveaux. Il est aussi quelquefois Philosophe et Cabaliste; mais il ne laisse pas de s'appliquer à la lettre, et cet Ouvrage peut n'être pas moins utile aux Chrétiens qu'aux Juifs. On voit même qu'il a lû les livres des Chrétiens, dont il se sert, mais plus rarement. Ceux qui aiment la littérature des Juifs, trouveront de quoi se satisfaire dans cet Ouvrage qui en est rempli.—*Dict. Hist. du Père Moreri édit.* 1718, vol. iv. p. 185.

THE CONCILIATOR, BY MANASSEH BEN ISRAEL.

This work shews that the author had a profound and intimate acquaintance with the Old Testament writings; and it procured for him the esteem and admiration of all the learned, as well Christians as Jews. It was recommended to the notice of Biblical Scholars by the learned Grotius.—*Rees' Cyclopedia.*

This work, which he afterwards finished, gained him the admiration and esteem of all the learned, both Jews and Christians; and it must be owned no Rabbi, either before or since, ever discussed these difficult points with so much erudition and solidity.—*Hist. of the Jews*, p. 436.

A learned and curious work, in which he reconciles those passages of Scripture which seem to contradict each other.—*Ency. Brit.*

### OPINIONS ON THE TRANSLATION.

We hail with pleasure every attempt to render the treasures which have been so long unheeded, more accessible to Christian students. "The Conciliator" will doubtless be thankfully received by many who have begun to feel interested in books of this class.—
*Jewish Intelligence.*

The object of this work, written by one of the most eminent Rabbins of modern Judaism, is to explain and reconcile the apparent inconsistencies in various parts of the Old Testament. It is a valuable collection of Rabbinical opinions, intermingled with many original observations, and deserves the attention of Biblical students.—
*Athenæum.*

The vast stores of erudition, research, and criticism in these volumes, impart to them a value of another sort, and render them well deserving of the attention not only of the Biblical student, but of every intelligent scholar.—*Literary Gazette.*

To some Biblical scholars, the present hint will be sufficient to lead them to examine a book, the title of which so plainly indicates its use. They will find it a work of much learning and research, giving the views of various learned men as to the mode in which apparently contradictory statements in Scripture are to be reconciled—
*Voice of Israel.*

CPSIA information can be obtained
at www.ICGtesting.com
Printed in the USA
LVHW011455150622
721317LV00002B/75

9 780343 964818